LGBTQ Politics in Nicaragua

Karen Kampwirth

LGBTQ POLITICS IN NICARAGUA

Revolution, Dictatorship, and Social Movements

THE UNIVERSITY OF
ARIZONA PRESS

TUCSON

The University of Arizona Press
www.uapress.arizona.edu

We respectfully acknowledge the University of Arizona is on the land and territories of Indigenous peoples. Today, Arizona is home to twenty-two federally recognized tribes, with Tucson being home to the O'odham and the Yaqui. Committed to diversity and inclusion, the University strives to build sustainable relationships with sovereign Native Nations and Indigenous communities through education offerings, partnerships, and community service.

ISBN-13: 978-0-8165-4279-6 (hardcover)

Cover design and digital collage by Leigh McDonald
Photo imagery from Unsplash.com
Typeset and designed by Sara Thaxton in 10/14 Warnock Pro with Hackett WF and Helvetica LT Std

Publication of this book is made possible in part by the proceeds of a permanent endowment created with the assistance of a Challenge Grant from the National Endowment for the Humanities, a federal agency.

Library of Congress Cataloging-in-Publication Data
Names: Kampwirth, Karen, 1964– author.
Title: LGBTQ politics in Nicaragua : revolution, dictatorship, and social movements / Karen Kampwirth.
Description: Tucson : University of Arizona Press, 2022. | Includes bibliographical references and index.
Identifiers: LCCN 2021053047 | ISBN 9780816542796 (hardcover)
Subjects: LCSH: Sexual minorities—Political activity—Nicaragua—History—20th century. | Sexual minorities—Political activity—Nicaragua—History—21st century.
Classification: LCC HQ73.73.N5 K39 2022 | DDC 306.7609728509/04—dc23/eng/20211217
LC record available at https://lccn.loc.gov/2021053047

Printed in the United States of America
♾ This paper meets the requirements of ANSI/NISO Z39.48-1992 (Permanence of Paper).

CONTENTS

ILLUSTRATIONS

ACKNOWLEDGMENTS

First and foremost, I am grateful to the many Nicaraguans who made this book possible through their generosity: letting me interview them, sometimes on multiple occasions, sometimes traveling a distance to meet with me, often answering my follow-up questions by email or Facebook Messenger, and even helping me by sending unsolicited information. I am deeply indebted to the following people: Tyrone Aburto, Katya Acuña, Helen Alfaro, Paholy Álvarado, Federico Avilés, Cristina Arévalo, Gaby Baca, Mary Bolt González, Amy Bank, Francia Misha Blanco, Erick Blandón, María Teresa Blandón, Roberto Bolaños, Silvia Carrasco, Donald Casco, Lola Castillo, Angélica Collins, Chester Córtez, Ana Criquillion, Carlos René Cruz, Marta Cuaresma, Mirna Cunningham, Dayanara Díaz, Ebén Díaz, Helen Dixon, Elyla, Evelyn Flores, Azucena Ferrey, Hazel Fonseca, Carolina Gallard, Digmari Gómez, Gio, Miguel Ángel Gómez, Yadira Gómez, Danilo Sebastián González, Franklin González, Natty González, Jaika Grádiz, Jeremy Grainger, Mística Guerrero, Mario Gutiérrez Morales, Norman Gutiérrez, Cristiana Huerta, Juanita Jiménez, Delphine Lacombe, Imara Largaespada, Luisa del Carmen Larios, Athiany Larios, David López, José Ignacio López Silva, Manoly Massiel López, Jorge Lozano, Carlos Luna, Rigoberto López Acuña, Harvey Vladimir Maradiaga, Juan Carlos Martínez, Julieta Martínez, Silvia Martínez, Marvin Mayorga, Cecilia Medal, Marta Meneses, Humberto Meza, Samira Montiel, Bismarck Moraga Peña, Feliciano José Morales, Lina Morales, Fidel Moreira, Tyler Moreno, Clara Murguialday, Aurelio Naranjo, Luis Ojeda, Patricia Orozco, Rigoberto Pérez Acuña, Karina Porras, Ana

Victoria Portocarrero, Ana Quirós, Carla Quirós, Elizabeth Ríos (Miss Gay 2013), Ricardo Ríos, David Rocha, Rocío, Patricia Romero, Elvis Salvatierra, Martha Sacasa, Lautaro Sandino, Wendy Salazar, Baltasar Sánchez, Harim Sánchez, la Sebastiana, Lupita Sequeira, Azahalea Solís, Millie Thayer, Doris Tijerino, Dora María Téllez, Elizabeth Torres, Aldrin Torrez, Juanita Urbina, Dámaso Vargas, Mario Vásquez López, Ludwika Vega, Marlene Vivas, Xochitl, Joel Zúñiga.

It is always hard to work in a country that is not one's native country—though there are great joys that accompany the challenges—and so I am particularly grateful to friends who always made Nicaragua a home away from home for this foreigner: Maria Dolores Álvarez, Manuel Aragón, Elena Cajina Quiñónez, Marvin Marenco, Teodora Morales Aragón, Maritza Silva, Carmen Quiñónez, Danilo Quiñónez, Elena Quiñónez, Aynn Setright, Guillermo Pérez Leiva, Maricruz Carrasco, Vondel Gámez, and Cielce Carrasco Gámez. Guillermo and Vondel were fantastic and very safe drivers, and Maricruz was a great research assistant. Jamileth Treminio has skillfully transcribed almost all my interviews since 2011. Finally, though they did not live to see this book, there is a part of Humberto Aragón and Silvia Carrasco in everything I think or write about Nicaragua. I will always miss them terribly.

It is a privilege to teach at Knox College, an institution that has stood for social justice since its founding by abolitionists in 1837, and from which I am proud to hold a bachelor's degree in political science and Spanish. In so many ways, big and small, members of the Knox community have supported me over the years it took to transform a set of ideas into a book. I am grateful to Laura Behling, Mariajose Bonilla, Chris Conner, Melody Diehl, Judy Donaldson, Liz Huerta, Mike Schneider, Katie Stewart, and Robin Venvertloh for their help. Anne-Marie Berk deserves a special mention for her critical role in the transformation of a series of ideas into a grant proposal that received funding. Ryan Lynch, who is truly an amazing librarian and historian, was with me at many stages, critically commenting on the proposal for this book and creatively tracking down sources from all over the world. Marcus McGee, my fellow Knox College alum, helped me think through issues of clientelism and LGBTQ politics through an article we wrote, later published in *Latin American Politics and Society,* by reading early versions of several chapters and by his willingness to engage in endless good-natured arguments about academia and politics. This is the first time in my life that a former student has become both a collaborator and a very good friend, which makes me feel fortunate.

This book was originally part of an enormous five-century project with the historian Victoria González-Rivera that took us more than a decade of work. It was published under both of our names as *Diversidad Sexual en el Pacífico y Centro de Nicaragua: 500 Años de Historia* in 2021 in San Diego, California. The English version of this project is in the form of two single-author books: the book you have in your hands and *500 Years of LGBTQ+ History in Western Nicaragua* (González-Rivera forthcoming). But even though they are distinct books, Victoria's imprint is all over my book.

One of the great joys of my life is that Victoria has been part of it since the 1990s, usually by phone, email, or Facebook Messenger, and on special occasions in person. We are a great team in that each of us knows things the other doesn't, each of us is fascinated by Nicaragua, and we are willing to argue things out, and eventually compromise, sometimes debating each word. This has not always been easy, but the most important things in life are not easy. Victoria is both brilliant and kind, one of my very dearest friends, and I can't imagine going through life without her.

In June 2014, Victoria and I met in Nicaragua for a prebook tour, having little idea how many years would pass and how much the world would change before the books (both the Spanish- and English-language versions) would be finished. It is hard to overstate how important those days were for the evolution of our thinking. Thanks to a grant from the Mellon Foundation (administered by Knox College) we were able to present an early version of this project to four audiences in three Nicaraguan cities over the course of less than a week. Feedback from the tour allowed us to share our initial findings and correct or add nuance to our interpretations. More than 150 people attended the presentations, including scholars and students, beauticians, nongovernment organization (NGO) professionals, working-class and middle-class people, and people of different sexual orientations and gender identities, many of whom are active in today's LGBTQ rights movement. During that week in June of 2014, we were also fortunate enough to be interviewed by one of Nicaragua's leading cultural figures, the journalist Carlos Fernando Chamorro, for what would be broadcast as an eighteen-minute interview on his television show, *Esta Noche*. Putting together that whirlwind tour of Nicaragua was no small feat, and we are very grateful for the contributions made by Helen Alfaro, Carlos Fernando Chamorro, Geni Gómez, Marvin Mayorga, Clara Murguialday, Ana Victoria Portocarrero and, especially, Ana Quirós who led the effort to organize over the months before we arrived in Nicaragua. I am grateful for her good humor and hard work.

I am indebted to Emily Hobson for information on Tede Matthews, to Florence Babb and Margaret Power for their hard work reading and offering insights regarding multiple versions of our grant proposals, and to Amy Bank and Ana Criquillion for making sure we met, despite the great geographical distances between us, and for their continuing friendship.

Victoria and I were awarded a Collaborative Research Fellowship for the 2017–18 academic year from the American Council of Learned Societies or ACLS, which literally transformed our lives, supporting each of us in a year of research and writing and, perhaps most important, making possible the translation and publication in Spanish (González-Rivera and Kampwirth 2021). It is very hard to get funding to publish in translation, a major reason why so many works on Latin America get published exclusively in English. That is a true moral failing, since publishing research in a language that the vast majority of Latin Americans do not read is yet another form of imperialism. We are grateful to the staff of ACLS for so many reasons, especially Rachel Bernard, Matthew Goldfeder, Anna Marchese, Cindy Mueller, and Tami Shaloum, for their generosity and great patience.

I am very grateful to Kristen Buckles, the editor-in-chief at University of Arizona Press. She had the vision to see that the English-language version of our five-hundred-year study would be published best as two manageable books rather than one enormous one. Throughout this process she has been enthusiastic, wise, and supportive. I also am grateful to other staff members at University of Arizona Press, especially Elizabeth Wilder for her cheerful editorial help, Leigh McDonald for the beautiful cover design, Jennifer Manley Rogers for copyediting, and Amanda Krause for carefully moving the book through production. I was very fortunate that the early version of the book was read by the best reviewers who have ever read a manuscript of mine. All three of them made suggestions that were—simultaneously—knowledgeable, insightful, and kind. The world of academia sometimes needs more kindness.

My family has been an important source of support and fun throughout the many years that went into the research and writing of this book. I am proud to be the mother of Sophie and Vanessa Oldfield, who have put up with my multiple absences to talk to interesting people in Nicaragua, and who have spent years watching me type in my "office" in a corner of the dining room. When I began the research for this book, they were still little girls, and they have grown into talented young women. Most importantly, this book would have been impossible without my husband, Duane Oldfield, who has been called "the heroic Duane" for good reasons. Far too many women see their careers slow down, or even end, when they have children. That did not happen in my case, thanks to Duane's cheerfully taking on far more than his share of the work involved in raising a family. After all these decades together, I still can't believe my luck.

ABBREVIATIONS

ADESENI Asociación por los Derechos de la Diversidad Sexual Nicaragüense (Association for Rights of Sexually Diverse Nicaraguans)

ADISEX Asociación de la Diversidad Sexual de Siuna (Siuna Association for Sexual Diversity)

AEDSN Arcoiris de Esperanza de la Diversidad Sexual del Norte (Rainbow of Hope for Sexual Diversity of the North)

ADISNIC Asociación Diversidad Sexual Nicaragüense (Nicaraguan Sexual Diversity Association)

ADMUTRANS Asociación de Mujeres Transgéneras Nicaragüenses (Association of Nicaraguan Transgender Women)

ADSO Asociación Diversidad Sexual de Occidente (Western Sexual Diversity Association)

AHCV Asociación de Hombres Contra la Violencia (Men's Association Against Violence)

ALN Alianza Liberal Nicaragüense (Liberal Nicaraguan Alliance)

AMGLIM Asociación Movimiento Gay Lésbico Trans Inter-Municipal (Inter-Municipal Gay Lesbian Trans Association Movement)

AMNLAE Asociación de Mujeres Nicaragüenses Luisa Amanda Espinosa (Luisa Amanda Association of Nicaraguan Women)

AMODISEC Asociación Movimiento de la Diversidad Sexual Costeña (Association Movement of Coastal Sexual Diversity)

AMTC Asociación de Mujeres Trans y Culturales (Trans Women and Cultural Association)

ANDISEX   Alternativa Nicaragüense de Diversidad Sexual (Nicaraguan Sexual Diversity Alternative)

ANH   Asociación Nuevos Horizontes (New Horizons Association)

ANICHTRANS   Asociación Nicaragüense de Chicas Trans (Nicaraguan Association of Trans Girls)

ANIT   Asociación Nicaragüense de Trans (Nicaraguan Trans Association)

ANJODISEX   Asociación Nicaragüense de Jovenes de la Diversidad Sexual (Nicaraguan Association of Youth for Sexual Diversity)

ASONIDHJO   Asociación Nicaragüense por los Derechos Humanos de los Jovenes LGBTI (Nicaraguan Association for the Human Rights of LGBTI Youth)

ASOTRACHI   Asociación de Transgeneros de Chinandega (Transgender Association of Chinandega)

ASTC or ATC   Asociación Sandinista de Trabajadores de la Cultura (Sandinista Association of Culture Workers)

ATC   Asociación de Trabajadores del Campo (Association of Farm Workers)

AVETRANS   Asociación Venus Trans (Venus Trans Association)

CDS   Comités de Defensa Sandinista (Committees for Sandinista Defense)

CEDEHCA   Centro de Derechos Humanos, Ciudadanos y Autonómicos de la Región Norte de Nicaragua (Center for Human, Citizenship and Autonomous Rights of the Northern Region of Nicaragua)

CEPRESI   Centro para la Educación y Prevención de SIDA (Center for Education and Prevention of AIDS)

CEI   Centro de Estudios Internacionales (Center for International Studies)

CENIDH   Centro Nicaragüense de Derechos Humanos (Nicaraguan Human Rights Center)

CEP-SIDA   Colectivo de Educadores Populares Contra el SIDA (Collective of Grassroots Educators against AIDS)

CISAS   Centro de Información y Servicios de Asesoría en Salud (Center for Health Information and Support Services)

CODISEX   Colectivo de Diversidad Sexual (Sexual Diversity Collective)

CONISIDA   Comisión Nicaragüense del SIDA (Nicaraguan AIDS Commission)

COSEP   Consejo Superior de la Empresa Privada (Greater Council of Private Enterprise)

DEIGEORSEX   Movimiento por los Derechos por la Identidad de Genero y Orientación Sexual (Movement for the Right to Gender Identity and Sexual Orientation)

ENABAS   Empresa Nicaragüense de Alimentos Básicos (Nicaraguan Staple Food Enterprise)

EPS   Ejército Popular Sandinista (Sandinista People's Army)

FCAM   Fondo Centroamericano de Mujeres (Central American Women's Fund)

FED   Fondo para la Equidad de Género y los Derechos Sexuales y Derechos Reproductivos (Fund for Gender Equality and Sexual and Reproductive Rights)

FER   Frente Estudiantil Revolucionario (Revolutionary Student Front)

FSLN   Frente Sandinista de Liberación Nacional (Sandinista Front for National Liberation)

FUN   Federación Universitaria de Nicaragua (Nicaraguan University Federation)

GAO   Grupo de Autoayuda de Occidente de Personas Viviendo con VIH-SIDA (Western Self-Help Group of People Living with HIV-AIDS)

GAY GAS   Grupo Gay de Actores Sociales para la Incidencia Municipal y la Integración Centroamericana (Group of Gay Social Actors for Municipal Politics and Central American Integration)

GEDDS   Grupo Estratégico por los Derechos Humanos de la Diversidad Sexual (Sexual Diversity Strategic Group for Human Rights)

GESIDA   Grupo de Educadores en la Lucha contra el SIDA (Group of Educators against AIDS)

IDSDH   Iniciativa desde la Diversidad Sexual para los Derechos Humanos (Sexual Diversity Initiative for Human Rights, also known as the Initiative)

ILGA   Asociación Internacional de Lesbianas, Gays, Bisexuales, Trans e Intersex (International Association of Lesbians, Gays, Bisexuals, Trans and Intersex people)

INDS VIH+   Iniciativa Nicaragüense de la Diversidad Sexual VIH + (Nicaraguan Initiative for HIV+ Sexual Diversity)

JOV JOV   Joven a Joven (Youth to Youth)

MAM   Movimiento Autónomo de Mujeres (Autonomous Women's Movement)

MDSMANAGUA   Movimiento de la Diversidad Sexual de Managua (Movement for Sexual Diversity of Managua)

MDS RAAS   Movimiento de la Diversidad Sexual Alexis Montiel Alfaro (Alexis Montiel Alfaro Sexual Diversity Movement; also known as the RAAS Diversity Movement)

MESC LGBTI   Movimiento Estudiantil de Secundaria de la Comunidad LGBTI (High School Student Movement of the LGBTI Community)

MINT   Ministerio del Interior (Ministry of the Interior)

MNACXDSSRR   Movimiento Nacional de la Diversidad Sexual, Por Los Derechos Sexuales y Reproductivos (National Movement for Sexual Diversity, Sexual and Reproductive Rights)

MODIVERSEX   Movimiento de la Diversidad Sexual de San Carlos, Río San Juan (San Carlos Sexual Diversity Movement)

MOJUDS   Movimiento Juvenil Diversidad Sexual (Youth Sexual Diversity Movement)

MOVFEMD or **MOFEM**   Movimiento Feminista por la Diversidad (Feminist Movement for Diversity)

MOVIDERSEX   Red Movimiento de Diversidad Sexual de Ciudad Sandino (Sexual Diversity Movement of Sandino City)

MRS   Movimiento de Renovación Sandinista (Movement of Sandinista Renewal)

MTGM or **MTG**   Movimiento Trans Gay de Managua (Trans Gay Movement of Managua)

NOVA ODISEA   Asociación Nova Odisea (New Odyssey Association)

ODETRANS   Organización de Personas Trans (Organization of Trans People)

PAC   Partido Alternativa por el Cambio (Alternative for Change Party)

PLC   Partido Liberal Constitucionalista (Liberal Constitutionalist Party)

RDS   Red de Desarrollo Sostenible (Network for Sustainable Development)

REDLACTRANS   Red Latino Americana y del Caribe de Personas Trans (Latin American and Caribbean Network of Trans People)

SHOMOS   Somos Homosexuales (We Are Homosexuals)

SITRADOVTRANS   Sindicato de Trabajadoras Domesticas y Oficios Varios Transgénero (Union for Transgender People who work in Domestic Service and Other Jobs)

TNG   Teatro Nueva Generación (New Generation Theater)

UCA   Universidad Centroamericana (Central American University)

UNE   Una Nueva Esperanza (A New Hope)

UNO   Unión Nacional Opositora (National Opposition Union)

LGBTQ Politics in Nicaragua

Introduction

In the 1980s, revolution was in the air. When the Sandinista guerrillas overthrew the Somoza dictatorship in 1979, they initiated a decade of rushed
social change that was carried out by hundreds of thousands of people.
Those people engaged in a variety of activities including teaching their fellow
citizens to read, immunizing children, and voluntarily or involuntarily fighting to defend the revolution against the U.S.-funded counterrevolutionary
guerrillas. It was no secret that all sorts of Nicaraguans—men, women, even
children—devoted some of the best years of their lives to the dream of the
revolution. What was rarely discussed is that many of those Nicaraguans
were what today would be called members of the LGBTQ (lesbian, gay, bisexual, trans, queer) community.

In the mid-1980s, some LGBTQ Sandinistas decided that they too wanted
a movement for their rights. They thought they should be able to fight for
their own liberation as LGBTQ people, just as other revolutionaries were
promoting the rights of women, urban workers, rural peasants, Indigenous
people, and children. So they quietly organized for about a year, meeting in
private houses, talking about strategies, and holding joyful parties. Once
they were discovered by officials in the security agency, the Ministerio del
Interior (Ministry of the Interior, or MINT), they were forbidden to meet
again. Moreover, some thirty of their leaders were detained, interrogated,
and threatened with violence and imprisonment. Many of them lost their
party membership and their employment. To make matters worse, state se-

curity agents told them that they were tools of the imperial enemy, that the revolution had no place for them, that Nicaragua had no place for them.

A generation later, the Sandinistas have changed and Nicaragua has changed. Since being voted back into power in 2006, the Sandinista party has passed laws forbidding discrimination due to sexual orientation, created LGBTQ-rights groups within the party, and featured trans women performers at events. Does that mean that LGBTQ Nicaraguans enjoy full civil liberties? Far from it, but the changes are real.

Those changes were obvious to me when I attended the 2014 Miss Nicaragua Gay pageant at Managua's Crowne Plaza hotel. That night, contestants performed to the beat of local music, asserting their own Nicaraguan identity and proclaiming themselves to be *pinoleros de corazón*.[1] The evening's entertainment included dramatic lip-syncing, sexual jokes, and a costume segment in which contestants showed off elaborate garments, implicitly telling stories of the historical clash of Spanish and Indigenous cultures. The costume winner was Brittany Wilson from the colonial city of Granada, dressed as a *conquistadora* in a skimpy suit of armor, holding a glittery sword. Finally, the pageant ended when Amerika Berdrinaxy, from León, was crowned Miss Gay in front of hundreds of enthusiastic supporters. Berdrinaxy—who won a tiara, $5,000, and a trip to compete in the Miss Queen International pageant in Thailand—planned to spend much of the following year traveling throughout Nicaragua, promoting human rights for the LGBTQ community (AP 2014; Gorgeous 2014; La Voz del Sandinismo 2014; RDS 2014).

This book offers a new way of understanding Nicaraguan politics. The last half century of resistance, revolution, democratization, and dictatorship has been the topic of many important studies (e.g., Close and Deonandan 2004; Close 2016; Vilas 1986, 1995; Walker and Wade 2011), but those studies do not analyze the role of LGBTQ people in politics, or even acknowledge their existence (for exceptions see Larracoechea Bohigas 2018; Babb 2020). By ignoring LGBTQ people, these scholars have made a mistake; politics looks different when everyone's experiences are considered.

For example, consider one of the central themes of Nicaraguan political history: the challenge of foreign domination. Outsiders have often preyed

---

1. *Pinol* is a Nicaraguan corn-based cold drink, so *pinoleros* are *pinol* drinkers. Translated loosely, *pinoleros de corazón* would be "Nicaraguans at heart."

on Nicaragua because of its unique geography and natural resources, or for geopolitical reasons. As Victoria González-Rivera (forthcoming) argues regarding the colonial period and the nineteenth and twentieth centuries, outsiders have sought to influence, dominate, and sometimes invade the country in ways that many Nicaraguans understood in terms of LGBTQ sexuality.

There has also been elite anxiety over foreign influences as a response to what are fundamentally local issues. As noted above, during the U.S.-funded Contra War of the 1980s, authorities within the Ministry of the Interior panicked in response to the country's first LGBTQ rights organization. Additionally, the 1992 antisodomy law, Article 204, ratified at a time of rising feminist and NGO activity, was a response to sexual and gender changes that Article 204 proponents thought were encouraged and financed by non-Nicaraguans. At other times, progressive policies regarding LGBTQ people were a way of cleaning up a party's international image with a veneer of sexual "modernity," something that happened in the 2007–17 period, under the government of Daniel Ortega and Rosario Murillo.

At times of rapid social change and heightened anxiety, elites frequently cracked down on "sodomites," lesbians, and transgender Nicaraguans. At other times, dictatorial politicians have tried to co-opt LGBTQ people in an effort to consolidate power and to make their governments appear socially liberal and modern. Nonetheless, despite these and other challenges, LGBTQ people often created considerable space for themselves.

Sexuality and Language

The default expression that I use in this book is LGBTQ even though that term would not have been used in Nicaragua until recently. When discussing the politics of the Sandinista Revolution in the 1970s and 1980s, or the politics of the 1990s and early 2000s, I often use the terms *homosexual*, *lesbiana*, and *gay* as those terms were frequently used at that time by LGBTQ people themselves.

Victoria González-Rivera (forthcoming) notes that before the Spanish conquest of the Americas, the Nahuat speakers of what is now Nicaragua used the term *cuylon*, which seems to have evolved over time into the ubiquitous Nicaraguan Spanish word *cochón*, a word that for much of the twentieth and twenty-first century was typically used in demeaning ways. Drawing on his fieldwork in Managua in the 1980s, U.S. anthropologist Roger Lancaster argued that *cochones* were defined by their "passive" role in anal sex, and by femininity or passivity in general. Yet even though the term *cochón* was generally derogatory, it could be used in a neutral or even positive way by men who did not self-identify as *cochones*. As an example, Lancaster offered the following quote: "We must go to the Carnaval this year and see the *cochones*. The *cochones* there are very, very beautiful" (Lancaster 1992, 238).

Some Nicaraguans referred to the sexual partners of *cochones* as *cochoneros*. Other Nicaraguans had no name for the male who played an "active" role in anal sex. Roger Lancaster referred to him as an *hombre-hombre*, a "regular" guy who suffered little or no social taint due to his sexual practice. If asked to label himself, Lancaster's *hombre-hombre* might have called himself heterosexual or even just "normal."

The word *cochona* could be used as a synonym for *cochón*, but it typically referred to a woman who had sex with women. But unlike a *cochón* who was defined by his supposed passivity, a *cochona* would be considered the "active" or more "masculine" partner in a sexual relationship between two women. The "passive" or "feminine" woman would not necessarily be considered a *cochona* nor would she necessarily be stigmatized in the same way (on stereotypes regarding *cochonas* and their feminine partners, see Howe 2013, 2, 19, 72).

For people who identified as members of the LGBTQ community, *cochón* and *cochona* could be used in an affectionate way, to refer to themselves and others like themselves. Similarly, the meaning of the word *cochonada* depended on the speaker and the context. *Cochonada*, the plural of *cochón* and/or *cochona*, was generally used in a derogatory way, as in "¡*Dejáte de cochonadas!*" ("Stop being so gay!"). But some members of the contemporary LGBTQ community have used the term *cochonada* in a positive way, simply meaning all that is nonheterosexual, much in the way that the formerly derogatory word *queer* has been reappropriated by many English-speaking LGBTQ people.

When LGBTQ Nicaraguans organized in the 1980s and 1990s, they often called their movement one of *orgullo homosexual-lésbico* or "homosexual-lesbian pride" (Sequeira Malespín and Berríos Cruz 1993). It was not until the turn of the century that the movement broadened to include a strong component of people who identified as *travesti*, *transgénera*, *transgénero*, and *transsexual*. *Transgéneras* and *transgéneros* also referred to themselves as trans women (*mujeres trans*),[2] and trans men (*hombres trans*), respectively (Moraga Peña et al. 2010, 11). They generally referred to themselves using the inclusive term *trans*, a term I use in a similar way.

By the end of the twentieth and into the twenty-first century, the most commonly used phrase to refer to people who did not identify as heterosexual (or not exclusively heterosexual) was *comunidad de diversidad sexual* (community of sexual diversity) or simply *la diversidad* (diversity). As of this writing, sexual diversity continues to be the most used phrase, though terms like LGBT, LGBTI, LGBTQ, LGBTIQ, and queer are increasingly used, especially by members of the community with strong international connections (either direct experience outside of Nicaragua, or knowledge through books, articles, and the internet).

Cuir is another word that is sometimes used. For some, *cuir* is a "Spanish-ization of the term queer" (del Val 2011), just as *gai* is sometimes used as a Spanish-ized spelling of "gay." When *cuir* is used that way, queer and *cuir* are basically synonyms (also see Viteri et al. 2016, 11; McCaughan and Rivera 2018). Others, like Ana Victoria Portocarrero, of the Nicaraguan art and activism collective *Operación Queer* (Operation Queer) thought that "for many of us *Cuir* is not the same as queer. I think *Cuir* is a way of placing ourselves in that which is queer but within the Latin American experience" (personal communication by Facebook Messenger, November 25, 2020; also *Managua Furiosa* 2019).

In the early twenty-first century, terms like gay, lesbian, trans, LGBTI, sexually diverse, and sexual diversity were often used as polite or positive alternatives to the older terms like *cochón*, *cochona*, and *cochonero*. Nonetheless, the emergence of new terms did not mean that the older terms ceased to be used, nor was the meaning of the older terms necessarily unchanging.

---

2. In an article that discussed the evolution of terminology and gender identity in Nicaragua, Patrick Welsh noted that some might "conclude that the term *cochón* is in fact synonymous with 'transwomen.' That, however, is not necessarily the case. Self-identifying transwomen in Nicaragua have undergone a conscious process of personal transition and social transgression that involves choices related to their own gender identity and expression and sexual orientation. *Cochón* is merely a label used to stigmatise 'feminised men' and for social control. In all likelihood, many of the self-identifying gay men included in [a study referred to in Welsh's article] would also have been branded as *cochones*, especially those whose gender expression (or elements of it) is culturally interpreted as feminine" (Welsh 2014, 43).

Elyla and Ana Victoria Portocarrero, both founding members of the Operation Queer collective, pondered the class and racial meanings attached to language. According to Elyla,

> For me, I think that *cochón* [and] gay have a super strong connection to class that I cannot leave out. A gay is a homosexual with a car, with a house, with a job, a position. A *cochón* is someone who lives, who struggles, who is in the street, who survives, who does not fit, who does not get work because he does not fit into the classist logic . . . who does not get work . . . because he is very black, who does not get work because he is very ugly, who does not get work because he does not have a proper education. The *cochón* represents all of that which is not the idea of gay for me, that is why I say that I am a dissident gay because I don't identify with the idea of being gay, and because I have been fluid in how I understand my sexuality and my identity. But for me that is how it is: there is a clear difference in class [and] race between . . . being gay and being a *cochón* (interview, July 14, 2017).

Portocarrero responded,

> But it is not the same for lesbians, I think that I would not make such a clear class distinction regarding women because I think that here in Nicaragua there isn't even much talk, there has hardly even been a discussion about lesbianism . . . Homosexual men have had more spaces to express themselves in general and to put forth their agendas and the differences between their agendas and those of women. They have more organizations. . . . If someone calls me a *cochona* I would not feel offended though I know that they would be trying to offend me. Nobody would say that to me, except perhaps [Elyla]. . . . And, it depends a lot on who says it to you and how they say it also, it depends a lot on that . . . the tone of voice, the context. . . . For example, in her concerts, Gaby Baca, who is an open lesbian musician, she always says "Long live the *cochonada!*" "Where are the *marimachas*?" "Where are the *cochones*?" . . . She also says it with great joy. . . . Everyone becomes very happy . . . when you make it your own, when you appropriate it, it loses the power to insult (interview, July 14, 2017).

Which term an individual chose to use depended, at least in part, on the audience. Roger Lancaster relayed a conversation he had with a nurse in the

1980s about a young man who died of AIDS, forced to spend his last year of life effectively imprisoned in a hospital. Lancaster's nurse friend explained, "He was a *co*—How do you say it? A homosexual" (1992 264).

In addition to questions of the audience, the term speakers chose could have as much to do with their own identities—such as class standing, age, ethnicity, sexual orientation—as the identities of the people to which they referred. Silvia Martínez, director of the trans rights organization *Red Trans* (Trans Network) made that point in the form of a joke: "What do you call a delicate [*fino*] young man who has money? Gay. And a delicate young man who is poor? *Maricón* [faggot]" (interview, June 8, 2011).

Though many believe the stereotype that LGBTQ activists are mainly middle class, that is not true in Nicaragua. Some of the activists in my study would be considered middle class in Nicaraguan terms but typically their lives were very precarious. In other words, to be "middle class" in Nicaragua is not the same thing as to be middle class in a country like the United States. However, most of the activists were from working class backgrounds, and many have faced great economic difficulties. For example, at the time of the interviews, many of the trans women had been sex workers or were sex workers. In some cases, activists were raised in middle class households but were downwardly mobile over the course of their lives, at least in part because of labor discrimination against LGBTQ people.

Methods

This book has a companion: *500 Years of LGBTQ+ History in Western Nicaragua* (González-Rivera forthcoming). The books may be read separately, but it would be best to read them together, for they are worth considerably more than the sum of their parts. Saying they are unique does not just mean that they cover a far broader sweep of time than anything that has been written on the politics of sexuality in Nicaragua, though that is true. Not only is there nothing like these two books, in terms of historical scope, regarding Nicaragua, there is very little like them regarding any country in the Western Hemisphere, with the important exceptions of *Intimate Matters: A History of Sexuality in America*, by the historians John D'Emilio and Estelle Freedman (2012), and *Historia de la Homosexualidad en la Argentina* (History of Homosexuality in Argentina) by the journalist Osvaldo Bazán (2016).

What is most unusual about our two volumes is the long collaboration between Victoria González-Rivera and me that made them possible. Our collaboration informs both books, as each has always interrogated the findings and prose of the other, often leading to significant rethinking of our interpretations of the written record of the past and the ethnographic present. While neither of us identifies as LGBTQ, we bring different experiences, along with a common love for Nicaraguan political history, to this project. We feel fortunate to have had the opportunity to become friends and work together, and we recognize that it is quite unusual for two people with such different personal experiences and methodological training—a historian who grew up in Matagalpa, Nicaragua, and a political scientist who grew up in Chicago, Illinois, United States—to collaborate over the course of more than twenty years. Our collaboration has resulted in sixteen joint presentations in the United States, Canada, and Nicaragua; two edited volumes (González and Kampwirth 2001; Kampwirth 2010); an ACLS Collaborative Research Fellowship (2017–18); and this two-volume set.

My book draws upon a total of two years of fieldwork between 1988 and 2017, especially between 2011 and 2017. During that time, I read published and unpublished documents related to LGBTQ life, conducted 120 interviews, and attended a variety of events including press conferences, film festivals, Miss Gay pageants, and LGBTQ organization meetings. Most of my research was carried out in Managua, the capital, and so Managua-based organizations are over-represented in my story. Since Managua, perhaps like all capital cities, dominates national politics—including social movement politics—this volume is fundamentally a story of politics in the capital, and politics that emerges from the capital.

That said, the story of LGBTQ politics is not confined to the capital, and in this book, I briefly consider the contributions of organizations and people based in fourteen of the seventeen departments (the Nicaragua word for states),[3] drawing on interviews with people who live and work in those departments, or written sources, or both. I very briefly refer to many organizations from across the country that belonged to national alliances, at least by the abbreviation of the organization's name in the list of alliance

3. Organizations and activists who appear in the pages of this book are based in the following departments: Boaco, Carazo, Chinandega, Chontales, Estelí, Granada, León, Madriz, Managua, Masaya, Nueva Segovia, Región Autónoma de la Costa Caribe Norte, Región Autónoma de la Costa Caribe Sur, and Somoto.

FIGURE 1 Presentation of preliminary findings from this study in Managua, June 2014. From left to right: author Victoria González-Rivera, CISAS director Ana Quirós, author Karen Kampwirth, IDSDH cofounder Marvin Mayorga. Courtesy of Ana Quirós.

members, and in the list of abbreviations. As the reader will note, the list of abbreviations is long since Nicaraguans often name their organizations with acronyms.

No one book can do justice to the richness and diversity of LGBTQ life in Nicaragua. It is different to live in a small city than in the capital, and the challenges faced by LGBTQ people in the countryside are quite different than those faced by their urban counterparts. Moreover, life in each of the departments differs from each other. The western and central departments share commonalities in that they were colonized by Spain, and Spanish is the dominant language today. Most people in those departments identify simply as "Nicaraguan," explicitly or implicitly alluding to being culturally and ethnically mestizo (of mixed European and Indigenous descent), what Jeffrey Gould (1998) calls the "myth of mestizaje," which portrays western and central Nicaragua as devoid of Indigenous peoples when that is not the case. This same myth erases Afro-Nicaraguans from the pacific and central regions and privileges these regions over the Caribbean regions of Nicaragua (Hooker 2005; González-Rivera 2020).

The history of the eastern parts of Nicaragua, known collectively as the Caribbean Coast, is quite different than that of the western and central portions of the country. The Caribbean Coast was colonized by Britain rather than by Spain and was incorporated violently into the Nicaraguan nation state in the late 1800s. Today it is a multilingual region in which many languages are spoken, among them Miskitu, Mayangna, Rama, Ulwa, Creole, Garifuna, English, and Spanish. It is a multiethnic region in which most inhabitants identify as Miskitu, Mayangna, Rama, Ulwa, Creole, Garifuna, Black, Afrodescendant, Asian, and mestizo. It is a politically autonomous region that is part of Nicaragua but which has its own distinct politics. All these factors shape LGBTQ life on the Caribbean Coast. To my knowledge little has been written on that topic (but see important studies of gender, sexuality, and race by Goett 2017; Morris 2016, forthcoming; and White 2014–15). In short, many stories from outside of Managua remain untold in this book. Hopefully future researchers will uncover them.

LGBTQ Studies in the Americas

By tracing the emergence of gay identities and politics in the Global North, sexuality studies scholars have told a captivating story. Historians John D'Emilio and Estelle B. Freedman's pioneering work on the history of sexuality in the United States documents how the meaning of sexuality in U.S. life has changed from a system centered on family and reproduction in the colonial era, to a romantic, intimate, yet conflicted sexuality in nineteenth-century heterosexual marriage, to an individualistic sexuality in the modern period, when sexual relations are supposed to provide personal identity and individual happiness, apart from reproduction (2012, x–xi). It was only in the latter period that changes in family life, urbanization, and the growth of a market economy created the conditions for widespread gay and lesbian identities (as opposed to same-sex sexual practices) in the United States.

Of course, this transition did not occur for all people at the same time and in the same way. The opportunities created by changes in family life, urbanization, and the market economy were available to a greater extent for people with more resources. That is, they were more available to men than to women, to white people than to people of color, and to upper- and middle-class people than to working-class people. Nonetheless, members of less powerful groups often saw their lives changed in significant ways (Chauncey 1994, 10).

Massive immigration to the United States in the nineteenth and early twentieth centuries was one of the factors that set the stage for the eventual creation of gay businesses and neighborhoods. At the same time, migration was a source of anxiety for many elites in the United States, especially as migrants increasingly came from southern and eastern Europe rather than northern and western Europe: "By the 1890s the majority of people immigrating to New York, in particular, were from Italy or Russia. . . . Almost a third of Manhattan's residents in 1910 were foreign-born Jews or Italians and their children . . . [leading] many Americans of 'older stock' to fear that they would lose control of their cities and even the whole of their society" (Chauncey 1994, 137). In the United States, fears of the foreign were constructed in terms of class and ethnicity but also in terms of sexuality, especially as many of these immigrants were single, settling into neighborhoods where they could find affordable furnished rooms to rent. Some of those neighborhoods ended up becoming gay, and later lesbian, enclaves (Chauncey 1994, 131–36; D'Emilio and Freedman 2012, 290–91).

It is worth noting that, in the United States, the catalyst for the emergence of gay and lesbian enclaves, according to D'Emilio and Freedman, was World War II.

> The war years pulled millions of American men and women away from their families, small towns, and the ethnic neighborhoods of large cities, and deposited them in a variety of sex-segregated, nonfamilial institutions. . . . It offered a dramatic, unexpected alternative to the years of isolation and searching for others that had characterized gay life in the previous half century. . . . [After demobilizing, many] gay men and lesbians, having experienced so great a transformation in their sexual and emotional lives, did not return to pre-war patterns (2012, 289–90).

The Contra War of the 1980s had a similar impact on some Nicaraguans during the war years. But in contrast with many demobilized U.S. soldiers and war volunteers who moved to cities where they could enjoy some freedom from their birth families, and the possibility to create gay and lesbian communities through consumerism (bars, bookstores, bathhouses, and the like), demobilized Nicaraguans did not enjoy such opportunities.

One reason for this was that the Contra War was on Nicaraguan soil. Hundreds of thousands of people were displaced (often as part of extended families) from their rural homes and forced to move into cities away from the fighting. This unexpected massive migration exacerbated a long-standing housing problem. Another factor impeding the creation of consumer-oriented lesbian and gay businesses was the U.S.-imposed embargo on Nicaragua. Scarcities of most goods led to greater control of their distribution by the Sandinista government, making a consumer culture practically nonexistent in Nicaragua during that period.

Given these factors, moving to a gay or lesbian neighborhood after military deployment was not an option for demobilized Nicaraguans, unless they were willing and able to leave the country. Instead, most gay and lesbian Nicaraguans returned to their extended families' households, typically living and sleeping in close quarters with parents, grandparents, and other relatives. Therefore, conditions that shaped the lives of gay and lesbian Nicaraguans were quite different from conditions that faced their U.S. counterparts. But that is not to say that there are two distinct models of sexual politics: a U.S. model and a Latin American model.

In fact, the sort of story I told regarding the United States can also be told of gay and lesbian politics in some of the wealthier, more urban, and more populous countries of Latin America. In countries that attracted large numbers of working-class European immigrants in the nineteenth and early twentieth centuries, like Argentina and Brazil, migration also helped create the conditions for gay communities. "Young and male were the dominant characteristics of the foreign population of turn-of-the-century Buenos Aires—in 1895, two-thirds of the immigrant population of the city were men; in 1914, nearly four-fifths of Buenos Aires' male adults were foreigners" (Encarnación 2016, 80). Many native-born residents of Buenos Aires feared that those disconnected young men would create "a world of immigrants and workers who were permanently or cyclically unemployed, [male] prostitutes, homosexuals and ruffians, anarchists who under the banner of radical political activism barely hid their delinquent pathology" (Jorge Salessi quoted in Bazán 2016, 114–15).

In Rio de Janeiro, mass migration of poor Afro-Brazilians from the countryside, and of new arrivals from Europe (especially from Portugal), had similar effects. During the last two decades of the nineteenth century, and the first two decades of the twentieth century, "men outnumbered women in Rio de Janeiro. . . . Amid the bustle of everyday life in Brazil's largest urban center, thousands of young single men roamed the streets in search of work, entertainment, company, and sex" (Green 1999, 17–18). All of those new arrivals were seeking opportunities, but they were not able to rely on the same survival strategies.

> The migration patterns of homosexual men from the Northeast to Rio and Sâo Paolo, or from the countryside to the city, challenge the standard model presented by sociologists and historians, according to which people relied primarily on kinship ties to move from one area of Brazil to another. For many young men who fled the control and condemnation of family, relatives, and small-town society to achieve urban anonymity in both cities, friendship based on shared identity and similar erotic experiences provided ties thicker than blood (Green 1999, 11).

In the biggest cities, a number of factors converged to create gay and lesbian subcultures. It was in the city where people found some relief from familial oversight through cheap rentals. The city was a place where gay men and lesbians had access to spaces where they could gather in relative anonymity, allowing them to "construct the multiple public identities necessary for them to participate in the gay world without losing the privileges of the straight: assuming one identity at work, another in leisure; one identity before biological kin, another with gay friends" (Chauncey 1994, 133–34; also Macías-González 2014, 2001).

Life in places like New York, San Francisco, Buenos Aires, Rio de Janeiro, and Mexico City offered some people more freedom to live alternate lives—or multiple lives at once—than earlier generations had enjoyed. Yet the growing gay and lesbian spaces also attracted a backlash in the form of antivice societies, religious campaigns, legal changes, and police raids on gathering places, a backlash that would eventually inform LGBTQ politics. Writing on Brazil and Mexico, sociologist Rafael de la Dehesa noted that in "both countries, state crackdowns on these spaces played a significant role in fostering organized resistance" (2010, 16).

The most famous example of resistance to police crackdowns—the moment observers often identify as the beginning of the modern gay and lesbian rights movement—was the riot at New York's Stonewall Inn beginning in the evening of June 27, 1969. Police raids were not new. What was new was the decision by bar patrons, especially trans women of color like Sylvia Rivera and Marsha Johnson, to fight back, and to continue to protest throughout the weekend. That marked a dramatic turn in LGBTQ life, and a new more radical politics. As I have noted, LGBTQ communities had been growing over the course of the century, and in the United States small gay and lesbian groups known as the homophiles had existed since the 1950s. Nonetheless, the Stonewall riots, and especially the ways in which the riots resonated, and were commemorated,[4] marked a new beginning, an assertion that to be sexually transgressive was a right, a good thing.

It was a beginning that could not have happened if not for earlier decades of migration, urbanization, and the development of gay and lesbian businesses and neighborhoods, all in the context of wars that were fought on foreign soil. Also, such resistance might have been unlikely if not for the political context of the time. The civil rights movement, the antiwar movement, the Black Power movement, and the second wave feminist movement were all sources of inspiration. Within weeks of the Stonewall riots, a group of gay men and lesbians founded the Gay Liberation Front (GLF), marking the organizational beginning of the movement for gay liberation, rather than for mere toleration (D'Emilio and Freedman 2012, 318–23; Encarnación 2016, 17–20; Epstein 1999, 37–41).

The Stonewall story is powerful, but its very power has distorted our understanding of gay and lesbian politics elsewhere in the Americas. According to political scientist Omar Encarnación, these distortions include

> the view that gay rights activism in Latin America is a post-Stonewall phenomenon; or the impression that the strategies of Latin American gay-rights activists to secure civil rights simply mimic those of their foreign counterparts, . . . Argentina, Brazil, and Mexico, among other Latin American nations, decriminalized homosexuality in the nineteenth-century, more than

---

4. Elizabeth A. Armstrong and Suzanna M. Crage (2006) argue that because of factors like the relationship of local LGBTQ organizations with the police, the nature of press coverage, and the ability of local organizations to commemorate the event, the Stonewall riots have been widely remembered. In contrast, similar (and earlier) protests, like the 1965 New Year's Ball Raid, and the 1966 Compton Cafeteria disturbance, both in San Francisco, are rarely remembered by the public.

a century before the United States and Britain got around to do it; and gay rights activism in Latin America developed independently of the Stonewall riots. (2016, 5)

In fact, *Nuestro Mundo* (Our World), believed to be Latin America's first gay rights organization, was founded in Buenos Aires in 1967, two years before the Stonewall riots (Bazán 2016, 335–39; Encarnación 2016, 40, 86–87).

Many gay and lesbian rights groups were created during the 1970s and 1980s, especially in the wealthier and more urban countries of the Americas. Political opportunities were also crucial. The existence of long-standing liberal democratic institutions in places like the United States created opportunities for activists to push for greater rights, especially for those whose demands were relatively moderate (Epstein 1999, 31–32, 45–46).

In places that had experienced recent dictatorships, democratization processes sometimes created similar opportunities. In other words, well-institutionalized democracy was not always a prerequisite for political gains. For instance, LGBTQ movements in Mexico and Brazil emerged in the 1970s in the context of what Rafael de la Dehesa called "semi-authoritarian regimes" (2010, 2), regimes that were in the process of slow and uneven transitions to democracy. Transition politics in Mexico and Brazil created spaces for activists, as LGBTQ groups in both countries were able to join with other opposition groups, and with emerging political parties, framing their demands in terms of human rights and democratization.

These strategies were somewhat effective in Mexico, especially in places like Mexico City, where trans people were granted the right to change their names to match their gender in 2004, and where marriage equality was implemented in 2010, including adoption rights for same-sex couples. They were very effective in Brazil where the LGBTQ movement, "arguably among the most successful in the Global South, has achieved an impressive body of legislation on LGBT rights, organized the largest LGBT pride marches in the world, and established a remarkably cooperative relationship with the state" (de la Dehesa 2010, 2; Diez 2015, 14–15; 152–95; Marsiaj 2006, 171–87).

The Argentine story is especially compelling. While LGBTQ groups in Argentina predated those elsewhere in Latin America, they were violently crushed following the 1976 military coup and did not reemerge until after the military dictatorship ended in 1983. Yet eventually, the movement in Argentina enjoyed considerable successes, and in 2010 Argentina became the second country in the Americas (after Canada) to extend marriage rights to same-sex couples. Part of the explanation, according to Omar Encarnación, is that Argentina "meets the two most noted preconditions for societal support for gay rights, especially same-sex marriage, a high level of social and economic development, and a low level of religiosity" (2016, 77). The recent history of Argentina also helps explain LGBTQ political successes. The horrors of the military dictatorship (1976–83) and the so-called Dirty War, in which the military "disappeared" (kidnapped, tortured, and usually murdered) up to thirty thousand people, as well as the organized resistance to the dictatorship led by the Mothers of the *Plaza de Mayo* had an impact on political culture. Today, the concept of "human rights" probably has more cultural resonance in Argentina than in any other country in the Americas. Members of the LGBTQ rights movement that reemerged after the dictatorship astutely framed their own demands in terms of human rights, and they successfully "built alliances with other movements confronting the Catholic Church, as it has struggled with the exploding issue of sexual abuse and proof of church involvement in Argentina's 'Dirty War'" (Friedman 2014).

Ultimately, the story of LGBTQ political successes in Argentina is one of impressive social movement politics. Without the structural, historical, and cultural factors I have identified, the successful campaign to change laws regarding marriage and other rights might not have been possible. But the campaign did not happen on its own. Rather, it was the result of years of hard work by LGBTQ rights groups. Those groups took advantage of opportunities created by the 2005 passage of a marriage equality law in Spain. In addition to the symbolic value of marriage equality in Spain, several veterans of the Spanish campaign did critical solidarity work, providing their Argentine counterparts with significant economic and organizing support (Bimbi 2010, 26; Friedman 2012, 29–31, 36–38, 40–43, 46–51).

Starting in 2005, and continuing for years, LGBTQ activists fought for expanded rights utilizing a number of tactics at once. Activists wrote articles and letters for newspapers; they sought television and radio coverage of their issues; they lobbied individual business leaders and politicians from all political parties; they held protests as well as public celebrations of LGBTQ family life; and they simultaneously sought change through the institutions of the judiciary, Congress, and the presidency (Bimbi 2010; Schulenberg 2012).

Finally, peculiarities of the Argentine transition to democracy provided opportunities, since there were really two transitions (Pousadela 2013, 702). The first began in 1983 with the end of the dictatorship and the election of

President Raúl Alfonsín and largely ended four years later with the passage of *Punto Final* (Full Stop) and *Obediencia Debida* (Due Obedience), laws that ended trials against those who had ordered or committed atrocities during the dictatorship. Nearly two decades passed before the second transition to democracy, beginning with the 2003 election of President Néstor Kirchner (and continuing through the presidency of his wife, Cristina Fernández de Kirchner, 2007–15). Under the Kirchners the *Punto Final* and *Obediencia Debida* laws were repealed, trials against those accused of Dirty War crimes started up again, and the state made unprecedented efforts to memorialize the victims of the military regime and to praise the Madres who had dared to resist the dictatorship.

The transformation led by the Kirchners (known as *kirchnerismo*) was important for the LGBTQ rights movement. "They were two processes that informed each other. Without the basic conditions created by the fact that *kirchnerismo* was in power, the uphill battle would have been far more difficult, but we were able to generate the conditions that made it possible for a government, that would have never addressed the issue on its own, to reach the point when it sat down to ask, 'What are we going to do about the gay marriage issue?'" (Bimbi 2010, 550).

Neither Néstor Kirchner nor Cristina Fernández de Kirchner were supporters of marriage equality until close to the end (Bimbi 2010, 158; Encarnación 2016, 77). Both took a long time to be convinced—Cristina even more than her husband Néstor. Ultimately, she did come around, as did many of her fellow citizens. "Cristina, as an indicator of our society, approached that position [in favor of marriage equality] first with indifference, then with doubt, and finally with determined support" (Bimbi 2010, 125). And in the end, the fact that she gave her full support to LGBTQ rights is what mattered. It mattered so much that even though her administration was replaced by the much more conservative administration of Mauricio Macri in 2015, the expanded rights that she signed into law were not in danger. They had become new Argentine values, embraced by the vast majority of Argentines.

On the Periphery of the Periphery

The combination of factors I just discussed (high degrees of urbanization, industrial capitalist development, extensive gay and lesbian urban networks, democratic or democratizing institutions) is infrequently found in the poorer countries of the Global South. As a result, those who study the politics of sexuality, especially those who write in English, have not spent much energy on Central America.[5] I hope this book is a step toward correcting that mistake.

Since Belize's Supreme Court struck down its antisodomy law in 2016 (Ring 2016), consensual nonheterosexual sex is legal in all the Central American countries. All of them have some laws on the books that prohibit discrimination for reasons of sexual orientation; however, as of this writing, only Costa Rica permits same-sex marriage and adoption of children by nonheterosexual couples (Kennon 2020). Still, every Central American country has its own unique LGBTQ history. In every country there are organized LGBTQ groups, as well as unorganized individuals who engage in resistance by living their lives as sexual dissidents, that is, by rejecting heteronormativity (Araya Molina 2019; Arévalo and Solorzano 2019; Berger 2006, 61–76; Córtez Ruiz 2019; Gardella 2019; Jiménez Bolaños 2017a, 2017b, 2016; Palevi 2017; Palevi Gómez Arévalo 2016; Portillo Villeda 2014; Restoy 2016; Thayer 1997; Ríos Vega 2020; Wundram Pimentel 2015).

Many wrongly assume that LGBTQ life in Central America has emerged recently and could only be due to "global queering" or the diffusion of LGBTQ culture—concepts such as gay, lesbian, and queer, symbols such as the rainbow flag, and traditions such as pride parades—from the Global North to the Global South. Political scientist Dennis Altman noted that during the final decades of the twentieth century, growing numbers of men throughout the world identified as gay, and as members of a gay community (in countries that were otherwise very different), sharing a common culture to a significant extent. In other words, global queering, according to this view, was driven by a series of influences including urbanization, international development agencies, economic globalization, the international film industry, tourism, and the internet (Altman 1997, 423–25).

Responding to the global queering argument, political scientist Peter Drucker contested the idea that LGBTQ identity and politics were largely an import from the Global North (or in his words, the imperialist countries): "If anything, Third World dependence on imperialist economies has helped to delay development of the material basis for Third World gay-lesbian communities" (Drucker 1996, 77).

---

5. The Central American countries are Costa Rica, El Salvador, Guatemala, Honduras, and Nicaragua. Together (along with what is now the Mexican state of Chiapas) they formed the *República Federal de Centroamérica* (Federal Republic of Central America), which existed from 1823 to 1841. Today, Panama and Belize are sometimes considered Central American because they share the isthmus with the traditional Central American countries.

Like Drucker, the philosopher Peter Jackson considered political economy to be key to explaining the emergence of a so-called global queer culture. For Jackson, thinking of global queering mainly as a transfer of queer culture from the Global North to the Global South (or from the colonizers to the colonized) was problematic.

> The import-export model does not explain why modern homosexualities emerged first in Asian societies that suffered the least direct impact from Western imperialism or why centuries of British and Dutch colonial rule in India and Indonesia, respectively, did not lead to those societies becoming the first in Asia with modern gay communities. Contact with the West, at least in its imperialist colonizing form, appears to have retarded rather than assisted the development of modern gay cultures in Asia (Jackson 2009, 366).

Instead, he argued, elements of modern gay culture seemed to emerge in many places at once due to the expansion of market capitalism in different cities at about the same time (2009, 362). Comparing his research on Bangkok with George Chauncey's work on New York City and James Green's work on Rio de Janeiro, Jackson found that sexual practices and identities evolved in remarkably similar ways in those places during the mid-twentieth century, even though individuals would have had little or no contact with their counterparts in the other cities (2009, 365, 371).

Globalization involves individuals and groups of individuals actively responding to and engaging with capitalism and global culture, even though there is no consensus on what constitutes "global culture." As anthropologist Martin Manalansan noted regarding his study of gay Filipino men in New York City, it is "apparent that even the gayest global spaces such as New York City are rife with cultural fissures and divides between various queer communities" (2004, viii). But Manalansan's ethnography was not mainly about how global queer culture influences people. Instead, it considered how a group of Filipino men made meaningful lives for themselves. He showed "how these men negotiate between Filipino and American sexual and gender traditions, more specifically between *bakla*[6] and gay ideologies" (2003, ix). To be bakla is not to be premodern; rather, it is "to assert a particular kind

---

6. "*Bakla* is the Tagalog term that encompasses homosexuality, hermaphroditism, crossdressing, and effeminacy. One of the bakla's singular attributes is a sense of self entrenched in the process of transformation" (Manalansan 2003, ix).

of modernity" (2003, x). Manalansan argued that we need to understand "the border between *bakla* and gay not in terms of self-contained modes of identity but as permeable boundaries of two coexisting yet oftentimes incommensurable cultural ideologies of gender and sexuality" (2003, 21).

Similarly, though the Nicaraguan border between *cochón* and gay, or between *cochona* and lesbian, is not the border between tradition and modernity, it is sometimes framed that way. As part of her ethnography of LGBTQ organizing in Nicaragua in the 1990s and early 2000s, the anthropologist Cymene Howe analyzed the explicit tactics, and implicit goals, of several urban and rural lesbian discussion groups. Those groups utilized much of the language and symbolism associated with global queering, and they sometimes received funding from international nongovernmental agencies.

> Nicaraguan lesbian discussion groups are invested in cultivating participants who are *bien educada*: women who are well-educated and well-mannered in how they speak about and understand sexuality. In lesbian discussion groups, women who historically have been designated cochonas can now subscribe to a new moniker: lesbiana. But who may count—or, better yet, who may want to be counted—as a lesbian is a question that remains unresolved in discussion groups (2013, 87, 61–91).

In short, global queer culture does not always transfer easily or well, nor should it necessarily.

In the Global North, one of the central strategies of the LGBTQ movement—coming out—has helped make decades of political accomplishments possible. It was all too easy for many heterosexuals to oppose rights for LGBTQ people when they thought they had never met such a person. Once coming out became a widespread strategy in the post-Stonewall era, and those same heterosexuals realized that LGBTQ individuals could be found within the circles of people who were dear to them (coworkers, friends, relatives), extending equal rights to the LGBTQ community struck many as the right thing to do.

While many individual residents of the Global South have benefitted from the coming out strategy, it is important to keep in mind that such a strategy is rooted in the history of the Global North, and that it is a strategy that may not work, or may not be desirable, in other historical contexts (Horn 2010, 174–76). Many LGBTQ people reject the goal of coming out, for reasons that are cultural as well as economic. Martin Manalansan has suggested that coming out is predicated on an individualistic U.S. expectation that to become an adult is to distance oneself from one's birth family, an expectation that is not shared cross-culturally (2003, 22–23, 27–35). Likewise, in her study of gay Cubans in Miami, scholar Susana Peña found that many saw coming out as strange and unnecessary, "because one's queerness is undeniable from a young age . . . an inborn trait that is, or should be, obvious to others" (2013, 88).

In his work on Mexican gay men, Héctor Carrillo has argued that families sometimes rely on "sexual silence" and "tacit tolerance as strategies for managing sexual diversity within family life" (Carrillo 2001, 73). Similarly, in his study of gay Dominican immigrants to New York, Carlos Ulises Decena noted that many see coming out to their relatives as unnecessary, as it was "already implied or assumed" (Decena 2016, 221). Yet for some of the men he interviewed, it was painful to stay silent regarding their personal lives. One tried to broach the subject, but his parents could not or would not "understand" the "gay topic" [asunto gay] (Decena 2016, 226–27). Others saw coming out to their families as unacceptably risky, given the economic and emotional support they received from them.

Paradoxically perhaps, many of Peña's subjects were closeted (i.e., they were not verbally "out"), yet their partners were incorporated into their families, illustrating the concept of "sexual silence." In the case of one couple, "both men and their respective families had all celebrated the previous nochebuena (Christmas Eve) together; the shared holiday was significant because Christmas Eve is traditionally spent with extended family of origin in Cuban culture [and throughout Catholic Latin America]" (2013, 125). In another case, "Miguel, who believed young Cuban gay men were making the 'biggest mistake of their lives' by coming out, was living in his parents' house with his partner at the time of our interview" (2013, 125; also see Decena 2016, 225, 227).

Despite these examples of tacit or implied acceptance, not all Latin American families have happily accepted the sexuality of their relatives if it remained unspoken. For instance, political scientists Javier Corrales and Mario Pecheny cited studies that found that 26.5 percent of participants in a Buenos Aires gay pride parade "felt excluded and marginalized by their families;" 29.8 percent of participants in a Santiago gay pride parade felt the same way (2010, 12). In high-income countries, a typical solution to the problem of "homophobia begins at home" is household exodus: LGBTQ youth leave their homes, sometimes their hometowns, in search of greater freedom, new experiences, and supportive friends. But for LGBTQ individuals in Central America, this exit option is considerably less prevalent.

For a series of reasons—housing shortages, low incomes, high unemployment rates, and cultural expectations that single adult children will live with and take care of older relatives—multigenerational households are common among working-class people across Latin America, especially in the poorer countries of the region.[7] Living with extended family can provide many benefits, but it can be complicated. One Nicaraguan woman, "Delia," told psychologist Mary Bolt González that her family members did not know she was lesbian. Then she qualified that claim.

> They suspect but nobody has the courage to ask me. Once my mother was brave enough, about four years ago, but I brushed her off. She called me and said, 'What are you—she did not say lesbian—a *cochona*? I did not say anything, I just laughed. . . . When my father was alive, he did not get involved, but he suspected. He did not say anything to me. The problem is with my siblings, because we are very close in age, and they are very sexist even my sisters. . . . Only one of my sisters knows for sure because she caught me with a person in my room [laughter]. . . . [S]he used to blackmail me a lot. . . . 'Either give me money or buy me a pair of pants or buy me a pair of shoes; . . . if not I will go and tell Mom everything that I know (1996, 70–71).

Delia's relationship with her brothers was even more difficult, as "they [said] they would make all those people into soap. 'Pure Hitler,' I told them. . . . Then I just insist[ed] that we respect each other, if you are going to think like that" (1996, 72).

Delia's experiences were not unique. One study of LGBTQ Nicaraguans found that 48.5 percent had been discriminated against by members of their own family (Moraga Peña et al. 2010, 21). Even some activists felt they could not live openly among their relatives and friends, as Cymene Howe found. One invited her to lunch at her office, warning her, "Do not tell anyone that we know each other from the lesbian discussion group." Even the facilitator

---

7. In Latin America, "The share of people living alone is less than one-third of those in the United States. Most of these live-alone youths are concentrated in the urban areas of Argentina and Uruguay" (Corrales and Pecheny 2010, 14).

of the group was not out at home. She invited Howe over to her house for dinner but "recommended that we mention homosexuality, lesbianism, and the discussion group only behind closed doors, where her mother would be out of earshot." A third activist told Howe that they used great caution in their organizing. "For example, we coordinate the meeting by phone. But we don't say who is calling. We have a secret message. The message just says 'Elisabet called,' but nothing more. Nothing about [the sexuality rights group] Xochiquetzal" (2013, 65).

Yet while I know of cases, from written sources and my interviews, in which relatives were hostile (in one case forcing an eleven-year-old boy to live on the street), I also know of cases in which intrafamilial relations were much warmer. Sometimes parents supported their LGBTQ children after a period of coming to accept their sexual orientation, or sometimes they immediately responded with hugs and professions of love when they learned their child was gay or lesbian (Bolt González 1996, 86, 112–14; Lancaster 1992, 259–60; Rocha Córtez 2012b). In recent years, some parents and relatives have allied themselves with the cause of LGBTQ rights, participating in poster campaigns, radio programs, and marching in gay pride parades.

In this range of experiences, Nicaraguans were like people elsewhere. For some, coming out helped them gain acceptance and respect within their families and social circles. But even though selectively drawing upon "global queer culture" (including the coming out strategy) might help many who remain closeted or semicloseted, the risks for economically vulnerable people who live with their relatives can be enormous. For many, the potential costs of coming out are all too real, while the potential benefits are much less obvious. So, while "global queering" has influenced life in contemporary Nicaragua, as it has elsewhere, it cannot completely explain the evolution of LGBTQ life in Nicaragua, with all its twists and turns.

LGBTQ Studies in Nicaragua

Victoria González-Rivera (forthcoming) discusses the small but insightful literature on the history of sexual orientation and gender identity in Nicaragua. Here I consider the scholarship on LGBTQ politics and culture during the past half century. The earliest of those works were written by foreigners who visited Nicaragua during the years of the Sandinista Revolution (1979–

90). In those pieces, which were published in English, they sought to describe LGBTQ life, and to analyze the political implications of the sexual practices they learned about during their stay in Nicaragua.

The philosopher Ann Ferguson wrote that the "social and economic preconditions for . . . a lesbian and gay rights movement simply don't exist, at least outside of the [very small] urban middle and upper class" (1991, 82), basing her analysis on the economy, the dominant cultural pattern she called "single mother patriarchy" (1991, 80), and the support networks of the lesbians she interviewed. Though sociologist Barry Adam studied gay men rather than lesbians, like Ferguson he argued that Nicaragua was characterized by "homosexuality without a gay world" due in part to a series of socioeconomic factors: the lack of privacy in small towns and city neighborhoods, the crowded multigenerational households in which most people lived, and the war-time economy of the 1980s.

> The inability to avoid family supervision is compounded by the usual architecture of houses and commercial establishments. Except for the houses of the small middle class, most people live in houses that open directly onto the street. . . . Though there is a bar owned by two gay men, it is separated from the street by no more than a metal grill, in common with other cafes and bars in the neighborhood, obliging those of its patrons who are homosexual to observe the norms of heterosexist propriety (Adam 1993, 173).

Like Ferguson and Adam, Roger Lancaster (1992) argued that the conditions for a gay and lesbian rights movement did not exist in the 1980s, but he based that claim on very different evidence, noting that traditional male same-sex sexual practices were constructed differently in Nicaragua than in places like the United States, with different political implications. According to Lancaster, while in the United States, both partners in a same-sex relationship would be seen as gay; in Nicaragua, the *cochón* played the "passive" role in anal sex. His partner was not seen as gay, but rather as what Lancaster called an "*hombre-hombre*," or manly man.

According to Lancaster, the manly man was not stigmatized by having sex with another man if he was seen to be the active participant. Indeed, such practices might have increased his status among his fellow manly men, as long as he was not seen as preferring sex with men to sex with women, and as long as he did not seem to identify with the *cochones* with whom he had sex.

This inclusive aspect of sex also has implications for the cochón's status as a political concept, for that category lacks the theoretical independence attributed to Western homosexuality as a distinct category of activity and personal identity. A cochón requires ordinary men, and his activity and identity can never be quite independent of them. Defined by passivity, the status is ever a dependent one (Lancaster 1992, 243).

Lancaster did not claim that individuals always followed these social "rules" in their private lives, nor did he claim to have done extensive research with men who identified as *cochones*. Instead, he analyzed general social rules largely from the perspective of the men in his circle of regular informants, most of whom identified as manly men (1992, 239). Still, general rules defining sexual practices had implications, regardless of what individuals did in private.

While twentieth century same-sex sexual practices in the United States stigmatized and excluded all who engaged in them (creating a common identity and the possibility for the emergence of gay businesses, neighborhoods, and politics), the stigmatization of the *cochón*, but not his partner, precluded the possibility of gay politics as understood in the United States. Lancaster argued that the construction of male sexuality made a Nicaraguan gay and lesbian rights movement unlikely. He also believed that foreign gays and lesbians, known as internationalists, who arrived in the wave of solidarity with the Sandinista Revolution, and who tried to support or "stimulate the formation of a variety of gay self-help groups, educational clubs, and political organizations," were engaged in suspect work by "duplicating the logic of colonialism," which inevitably centers the West (1992, 272). In a later piece, Lancaster seemed to qualify his position, noting that "the slow emergence after 1990 of an open gay liberation movement in Managua would seem to mark an important turning point in Nicaragua's political culture" (1995, 110).

Antonio Velásquez Villatoro and Patrick Welsh both differed with Lancaster, but they drew upon different sorts of evidence. Velásquez Villatoro considered the way in which homosexuality was portrayed in literature, specifically in the Nicaraguan author Lizandro Chávez Alfaro's novel, *Trágame tierra*, published in 1969. The complexities in the novel led Velásquez Villatoro to argue that binaries such as active versus passive and macho versus *cochón* were oversimplifications (Velásquez Villatoro 2015, 53).

Patrick Welsh critiqued Lancaster's argument from an ethnographic perspective. For Welsh, Lancaster's claims regarding sexual practices and their political implications were based on a real but exaggerated distinction between the Anglo-American model and the Nicaraguan model, noting that in contemporary Nicaragua the

> *cochón-cochonero* paradigm has never really existed as an exclusive model of homosexuality between men. During the 1980s, for example, in the midst of the Sandinista Revolution, a "gay" collective emerged in Managua that brought together a group of young revolutionaries who self-identified mostly as lesbians and gays. The latter category, however, integrated at least two sub-groups of homosexual men—those who had been culturally labeled as cochones, and those whose self-identification was as "gays," within a modern conceptualization of the term. To some degree, the distinction between the two sub-groups was also related to issues of social class, formal educational achievements, the influence of religion, economic capacity, access to other cultures and urban/rural origins (Welsh 2014, 42–43).

As Welsh noted, during the mid-1980s a group of up to one hundred Sandinista Nicaraguans participated in a gay and lesbian pride group. That organization, known by some as *Grupo Inicio* (Initial Group) was eventually crushed by the ruling *Frente Sandinista de Liberación Nacional* (Sandinista Front for National Liberation, or FSLN), only to reemerge in the form of the HIV-AIDS education collective *Colectivo de Educadores Populares Contra el SIDA* (Collective of Grassroots Educators against AIDS, or CEP-SIDA). So, despite Ferguson, Adam, and Lancaster's claims that conditions did not exist for the emergence of an LGBTQ movement in the 1980s, scholars now know that is largely untrue.

It is not surprising that scholars who worked in the 1980s thought conditions did not exist for LGBTQ politics since the participants in Initial Group agreed not to talk about what happened to them while the revolution was under threat from the U.S.-funded Contra guerrillas. It was not until after the revolution ended in 1990 that this major turning point in Nicaraguan history—when LGBTQ people first sought political rights—was analyzed in film or print. Still, that work was almost all in English, and so it was inaccessible to most Nicaraguans (Aráuz 1994; Babb 2003, 2004; Broadbent 1991; Hobson 2016; Howe 2013; Kampwirth 2014; McGee and Kampwirth 2015; Thayer 1997; Randall 1993).

The one book written in Spanish on LGBTQ life in the late twentieth century was Mary Bolt González's pioneering book *Sencillamente diferentes . . .*

La auto estima de las mujeres lesbianas en los sectores urbanos de Nicaragua
(Simply Different . . . Lesbian Self-Esteem in Urban Nicaragua). The book,
based on interviews with thirty lesbians in 1994 and 1995, addresses themes
like family life and personal identity. Additionally, many of the women who
told their stories in that book referred to their political experiences and opinions, and Bolt González concluded with a brief overview of LGBTQ politics
in the 1980s and 1990s (1996, 294–97). In the years after the publication
of Bolt's book, the only Spanish-language publications on contemporary
LGBTQ politics in Nicaragua appeared as two book chapters (Aráuz 1999;
Kampwirth 2012). Given the limited nature of the literature in Spanish, it
was not surprising that, when I began the interviews for this book in 2011, I
found that almost no young LGBTQ activists were aware that there had been
organized LGBTQ politics in Nicaragua in the 1980s.

The early 1990s were a complicated time for members of the LGBTQ
community. Sandinista President Daniel Ortega's electoral loss to conservative Violeta Barrios de Chamorro in 1990, followed by the United States'
withdrawal of economic and political support to the Contra rebels, meant
that the Sandinista Revolution and the Contra War ended almost simultaneously. The end of the war and the new neoliberal regime created economic
hardships as well as political opportunities for some LGBTQ Nicaraguans. It
was somewhat easier to organize openly, without the pressures of the Sandinista state, and new organizations and events were created, often in alliance
with the emerging autonomous feminist movement.

But that brief period of political openness ended in 1992 when Article
204, the most restrictive antisodomy law in the hemisphere, was passed
by the National Assembly and signed by President Chamorro. Many activists feared that they could be imprisoned for even speaking out in favor of
LGBTQ rights. That did not make all of them stop, but it did require creativity on their part (on LGBTQ organizing in the 1990s and early 2000s see
Babb 2003, 2004; Howe 2013, 2002; Thayer 1997; on sexuality see Montenegro 2000; for a novel inspired by the most well-known victim of Article 204,
Aura Rosa Pavón, see Sirias 2009; for an anthropological account of Pavón's
story, see Howe 2009).

The most recent period—from Sandinista Daniel Ortega's inauguration
as president in 2007 to the present—was a time of rapid growth for the
LGBTQ movement, not only in terms of numbers of organizations, but in
terms of the social presence of the LGBTQ community through beauty pageants, music, performance art, conferences, social media, and pride parades.

It was a complicated time as under the Sandinista government a new Penal Code went into effect in 2008, simultaneously eliminating the infamous Article 204, and banning abortion under all circumstances, even to save a woman's life.

The relationship between the Sandinista Front and the LGBTQ movement had changed dramatically from that of the years of the revolution: instead of responding to LGBTQ organizing mainly with repression, the FSLN sought to draw members of the LGBTQ community into its clientelistic networks. As of this writing, there are a few publications that address LGBTQ issues during the years of the "second Sandinista revolution" (Heumann et al. 2017; Kampwirth 2014, 2012; McGee and Kampwirth 2015; Moraga Peña et al. 2010), and one award-winning gay coming-of-age novel (Luna Garay 2013). Also worth noting is the literature on sexually transgressive traditions in public festivals in the cities of Masaya (Blandón 2003; Borland 2006; Palma 2004), and Managua (Guevara 2014; Lancaster 1988; Petrus n.d.).

In the twenty-first century, many important sources were websites. Though sometimes ephemeral, they often reached a much wider audience than formal publications. For instance, Elvis G. Salvatierra's column "A propósito de . . ." on the website *Managua Furiosa* (Furious Managua) regularly posted from 2014 up to this writing, was notable for its thoughtful commentary on Nicaraguan life. His essays addressed a variety of themes including women in advertising, gay pride day, the massacre at the Orlando Florida nightclub, gay men's misogynistic "jokes," heterosexual men's homophobic "jokes," LGBTQ people in public life, journalistic coverage of LGBTQ issues, gender binaries, activism, and employment. One of the main themes that ran as a thread through most of Salvatierra's work was the relationship between LGBTQ and feminist thinking:

> When I learned about the feminist movement my understanding of sexual diversity changed. Feminist proposals, both collective and personal, helped me to understand that there is not just one way of existing and being in the world, that every person should be recognized as unique, and as a result respected and considered in all areas of existence (Salvatierra 2015a).

If the relationship between feminism and LGBTQ rights was one of the most important themes that informed Salvatierra's work, the other was family relations. He concluded an essay mocking the idea that boys become gay because "they were not treated with a heavy hand" or girls become lesbian because "their mothers did not teach them how to be women," with a poem by the gay Chilean writer, Pedro Lemebel.

> There are so many children who will be born
> With a broken wing
> And I want them to fly *compañero*
> May their revolution
> Give them a piece of red sky
> So that they may fly
> (Pedro Lemebel, quoted in Salvatierra 2015b)

The online magazine in which Salvatierra's column, *Managua Furiosa*, appeared was not exclusively an LGBTQ magazine—that was just one theme among many. But there were blogs that were devoted mainly, or exclusively, to LGBTQ life. One of those blogs was *Comunidad Homosexual de Nicaragua* (Homosexual Community of Nicaragua), which regularly posted information on events within Nicaragua, academic studies, political accomplishments, or crises that faced LGBTQ people internationally as well as nationally, and sometimes detailed reports on conflicts within Nicaragua's LGBTQ community. While not claiming journalistic neutrality, Homosexual Community of Nicaragua was an invaluable source of information during a period of rapid growth in LGBTQ organizing (*Comunidad Homosexual de Nicaragua* 2010–14).

From 2007 to 2017, Mario Santiago Vásquez López was the main creator of two blogs: *Espacio Comunicación Alternativa* (Alternative Communication Space) (2007–11), which was a project of the *Grupo de Diversidad Sexual de Carazo* (Sexual Diversity Group of Carazo), followed by *El Blog de Mariosvl* (Mariosvl's Blog) (2011–17). Taken together, these two blogs were the most extensive websites on LGBTQ issues in Nicaragua. Over the course of hundreds of posts, viewers could read about global and Nicaraguan LGBTQ history, select from a large collection of video interviews with members of Nicaragua's LGBTQ community and their allies, learn about film festivals, television shows, pride parades, and other community events, read about the Nicaraguan LGBTQ community's political accomplishments and challenges, and follow the Miss Nicaragua Gay and Miss Nicaragua pageants in detail (Vásquez López 2011–17, 2007–11).

David Rocha Cortez 's *Crónicas de la ciudad* (Narratives of the City), published online from 2012 through this writing, was the most literary of the blogs, addressing themes that included family, friends, work, the history of LGBTQ Nicaragua, contemporary politics, and—especially—the city of Managua. Some of the posts are essays, some are poems, and many are prose poems. For instance, the first stanza of his prose poem, *"Lirismo Cochón"* (*Cochón* Lyricism) reads:

> This *cochón* lyricism smells of sweating men, a *macho* and a *loca* sweating in a public bathroom as though life were vanishing through their pores. This lyricism that will be confused with a cowardly and feminine poetic voice, with a subject that unfolds with who knows what words. This lyricism that will remain forever written in my notebook. This lyricism that is not tethered down in monuments, progressive buildings, cards, coat of arms, neon lights, public kisses, Sunday afternoons. (Rocha Córtez 2017a)

Rocha's prose is often stunning, taking the ordinary, even unpleasant, details of everyday life, and turning them into brilliant images, like the lyricism of the public bathroom in the passage quoted above. Or as in these lines from the *"Segunda carta de amor"* ("Second love letter"), inspired by a ride on one of Managua's crowded buses: "This dead city that only knows the price of forgetting, that knows the price of a forgotten memory, seduces me with its traffic circles since in them there are remnants of your embrace. . . . We go over one bridge, two and three, and as we go over your underarm is drawn on my window, your woody scent slipping by my nose" (Rocha Córtez 2012a; also see Rocha Córtez 2019).

Overview of the Book

Chapter 1, "LGBTQ Memories of the Sandinista Revolution," opens with the experiences of some of the gays and lesbians who participated in the guerrilla uprising against the Somoza dictatorship. Once the Sandinista Revolution (1979–90) had begun, the FSLN's efforts to consolidate power were complicated by sexuality. Considering accounts of theatrical productions, practices of the Ministries of Culture, the Interior, and Education, and mass mobilization within the literacy campaign, I find that the Sandinistas had no single LGBTQ policy, instead promoting many, often contradictory, policies.

This is nicely illustrated by the experiences of men who served in the war against the Contras. For them, the war was simultaneously frightening and liberating; some were intentionally put in danger by homophobic commanders while others found that the homosocial environment of war provided sexual opportunities.

In chapter 2, "The Wizard of the Revolution and Other Stories," I consider the cultural revolution of the 1980s, analyzing the television personality and close confidant of the first lady, Donald Casco, an openly gay artist, astrologer, and "Wizard of the Revolution." Casco's story, and the revolution itself, was shaped by the old politics of U.S. domination (manifested through the Contra War) as well as a new entanglement with Cuba and the Soviet bloc states. Many gay and lesbian Nicaraguans studied in Cuba or the Soviet bloc, while thousands of gay and lesbian foreigners visited Nicaragua in solidarity with the revolution. Inspired in part by those experiences, LGBTQ Sandinistas formed the first gay/lesbian pride group in the mid-1980s, which was crushed by members of the Cuba-influenced Ministry of Interior, claiming that such organizing was a way the empire would destroy the revolution from within. Late in the 1980s, the group reemerged to do HIV/AIDS education under the protection of Minister of Health Dora María Téllez. They also formed some small groups and even participated in the official parade that marked the tenth anniversary of the revolution.

Chapter 3, "After the Revolution: 1990–2006," starts after the FSLN's Daniel Ortega lost the 1990 election to conservative Violeta Barrios de Chamorro who, like most Latin American leaders at the time, oversaw a transition to neoliberal democracy. Her government also chose to crack down supposed sexual licentiousness through Article 204, penalizing "sodomy" and pro-LGBTQ rights speech with three to five years in prison. In response, FSLN Congresspeople voted unanimously against Article 204, despite the party's LGBTQ policies in the 1980s, and more than twenty-five organizations joined in the Campaign for Sexuality Free of Prejudices. From 1992 to 2008, Nicaraguans lived under the shadow of the worst antigay legislation in the Americas. Yet, these were also good years for the movement, as festivals, an LGBTQ church, support groups, and rights organizations emerged, often with the support of organized feminists. This chapter traces the movement from the early 1990s when it built on previous HIV-AIDS work, to the mid-2000s, by which time it had a clear transgender as well as gay and lesbian character, focusing on rights more than health.

In chapter 4, "The Return of Daniel Ortega," I show that the party that Ortega headed in the 2006 campaign bore little resemblance to the guerrilla coalition that overthrew the Somoza regime and governed from 1979 to 1990. It now claimed to be Christian rather than secular, antifeminist rather than feminist, and it incorporated LGBTQ people into its coalition rather than rejecting them. Moreover, its new alliance with the Catholic and evangelical churches was confirmed by Ortega's wife (and campaign director), Rosario Murillo, when she denounced abortion, even to save a woman's life. This new Sandinista policy was ratified through a law banning abortion under all circumstances, which was passed in the National Assembly thanks to Sandinista votes, weeks before Ortega was reelected in November of 2006.

In this chapter, I analyze this transformation of the FSLN and tell the story of the rise of a significant LGBTQ rights movement. I refer to that period as the decade of the LGBTQ boom, for never in Nicaraguan history had so many LGBTQ rights groups worked for so many different issues, in big cities and small towns across the country. I analyze the emergence of twenty-nine individual LGBTQ rights groups and coalitions over the course of the decade, groups that added their forces to the many older organizations that had been founded in the 1990s or early 2000s. These groups all shared some goals, such as greater LGBTQ visibility; full civil rights for all members of the LGBTQ community; and the right to be treated with respect, obtain decent work, and live lives free of violence. At the same time, they worked on a never-before-seen variety of issues. Some organizations conducted research while others produced radio shows or theater and art installations. Still others provided space for socializing and self-improvement. Some provided legal clinics and job training. Others promoted equal working conditions for members of the LGBTQ community, while others lobbied for laws that were more just. As a result of their courage and hard work, Nicaragua was a different place than it had been at the beginning of the decade of the boom.

Chapter 5, "A Sexually Diverse Decade," opens by considering the reasons for the boom in LGBTQ organizing, including new laws, a new approach from the ruling FSLN, an increase in the availability of funding for new organizations, and the role played by Zoilamérica Ortega Murillo in supporting the movement, helping activists make connections and get access to resources that they would not have had otherwise. In this chapter, I evaluate the many accomplishments, and the real costs, of life during the boom years. That era began with regular and audacious demonstrations, talks on college campuses, participation in feminist events, and the hosting of international conferences in Nicaragua. During those years, the movement got its own buildings—in the cities of Managua, Masaya, León, and Matagalpa—providing offices for many organizations, and spaces that could be used by other groups and individuals. The importance of physical safe spaces cannot be overstated. That was the time when the impressive study *Una mirada a la diversidad sexual en Nicaragua*, (A Glance at Sexual Diversity in Nicaragua), by far the most extensive study on sexual diversity up until that point, was researched, published, and made available online in PDF form. In 2009, the Office of the Attorney General for Human Rights named Samira Montiel as *Procuradora Especial de la Diversidad Sexual* (Special Ombudsperson for Sexual Diversity), the first state advocate for LGBTQ rights in Central America. Then, in April 2012, for the first time, the Miss Gay Nicaragua pageant was held in Nicaragua's most prestigious venue, the Rubén Darío Theater. Yet despite all these accomplishments, many LGBTQ activists worried rightfully that they had gained visibility without gaining rights.

In my conclusion, "Nicaragua's Family Regime in Comparative Perspective," I consider that while in some parts of the world, urbanization, capitalist development, and increasing LGBTQ visibility provided opportunities for those who sought greater rights for LGBTQ people, in other places homophobic politicians found that those same factors provided opportunities for themselves at the cost of the LGBTQ community. By scapegoating LGBTQ people as foreign agents or threats to traditional family values (or both), some politicians consolidated their power at the cost of the rights—and sometimes the lives—of LGBTQ people. Here I evaluate the politics of backlash in the United States, Indonesia, Egypt and, especially, Russia. I argue that, like Vladimir Putin, President Daniel Ortega, and his wife Rosario Murillo concentrated power in their own hands over the course of more than a decade in power. Like Putin, they invoked gender and sexuality to lend legitimacy to their rule, but, unlike Putin, they did not attack the LGBTQ community. Instead, they sought to incorporate members of that community into their clientelistic networks rather than ceding to their demands for full civil rights or outright repressing them.

Attempts to co-opt the LGBTQ movement through public policies and clientelistic benefits played an important role in the Ortega-Murillo government's strategy to build legitimacy. In concluding, I consider the ways in which Ortega-Murillo consolidated power: pact-making with the opposition, legal changes, electoral fraud, control of the mass media, economic growth, clientelistic policies, and co-optation or repression of civil society, especially the business sector, the Catholic Church, and the feminist movement. I suggest that the story of Ortega-Murillo's consolidation of power cannot be fully understood apart from their LGBTQ policies, for such policies served the project of creating a single-party and single-family state, particularly by reducing the threat of the feminist opposition, which has been historically allied with LGBTQ groups. That project draws upon a strategy called "pinkwashing," in which liberal LGBTQ policies create a modern image for international donors and draw attention away from problematic policies, in this specific case, the FSLN's poor record regarding reproductive rights and civil liberties.

The decade (2007–17) in which the Ortega-Murillo government consolidated its power was also what I have called the decade of the LGBTQ boom. At the end of the conclusion, I return to the boom and June 2017, which was marked with a series of pride events across the country. The pride parade that year was the largest in the history of the country, as thousands of colorfully attired people waved from vehicles, rode skateboards, pushed baby strollers, marched down the streets, or danced while accompanied by drums and brass bands. Finally, they stopped at the Metrocentro traffic circle, the site of so many demonstrations during the previous decade. There they listened to music and speeches, including an essay written and read by David Rocha titled "Our Memories, Our Revolutions: Nicaragua, Another Zero Hour" (Rocha Córtez 2017). As Rocha noted, the date of pride day—June 28—marked the anniversary of the Stonewall uprising, far away in New York City. That day many Nicaraguans, like many other people all over the world, celebrated one of the most important holidays on the global queer calendar. Yet, as Rocha also recognized, while the day commemorated an event in New York, what they remembered on that day was not global history but rather Nicaraguan history. At the march, they celebrated their country's history as they demanded a more just future.

In the epilogue, I briefly consider the events of April of 2018, when what was a hybrid regime (one that manifests both democratic and dictatorial elements) turned almost overnight into a full-fledged dictatorship. In response to demonstrations against changes in social security and in favor of democratic institutions, the Ortega-Murillo government hit back with force. One of the first protesters who was attacked was Ana Quirós, a well-known lesbian feminist activist in her sixties who suffered severe head and hand injuries. In the months that followed April of 2018, hundreds were killed, thousands were injured, and hundreds more were imprisoned, including many LGBTQ activists. Several trans women were jailed in men's prisons, where they and other prisoners were tortured.

As of this writing, demonstrations of any sort (except those supporting the government) have been banned, multiple nongovernmental organizations—including those that promote LGBTQ and women's rights—have been stripped of their legal standing and their property seized; opposition media offices have been ransacked, and their shows were taken off the air. In some cases, television broadcasters were imprisoned and charged with terrorism. Dozens of journalists have fled the country rather than waiting to see if the death threats they received would be carried out. Those attacks have contributed to the relative silence of the international press regarding the brutal crackdown in Nicaragua, making this book more urgent than ever.

CHAPTER ONE

LGBTQ Memories of the Sandinista Revolution

"¡Que se rinda tu madre!"[1] Those were the final words of poet Leonel Rugama, who died on a hot January day in 1970 while defending a safehouse against the bullets, tanks, and helicopters of Somoza's National Guard. Upon his death, twenty-year-old Rugama entered the pantheon of saints of the revolution. He was a hero of the clandestine struggle, what he called life in the catacombs, linking early *Sandinismo* with early Christianity. Like thousands of his fellow Sandinistas, Rugama tapped into a cult of martyrdom, a cult with deep roots in Marxism, Christianity, and even older traditions. Former Sandinista vice president Sergio Ramírez explained,

> The cult of the dead was never an order anyone gave from the revolutionary chain of command. It was the consequence of an intimate conviction nourished by example, with roots in Catholic and also indigenous traditions, which the rigors of clandestine struggle came to exalt. Christ, who calls to sacrifice, to eat his body, and Mixtanteotl, the Nahuatl god of the dead who demands live sacrifice (Ramírez 2012, 25).

All the fallen were secular saints, but not all are remembered like Rugama, who perhaps is remembered because of his audacious last words, perhaps because his words live on in poems such as this:

---

1. *"¡Que se rinda tu madre!"* is often translated as "Let your mother surrender," but just what does that mean? What is she being asked to surrender? Rugama's words make more sense if thought of as a sexual slur, better translated as "Let your mother give [it] up!" (Perla 2016, 1).

"THE EARTH IS A SATELLITE OF THE MOON."
Apollo 2 cost more than Apollo 1
Apollo 1 cost a lot.

Apollo 3 cost more than Apollo 2
Apollo 2 cost more than Apollo 1
Apollo 1 cost a lot.

Apollo 4 cost more than Apollo 3
Apollo 3 cost more than Apollo 2
Apollo 2 cost more than Apollo 1

Apollo 1 cost a lot.

Apollo 8 was really expensive, but nobody noticed
because the astronauts were Protestants
and they read the Bible on the moon
filling all Christians with wonder and joy,
and upon their return Pope Paul IV blessed them.

Apollo 9 cost more than all the others put together
including Apollo 1 which cost a lot.

The great-grandparents of the people of Acahualinca were less hungry than
                                                              the grandparents.
The great-grandparents died of hunger.

The grandparents of the people of Acahualinca were less hungry than
                                                              the parents.
The grandparents died of hunger.

The parents of the people of Acahualinca were less hungry than
                                                the children of the people there.
The parents died of hunger.

The people of Acahualinca were less hungry than
                                                the children of the people there.

The children of the people of Acahualinca are not born due to hunger, and
    they hunger to be born, only to die of hunger.

Blessed are the poor for they shall inherit the moon. (La Voz del Sandinismo
    2020)

Rugama's most famous poem spoke of the injustices in Managua's Acahualinca neighborhood. It spoke of an inequitable international system in
which the U.S. government supported extravagant space exploration programs and a brutal dictatorship in Managua. As for the dictatorship, the
Somoza's actions spoke for themselves.

> Birthday parties for Dinorah Sampson, Anastasio Somoza's lover, were
> enlivened with mariachis brought in from Mexico. She stood at the door
> to her mansion receiving hand kisses adorned with a three-layer hairdo,
> like a wedding cake. Then there was the more refined kitsch reserved for
> the official first lady, Hope Portocarrero, skinny like an aged Vogue model.
> For the inauguration of the international airport terminal, she ordered an
> express plane from Miami to bring even the tomatoes, heads of lettuce,
> and celery for the formal buffet served in the waiting area to guests dressed
> with rigorous etiquette. It was a party that was spoiled by her own hus-
> band who, full of rage and vodka, ordered the clock to be yanked from the
> wall that showed the local time in the Soviet Union, among other places
> (Ramírez 2012, 28).

In response to those excesses, Rugama chose to live, and die, in the catacombs. His audacious final words *"que se rinda tu madre"*—reproduced on
monuments, posters, murals—captured the reckless daring of the revolutionaries, vastly outnumbered. Their legacy shows that miracles can happen,
for what but a miracle could explain the flight of the all-powerful dictator
less than a decade after Leonel Rugama's death?

Founded in 1961, the FSLN was a product of its times. It was the age of
dictatorial governments, in Nicaragua as elsewhere in Latin America. It was
the age of U.S. dominance and nowhere more so than in Nicaragua, where
the Somoza dictatorship (1936–79) had ruled comfortably for decades with
support from Uncle Sam. It was the age of the triumphant revolution in
Cuba. Not coincidentally, it was also the age of small guerrilla movements,
almost all doomed to be crushed by the dictatorships they challenged.

That is what nearly happened to the FSLN. When Leonel Rugama wrote
his poems of guerrilla struggle, he seemed to expect such a fate. Rugama,
who was born in poverty and had studied to become a priest, was known
for his "shyness and innocence with girls" (Francis 2012, 240). His poems
reflected those experiences: the themes of injustice, saintliness, sacrifice, and

death predominated in his poetry. The theme of victory did not. That is what Rugama wanted of course, but it seemed too much to expect in 1970.

Why did the Sandinistas—alone among the Latin American guerrillas of the 1960s and 1970s—succeed in overthrowing their dictatorship? One reason was a shift in thinking. Until the late 1960s, the FSLN looked to the Cuban Revolution and Che Guevara's new man. According to Omar Cabezas (1986, 11–12), Leonel Rugama told his comrades that they needed to "be like Che": one of a small band of highly trained, egalitarian, self-sacrificing fighters who would bring down the dictatorship through sheer force of will. This approach, called the *foco* theory, seemed to work in Cuba, though it never worked anywhere else. Following the 1967 massacre at Pancasán, the FSLN switched to a mass mobilization strategy.

That strategic switch had implications for the kind of people the Sandinistas sought to mobilize, creating a "before" and an "after." Before, they recruited only young, strong, apparently heterosexual men. After, they tried to recruit everyone. As a result, there were big changes in the number of women who participated in guerrilla struggles, estimated to be about 30 percent of recruits in Nicaragua compared to only 5 percent in the earlier movement in Cuba, though there is debate regarding those figures (Kampwirth 2002, 2, 118). The new strategy also unintentionally changed the sexual identity of the revolutionary coalition.

Erick Blandón knew he was gay from the time he was a boy growing up in the city of Matagalpa. It was something that he never discussed with his family, though he thought that they all knew. "They reacted well, better than well; they reacted with love. They have always been very proud of me. They have always encouraged me to succeed" (interview, December 4, 2013). The FSLN had much the same reaction to his sexuality: it was an issue that was not discussed.

Blandón's activism began in 1969, when he was still a high school student. He was active "in defending human rights and liberty for the political prisoners . . . regarding the imprisonment of Doris Tijerino Haslam. Doris is from Matagalpa. I was a friend and classmate of her younger sisters, [and her imprisonment] made all the young people act . . . and later we participated in demonstrations, to demand her liberty. I participated in sit-ins, and I was one of the leaders of the sit-in at Matagalpa's cathedral and later, around that same time, I was involved in solidarity work with the Nicaraguan teachers who went on strike against Somoza" (interview, December 4, 2013). Later, as a college student, he joined the FSLN-affiliated student organization, the *Frente Estudiantil Revolucionario* (Revolutionary Student Front or FER), becoming a collaborator and finally a member of the party.

What was it like to be a gay man in those organizations?
I want to tell you something that is important to keep in mind, which is that in the 1970s, during the years of struggle, the FSLN never had a policy of marginalizing people because of the issue of sexuality, in fact there were many *compañeros* who were obviously gay, though they were not out, it was obvious that they were [gay] and at no time was there a policy of discrimination (interview, December 4, 2013).

Like Erick Blandón, Mary Bolt was a student when she was recruited. She was also lesbian. "I joined the FSLN in 1974. And the truth is that at that time I never concerned myself with lesbian organizing. For me the most important goal was to overthrow the dictatorship." When asked whether she was an open lesbian she replied: "They never asked me: what sort of thing are you? Never [laughing]; you simply joined and that was it; it was not like they asked me what I thought; what I believed. I just joined. So before the overthrow of Somoza, I never had problems; well, I just worked" (interview, July 5, 1994).

"Xochitl" was another lesbian whose contributions were critical. Though she was not completely open about her sexual orientation, she did not try to hide it either. When we talked years later, her hair was very short, and she wore jeans, masculine shoes, and a button-down shirt. She had always dressed that way, "always as a lesbian." She shared, "About in 1976 I began to work as a nurse in some of the hospitals of León, because I am a nurse. There I worked directly with the clandestine revolutionary movement: I stole instruments. . . . I stole anesthesia, which was sent to [the place] where my brothers were participating, that is, almost my whole family participated in that. . . . Later I started to realize that there were a huge number of women who were lesbians. . . . The presence of lesbians was significant" (interview, July 5, 1994).

Magaly Quintana also participated in the anti-Somoza struggle, explaining, "I was a student leader for many years; I was vice president of the FUN *Federación Universitaria de Nicaragua* (Nicaraguan University Federation). . . . I was a member of the Revolutionary Student Front and later I worked for many years with the Proletarian Tendency of the FSLN. With the Tendency I worked on everything related to propaganda and with the social movements, working with youth movements and with workers movements, trying to organize the world of the workers" (*Cuerpos Sin-Vergüenzas* 2014b). Like the others, she knew that many Sandinistas, including student activists in León, were gay or lesbian. Unlike them, she did not think that FSLN leaders ignored their sexuality.

> León was a place where the student movement did not just question political issues, rather it questioned the existing moral culture, and we began to try to create different relations. . . . So specific houses were formed where we lived. They were like shelters, very profoundly our own, when in that movement for example lesbian relationships began to flourish and of course gay relationships. They [in the FSLN] had just realized what was going on and they started to profile us. Obviously that is what happened; they immediately began to send people to psychiatrists or psychologists. . . . The FSLN had organized its own psychologists. . . . I am talking about 1971 or '72 (*Cuerpos Sin-Vergüenzas* 2014b).

Quintana was not sent to a psychologist, but she had to comfort a close friend (and former girlfriend) who was forced into treatment.

> One day I found her sobbing, and I asked her what happened. "They sent me to see a psychologist." The psychologist's treatment was to first require that she wear skirts and dresses, that was the thinking of psychologists. Of course, I laughed. I didn't know who needed a bump on the head, whether it was the psychologist or [my friend] because it seemed so inept to me. . . . That sort of thing was done throughout the whole revolutionary process before July 19th [the overthrow of Somoza], obviously one did not feel it so strongly [then] because many people in one way or another were clandestine. They went off on their own, and so the repression was not so visible (*Cuerpos Sin-Vergüenzas* 2014b).

People like Erick Blandón, Mary Bolt, Xochitl, and Magaly Quintana were important members of the Sandinista coalition who identified as gay or lesbian, though they were not completely open regarding their sexuality. But sometimes the FSLN was offered—and happily accepted—support from openly gay people. Rita Aráuz, a Nicaraguan who spent part of her teens and early twenties in the United States, explained:

The FSLN eventually recruited me there in San Francisco. And they recruited me as an open lesbian feminist. That was in 1976, '77. And it was
within the gay community that I began to organize a movement in solidarity
with the Sandinistas in their war against Somoza. . . . [Later, when the Sandinistas had taken power] Aura Lila Beteta, the first Sandinista consul in San
Francisco, gave us a letter strongly recognizing the work we did. . . . We had
open and extensive support from the FSLN and that is an indicator of the
political nature of the FSLN at the time (1994, 288).

Since Aráuz worked for the revolution, the leaders of the FSLN accepted the
fact that she was an open lesbian, and that her organization, "Gay People for
the Nicaraguan Revolution," was (obviously) a gay solidarity group (Hobson
2012, 5, 8; 2016, 98, 103–12). Of course, the fact that she worked from afar
probably contributed to the difference between her experience and that of
some LGBTQ Sandinistas who lived in Nicaragua (on LGBTQ people in El
Salvador's FMLN, see Córtez Ruiz 2019).

The work of thousands of LGBTQ people helps explain the eventual
overthrow of the dictatorship, but some chance occurrences also mattered.
When some ten thousand people died in an earthquake in Managua in December 1972, Anastasio Somoza could have demonstrated concern for his
people, hundreds of thousands of whom were injured and homeless, many in
mourning. Instead, he further enriched himself and his cronies by pocketing
much of the disaster aid that poured into the country (Wilkinson 1992). He
even forced residents of Managua to rebuild their own streets in exchange
for food, laying down heavy cement blocks by hand. That was when many
began to support the kids of the FSLN, motivated more by disgust with the
Somozas than by confidence in the Sandinistas.

Still, many held out, thinking the guerrillas couldn't succeed, or worrying
that the Sandinistas were reckless, or maintaining suspicions that they were
Marxists. Then in January 1978, eight years after Leonel Rugama fell to the
dictatorship's bullets, a very different opposition figure fell. Pedro Joaquín
Chamorro, editor-in-chief of the daily newspaper *La Prensa*, had opposed
the Somoza family since the 1950s. He had been imprisoned and had been
tortured, personally, by Anastasio Somoza Debayle, as he wrote in *Estirpe
Sangrienta* (1980 [1957], 70, 72–81).[2]

---

2. Similarly, Doris Tijerino noted that in the late 1960s and early 1970s, Anastasio Somoza
Debayle and his sons sometimes personally raped or tortured political prisoners (Randall 1978,
79, 103).

People like Pedro Joaquín Chamorro—wealthy, educated, internationally prominent—are normally left alone by dictators, at least by the smart ones. It turned out that Anastasio Somoza Debayle, or perhaps his son (also Anastasio), were not so smart. While the intellectual author of the crime was never confirmed, there was no doubt about the crime itself: as Pedro Joaquín Chamorro drove to *La Prensa* one morning, his car was strafed with bullets, marking the beginning of the final insurrection. Most Nicaraguans thought that if Pedro Joaquín Chamorro's money and prestige could not protect him then none were safe. In the months that followed, the FSLN, which had been divided into three groups, known as tendencies, reunited. Also in the months that followed, the Somoza regime, which had governed for decades through a combination of clientelism and violence, shifted to an all-violence strategy, ultimately dropping bombs on poor neighborhoods in several cities.

That strategy could have worked if not for the Carter administration's ambivalence: committed simultaneously to an old U.S. policy of resisting communism and a new U.S. policy, supporting human rights. But it was not possible to support both anticommunism and human rights, at least not in Somoza's Nicaragua. Then, in June 1979, ABC correspondent Bill Stewart was murdered by a National Guardsman. The murder, which was captured on film and repeatedly shown on the nightly news in the United States, was the last straw that led Carter to cut ties to the dictatorship. Less than a month later, Somoza fled and Leonel Rugama's comrades took over.

The Sandinista Revolution (1979–1990) had begun. To their great joy and surprise, the Sandinistas had their chance to make a revolution. But what did that mean? In its simplest sense, it meant reacting against all that was brutal and unfair in the old regime. The FSLN sought to make Nicaragua more equitable through free health care, legal reforms, the mobilization of young people and women, the redistribution of land. Land reform, especially in the first couple of years, was greatly facilitated by the fact that Anastasio Somoza had owned 25 percent of the land in the country (LaFeber 1986, 226). Since he could not take that land on the plane with him, it was available for the creation of cooperatives and state farms, giving many rural people access to land for the first time.

The finest hour of the revolution was the 1980 national literacy campaign. When the FSLN took power, literacy rates were low, especially in the countryside, and so universal education was a revolutionary priority: over the course of five months, eighty thousand literate Nicaraguans fanned out across the country to teach their fellow citizens to read. As a result, illiteracy dropped from 50.4 percent to 12.9 percent nationwide, and Nicaragua won UNESCO's annual award for excellence in education (Vilas 1986, 214, 218).

Much of the revolution was considerably less glorious. Within a year, the revolutionary coalition, forged in opposition to the dictatorship, started to fall apart. The one thing that united everyone—opposition to Anastasio Somoza—was gone. Violeta Barrios de Chamorro, widow of Pedro Joaquín Chamorro, and businessman Alfonso Robelo resigned from the ruling Junta, leaving it less representative of the many currents within Nicaraguan society. Upon the inauguration of Ronald Reagan as president of the United States in January of 1981, the Contra War—mainly directed by former officers from Somoza's National Guard (Morales Carazo 1989, 126)—began in full force. Fifty-eight thousand people, out of a population of three million, were to die in that war (Vilas 1995, 138).

Yet despite the brutality of war, despite shortages and eventual hyperinflation, the Sandinistas instituted the first free and fair elections in Nicaraguan history. There was an election in 1984, which they won, and another in 1990, which they lost. And then they stepped down. As Sandinista President Daniel Ortega handed the presidential sash to the newly inaugurated Violeta Barrios de Chamorro, the FSLN became what was probably the only revolutionary movement ever to take power through armed struggle only to give it up through an election.

The revolution challenged the legacy of the Somoza dictatorship and all the dictatorial governments that preceded it, but it was also a product of those dictatorships. It simultaneously rejected and embraced the old culture, something that was to shape the role of homosexuality within the revolution. Speaking in 1992, Erick Blandón observed,

> During [Somoza's] time, just as now, there was a lot of social, religious, and institutional repression against sexual options other than heterosexuality.... It seems to me that the government responded to a moral order.... [T]here were norms that were accepted by the whole society including by gays and lesbians themselves. Gays and lesbians have even caused shame to their own families. I think that at the time of the triumph of the revolution one can say that within the FSLN ... there was no unanimity about how gays and lesbians should be treated, and the majority of the leaders saw them with the same conservative prejudices that were held by the majority [of Nicaraguans]. (Interview, October 23, 1992).

The dictatorship that the FSLN rebelled against endorsed a Catholic moral order. But the Somoza dictatorship was also a "liberal dictatorship," one in which gays and lesbians could sometimes make spaces for themselves.

One common memory of the Somoza era was that it was a time of sexual disorder, a time when people like Anastasio Somoza's gay nephew Bernabé Somoza Urcuyo patronized the gay and gay-friendly bars, such as *Lago de los Cisnes* (Swan Lake) and the *Tortuga Morada* (the Purple Turtle), which flourished in Managua. There were years when the dictatorship protected LGBTQ Nicaraguans like *la Caimana* (Alligator Woman), as long as they were loyal to the regime, and willing to participate in its clientelistic networks. There were years when many National Guardsmen made a good living through the prostitution industry (González-Rivera, forthcoming). For many Sandinistas, to reject *Somocismo* was to reject sexual disorder. So, they sought to impose order by banning prostitution, providing job training for (female) sex workers, shutting down gay bars, and making life difficult for some LGBTQ Nicaraguans (INSSBI 1987).

At the same time, the revolution promised emancipation. For most Sandinistas, emancipation did not mean gay liberation, but in its earliest days, the Sandinista Revolution was not particularly antigay either. There were even brief moments when revolutionary transformation was linked to gay and lesbian rights. For instance, during the last half of 1979 "Aura Lila Beteta, the FSLN's new consul in San Francisco . . . attended a GPNR [Gay People for the Nicaraguan Revolution] meeting and issued statements of support for gay and lesbian freedom" (Hobson 2016, 109). At the First National Third World Lesbian and Gay Conference (held in Washington, D.C., in October 1979), Gay Latino Alliance member Rodrigo Reyes read a message from Beteta on behalf of the Nicaraguan government: "To the first national conference of Third World lesbians and gay men, revolutionary Sandinista greetings. May from your conference be born a movement that identifies, that unites and struggles with the liberation movements of all oppressed people" (quoted in Hobson 2016, 112).

Eventually some gay and lesbian Sandinistas decided to claim emancipation for themselves. They did this early in the revolution by seizing the opportunities that social upheaval provides and later in the revolution by trying to create a gay-lesbian pride movement. But in ways that run parallel to the role of women's issues within the revolution, the most common response to the issue of gay rights was that they should be postponed: until poverty was overcome, until the country was reconstructed, until all other goals were met.

Tim McCaskell, who spent a month in Nicaragua in late 1979 and early 1980, described his first conversation with a university student. Such conversations, with small variations, were repeated during his visit.

> I explain that I am from a Canadian gay newspaper and that I want to know about how the revolution has affected the lives of lesbians and gay men. He seems slightly perturbed by the question. The country is in desperate economic straits, he says. . . . I repeat that I want to know how these economic and social transformations affect people's emotional and personal lives— relations between men and women, for example, or homosexuals. He replies that here are all sorts of backward cultural phenomenon, especially between men and women, and that these can be traced to the misery arising from the country's dependence on imperialism. I agree, but want to know how machismo itself is being challenged. He talks some more about the economy. (McCaskell 1981, 19)

Later that afternoon, as they toured the university where the young Nicaraguan studied, McCaskell asked his question from a new angle. "I ask my guide directly if there are any gay organizations on campus. 'No, not that I know of,' he replies. 'Some people look upon that kind of thing with distaste. But myself, most people I think, feel that it's part of private life. Why would you want to organize around that? There are so many much more important things to be done'" (McCaskell 1981, 19).

The Sandinista Revolution, one of the great political movements of the twentieth century, has been remembered in many ways. Sergio Ramírez notes that he owns more than 500 books on the revolution, written in multiple languages (2012, 2). But those hundreds of books did not capture everything. Among other things, they missed the memories of contested sexuality that ran underground through the guerrilla years, and the years of revolution. Here are some of those hidden stories.

Many Gay Policies

It was going to be an enormous cultural event, marking a new era. Just weeks after the FSLN overthrew the Somoza dictatorship, the colonial-era play *El*

Güegüense o Macho Ratón (The Old Man or Male Mouse) was to be presented at the Rubén Darío Theater. It would be hard to overstate the symbolic significance of that event because of the nature of the play and the theater in which it was to be performed.

The main character in the play, which is accompanied by music and dance, is the *Güegüense*, who most scholars identify as mestizo.[3] He gets the best of the colonial authorities, despite the authorities' far greater power, because the *Güegüense* and his relatives are more intelligent. *El Güegüense* may be interpreted in many ways, but certainly a revolutionary interpretation is possible, a reading in which the colonial play is a metaphor for the overthrow of the dictatorship. As in *El Güegüense*, in 1979 ordinary Nicaraguans got the best of the authorities of the day—the Somoza dictatorship and its U.S. patrons—because they were so courageous, and so clever.

The setting also mattered. The opulent Rubén Darío theater had been inaugurated in 1969 by Anastasio Somoza and his wife, Hope Portocarrero de Somoza. She wanted a theater like Washington, D.C.'s Kennedy Center, and she got what she wanted, a theater so well built that it was one of the few buildings in downtown Managua to survive the 1972 earthquake (Holiday Travel 2021). With its crystal chandeliers, red velvet decor, multiple balconies, and excellent acoustics, it was quite a grand theater for such a poor country.

Of course, the theater was not built for the impoverished majority; it was built for the elite, mainly people associated with the dictatorship. Now it was going to be opened to the public so they could see Nicaragua's most famous play, in a version that was first performed in 1978, under the direction of Alberto Ycaza. That version "was conceived of as a tragedy, due to the '[c]lash of two mentalities: Gentlemen Leaders of a civilization whose destiny is governed by knowledge of the cosmos, invaded by the Royal Council of another civilization in which individual power is utilized as an element of domination, and whose norms are promulgated *in contrast with the laws of nature*'" (quoted in Blandón 2003, 127–28, emphasis added by Blandón).

But there was a problem. "In the staging of that performance the actors emphasized points with homoerotic gestures" (Blandón 2003, 128). To ridicule the authorities, the *Güegüense* pronounced his words with a feminine lilt, "as if the language spoken by the Spanish were a language of faggots

---

3. According to some interpretations, the *Güegüense* and his relatives were Indigenous rather than mestizo (Blandón 2003, 41, 119–56).

[*maricones*]" (Fernando Silva, quoted in Blandón 2003, 128). In September of 1979, Erick Blandón was general director of the Culture Ministry and in charge of the production when Ernesto Cardenal, the national head of the Culture Ministry, spoke to him. He told Blandón to stop working on the play, explaining that "Sergio Ramírez, a member of the National Reconstruction Government Ruling Council, had told him that the revolution could not promote homosexuality" (Blandón 2003, 225, n. 9).

It seems that, shortly after the fall of the dictatorship, the revolutionary leaders thought about the question of homosexuality, and the answer was "no." Yet, looking back on the revolution, many people observed that the FSLN did not have a "gay policy" (Erick Blandón, interviews, October 23, 1992, and December 4, 2013; Dora María Téllez, personal communication, October 9, 2010; Mario Gutiérrez, interview, November 30, 2012; Lancaster 1992, 262–64; Levins Morales 1983, 1; Randall 1993, 919–21). According to former guerrilla Commander Dora María Téllez, the issue was debated only once.

> In the middle of the 1980s . . . the Sandinista Assembly took up a resolution. . . . [T]he debate was very heated, and the resolution was that there could be lesbians and gays . . . within the party but not in leadership positions. . . . It could have been 1987, something like that. There was the debate and the resolution . . . which ended up being ignored because when it comes down to it everything is a game of correlation of forces. Nobody had the nerve to fire leaders who were closeted gays or closeted lesbians. . . . The discussion had been to satisfy the vindictive demands of a segment of the Sandinista Assembly against certain people. With that I mean that there was a resolution that explicitly said that they [gays and lesbians] can be members of the FSLN but not in leadership positions, which was never enforced, and we continue with the practice of "I do what I want but I don't disclose it" (public comments, *Hispamer*, June 18, 2014).

Revolutionary leaders were hardly indifferent to questions of sexuality. They simply did not agree, so instead of a single gay policy, there were gay policies.

On occasion, the range of policies and opinions regarding LGBTQ Nicaraguans were expressed in writing. "In the MINT, Tomás Borge repressed bureaucrats who were gay or lesbians. Even . . . Tomás Borge's book, *The Patient Impatience*, is full of prejudice against homosexuals" (Erick Blandón, interview, October 23, 1992). Though Borge often ridiculed homosexuals, there is one passage in *The Patient Impatience* in which he described one of the gay residents of his childhood neighborhood with something like admiration. "There was another homosexual, much beloved by the neighborhood women because of the sympathy he displayed for others' afflictions and because he was opposed to Somoza. He built altars. His Saint Joseph and Nazarene altars resembled exteriorist poems and delighted the children" (Borge 1992, 33). But the deprecatory tone of the following was more typical.

> One evening . . . I saw my chubby friend, Cristóbal Alvarado, approaching. . . . I was about to introduce him to my girlfriend, when his demeanor, something about his shoulders and his eyes, aroused my suspicions. Sure enough, Cristóbal, with effeminate voice, teary eyes, and exaggerated gestures, denounced my betrayal and reproached the horrified Angélica María for flirting with an engaged man. "Engaged to whom?" she asked. "To me, darling, who else?" the son-of-a-bitch minced. Angélica María turned red, then pale, then methylene blue; she called me a degenerate. I had to use all my powers of persuasion to convince Cristóbal to explain he was joking. (Borge 1992, 86–87)[4]

Borge's book was mainly about his experiences within the guerrilla struggle. But as though to prove that all politics is gendered, the homophobic themes in the book were accompanied by many stories in which he and other Sandinista men impregnated women, only to abandon them and their children (1989, 145–46, 160, 180, 295–96, 307, 309, 315, 321, 385).

Tomás Borge was an extremely powerful and influential person. The only official founder of the FSLN who survived to see the overthrow of the dictatorship, he wielded formal power as a member of the National Directorate and head of the Ministry of the Interior, as well as a great deal of informal power. He was also known to be quite homophobic.[5] While suggesting that his attitudes were fairly typical of the top leadership of the party, Rita Aráuz

---

4. Borge's girlfriend Angélica María seemed to believe that Cristóbal's claim to be his boyfriend could possibly be true. Had she thought it were impossible, she would have recognized it as a joke.

5. For an entertaining story of the writer Julio Cortázar attempts to challenge Borge's homophobia, see Peri Rossi 2001, 49–50.

also thought that he sympathized with LGBTQ Sandinistas to some extent. "His line was that he supported us, that gay rights had to be part of the overall struggle; but he personally was just too sexist to internalize it on a more personal level" (Aráuz 1994, 271).

Most LGBTQ Nicaraguans were not as generous as Aráuz when looking back at Borge's treatment of gays and lesbians. But they did agree that Borge's vision was not the only vision, and he was not the only Sandinista with the power to persecute or protect people. Catholic priest Ernesto Cardenal directed the Ministry of Culture, overseeing the work of many men and women whose homosexuality could make them vulnerable.

> Often when people were fired . . . there were allegations about their sexuality: that happened to various people. . . . I cannot say their names, as I have not been authorized to do so, but there were cases of bureaucrats from the Ministry of Culture who participated in the coffee harvesting brigades and who were fired because it was discovered that . . . they had sexual partners of the same sex during the coffee harvests. That caused a constant crisis in the world of culture. (Erick Blandón, interview, December 4, 2013)

That is not to say that all gays and lesbians were forced out of the Ministry of Culture, and Cardenal wrote critically about the persecution of gay people—some forced into internment camps—that had occurred in Cuba (1974, 20–21, 31, 49, 236). Nonetheless, the situation in the Ministry of Culture was sometimes tense, and Blandón suggested that this conflict over sexuality was one of the roots of a conflict in the early 1980s, which was resolved by many leaving the Ministry of Culture to join the *Asociación Sandinista de Trabajadores de la Cultura* (Sandinista Association of Culture Workers, or ASTC, sometimes called ATC), headed by Rosario Murillo, the common-law wife of Commander (and later president) Daniel Ortega. Many Ministry of Culture employees who had felt vulnerable because of their sexual orientation felt a bit freer working at the ASTC.

> What I mean is that it wasn't an official policy; it depended on which leader was in charge. . . . [W]hat was contradictory was that in the ranks of the top leadership of the FSLN, in the departments that were part of the structure of the party, there was no such policy. . . . [T]here were cadre who were openly gay within the department of International Relations, within the department

of Propaganda, [the department of] Organization; in some of the departments that problem [of discrimination due to sexuality] did not exist. (Erick Blandón, interview, December 4, 2013)

Occasionally, top leaders of the party even went out of their way to publicly defend freedom of sexual orientation. When Bayardo Arce, a commander of the revolution and member of the National Directorate, defended LGBTQ people, it was an important moment for Erick Blandón,

Once there was a conflict at the television station with one journalist . . . who had been a collaborator or member of the FSLN [during Somoza's time] and who had a conflict with the other workers. The workers accused him of being gay, and the leaders of the television station decided to fire him. . . . The National Directorate member who oversaw television was Bayardo Arce. . . . I was at Bayardo Arce's house when the official from the television station informed Bayardo that they had decided to fire the journalist. "But why?" he asked. "Because he is gay." Bayardo said, no, no, that is not a reason to fire anyone, because—these words strike me as very important—"in the FSLN during the years of struggle we never asked people, with whom, nor how they had sexual relations, and now that is not going to be a reason [to fire anyone]." I think that was like a policy of tacit acceptance, without saying anything openly, but it was obvious that there were many lesbians, many gay kids, so that [sexuality] was not an impediment. . . . [T]hey just asked if one was against Somoza and that was the only requirement. (Interview, December 4, 2013)

Bayardo Arce was not the only leader who sometimes defended gay and lesbian revolutionaries. Others including José Benito Escobar, Ricardo Morales, and Daniel Ortega were remembered for their respect for gay and lesbian Sandinistas (Erick Blandón, email communication, June 12, 2014; Dora María Téllez, personal communication, October 9, 2010; Broadbent 1991).

In *Adiós Muchachos*, Sergio Ramírez wrote of the experience of his wife, Gertrudis Guerrero Mayorga, known as Tulita. She spent two months as headmistress of a cotton-picking brigade, comprised of professors and students from the UCA (*Universidad Centroamericana*, Central American University). The long days picking cotton in the hot sun were exhausting, yet they found energy for other activities in the evenings.

Ramírez explains that Tulita was expected to keep "careful watch at night so that the young men would stay out of the women's quarters. It was, after all, a contingent from a Catholic University. Even so, the couples found ways to meet anyway, in the cotton fields or on the cliffs by the sea" (2012, 9). Ramírez's story—a struggle between two models of heterosexual culture, one more sexually constrained and the other more licentious—hardly surprises. But then he went on,

> There is also the story of the wedding party one night between two men who wanted to get married, one with a mosquito net veil and a crown of wild-flowers. The couple, along with everyone else, refused to eat anything but the same ration consumed by the cotton pickers—steamed plantains, rice glop, and a stale tortilla—because it was time not only to fight for others but to live as others did. (Ramírez 2012, 9)

Was that wedding endorsed by the revolution? Hardly. And yet, Tulita Guerrero Mayorga, headmistress of the brigade and wife of the vice president, did not stop the ceremony. Writing many years later, the lesson that Ramírez drew from that vignette is that the gay wedding was incorporated into the revolutionary ethics of the time, a time of sacrifice.

Those different currents—Tomás Borge's Cuban-style homophobia, Ernesto Cardenal's conflicts with his gay employees, Bayardo Arce's defense of LGBTQ Sandinistas, Sergio Ramírez's gay wedding story—flowed together in a conversation Tim McCaskell had at a New Year's Eve party ringing in 1980, a private party for gay men.

> "One of the commanders tried to introduce an anti-gay law to have it proclaimed by the junta here, just like in Cuba," I am told by one of Pablo's friends. "But they wouldn't go along. They said there was no need for that kind of thing here. There are a number of gay men and lesbians among the new leaders. Of course, they aren't open, but we know. That's stopped any anti-gay laws so far" (McCaskell 1981, 21).

The working-class and upper-class men at the party were divided over the new revolution, not even six months old at that point. The working-class men thought things were better than under Somoza, for various reasons, including that people were safe from the practically random violence of the last months of the dictatorship. Some had participated in the guerrilla struggle and even had jobs within the revolutionary government, though none were open about their sexuality at work. In contrast, the upper-class men tended to be suspicious of the new revolution; some even considered leaving the country.

But no matter their economic situation or view of the revolution, none hoped for more than to be left alone. "When I suggest that it might be important to organize to give gay people a voice to avoid the repetition of the Cuban experience, someone jokes, 'a gay Sandinista group,' and it is a great laugh. The idea that sexual politics might have a place in the Nicaraguan revolution seems completely alien to gay and straight alike" (McCaskell 1981, 21).

Mobilizing Gays and Lesbians in the Revolution (Quietly)

As I discussed in the introduction, in places like the United States a series of late nineteenth- and early twentieth-century social changes, including urbanization and the diminishing role of agriculture, created the conditions that allowed some people (who in earlier centuries might have engaged in same-sex relations without building an identity around that experience) to come to identify as gay or lesbian. In the relative anonymity of the city, gay men and lesbians found ways to meet and create community, first in bars and similar spaces and later in whole neighborhoods (D'Emilio 2007, 252–53). "By the time of the Stonewall Riot in New York City in 1969—the event that ignited the gay liberation movement—our situation was hardly one of silence, invisibility, and isolation. A massive, grass-roots liberation movement could form almost overnight because communities of lesbians and gay men existed" (D'Emilio 2007, 254–55).

Nicaragua's history was quite different. In the twentieth century, Nicaragua was integrated into the world capitalist economy, as was the United States, but it was integrated in a subordinate way, what social scientists often call dependent development (Saldaña-Portillo 2003, 54–57). Even in urban Nicaragua, very low wages for the vast majority mean that households continue to be economic units, with multiple generations living under one roof and pooling their resources. As a result, to this day there are no gay or lesbian neighborhoods as there are in most major cities in the Global North. Those would not seem to be propitious conditions for the development of gay identities, much less a gay rights movement (Adam 1993, 172–74; Horst 2010).

But in Nicaragua there was a revolution. The anthropologist Florence Babb argued that despite the absence of the sort of capitalist development analyzed by D'Emilio, the nearly eleven years of social transformation that followed the overthrow of the Somoza dictatorship created new identities and consciousness.

> When young Nicaraguans left home to participate in the revolutionary movement in the late 1970s and, again, left families in the early 1980s to participate in health and literacy brigades, they found needed opportunities for independence and privacy. . . . A number of individuals were able to explore more intimate aspects of their sexual lives as a result of their collective participation in work and political activism. (Babb 2003, 307; Thayer 1997, 399, makes a similar argument)

Thousands of LGBTQ Nicaraguans participated in the revolution. But in some sense, each had his or her own revolution. Their experiences varied greatly depending on factors including how long they had belonged to the FSLN, their gender, their class background, who their direct superiors were, and simple luck—perhaps mostly luck.

Mary Bolt, the student activist who joined the Sandinista movement in 1974, was born in February 1953, so she was twenty-six in July 1979, when the revolution began. Her relatively advanced age (compared to many other veterans of the war against Somoza), and her long history within the FSLN, meant that she was immediately appointed to positions of responsibility in Matagalpa, her hometown.

Like the men who laughed at the idea of a gay Sandinista group, Mary Bolt was not interested in organizing for lesbian rights. Instead, she simply wanted to defend the revolutionary project, which needed defending. From the very beginning, the revolution was threatened by the old leaders of Somoza's National Guard, who within a year or so regrouped as a violent counterrevolutionary movement, the *Contra*, organized and generously funded by the Reagan administration of the United States. But despite her disinterest in promoting lesbian rights, Mary Bolt's sexual identity came into conflict with her revolutionary identity.

> In '81 I had problems. I worked in a sector in Matagalpa that was, let's say, quite conservative. I had problems regarding comments that people would

make. People would gossip and say things that were not true. They said that I had orgies, things like that. I was shocked when I heard what they said about me because such a thing had never even occurred to me, right? And due to all that, the National Directorate of the FSLN—I was the political secretary of the party there in Matagalpa—due to that, they transferred me to Managua. But I talked it over with the National Directorate and they told me that it was due to the social situation that they transferred me, that they absolutely had not lost their trust in me. I accepted [the transfer;] I accepted it because it was a new leadership position. They were not—at any point— reducing my responsibilities. (Interview, July 5, 1994)

Mary Bolt was transferred to Managua to work at the Ministry of Education, where she enjoyed a little more freedom. Nonetheless, she had to be very discrete about her personal life when at work, the sort of silence that would never be expected of a heterosexual. Though the way she told the story, it was her decision rather than something imposed from above.

I was the one who decided to be very cautious . . . and to separate my private life from my work life, but not because my superiors told me to do so, rather because of the significance of the Ministry of Education. There is a sector within it that is very conservative, so I had to earn authority because I did not have a prior history within the Ministry. . . . I had to be careful so as to gain authority and recognition from the teachers. In this sense the only problem, so to speak, that I had was one I had in Matagalpa. (Interview, July 5, 1994)

Before the decade ended, some of her friends tried to organize a gay-lesbian pride movement. Despite her initial disinterest in lesbian rights, she attended some of those meetings, held in a house in Managua's Centroamérica neighborhood, though she was not very deeply involved: "I became fully involved in 1991, '92 [after the revolution was over]" (interview, June 6, 2011).

Like Mary Bolt, "Xochitl" was an active Sandinista from the early 1970s. Also like Bolt, when the revolution came to power in 1979, she joined in, participating in the industrial brigades as well as the EPS (*Ejército Popular Sandinista* or Sandinista People's Army). "I never had problems because I was a lesbian. Never. . . . And I continued within the Sandinista Front, they made me a member of the *Juventud Sandinista* (Sandinista Youth), and I have kept my membership, I continue even now. Despite my age they have not yet made me a member of the party; I continue to be a member of the Sandinista Youth. I still have my membership card from a long time ago" (interview, July 5, 1994). Someone who had been such a loyal Sandinista for so many years typically would have been invited to become a member of the party itself, especially once she was a middle-aged woman, well past the average age of a Sandinista Youth activist. It is possible that this oversight was discrimination against her for being a lesbian, but if it was discrimination, she did not seem to see it as such.

Ana Quirós was born in Mexico in 1956, the daughter of Costa Rican parents. Raised in Costa Rica, she was involved in the Nicaraguan solidarity movement in the 1970s, and once the Sandinistas overthrew the dictatorship, she moved to live in Nicaragua in 1979. It was in Nicaragua that she was first romantically involved with a woman, around 1982. "From the beginning my friends were like 'you like fish, I like chicken, so what.' . . . [T]he majority of people didn't say anything because there was something like the equivalent of the gringo policy [don't ask, don't tell;] . . . within the ranks of the FSLN there were sexually diverse people. I especially knew lesbians, not as many gay men. I had something like a support group among those women, but it was not the sort of thing people talked about" (interview, December 5, 2013).

Yet some lesbians of the same generation as Bolt, Xochitl, and Quirós did feel discrimination. Like Mary Bolt, Magaly Quintana was sent to work in Matagalpa after the FSLN came to power. For reasons that she could not explain, she found herself in the midst of a large community of lesbians. Maybe it was just a coincidence but there were approximately thirty Sandinista lesbians in Matagalpa, which came to the attention of Lenín Cerna, the director of state security within the Ministry of the Interior. Once he recognized this "problem," Cerna tried to do something about it. He sent "a group of the most handsome men, those that the FSLN considered to be the most macho to convince and convert us. So look how mixed up it was . . . breaking up all the lesbians because [they were] a terrible danger. It was very funny" (*Cuerpos Sin-Vergüenzas* 2014b).

That is, it was funny that the Ministry of the Interior wasted energy in an effort to convert a bunch of lesbians to heterosexuality. It was almost funny that they thought they could be converted, if only they met men who were handsome enough. But in some ways, it was not at all funny to be pursued by the crowd of handsome men. Quintana explained: they followed us around and "additionally [they were] bullies, because their job was to convince us; of course some of them knew that we could not be convinced [to become heterosexual,] but there was a mix of political game, political power, which was very intense. It was not easy" (*Cuerpos Sin-Vergüenzas* 2014b).

The staff at the Ministry of the Interior also tried to break up the group of lesbians. In some cases "they rewarded them and sent them on vacation for like six months, to the Soviet Union, but on vacation, to soften the blow, others went to the war zone. . . . [T]hey sent two to the war zone so obviously the message was clear: 'here they will disappear.' In my case, they sent me to Managua. . . . [T]hey broke us up, but then later they sent other women, and another group. That happened in Matagalpa; there is something about Matagalpa" (*Cuerpos Sin-Vergüenzas* 2014b).

Like Magaly Quintana, Marta Villanueva was active in Sandinista politics from a very early age. Born in 1956, she first became involved as a high school student, when she participated in a strike. "I studied at the Ramírez Goyena Central National Institute, which was a seedbed for many activists who later joined the struggle against the Somoza dynasty. In a student strike—I would have been in my second or third year—and I participated in the strike, that was the first time I had some contact [with the movement]" (interview, June 2, 2011). Later, as a university student, she joined the Sandinista Youth, and still later she joined in the mass campaigns of the early 1980s: "I participated in the coffee and cotton harvesting brigades, [and] in the literacy campaign" (interview, June 2, 2011).

During all that time, even from the age of six or seven, she felt she was different from other girls. And she felt alone both in the private world of her family and in the public worlds of the university and the revolution.

When I was a teenager [my relatives] insisted that I had to follow the pattern that had been established within my home[,] because all of my sisters were married[;] they had children, and I was the youngest[;] so, in a certain way they pressured me into having a boyfriend so as to . . . reduce the pressure on me, but when I entered the university I felt that really I could not continue maintaining the appearance that they wanted, that I would get married and all the rest. The university for me was liberating[;] my schoolwork permitted me to be out of the house[;] . . . [but] it was a difficult time because wherever I looked for answers for my situation nobody could give me an answer, because even though it is true that in Nicaragua there were some people, the only ones that I had seen were gay men[;] I never saw a lesbian which would have allowed me to identify with the word "lesbian." I did know that in the 1960s there had been a very famous person in Managua who was called *la Caimana* [Alligator Woman]. (Interview, June 2, 2011)

Villanueva had never met the famous *Caimana*, though it was encouraging to her to know that such people existed (on *la Caimana*, see González-Rivera forthcoming).

But it was not enough. When Villanueva consulted a psychologist at the UNAN of Managua, he recommended conversion therapy for her and for a gay male student. Instead, on her own, she searched in the library.

All I could find were books that spoke of homosexuality as a sin, because I searched for bibliographies, literature, someone who could help orient me or identify with me, with someone who was in the same boat, and that search was very difficult. The only thing that was nearby was the Catholic religion. My whole life my family was very Catholic: we went to mass on Sundays, we celebrated *Purísima* [the feast of the conception of Mary] in the house. In all those activities I was always very involved. There was a time when I felt very guilty. I questioned myself a lot, and I said to myself, why am I different than my sisters, why am not I the same as them? I went through that whole process feeling very alone, very alone. (Interview, June 2, 2011)

Finally, in 1982 she graduated with a degree in educational psychology and went looking for a job. Villanueva found a job, or rather various jobs, mainly in schools, but she chose to leave several of them because she could not take the social pressures. "I felt a lot of social pressure at work, because everyone had a partner except for me. In the parties, in the activities, they asked me why I was alone. That had quite an impact on me because I had nobody with whom I could talk, nothing. In the case of my last job, I decided to leave because there was so much pressure on people who worked for the state. . . . The job that I left in 1987 was in the National Institute of Water and Sewage. There was so much social pressure that I decided it would be better to quit" (interview, June 2, 2011).

She left because she could not stand the constant pressure from her fellow workers who wanted to know why she had not looked for someone. In fact, she had looked for—and found—someone, a girlfriend with whom she lived for eleven or twelve years. But while it was wonderful to live with her, having a girlfriend caused its own problems. If her fellow workers were rude, her neighbors were worse.

> We suffered a lot. That ended up leading to our breakup because of our trouble finding a place to live together. . . . We faced many incidences in which people wanted to break into our house, some of the neighbors near the place where we went to buy things, just to bother us. They would wait for us outside the store with hostile attitudes, [and] the harassment was so great that we had to file a complaint with the police. So then the police at that time said to us why were we living together, just two women alone? They said that was why people were harassing us because we were attacking social norms. (Interview, June 2, 2011)

When she sought help from friends in the FSLN, they suggested that she should just stop acting that way. Instead, she and her girlfriend hired a lawyer.

> The lawyer said that to win the case we could not say that we were lesbians, and that we were a couple. We would have to say that we were not anything like that. If not, we would lose the case, but [still] the police were very aggressive, and they treated us very badly. Later they told us, if we wanted our neighbors to leave us alone, they could go by with their patrol car, but we would have to give them something. So that was the way it was, that extreme, we ended up selling the house where we were living. All of that is part of what I have lived through because of my [sexual] preferences or sexual orientation. (Interview, June 2, 2011)

After the revolution, in the 1990s, Villanueva became active in lesbian rights organizing as a founding member of *Grupo Safo* (Safo Group).

Juan Carlos Martínez was another gay revolutionary, born in Managua in 1970. The sixth of seven children, he was raised by his parents in a working-class neighborhood. There were some economic limitations, but his childhood was "normal," and he had good relations with his parents, neighbors, and siblings, especially his sisters. Since he was barely nine years old when the FSLN overthrew the Somoza dictatorship, his childhood was a revolutionary childhood.

I was a member of the *Asociación de Niños Sandinistas* [Association of Sandinista Children]. . . . Additionally there was something that was part of my
life, and which has had a permanent impact on my life, [which was] that I
worked with liberation theology, with the *comunidades eclesiales de base*
(Christian base communities)[.] I was very close to the congregation of *La
Asunción* who work in San Judas, they are very advanced, that shaped my
political activities, partisan activities within the Association of Sandinista
Children, that was part of the work of evangelization, catechism, but shaped
by the theology of liberation. (Interview, December 6, 2012)

It was exciting for Juan Carlos to be involved, along with his classmates, in an
important mission at a young age, but he also felt that he was different from
his classmates, a feeling he had experienced from the age of four or five. That
feeling evolved into a realization that he was gay, a fact he felt that he had to
hide while participating in revolutionary campaigns. "In the campaigns as
in any other area of life at that time I had to hide my sexual orientation; at
that moment our society was much more intolerant" (email communication,
August 9, 2013).

As Martínez became a teenager he continued his revolutionary and religious work. "Our group went to harvest coffee, cotton, [and we participated
in] the people's health campaigns" (interview, December 6, 2012). In recognition of his years of participation, he was invited to join the Sandinista
Youth, yet despite that recognition, he still felt that he needed to disguise his
sexual orientation. He knew many other gay men, lesbians, and trans people
who played a part in the revolution but who were also silenced. "The strategic
thing was not to speak, not to mention this issue, an issue that was considered to be a legacy of capitalism" (email communication, August 9, 2013).

Homosexuality was understood by some Sandinista leaders as a leftover
from the capitalism of the Somoza era, a problem that would cease to exist
once Nicaragua had made the full transition to socialism. And Juan Carlos
Martínez's perception was hardly unique. Florence Babb (2004, 28), Erick
Blandón (2003, 57), Silke Heumann (2014, 337–38), Tim McCaskell (1981,
19), and Joel Zúñiga (interview, June 18, 2014) all described similar versions
of this "legacy of capitalism theory," a theory that informed a lot of Sandinista thought during the 1980s (and twentieth century Marxist thought
in general). According to the theory, class dynamics drove social change,

so social inequality based on factors like gender, race, or sexuality would disappear—almost magically—as capitalism was dismantled and socialism was implemented. Not only was it unnecessary to address gender, race, or sexuality, but paying attention to such things was a deviation from the real struggle that would make social progress more difficult.

Certainly that is how Martínez perceived it at the time, that it would be impossible to address the issue of gay rights, or even gay toleration, within the revolution. There were some Sandinista activists who were more open than he was, but whether that is because they had more seniority in the party or because they had more sympathetic superiors, or simply because they were less fearful, is difficult to tell. The fact that he was a gay man, and most of the other cases I have discussed so far regarded lesbians, may be significant. Many (though certainly not all) lesbians have an easier time "passing" as heterosexual than do gay men, and that was almost surely true in revolutionary Nicaragua (Howe 2013, 6; Peña 2013, xxvi; Welsh 2014, 45, n. 10).

Another view of the lives of gay men in revolutionary Nicaragua was provided by Ian Scott Horst, based on his experiences in 1986. A gay-rights activist in New York, he hoped to learn about gay and lesbian life during his time in Nicaragua, though he was unable to meet any lesbians. Instead, he spent many days in Managua's city center, a place where unemployed young men, especially gay men, hung out, gossiped, and sometimes hooked-up with other men.

The central park, also called the Plaza of the Revolution, was framed on one side by the ruins of the cathedral. The cathedral, which was largely destroyed in the 1972 earthquake, was a favorite location for men to have sex with men (until the mid-1990s, when its doors and windows were sealed with iron bars by the government of Violeta Barrios de Chamorro). On another side sat the National Palace, and its third side was marked by the grave of FSLN founder Carlos Fonseca, along with a large gazebo. Horst liked to spend time in the gazebo, escaping the full force of the tropical sun, and learning about gay life during the revolution.

During the month of June 1986, the Plaza was a relaxed place. When young Nicaraguans got tired of chatting with each other they would sometimes wander over to the gazebo to talk to Horst, sometimes about gay life, sometimes about the war, the draft, the price of running shoes, or the merits of Boy George's music.

FIGURE 2   Members of ANIT pose in front of the old cathedral of Managua, a popular meeting place for LGBTQ people, c. 2015. Courtesy of Ludwika Vega.

But while all this takes place right out in the open amidst mothers dragging their two-year-olds along by the wrist and clerks rushing home from work in the nearby National Palace, there is a tension. As Managua filled with foreign dignitaries and tourists for the revolution's seventh anniversary celebration [to be held on July 19th], some officials of the MINT, the Ministry of the Interior, began to complain that the presence of queeny young gays in the park was a desecration and disrespect toward the remains of Carlos

Fonseca lying nearby. In early July a beefed-up police and army presence in the park and plaza effectively—though surely temporarily—discouraged the gay presence in the park, and definitely halted gay people from using the ruins of the cathedral for sexual liaisons. (Horst 2010)

Surprisingly, perhaps, some gay people seemed to agree with the MINT. After all, the Plaza was the final resting place of Carlos Fonseca, the most revered of all the heroes and martyrs in a country that has had far too many heroes and martyrs. "An 18-year-old shop clerk . . . spoke disparagingly of his fellow gays who had no respect for places like Fonseca's tomb. . . . [H]e denounced those gays who would loudly carry on in the shadow of one of Nicaragua's greatest heroes. '*Son vulgares*,'" he said (Horst 2010).

Referring to people who had sex in the cathedral as *vulgar* was probably a comment on the unacceptability of having sex in public. To be *vulgar* was to be disrespectful, but it did not refer to any sort of disrespect. It had a strong class content. In fact, had the eighteen-year-old clerk been better versed in Marxist terminology he might have called them lumpen.

It refers to the poorest layers of society; those who eke out a living from their homes in the ruins selling sodas dispensed into baggies or trading on the black market. *Los vulgares*, the vulgar ones, are those people who the Sandinistas have not managed to reach in seven years of the revolutionary process. They are the people who by and large do not see the revolution as their own: who watch in bewilderment as the political storm rages past them, offering few concrete solutions to their poverty and disempowerment. To many gay people, those fellow gays who spend their afternoons in the parque central or climb through the ruined office buildings cruising for sex are vulgar. They are defined outside of the revolutionary process and looked down upon. (Horst 2010)

Of all the ironies of the revolution, not just the Sandinista revolution but all the twentieth century Marxist revolutions, this was one of the big ones. To be a revolutionary meant to disdain class inequality, to work for social justice. But it also often meant to disdain those at the very bottom of the class pyramid, a bottom that—in Nicaragua—was and is quite large. According to Marx (1848), the lumpen proletariat cannot be trusted. The vulgar ones are so desperate that they are easily bought off. They are the strikebreakers, the counterrevolutionaries. The vulgar ones were those for whom the revolution was made and often the least likely to voluntarily join revolutionary activities.

> Tony, at age 19, is already a veteran of service in the army. He lives with his family in one of the poorest sections of Managua, occasionally helping his father cart and sell soda. He doesn't think too much of the revolution, and one of his most often repeated phrases is, "Antes, cuando Somoza . . ." Before, under Somoza, the lake was so clean you could swim in it. Before, under Somoza, you could buy good clothes. Before, under Somoza, life was beautiful. Too young to really discern which of these fantastical notions embody reality, he's watched close friends [get] killed and seen his life and that of his family grow no easier. He is one of the *vulgares*. Arrested by the police for having sex with another man in one of the ruins, he spent days in jail without being able to contact friends or family. Until his release his family was frantic. What had happened to him? Had he been kidnapped by the contras? Killed? Arrested? After a few days he was released and told never, never to go to the park again. Afterwards, even a block or two away he begins looking nervously around him for fear of being spotted by the same police officers. If asked, Tony will say he was arrested for being gay; that being gay is illegal in Nicaragua. (Horst 2010)

Horst told Tony's story to Walter, a young gay man from a middle-class family. Walter studied history in college, sympathized with the revolution, and was a member of the Sandinista Youth. Walter told him that this could not have happened, that it was legal to be gay in Nicaragua. But then he heard more details, and he understood. "When told of who Tony is, he says, as if it explained everything, 'He's vulgar, then'" (Horst 2010).

Walter, of course, did not go to the Plaza to meet people. Instead, he recommended that Horst join him at his favorite hangout, *Lobo Jack*.

> Lobo Jack is a whole other world from the Plaza and its park. With a cover charge that might be Tony's family's food budget for a week, it's filled with well-dressed young people. It doesn't look like a gay bar. The dance floor is crowded with male-female couples dancing to a tape of alternating North American disco and Latin American salsa. Amidst this crowd of seeming heterosexuals, though, Walter can point out half of a couple here and there

saying, "He's gay; I think she is too." At which point Walter goes off to dance with a Sandinista army reservist called Martha, also gay. (Horst 2010)

For young men who could not afford to dance at *Lobo Jack* and to participate in Sandinista student groups, the revolution was not always emancipatory. Sometimes there were terrible consequences for men and boys who challenged heterosexual norms during the 1980s.

Manoly López identified as a transwoman and as a Sandinista at the time of the interview in 2012. Born in 1968, she explained how she had been a boy who liked to wear miniskirts. "In the 1980s, when the FSLN party came to power, there was terrible discrimination, there has always been discrimination, but at that time I could not even walk a half a block dressed as a woman because they arrested me, they beat me up. . . . It is true that everybody has their own personal and political beliefs, [yet] I am not sure what has attracted me to that party, to the FSLN; . . . but I have seen the advances that we have made here in Nicaragua" (interview, December 6, 2012).

She almost did not live to see those advances. In the early 1980s, Manoly often left the house dressed in her masculine school uniform, only to change, after school, into feminine clothing borrowed from her sisters. One such afternoon, when she was twelve years old, she went out drinking with an older gay friend. After a few drinks she left with a man she had just met, who seemed romantically interested in her. The next thing she remembered was waking from a coma in a hospital bed. She had been found in a sugar cane field, lying in a pool of blood.

If not for the Spanish doctor who was living in Masaya, in solidarity with the revolution, Manoly doubts that she would have lived. Finally, after many surgeries to reconstruct her intestines and anus, and a total of two and a half years in the hospital, Manoly went home, eventually becoming a trans-rights activist. "My Mom sobbed terribly, I almost died, but 'weeds never die' is what I tell my mom" (interview, December 6, 2012).

Based on fieldwork in Managua in the 1980s, the anthropologist Roger Lancaster observed that

> In its early years, the revolution constrained homosexual practice. The na-
> ture of socialist revolution, and perhaps particularly that variety influenced
> by liberation theology, entails a strong normative or corporatist compo-
> nent . . . [producing] a cultural atmosphere in which homosexual practice

(and sexual transgression in general) was at least publicly regarded as more suspect than before, tainted with the image of indulgence or corruption, and was perhaps even somewhat less readily available. (1992, 253)

But the revolution was a complicated thing. On the one hand, it depended on social pressure to get people to join a movement bigger than themselves, to emulate Che Guevara's new man, to sacrifice personal comfort for the greater good. On the other hand, the revolution created opportunities for many people, including LGBTQ Nicaraguans. Lancaster suggested that sometimes it created opportunities *especially* for LGBTQ Nicaraguans, citing the example of a gay man who was elected to the highest position in the local neighborhood organization, the *Comités de Defensa Sandinista* (CDS) (Committees for Sandinista Defense). "Having fewer family responsibilities and dependents appears to have freed many politically conscious *cochones* to work for the revolution. In the process, some have gained recognition and status in the community, much as priests drive charisma from a life of celibacy and service" (1992, 254).

The War Years

If the revolution was too often a time of sacrifice, never was that more true than with regard to the Contra War. From 1983 until the end of the war in 1990, military service was obligatory for young men. Thousands of gay men served—and many died—defending the revolution. Mario Gutiérrez noted that neither the army nor the FSLN, nor any of the smaller parties that trace their roots to the Sandinista movement, have publicly recognized "the courage, the daring, and the role in combat of gay men who as members of the FSLN or as Nicaraguans also gave their lives for the revolution. They should make a monument specifically to remember them" (interview, November 30, 2012).[6]

---

6. It is likely that some gay men and lesbians fought on the side of the *Contra*. But I have not been able to locate any of them, nor have I found any written evidence of their existence, except for one brief comment by Commander Edén Pastora regarding the southern front of the Contra forces or ARDE (*Alianza Revolucionaria Democrática* or Democratic Revolutionary Alliance). In an interview with Lola Villas, Pastora (who fought on the side of the Sandinistas in the 1970s, and the Contras in the 1980s), said that, despite accusations to the contrary, he had never been involved in executing homosexual guerrillas. "'I never killed homosexuals, I never imposed violent punishments upon homosexuals. Not at all!' he insisted. 'We were not

Women also served in the armed forces and in two all-female battalions (named after Erlinda López y Digna López). But their experience was quite different than that of men. Despite the significant participation of women in the struggle against Somoza, once the Sandinistas took power, women played more limited roles within the armed forces, especially once the Contra War began and the Sandinistas implemented a draft. Men were drafted; women were not, despite lobbying efforts by the *Asociación de Mujeres Nicaragüenses Luisa Amanda Espinosa* (Luisa Amanda Association of Nicaraguan Women, or AMNLAE) in favor of including women in the draft.

Even after they were excluded from the draft, women were permitted to serve in the army as volunteers (Molyneux 1985, 149–50), and as Ian Scott Horst observed during his 1986 visit, "female soldiers [were] a common sight" (2010). But those women were a minority, and since they were volunteers their experiences were different from those of men, who usually were drafted. Also, as Emily Hobson noted regarding images that were used by the U.S. gay and lesbian solidarity movement, "Such images indicated the constraints of revolutionary gender norms, which opened the door to female masculinity while tightening the lock against effeminate men" (Hobson 2012, 5; James Green 2012, 455–56 made a similar argument regarding the Brazilian left).

I interviewed a number of lesbians who served in the armed forces but none of them were out at the time, not even to themselves. As a result, the stories here are of men's experiences. The story of lesbians' and bisexual women's experiences in the war is yet to be told.

That many gay men served in the Sandinista army, and that many were treated badly, is clear. Erick Blandón noted that,

> on the one hand there was a notable persecution in the military against young gay men who were drafted during the war. For example, they were repressed, imprisoned, or dishonorably discharged from the troops. When one of the superiors discovered that there were gay couples, normally they punished the one who had a passive attitude. It was even the case that when the draft board was recruiting, many young men pretended to be gay with

concerned about homosexuality. It is a social problem, and we were concerned with addressing other social problems.' Were there gay guerrillas? 'At that time, no,' he responded. 'In the last guerrilla movement (ARDE) I did see homosexuals. In that guerrilla movement I did not see problems with homosexuality'" (Villas quoted in Medina 2013b).

the support of their parents to avoid going to the war front. . . . Julio López [Campos] who was the head of the DRI [Office of International Relations or *Dirección de Relaciones Internacionales*] believed that gays and lesbians should not be permitted to work in foreign relations. And leaders like Tomás Borge defended that rule because he believed that gay men—not lesbians— but gay men should not serve, because their sexual orientation made them easy to blackmail within the army. (Interview, October 23, 1992)

Yet for all the claims that they could not be trusted, Blandón concluded noting that "no gay Sandinista ever went over to the side of the enemy and infinite numbers of heterosexual Sandinistas" deserted and joined the *Contras* (interview, October 23, 1992).

Were gay men supposed to be drafted? There was no written policy, but many believed that the answer was no. Fidel Moreira, born in 1974 in Managua, was too young to serve but he was old enough to hear stories. "People who were young men at that time have told me that they lined up dressed as gay men, [and] the chief of police told them no. Young heterosexual men who did not want to be drafted arrived and acted as though they were gay because homosexual and gay men who were open were not accepted in the military service. It was paradoxical, because there were heterosexuals who did that and there were gay men who wanted to complete their military service" (Fidel Moreira, interview, December 3, 2012).

There were various reasons why gay men might want to serve in the military. For those who were closeted, serving could help disguise their homosexuality, and in fact, many framed military service as proof of heterosexuality. Roger Lancaster described a 1986 conversation with Charlie, asking him what he would do when he reached the age of mandatory service, only a year or two off. "When it's my time, I'm not going to run. I'd rather stay in school and study, but when I have to, I'll go into the service, and do my time. Only the *cochones* run" (Lancaster 1992, 197). Similarly, young men were shamed by graffiti painted on a wall in the city of Granada: Only fags dodge the draft; "*Sólo las maricas son evasores*" (quoted in Lancaster 1992, 197).

Of course, those threats were not the only reason for serving. Many gay men, like many heterosexual men, served because they supported the revolution, and because they feared what could happen if the *Contras* won the war. Moreover, there were serious consequences for not serving. In addition to the stigma of being a draft dodger, it was difficult to obtain work or to enroll in school without written proof that one had completed military service.

Norman Gutiérrez came from a revolutionary family, dating back to the Somoza era: his older sisters were members of the GPP tendency within the FSLN, and his grandmother ran a safe house (that is, she hid arms and people in her house). Born in December 1966, Gutiérrez was only twelve years old when the FSLN overthrew the Somoza dictatorship, and he immediately became a revolutionary activist. "I began to participate in some of the organizations of the revolution, in the Committees for Sandinista Defense. I was the coordinator for my block from a very young age . . . and then they called me up for military service" (interview, June 8, 2011). At age seventeen he joined the army because he was a Sandinista, which is not to say that it was exactly voluntary.

> I had the opportunity to spend three years at war, to participate in what were really the worse years of the war, in 1984 to 1986[;] I fired rocket launchers, and I also was a heavy machine gun operator. When I tell people this, they don't believe it. They always think that I had to be in the kitchen for the battalion, or in the regular battalion, but I was directly on the war front. I was in the Sandinista Youth. I was a political official of the battalion. I played a very important role within the structure of the battalion. I did all the work that was necessary at that time. An amnesty law for the counter-revolutionaries was created, and I did political work with the peasants doing consciousness-raising in preparation for demobilization. There, on the war front, was where I obtained my membership [*militancia*] in the FSLN. It was interesting to participate; evidently during those times there was more revolutionary mystique; there was more commitment. To be a revolutionary in the 1980s was very different from being a revolutionary now. (*Cuerpos Sin-Vergüenzas* 2014b)

Gutiérrez noted that, from his perspective, "there was not persecution within the military service, there were many homosexuals in the military service, many gay kids, some who were openly gay and others who were not." At one point, he belonged to a battalion named after Miguel Ángel Ortiz within which most of the gay soldiers worked in the kitchen. But he personally did not work in the kitchen, "I never thought about staying in the kitchen, because that was not for me. Evidently in my case I did not associate homosexuality with playing a role in the kitchen" (*Cuerpos Sin-Vergüenzas* 2014b).

At the age of sixteen, René Villalobos served in the Sandinista military. While serving he rose through the ranks: "I was the assistant to the chief of a brigade who trusted me." Being competent and honest with large quantities of money, and thus gaining the respect of his peers, allowed him some social freedom. It was then that he started to become more feminine in his presentation. "I did not wear a uniform like everyone else; rather I wore clothing that gave me a feminine appearance. . . . the military service was what helped me." Upon returning from the war she was a new person telling her family that she was no longer René the man; rather, she was René the woman (*Campaña Somos Iguales a Vos* 2016).

But some soldiers experienced the war differently than Norman Gutiérrez and René Villalobos. Mario Gutiérrez explained that because he was college educated and due to his vision problems, he was placed in decision-making positions rather than on the front lines. From those positions he could see what homophobic commanders tried to do to gay recruits, and sometimes he was able to intervene to protect them.

> There were homophobic men within the army who would send gay kids to become cannon fodder at the war front, and I was aware of it. I was one of those who stopped the officers. I said to them, if you send this kid to the war front because you are a homophobe—that was not the word that was used—because you hate homosexuals, I will let everyone know that you had a sexual relationship with me. That was the way I had to threaten them, [and] because of that all the officers of the army knew me. . . . For example, we would be near the *Contra* and they would send the kids to be assassinated. They killed them because they knew they were not going to have a way to escape. It is a way to say, he died in combat; but no, you sent him to be killed—he did not just die in combat. Am I being clear about the military commanders' ability to manipulate? But I need to say that on the other hand the army did not have [an official] policy against homosexuals; that did not exist. (Interview, November 30, 2012)

While fighting deep in the mountains in the northern departments of Matagalpa and Jinotega, in such isolated places that Gutiérrez often wasn't sure where they were, "all of us had sex with men, the officers and the kids themselves, everyone. . . . That is why we say that the golden age of the *cochonada* in Nicaragua was in the 1980s. . . . We had sex with all the men of Nicaragua. That is why when many of the officers see us today, they signal to us. They say be quiet; don't say anything. Now they are grandfathers; the war veterans today know many things about that past" (interview, November 30, 2012).[7]

Similarly, Florence Babb observed that "in revolutionary Nicaragua an unintended consequence of service in the military and the brigades was the discovery of same-sex desire among a number of young women and men" (Babb 2003, 307). Fidel Moreira said that "there were gay men who wanted to serve in the military, because of all that implied, being in the mountains with so many men; there are many stories like that" (interview, December 3, 2012). But while that was true for some people, for many young recruits, military service did not necessarily offer such sexual opportunities.

Joel Zúñiga began his military service in 1985, when he was nineteen or twenty years old, and for him "it was quite hard. One could sense if another person was gay, but nobody said anything. There was a lot of fear [and] you could not trust people" (interview, June 18, 2014). Often he suspected that a fellow draftee or an officer was gay. He knew that some men had sex with other men within the army, but it was a risky thing to do. There could be serious consequences including, sometimes, immediate expulsion.

Juan Carlos Martínez, who began his military service in 1987 when he was sixteen or seventeen years old, also feared that he might be discovered. And if discovered, he could get a dishonorable discharge, which would make work and study very difficult (interview, December 6, 2012). So many young men found themselves in an ambiguous and often uncomfortable position within the Sandinista Popular Army: not sure if they belonged there, sometimes threatened by homophobic superiors, sometimes enjoying new opportunities for same-sex relations.

---

7. It is worth noting that Gutiérrez was unusually courageous in his defense of gay rights in the 1980s. Barry Adam recounted a debate that ran in the pages of *El Nuevo Diario* in 1985. The debate ended with a letter from Gutiérrez, published under his full name (Mario José Gutiérrez Morales), in which he eloquently condemned homophobia as "an ultra-reactionary ideology . . . denying democratic liberties, human rights, the right to participate in the construction of a pluralist, revolutionary and democratic society" (quoted in Adam 1993, 178).

CHAPTER TWO

The Wizard of the Revolution and Other Stories

"The FSLN respected me; it made a space for me. . . . That was something that I liked about the FSLN, the way it welcomed me, the television [show] that made me famous."

—Donald Casco

One never knew quite what to expect from Donald Casco. Starting in 1986 and continuing for another seven years or so, the Donald Casco show appeared on channel 6, that is, Sandinista television.[1] One day featured card reading, another considered crystals, another reviewed cultures of the ancient world. While the show was not about sexuality in any overt way, Casco appeared to be gay. According to Casco, everyone knew he was gay: "When they saw me on television, with the gestures I made, the way I was made up, with all my shtick" (interview, November 28, 2012). In fact, he soon acknowledged to the press that he was gay. And he was the star of the show.

> Since I like culture, I did not want it to be an esoteric thing, a thing about witchcraft; [rather] I brought high culture to the show. . . . I would speak about extraterrestrials, about the ancient Mayans—that was a novel thing because no television station in the world did that sort of thing. . . . The shows addressed the discovery of Machu Picchu, how Tutankhamun's tomb was discovered. The hour-long program was divided up; first at the beginning I would read cards to predict people's futures. I was always wearing exotic robes . . . feathers; I would dress like a Nicaraguan *cacique*, the next day I was dressed like the Pharoah, the day after that I would come out dressed as a robot, the day after that the show appeared at the seaside. . . .

---

1. At least as late as 2004 Casco continued to be a television personality in a short astrology segment on channel 23's Bolsa Visión news program.

I was very original in my program. (Interview, November 28, 2012)

With the help of technically skilled people who had come to support the revolution from places like Germany and Brazil, the show was quite advanced, using the sort of makeup, costumes, and lighting that had not been seen in local programming up until then. Once, he was made to disappear on camera, just like a real magician. "The revolution looked kindly upon me, the people [too]. That was the most extraordinary thing, members of the National Directorate itself called me; they reached out to me so that I could help them" (interview, November 28, 2012).

FIGURE 3   Donald Casco, dressed for his television show, mid-1980s. Courtesy of Donald Casco.

Guerrilla struggle, the literacy and health campaigns, land reform, defending the country against the *Contras*: those are standard images of what the Sandinista Revolution was *really* about. But not all Nicaraguans experienced the 1980s in such dramatic ways. For many, especially children, or retired people, or women who worked at home, the events of the revolution were observed from afar, often filtered through a television screen. Those were the sort of people who often remembered Donald Casco decades later.

That may have been especially true for kids who suspected that they were gay or lesbian or trans. Ludwika Vega, born in 1983, grew up to become a transgender rights activist. She laughed when I asked about the cultural role that Donald Casco had played, as an openly gay man. "Yes, he is open, he has always been open. I remember how he used to wear short-shorts" (interview, November 29, 2012).[2] In contrast, people who were of the age to be mobilized within the revolution often did not remember him. Too much was going on in their lives for a melodramatic TV astrologer to make an impression.

---

2. In referring to his "short-shorts," Ludwika Vega must have been thinking about Donald Casco's later career (after the end of his astrology television show) as a weight lifter when he, like all weight lifters, would have worn short-shorts. According to Casco, he did not have a weight lifting TV show, but his weight lifting work, at various gymnasiums in the United States and Nicaragua, did sometimes receive media coverage (personal communication by Facebook Messenger, August 3, 2017).

But we should not forget him, for Donald Casco was another facet of the social transformation that was the revolution. The first openly gay television personality in the country, Donald Casco was transmitted into Nicaraguan homes on Sandinista television. One might say that the gay astrologer's program was endorsed by the revolution, though some would say that goes too far. Mario Gutiérrez agreed that Casco was open about his sexuality but thought that "it is not right to say that he was endorsed by the revolution . . . for the Nicaraguan as long as you are goofing around, screwing around, joking, mocking, and making jokes, Nicaraguans love that, and also they love gossip just like people everywhere. . . . [Donald Casco's] program was permitted because it fit well within the idiosyncrasy, the atmosphere, the scandalous way of being of a Nicaraguan. The program was a big hit . . . but that does not have anything to do with the policies of the revolution. The revolution never had a policy of defending gay rights" (interview, November 30, 2012).

Donald Casco's story started in 1951, when he was born in Matagalpa, a small city in Nicaragua's mountainous north. One of seven siblings in a middle-class family that belonged to the Assembly of God (*Asamblea de Dios*), he went to good schools. Not only was he an excellent student, but from the age of about five, he seemed to be a very unusual child. As Casco explained:

> During that period many of my abilities were discovered . . . exotic abilities, clairvoyance, paranormal abilities. . . . I would predict things [I could not know;] my mom was an evangelical, and my father was a man with Muslim tendencies. I was very different, an extraordinary thing. . . . At the age of 16 I became sick with something that they blamed on demonic things, at 16, but the Lord appeared to me and said that he was going to cure me, and I was cured. It was a fatal illness: they had even already purchased the coffin and everything; I saw it. . . . I dedicated the next 16 years of my life to the Lord's things. You know what the traditional evangelical churches are like—no movies, no sex—and I was a very devout person. During this time, I had the chance to study many languages, the Bible, all of that helped me with culture, the Bible, the piano. . . . What I want to say is that I practically lived a mystical and very religious life. I was like an example for many. (Interview, November 27, 2012)

At that time, he did not think of himself as gay; he even had girlfriends. "Maybe I was a little attached to my mother, like people say, spoiled, but I did not feel like I was gay because when the Lord cured me, when I felt that I was going to die, I spent 16 years in the church as a follower, without going to the movies, [or] to dances, without thinking about sex, [as an] evangelical, in the Assembly of God. My family was evangelical, [and] it was among the first converts in Nicaragua. I was the pianist at the church. . . . I was the principal musician at the church. I was also the president of the youth group [and] the Sunday school; the only thing I did not do was to be the pastor" (interview, December 1, 2012).

A visit to the United States, where he had relatives, was the beginning of a new stage in Casco's life. "When I went to the United States, I was 24 years old; I began late. I had my first complete homosexual relationship in the United States, not here in Nicaragua. The people of my home city Matagalpa do not know me as gay, except for a few who now know I am gay, but in my hometown, I was never gay. I had a girlfriend and everything. I lived a normal life" (interview, December 1, 2012).

Upon his return from the United States, the guerrilla movement was growing, and the FSLN recruited him. The FSLN did not recruit him as a gay man, for he was not yet openly gay, since it was difficult to be open in the Nicaragua of his youth. For one thing, his family was unsympathetic. Then there was the issue of other people, especially in Matagalpa, his hometown.

Gay people existed but to be gay was a taboo, [and] people talked about them, [and] they were there but they were shocking. Seeing a gay person was like seeing a leper, [and] if a gay person was coming, people crossed the street to avoid him, [and] the bad vibes that came from those people. Today we live with them at home, at work, in the family—it is totally and completely different in every way. [Back then] women did not have important positions; today they are lawyers, businesspeople, in the top positions, even president. In Nicaragua nobody expected that; women were relegated to their homes to knit and do things like that. Men were in charge of bringing money home, and gay people were discriminated against. (Interview, December 1, 2012)

When he was recruited by the FSLN, he was asked to design the front page of the FSLN magazine *Trinchera*, a job he did for three years. Casco collaborated, along with several his relatives, including his sister Lourdes, who was involved in the takeover of the cathedral. Casco moved between

Managua and Matagalpa as opportunities arose for him to work as an art
teacher and for reasons of safety. After the assassination of Pedro Joaquín
Chamorro in January 1978, he and his sister returned to Matagalpa. A few
months later, in September, there was a massacre in Matagalpa's Soza Hotel.

> The National Guard killed the whole family, and everyone who happened
> to be there. So then all the people rose up. My house was up on a hill; my
> mother was almost shot; they fired at her head but did not hit her. There was
> a lot of fear and to be safe they said to me, let's go to Managua; my sister lived
> here in Managua, so we came here and we left the house [in Matagalpa] to
> the FSLN; we left food and everything. It worked well for them because from
> my house you could see everything, [and] it was like a tower. From there they
> could fire their guns, [and] they could fight with the National Guard from
> there. (Interview, November 27, 2012)

Casco was not yet a member of the party—that would come after the revolutionary triumph—but he was an important collaborator, in part because of
his class background. As Lynn Horton observed, though the FSLN fought in
the name of the poor, and many who fought were poor, the revolutionaries
could not have succeeded without members of the middle and upper classes.
Elites had the ability to mobilize the poor people who participated in their
clientelistic networks, something that was not true the other way around
(Horton 1998, 68–71). Also, elites had the ability to move in certain circles
without attracting attention.

In 1979, the FSLN asked Casco for more help. At that time, he was taking piano lessons in the same building in Matagalpa where Somoza's party
had its office. His contact in the FSLN told him, "'The revolution is coming,
the war is coming; Donald, do us a favor.' I was not directly involved, but I
supported them, [so I said] of course, I would be happy to help.... I told the
political boss there, lend me this building, we are going to clear out the con-
servatory this weekend, we want to be able to save the piano, furniture, all the
musical instruments, because they were going to burn down that building,
and they didn't want to lose everything" (interview, November 28, 2012).

Under the pretext that the building was to be painted, Casco helped to
move the piano and the furniture to his house, so that they would be protected from the fight that was to come. "They told me, the war is going to
start on a Friday at five in the afternoon, in June; everything has been five

with the FSLN. [I told them] I am not a military person. I have had no military training; but you know that I am with you. I am a Sandinista one hundred percent, and I will give you my house to be used as a hospital. . . . I gave them the keys, and we went to our country house. . . . We had a little house in the country, not very far away, like about seven kilometers" (interview, November 28, 2012).

So began the revolution, and, along with it, Donald Casco's life as a gay man. He had been involved sexually with a few men earlier in his life, but the revolution provided many more sexual opportunities, especially the Contra War, in which he served as a volunteer, in the "32–36 battalion, and [he] called it the 69–14, it was the Conchita Alday [battalion]" (quoted in Agüero 2004).

> When I was with the soldiers, we slept in the same place. In the middle of the war there was an airplane that shot down upon us. . . . One of the young men talked to me, he hinted about sex, I don't know why, if he was so inclined, and we began to do it. . . . I was distancing myself from the church because I knew what I had done, I was distancing myself [from the church] and involving myself more in the revolution. When I was off at war, I had sex with many [men] in the war and after the war was over, in my house. That was something that happened with everyone in the war: important Sandinistas, commanders, they were hypocritical because they spoke out against that, I don't know if I can give you names, but they were important people, their rank was from commander all the way down. I was almost always around the center of power, with that sort of person. I was with a lot of internationalists, Europeans, foreigners who came from all the countries of Europe and South America. I also had sex with famous guerrillas. (Interview, November 28, 2012)

Right after Somoza's fall, in recognition of his collaboration and his class status, Casco explained that "they gave me power . . . naming me representative of the Ministry of Agriculture in Matagalpa" (interview, November 28, 2012). Like tens of thousands of other Nicaraguans, Casco participated in the Literacy Crusade during the first five months of 1980. Sent to the north of the municipality of Moyogalpa, that municipality was honored as the first *Unidad Alfabetizadora Sandinista* (Sandinista Literacy Unit) to be "liberated," that is, to be free from illiteracy. That neighborhood was rewarded for its hard work with newly paved roads, titles to houses, and electricity. A film was even made about the neighborhood by a team from Holland.

After the excitement of the Literacy Crusade, Casco was not too happy to return to the Ministry of Agriculture, in part because his real love was for the arts. Eventually he was given what he called "the prize." He was named director of culture for the city of Matagalpa, running activities out of an expropriated house named after one of the martyrs of the revolution, Carlos Pineda. For more than two years Casco ran the *Centro Popular de Cultura Carlos Pineda* (Carlos Pineda People's Culture Center) in Matagalpa, offering piano lessons, art lessons, exhibitions of art, handicrafts, knitting classes—all for free. When ballet dancers from Cuba and Russia arrived to assist them, they added dance classes.

In late 1982, Casco visited the state of Texas in the United States to see relatives and friends. While there, people from the CIA wanted to talk to him.

> They detained me there and they interrogated me. . . . They knew very well that I was a very well-known person in [Nicaragua] and they were intelligent, because when I was at the house of a North American friend, they just spoke in English. The CIA is looking for you, they told me, the FBI. [My friend said] probably they want you to make drawings, something like that. I did not say, you don't know anything about what is going on in Nicaragua, how would a North American know what is going on here? I called [Nicaragua] and I spoke with various people, with Doris Tijerino, with various people, and I told them what was going on. I knew there were people who had recanted; I knew of people in the United States who had denounced me, people who had seen me rise in the ranks of the FSLN; they gave me their names. The FBI took me to a Holiday Inn. . . . They treated me as a person at the level of a Minister—they did not take me out to any old dinner, rather to a special dinner; they were also very well-dressed. I was prepared, because [people in Nicaragua] had given me guidelines; they said tell them everything; base your testimony in the law. I had read a lot about the FSLN, [and] I was very politically secure; I answered everything. You did such and such a thing? Yes. Why? Because those are our laws, and one must respect such things, the way we have made them. (Interview, November 28, 2012)

That was the end of the interrogation. Perhaps he did not give up any new information, or perhaps the real purpose of the special elegant dinner was to convince him to defect to the United States, as many middle- and upper-class Nicaraguans had done. But if that was the goal, it did not work, in part because while he was in the United States a big event occurred at home: the birth of a child who became his adopted son, the child of a woman who worked for his mother. So in late 1983 he returned to Nicaragua, to help raise that child, and later to raise his sister: Casco's adopted daughter. "I adopted one of them who is named Aron, and the other is called Claudia, a little girl; I raised the two of them from when they were born. I took care of everything: their material needs, their education, primary school, high school, [and] university."

They all lived in the big house in Matagalpa: Donald Casco, his mother, the biological mother of the children, along with Aron and Claudia.

> My mother provided them with affection, they called her *mamita*. . . . We had to prepare the road for their education, [and] they studied grade school, high school, [and] he graduated with a bachelor's degree in computer science. My daughter is currently studying marketing. . . . Also [my daughter] has a child; she is married. My son is an evangelical pastor; he is married to a woman who is also an evangelical pastor, [and] he is a Christian. You can see that a gay person, who I was, gave them an education. . . . Would it be because of my mother since they were at her side, not because of me? They stayed with me; we would go on trips, to the sea, to everyplace. They knew about me; it is not like [now in some countries] . . . that there is a right to adopt children. In that time gay adoption did not exist. This is a total contradiction that I can prove with my own children, that they sought out their own path and not mine. They are totally heterosexual, but they never opposed me in my decision. Never, they never complained, everybody knew. They respected me and they respect me now. I think society has learned how to be respectful. I am like a standard-bearer in this country, because I was one of the first people to publicly say it and without fear of anything. (Interview, December 1, 2012)

He went on to explain that since "since I am no longer involved with that [he is no longer sexually active] . . . all of that has been reduced; there is a sphere of respect, also gay people are more accessible, more respected; people have changed; they do not bother me; there are no problems. Those who valued my work as an artist, value me as an artist, Christians see me as a man of

God, which makes me happy. I do not feel poorly treated by society. I enjoyed being part of the world of celebrities" (interview, December 1, 2012).

Though he returned to Nicaragua, he did not return to government work, dedicating his time to painting, while offering piano and art classes, until 1986, when a girl came looking for a "a nice young man, a light-skinned guy." She was interested in his painting and invited him to exhibit his work at the *Alianza Francesa*, in honor of the anniversary of the French Revolution. While showing his work, he received a phone call. It was the television producer, Dennis Schwartz.

> He called me on the phone, and he said to me: "Donald those paintings, they are so pretty, that exposition will be very beautiful". . . . But he [also] said, "you are an esoteric, a person who reads palms. . . . Could you give us a demonstration of your powers here?" Such things have never happened, no leftist communist revolution has ever seen such things, a thing that is like a myth, to do things like this in a world that was atheist, such a pragmatic world that was the revolution. (Interview, November 28, 2012)

Word got out fast, for when he arrived home his mother said to him "what is happening to you, what is that commotion? You came home and it is as though there had been a death." There was "a crowd, cars, and everything at my house. They wanted me to read cards, [and] that is how the boom of Donald Casco began. They said I was a witch, the wizard of the revolution; that was what they called me; they celebrated it, and everything. As I was very famous [because of] the television program, it was extremely famous. The television show's ratings were extremely high, and the shows were on during prime time" (interview, November 28, 2012).

Donald Casco's life had changed. He had been a member of the Sandinista party, a father, a teacher, an artist, and an evangelical who read cards on the side. Now he had been discovered, and not just by television viewers. He was also discovered by the first lady, Rosario Murillo. He knew who she was of course, and she knew who he was, since they both moved in Sandinista circles. But they did not know each other well until Rosario summoned him to the presidential residence through a phone call from a friend. They ended up hitting it off, and Donald Casco was to become a close confident of the first lady, a regular member of the presidential household, who "practically lived in their house."

She told me all her problems; . . . at the same time [I was] her court magician, [and] we traveled to various countries; I was her friend: she gave me many gifts, royalties, [and we were] very close. When I arrived, she would take me to the theater. She is very informal [and would say]: "Donald Casco you should not be seated over there; sit down with me, with the president" right in front of everyone, things like that that one does not normally see, without any social protocol. That way I came to know and brush with great personalities. (Interview, November 28, 2012)

Donald Casco came to know many famous people: Bianca Jagger, Hortensia Allende (the wife of the late Chilean president), the mother of Muammar Gaddafi, the actor Nick Nolte. Casco even read cards for Jimmy Carter. Donald Casco had a big public presence as a television personality, along with a big private presence within the house of the first family. So many called him the "wizard of the revolution" (Agüero 2004). But how could the Sandinista Revolution have a wizard?

On one level that seems contradictory, as the Sandinista Revolution was Marxist. But most Sandinistas were not atheist, and the revolution had roots in Catholicism along with other spiritual traditions. In an interview with the journalist Arnulfo Agüero, Casco was asked about the apparent contradiction between Marxist politics and esoteric belief. He pointed to the influence of Cuba: "Remember that this Revolution was very influenced by the Cubans, and the Cubans are great believers. They are followers of the palo religion, they believe in *la orichá* [from *Santeria*], in spiritual cleanings and all those things. In fact, the commander of the Cuban Revolution, Fidel Castro, went to visit a famous witch from one of the Cuban provinces. . . . I cannot give details, for reasons of esoteric ethics. But I do know that he sought her out for spiritual cleanings" (quoted in Agüero 2004).

The Sandinista Revolution was hardly the first political movement to be guided by esoteric beliefs. "Remember that all the European courts had their court magicians. The pharaohs had their astrologers, so I was the 'Imperial Wizard of the government.' And nobody else was in such a trusted position" (quoted in Agüero 2004). Indeed, nobody has to look back as far as the European courts to find an official astrologer. In the 1980s, when the United States and Nicaragua were effectively at war with each other, Nancy Reagan and Rosario Murillo, the first ladies of their respective countries, were, ironically, united in their firm belief in astrology (Seaman 1988).

Though he rose to prominence during the 1980s, Donald Casco's work did not emerge from whole cloth during that decade. Instead, his show was a new example of a deeper Nicaraguan tradition. Casco rested on the shoulders of earlier sexually transgressive Nicaraguans who enjoyed local fame during the days of the Somozas, figures like *la Caimana* or *la Sebastiana* (González-Rivera forthcoming).

From another perspective, his work built on a regional tradition of famous performers whose sexual orientations were ambivalent, like the Mexican singer Juan Gabriel. Donald Casco also drew fairly explicitly on the work of the internationally famous Puerto Rican astrologer Walter Mercado. Tace Hedrick (2013, 181) argues that "Mercado's queer sexuality is an open secret, of the kind other Latin American figures, such as Gabriela Mistral, have managed so well that it becomes part of their working persona. . . . Mercado's queerness is of a piece with his ownership of (Oriental) 'spiritual capital.'" According to Hedrick, Latin American fascination with the spiritual traditions of the "Orient" emerged out of the colonial dependency of Puerto Rico. Mercado's "performances, and his success are in large part a sign of Puerto Rico's imbrication with United States socio-political hegemony; he depends on a late capitalist global economy for his widespread fame and financial success; he is pro-statehood and anti-Communist" (2013, 184–85).

Like Mercado, Casco drew upon a wide range of spiritual traditions, many of which might be called "Oriental." Like Mercado, Casco rose to fame in a country shaped by a colonial and neocolonial relationship with the United States. But unlike Mercado, Casco lived a life that was constructed in at least partial resistance to the United States and within the Sandinista Revolution.

Was Donald Casco a significant player in the revolution? As a collaborator in the 1970s and 1980s, his role was important, since the revolution would have never happened without the thousands of people who collaborated with the FSLN. But was he a significant gay player in the revolution? There was an effort to organize a gay and lesbian pride movement in the 1980s, as I will discuss shortly. He did not participate in that effort, though he knew some of the people who did, and he supported them. Nor was he active in efforts to organize for LGBTQ rights after the Sandinistas' 1990 electoral defeat, for the most part,[3] not even after his falling out with Rosario Murillo.

3. In 1992 a reporter for a Peruvian newspaper identified "the painter Donald Casco" as one of Nicaragua's "gay leaders," citing Casco's criticism of the 1992 antisodomy law (*Conducta Impropia* 1992).

And yet . . . for the queer kids who watched television during the revolution, or during the decade that followed it, he was a sort of a role model, albeit an esoteric and fantastic role model who was sometimes mocked on *Camara Matizona*, Nicaragua's version of *Candid Camera*. But despite the limits of his image, Donald Casco was there: a television celebrity, a Sandinista, and a close confidant of the first lady who was open about his homosexuality. And that, in the end, was real cultural change.

Lesbians, Gays, and the International Solidarity Movement

The revolution changed Nicaragua's role in the world. It had been part of the global system for a long time, first as a colony of Spain, and later in a neocolonial relationship with the United States. The overthrow of the Somoza dictatorship was a slap in the face to the Somozas' international patron, the United States, and it reacted in kind, especially after Ronald Reagan's inauguration in 1981. The brutal eight-year-long Contra War could be seen as payback for the Sandinistas' rejection of U.S. ally Anastasio Somoza. In defense, the Sandinistas sought help from people in Western Europe, Canada, and, most famously, Cuba and the Soviet bloc.

Nicaragua's relationship with the world changed in big and abstract ways, the ways of geopolitics. But it also changed in small and intensely personal ways. Even before the revolution, some Nicaraguans—typically from the upper and middle classes—left their homeland to get a degree, often returning afterward. Mario Gutiérrez, who was born in 1957 into a *Somocista* family, was one such Nicaraguan. By 1974, when he was only seventeen he "was studying architecture in Brazil. It was another world, with a lot of autonomy, independence. My parents just sent me money." Living in Brazil was what he called "a very influential factor in my life" (interview, November 30, 2012).

As a teenager in Nicaragua, he had sexual experiences. "Initially, like all men, I had a bisexual life; I loved women a lot as well, until there was a moment in which I could decide. I accepted my condition as gay despite the possible ways that would affect my life." While in Brazil he rethought his sexuality, and his politics.

I quickly became involved in gay initiatives, in Brazil. I began because of some [female] friends who were students and feminists; . . . that was a determining factor in my life in terms of a change in mentality and everything, in cultural terms. I often traveled to Argentina. I became familiar with the dictatorship in Argentina. I was able to see the horror of the dictatorship which persecuted the homosexual community, in Chile, Argentina, how the dictatorship assassinated people in Chile, and the same in Uruguay. Brazil is another thing entirely. . . . Brazil is like, more open. (Interview, November 30, 2012)

Even though Brazil, like Nicaragua, was under dictatorial rule, in Brazil he came to oppose dictatorships. Perhaps that was because of what he learned in South America, or perhaps simply because he was far from the pressures of his family and their social circles.

In Brazil he began to identify as a leftist and as gay, which caused problems. Gutiérrez tried to join the Brazilian Communist Party but was rejected because they thought he was gay. He could not join the party, since homosexuality, in the Marxist discourse of the time, was the equivalent of being capitalist, imperialist, decadent (Green 2012, 440–42, 450, 456–60).

Although Gutiérrez never became a communist, he did find a home in the antidictatorial movements of the 1970s: the feminist movement, the Black rights movement, the early days of what would become the Worker's Party or the PT. Many years later, after being elected president of Brazil, PT leader Luiz Inácio da Silva, known as Lula, was to promote an array of gay rights policies (Friedman 2009, 428–29). Back in the 1970s, "it [wasn't] that [Lula] was exactly pro-gay, but he was to some extent. . . . Lula's ideas were very open-minded" (interview, November 30, 2012; Green 2012, 466).

After five years in Brazil, just as he was completing his architecture degree, the Somoza dictatorship fell. Gutiérrez returned to Nicaragua in October 1979. Of course, home was different, and so was he. He now identified as gay, and as a leftist. Neither change pleased his parents, but the political change might have been harder to take.

Almost immediately, he joined the revolution, to his parents' horror. "I went with the literacy campaign to *Rio Coco* and for my family that was a scandal; because I was a communist, [they thought] I had become a communist, which I was not, because in Brazil I was never allowed to be a communist. Do you understand the contradiction? For them I was a communist, but I never was able to be a communist, because [the communists] never were going to let me join because I was gay. How terrible. I did not know where the hell to go; ideologically I was part of the left but didn't know where to locate myself" (interview, November 30, 2012).

During the revolution the numbers of young people who left the country to study increased dramatically. Moreover, their class background changed. Due to generous scholarships to study in Cuba, Eastern Europe, or the Soviet Union, thousands of working-class kids (who before the revolution might not have gone to college of any sort) found themselves doing things like studying math in Bulgaria, technology in Cuba, or oceanography in the Soviet Union. Many who become activists in the 1990s first came out while studying abroad in the 1980s, including some who went to Cuba (probably the country that offered the most scholarships).

Marvin Mayorga was one of those students who came out to himself and to a circle of friends while studying in Cuba. Born in May of 1970, Mayorga was nine years old when the Sandinistas overthrew the Somoza dictatorship, soon becoming an activist: a member of the *Asociación de Niños Sandinistas* (Association of Sandinista Children), a member of the Sandinista Youth, an announcer on a Radio Sandino program called "*Voces Infantiles*" (Children's Voices), a militia member, and a participant in a neighborhood health brigade (interview, June 3, 2011).

He would have been drafted in 1987, but his older brother, Mauricio, had been killed in combat in 1985, and "there was a 'rule' that if in a family a son had been killed in the war, the others did not have to serve in the war zones. Since I had good grades, they offered me a scholarship to study in Cuba, and I accepted it." Up until then, he explained, "I was not sure if I was gay; I was searching for my identity, but I had heard rumors about the homosexual disease: AIDS; it was like a sickness of capitalism. I remember that once I heard about the 'ideological deviance of homosexuals' from the USA (now I laugh about it . . . but then part of being a committed revolutionary was not being 'like that')" (personal communication, Facebook Messenger, August 23, 2013).

Ironically, given Cuba's history of oppressing its own LGBTQ citizens (Guerra 2010), it was in Cuba where Mayorga first was able to live openly.

> Personally, I think that my three years in Cuba were the best years of my life. . . . Contradictorily, it was in Havana where I came to understand the life of gay couples. Some six couples of different ages, who lived with each other, showed me how various gay professionals lived and enjoyed the incipient gay

life at carnivals, et cetera. . . . The theaters were always full of people from the 'gay world' of models from Cuban TV and magazines. It was common after seeing famous plays performed that we gays would go to the area around the Capital, or to the benches of Paseo Avenue, or to walk along Carlos III Avenue until we got to *Coppelia* where we could eat ice cream at 1:00 a.m. (personal communication by Facebook Messenger, August 23, 2013)

Being a foreigner probably gave Mayorga freedom that locals did not enjoy. No doubt the fact that he was far from the gaze of family and old friends made a difference. In any case, the chance to study in another country was something that would give a certain international flavor to gay and lesbian politics long after the revolution had ended (José Ignacio López Silva, interview, December 7, 2012; Marvin Mayorga, interview, June 3, 2011; Hazel Fonseca, interviews, June 10, 1991, and December 10, 2013).

Due to the revolution, many Nicaraguans left their country for the first time in the 1980s. Also due to the revolution, many foreigners went to Nicaragua for the first time in the 1980s. They came from many countries, including an estimated one hundred thousand U.S. citizens who visited or lived in Nicaragua to express solidarity with the Nicaraguan people, as well as rejection of the Reagan administration's Contra War policy (Kaufman 2014). Sergio Ramírez explained,

The Sandinista Revolution was a collective utopia. Just as it defined a generation of Nicaraguans who made it possible and who fought to sustain it, it also gave a generation around the world a reason to live and believe. That same generation fought to defend it in the trenches and on many fronts when the war against the Contras and the embargo from the United States began. They came from Europe, the United States, Canada, and Latin America, promoting solidarity committees; collecting funds, medicine, school supplies, farming equipment; and writing in newspapers, gathering signatures, pressuring legislatures, and organizing marches (Ramírez 2012, 2).

Amy Bank was one of the U.S. citizens who arrived through the solidarity movement, though she was more audacious than most; in fact, in 1985, at the age of twenty-six, she agreed to direct the *Casa Nicaragüense de Español* (Nicaraguan Spanish House) just for a year. "What could happen in one year?" she mused in Managua, where she still lived in 2013.

By 1985, Bank had been involved in solidarity work for several years. She had visited Nicaragua, briefly, and she spoke Spanish, though not well enough to be the translator (which was part of the job). Plus, she was an open lesbian. None of that was a problem for the people who interviewed her.

> They interviewed me on the phone and one of the questions was, Amy, you know that Nicaragua is a very sexist country, [and] you are a lesbian. How do you think it will go? Are you ready for that? I said, look, I am single now. I am not going to arrive with a banner saying that I am gay. . . . I am going for one year; what could happen in one year? I said . . . one of the benefits of being a lesbian In a sexist country is that I can work with men without there being any spark [or] sexual tension, because I am not interested in them, and they are not normally interested in me. I have more opportunities to work with men; because of that, in a certain way, it is an advantage. I think they liked that part of my answer because . . . they offered me the job (Interview, December 7, 2013)

In November of 1985 Bank arrived on a plane with her first group of students, and together they went to meet their host families in *Máximo Jerez*, a working-class neighborhood of Managua. Bank's Nicaraguan host family was an older woman named Sonia.

To ease her transition, the former director of the school, a U.S. citizen named Silvia, introduced her to some friends. "I think she showed me some photos and explained about Mayra, Marta, and Lupita. She said they are gay and lesbian, but they are not out of the closet; probably they will not say anything the first time, but I am giving . . . a letter of introduction to you and another one to them, so that you will get to know each other. . . . Joel, Mayra, and Lupita knocked on the door during the second day when I was at Sonia's house, and they invited me to have a beer. We went and everything was great. Nobody said anything about being gay" (interview, December 7, 2013).

Things were going well: it was just her second night in the country, and she already had new friends. That is, things were going well until she returned to Sonia's house to find Sonia waiting with a local leader (*responsable*) from the FSLN.

> They sat me down, [and] they said to me, Amy, we want you to know that your position here in the neighborhood gives you . . . a position of author-

ity . . . and you have to be very careful about who you get involved with. . . . They did not say that [Joel, Mayra, and Lupita were] gay; they just told me that we are watching you and you must be careful because you are a leader, you are a de facto leader. I listened and that night I was sharing a room with Sonia, because we just had one bedroom and two cots. . . . I had said that nothing would happen in a year, that I wouldn't carry a banner, that nothing was going to happen to me. . . . It was the second night there, and I am pressed up against a wall. I said [to myself,] I don't know if I am going to last. (Interview, December 7, 2013)

Despite the ominous warning, she became friends with Sonia and the FSLN official, and she became well-integrated into the neighborhood. As Sonia's health worsened, making it impossible for her to fulfill her household's nighttime vigilance duties, the duties fell to Amy, since she was the only other member of the household.

None of the obvious problems—she was a U.S. citizen during the Contra War and someone who hung out with suspicious people—seemed to matter. Her household was obliged to defend the neighborhood from counterrevolutionary activity, so that is what she did, at the same time as she worked more than full-time directing Nicaraguan Spanish House.

My work hours were from 7:30 in the morning until 6:00 in the afternoon, Monday to Friday, and 8:00 in the morning to 6:00 on Saturday. On Saturday we took trips outside of Managua. I was always exhausted; even at the age of 26 I was super tired and afterwards I had to do the neighborhood watch [*vigilancia*] from 11:00 to 2:00. Mayra and Joel and Marta [and Carolina] began to join me in the neighborhood watch, which involved sitting at the street corner. . . . I began to smoke; I had people who sent me popcorn. I would make popcorn. . . . We made popcorn for the neighborhood watch which became a ritual: to smoke and eat popcorn, that was the party every Friday. We had lots of time to talk and as a result, Mayra and I began to make eyes at one another. (Interview, December 7, 2013)

By the second day in Nicaragua, she was warned to watch her behavior, by the sixth week in the country she had a Nicaraguan girlfriend. That did not go unnoticed. As Bank felt more pressure from her neighbors, and more warnings from local FSLN leaders, she wished she could leave her suffocating household and neighborhood.

Some of Bank's friends had the same idea. In that wartime economy, it was easy to buy property if one had access to dollars. So, she and three others bought a house, complete with an enormous living room and patio, in Managua's *Centroamérica* neighborhood. Moving turned out to be more complicated than expected, as Bank learned that her employer, Nicaraguan Spanish House, was a project of the Sandinista state, overseen by the Department of Finances.

The purpose of the school was twofold: First, to expose U.S. citizens to life in Nicaragua, motivating them to pressure the U.S. Congress to end the Contra War. Students met with people from all walks of life (including Sandinista opponents) during the first half of each day, before afternoon Spanish classes, and through the homestays they would make friends and learn how ordinary people lived. The second purpose of the school was to get access to U.S. dollars, which were desperately needed due to the Reagan administration's embargo on the country.

As an employee of the revolutionary state, Bank could not just leave Sonia's house in *Máximo Jerez*; living there was part of her job. She needed permission to move, but permission was granted, so she moved into the new house in August 1986 while she continued to direct the school and oversee home-stay students in *Máximo Jerez*. That house in the *Centroamérica* neighborhood would witness the first attempts to organize a gay and lesbian pride movement, to which I will turn shortly.

Amy Bank was one of many LGBTQ foreigners who shaped the revolution and who in turn were shaped by it. Some, like Bank from the United States and Ana Quirós from Costa Rica, would eventually settle down in Nicaragua. Others, like Tede[4] Matthews from San Francisco, went back and forth, providing social, political, and economic support throughout the 1980s and into the early 1990s. Still others visited briefly, or never visited, doing solidarity work from afar.

According to Emily Hobson, the images used by gay and lesbian solidarity activists were often sexually charged.

> Through fliers, posters, and similar materials, activists visualized the Revolution and their solidarity through female masculinity and women's affection. Lesbians outnumbered gay men in solidarity work, yet even mixed-gender groups centered images of women and celebrated women's revolutionary

---

4. Tede Matthews pronounced his first name "Teddy."

leadership through a lesbian homoerotic. Moreover, many U.S. lesbians spoke about the affective pull of the Revolution and of Sandinista women in highly charged terms—"seduction," "gorgeous," falling "madly in love" (Hobson 2012, 2, also 6–10, 16).

Some gay and lesbian solidarity activists visited early in the revolution. Ana Quirós moved to Nicaragua from Costa Rica in 1979, founding the *Centro de Información y Servicios de Asesoría en Salud* (Center for Health Information and Support Services, or CISAS) in 1983. She recalled that foreign delegations arrived for medical conferences that were held in November 1983, and within those delegations "there were a huge number of men and women from the U.S., many of them LGB; T were not there, T is a much newer thing for activism." The presence of foreign lesbian, gay, and bisexual health professionals led some Nicaraguans to aspire "to have different lives" not so much in political terms as "to have discos, parties, and things like that" some of which had been banned during the early years of the revolution (interview, December 5, 2013).

Roberto Gurdián (a Nicaraguan who had lived in the United States from the mid-1970s) moved back to Nicaragua in 1980 where he was already "notorious" as a gay-rights activist. When he arrived, he looked for work.

> A friend and I both applied for jobs at the Tourism Bureau, *Inturismo*—two gay men! . . . I heard from a friend who was at the meeting they had about hiring us, [and] that my boss said, "Look, we can't hire both of them, because then the rumors will start up again, they'll say *Inturismo* is full of queers. So let's just hire one of them." So I was hired. But, you know, it's true. . . . *Inturismo* is full of queers, and the Ministry of Culture, and the airline. (Quoted in Levins Morales 1983, 1)

While working for the tourism bureau, Gurdián made some efforts to encourage gay and lesbian organizing.

> When I was there in 1980 I talked to some people I know and suggested we try to start a newsletter, to be distributed to a very small circle in Managua of people we thought were not necessarily gay, but receptive to this kind of information. I got no support at all. That's the biggest limitation a future gay movement has to overcome in Nicaragua. The people who have the political

basis for doing it are not yet willing to. They're afraid of our small society. It's very scary because there's no anonymity. But these are people who are known to be gay, and they aren't making the effort to get more cohesion among themselves, to begin talking with people who might be sympathetic to the cause, to see if they can achieve some kind of political support among people who are influential in the revolution. And there are such people who might be receptive. (Quoted in Levins Morales 1983, 1)

Gurdián returned to the United States within a year or two, where he continued to be active in Nicaraguan solidarity work (Hobson 2016, 106). But many more gay and lesbian people followed him to Nicaragua.

Following the 1983 health delegation discussed by Quirós, there were various delegations that were explicitly feminist or LGBTQ, or both. In September 1984, eighteen women from the Bay Area feminist group *Somos Hermanas* (We Are Sisters), many of whom were lesbians, visited Nicaragua. Months later, the Philadelphia Lesbian and Gay Work Brigade helped "construct a school for agricultural workers" (Hobson 2012, 9). In May and June 1985, the entirely lesbian and gay Victoria Mercado Brigade, comprised of thirteen people (mainly people of color, and majority female) visited Estelí and Managua, where they "built a neighborhood center and held informal meetings with Nicaraguan lesbians and gay men" (Hobson 2012, 9). Members of those delegations had many interesting conversations. For instance, "on the Somos Hermanas delegation and on a trip she made with a girlfriend in 1985, [Lucrecia] Bermudez met lesbian, gay, and straight Nicaraguans, women and men, eager to discuss sexuality and sexual politics" (Hobson 2012, 12).

In various ways, Nicaragua's place in the global system changed following the revolution. In the most negative way, the fall of the Somoza dictatorship led almost directly to the Contra War as the remnants of the dictatorship regrouped, with economic and political support from the Reagan administration. The war wreaked havoc on the lives of millions of Nicaraguans for eight long years, a situation that was particularly complicated for gay men and lesbians who fought in the war. In a positive way, the revolution made it possible for thousands of working-class Nicaraguans to study in other countries, especially Cuba and the Soviet bloc.

The revolution also led to an international solidarity movement, with the revolution and against the Contra War. Among the 100,000 US citizens who visited briefly, or who lived in Nicaragua for months or years, thousands were gay or lesbian. Without the revolution, it is unlikely they would have ever visited Nicaragua, except perhaps as tourists who rarely have contact with people outside of the tourist industry. Because of the revolution, they made friends with ordinary people, including gay and lesbian Nicaraguans. Some of them provided their new friends with critical material support.

These global experiences—the war, study-abroad, meeting with delegations of foreigners—had an impact on grassroots organizing. They inspired a number of LGBTQ Nicaraguans who decided, by the mid-1980s, that it was time for them to organize, not just for the revolution but also for themselves, within the revolution. It would be a terrible mistake to claim that foreigners gave them ideas that they could not, or would not, have come up with on their own. But it would also be wrong to deny the part that global factors played in the story of the attempted movement, to which I now turn.

Why Not a Movement for Our Rights?

Martha Sacasa was one of many who tried to organize for LGBTQ rights within the revolution. Though her official birth date was July 30, when she was a teenager her family celebrated her birthday on July 18, because in 1979, when she turned fifteen, she received a big present: the fall of Somoza and the arrival of the FSLN. "From the seventeenth [of July] when the FSLN arrived that was my present" (interview, December 12, 2012). She was so excited that she volunteered to serve in the neighborhood militia, followed quickly by the army where she worked as a radio operator: "I was in the army for a year. I left the army mainly because I was very young. . . . I wanted other things; I wanted to study" (interview, December 12, 2012).

After leaving the army she studied "graphic design and communications" at the Polytechnical University of Nicaragua while participating in revolutionary activities and making friends with other LGBTQ people. Initially, they had no place to meet.

> We would meet in a park, in a garbage dump. . . . Mayra, Carol, Joel, and me, [and] later on Lupita joined us; some years later we met Amy from the Nicaraguan Spanish House, [and] . . . we met the people from the Victoria Mercado Brigade. There were various organizations, various people who encouraged us and talked to us about what the organizations in the United States

were like, and we saw an opening for us. We were thinking that because we were revolutionaries, because we were all part of the FSLN's struggle, that we were going to have opportunities. (Interview, December 12, 2012)

Sacasa eventually found a place to meet. When Amy Bank and her friends bought the house in the Centroamérica neighborhood in 1986, two of the owners quickly returned to the United States, visiting only occasionally, and making a space for Sacasa. Five people ended up living in the house: Martha, Mayra, and Joel (from Nicaragua), along with Julie and Amy (from the United States). Dozens of others visited regularly, including Lupita Sequeira, one of the people who had gone out with Amy Bank during her second evening in Nicaragua.

Born in August of 1960, Sequeira was an activist from the age of thirteen, when she organized events at her high school to raise funds for the FSLN guerrillas. They were in so much need that they had to lubricate their weapons with coconut oil. As she raised money for the clandestine movement, she also organized protests against the Somoza dictatorship.

Once I was a little older, in 1976, 1977, I started organizing with the Popular Action Committees.... My work was to identify people who had weapons to take them away from them. At that time, we called that recuperating weapons. . . . We made Molotov cocktails, contact bombs, [and] we had training.... Two other women and me were assigned to our group to be ready for the hour of the insurrection. We were not supposed to be in combat, rather we were supposed to be messengers. . . . To be a messenger at that time meant that one was proven to be extremely trusted politically, trusted militarily also. In other words, we had to be disciplined, punctual, well trained so we could enter into combat at any moment if we were caught. . . . We trafficked arms, correspondence. . . . Sometimes there were tiny papers that were all folded up, hidden in the most intimate parts of our bodies. . . . We managed to pass right under the noses of the [National] Guard, through all the military roadblocks. Imagine that sometimes we had to transfer arms to the other *compañeros*. . . . We would hide them in bags of vegetables, bags of food, to camouflage what we were carrying. . . . [In June 1979] there was a tactical retreat to Masaya, and we were left in the city amidst the roadblocks of the National Guard so as to be able to pass information back and forth. . . . We were also left there so we could continue to harass the National

Guard. . . . Now I realize that was crazy; we were David fighting against Goliath. I would not do it again; there are some who say they would, but not me. I thank God that I ended up alive. (Interview, December 2, 2012)

When the revolution came to power in July 1979 she was almost nineteen years old and a trusted Sandinista, so she was sent to the *Asociación de Trabajadores del Campo* (Association of Farm Workers, or ATC), to plan for the literacy campaign. Disappointed that she was not going to teach, she protested: "It got to the point that the top leaders called me. I remember that Commander Dora María Téllez said to me 'Understand that you will do more important work directing everything than teaching literacy.' That is what she told me—'along with some others you are in charge of the literacy campaign in an important area of Managua.'" So Sequeira followed orders and oversaw the literacy campaign, but she also secretly taught people to read: "I directed the campaign and I taught as well" (interview, December 2, 2012).

After the literacy campaign Sequeira was transferred to the Ministry of the Interior, referring to herself as a "soldier," though she worked in state security, the rough equivalent of the U.S. Federal Bureau of Investigation (FBI). Her work was engrossing, so during her teens and early twenties she had no private life, only a public life, "I never thought about having a family; that was not on my agenda" (interview, December 2, 2012). In 1985, she found time to reflect because a broken tailbone left her hospitalized for five months and recuperating for most of a year. During that involuntary hiatus she fell in love with a female friend and realized that she was lesbian.

When Sequeira returned to the Ministry of the Interior, she had changed. She was hanging out with new friends and thinking about how to transform the revolution from within.

We began to want to organize ourselves, because political organizing was in the atmosphere in Nicaragua. At that time women, children, neighborhood groups were organized. . . . So we said to ourselves, why not us? But there was something that made us hold back for sure, to stay a bit hidden away. And that is when we started to reflect on what was going on, why this would be if we are in a society where we said that there was freedom of speech. There was also freedom to organize, so why couldn't we organize in that way? So little by little we started to share; we started to realize that there was . . . a taboo, social oppression, right? (Interview, July 5, 1994)

By 1986 the revolution was more than half a decade old, so many gay men and lesbians had organizing experience within the revolution, and many had also been involved in the guerrilla struggle. Not only did they know how to organize but they expected to organize. They believed the revolution's rhetoric of social justice. Reasonably enough, they thought it should apply to them too.

By August of 1986 they had a safe place to meet: the big house in the Centroamérica neighborhood. Amy and Julie were not Nicaraguans, so they retreated to the kitchen during the political part of the meetings and only joined in once the party started. Another precaution was to make sure all participants were Sandinistas; not simply that they sympathized, but that their political histories were beyond reproach (Amy Bank, interview, December 7, 2013). Members of the new group, which some insisted had no name while others called *Grupo de Orgullo Gay-Lésbico* (Gay-Lesbian Pride Group), and still others called *Grupo Inicio* (Initial Group), could not be accused of being CIA spies.

In this way people began to meet regularly. Ana Quirós explained "that it was a mix of a self-help group and a deliberation group and a wild party [*bacanal*] group. I remember that all the meetings ended in a wild party, and all the parties ended with men putting on a strip-tease show" (interview, December 5, 2013). Eventually, a coordination committee was formed, and large numbers of people attended some of their events: estimates ranged from up to fifty or sixty to as many as one hundred (Aráuz 1994, 271–74; Randall 1993, 912; Lupita Sequeira, personal communication, June 19, 2014).

Norman Gutiérrez participated in those events in the house in Centroamérica and a few other private homes. Not yet twenty when the group began to meet, he already had a long history as a revolutionary activist, and he was a veteran, having completed two years of military service in 1986. While serving in the military, he had become a member of the Sandinista Youth. "When I demobilized in July of 1986, I was part of the Julio Buitrago contingent within the Sandinista Youth; it was one of the most famous contingents of the war. So, it was somewhere near the end of that year when I began to be in contact with a sexual diversity group. . . . Joel Zúñiga, Rita Aráuz, Lupita Sequeira, Alfonso González, [and] Marcos Guevara were in that group, and they started to invite me to meetings that were held at Joel and Rita's house, and I began to participate" (interview, June 8, 2011). He explained that the group had several goals.

There was the issue of prevention [of AIDS], but more than prevention there was interest at that moment in the rise of the revolution and the struggle to promote rights, and really because very profound changes were occurring in the social system, especially regarding the issue of women's rights. The lesbians in the group—who were in the majority—were members of the FSLN; they thought that we could promote a sexual diversity movement, a Nicaraguan lesbian-homosexual movement. (Interview, June 8, 2011)

But they were wrong. Though they were all loyal Sandinistas, though all they did was talk about gay and lesbian rights (along with dancing and strip-teases), their very existence was unacceptable to the FSLN. "The group was growing and growing until the point when the people of the FSLN saw it as a dangerous thing, dangerous because any organization . . . more or less like now, any organization . . . that they could not control, and they did not have direct control over the group, what happened is they did not even discuss it. That was the beginning of a witch hunt or *loca*[5] hunt" (Ana Quirós, interview, December 5, 2013).

That social group violated the logic of what were called popular organizations: such groups were to be overseen by an all-knowing vanguard party, the FSLN, acting as transmission belts with information passing—at least in theory—from party to popular organization and back again. Through its independence, Initial Group violated the logic of the transmission belt organization.

There was another problem with the group: some of its members had ties to the United States, either because they were U.S. citizens who lived in Nicaragua or because they were Nicaraguans who had lived in the United States. All the foreigners supported the revolution and rejected the Reagan administration's support for the *Contras*, at that point responsible for a brutal war that had killed tens of thousands. It was *because* they opposed the Reagan administration that they lived in Nicaragua; their presence was a sign of solidarity with the revolution. Nonetheless, "it looked very bad since obviously there was a context of aggression, and so it did not look good. It was thought that, even though all the women were members of the FSLN and some of the men were members of the FSLN, it was thought that those

---

5. "*Loca* is a feminine-gendered noun and vernacular expression that literally translates to 'crazy woman' and is used to denote an effeminate homosexual man" (Peña 2013, xi).

ideas came from the CIA since at that time everything was a synonym of the CIA, and the group fell apart" (Norman Gutiérrez, interview, June 8, 2011).

But the group did not fall apart on its own. It was forcibly dismantled. Gutiérrez was young, and he was not one of the leaders, so he was not jailed. But almost all the leaders of the group were jailed, at least briefly. On March 13, 1987, Marcos Guevara and Aníbal López were among those who were called

> to state security House Number 50 where they were interrogated and threatened by the official, Jacinto Suárez. López, who had joined the [Sandinista] movement at the age of 16[,] added that without considering that we were Sandinista revolutionaries, Suárez told them that Nicaragua was not ready for that sort of movement[,] and that also because we were homosexuals "there was no identity or space for us within the revolutionary process because the new man was not a *cochón* nor a *cochonero*[6] and because of that it was easy to confuse us with the enemy." (*El País* 1992, 8)

Something like thirty people were interrogated in House Number 50 by a group that included Cubans who collaborated with the Sandinistas. One of those Cubans "told us that they were going to give us elephant kicks . . . [adding that] society was not going to accept us, that we did not have permission to meet nor to even be near each other. They banned a lot of things. We all felt bad because we had all given so much [to the revolution,] but they wouldn't even give us a chance" (Martha Sacasa, interview, December 5, 2012; also, Aráuz 1994).

The interrogations were frightening and disheartening. The Initial Group activists who were interrogated had given many years of their lives to the Sandinista Revolution, often at literal risk of death. Nonetheless, they were treated as though they were *Contras* or foreign spies. Ironically, they were accused of being tools of foreigners by Cubans, themselves foreigners. Most Initial Group activists were not out to their families and friends, and so they feared the consequences of being outed by the Ministry of the Interior. And many of the questions were prurient and weird, like being repeatedly asked what they did in bed with their partners.

Lupita Sequiera was one of the leaders of the group who was punished.

---

6. See the introduction for a discussion of the terms *cochón* and *cochonero*.

They fired me from my job, and they also threw me out of the party. I was a member of the FSLN. And from that point on I began to have an . . . attitude questioning the party. Why were they throwing me out of the party since my political, military, party record was good? . . . At that time the Ministry of the Interior prohibited us from having political meetings. We could not exist politically, but we could exist socially. At the same time, we were threatened severely . . . including the threat of going to prison. But since they knew that we were all involved in the [revolutionary] process, in the end they did not do anything to us. (Interview, July 5, 1994)

Sequira was told that nothing would happen to them in recognition of their years of service to the revolution. That was true in the sense that none of them spent much time in prison, but they were punished in many ways. Some activists who were serving in the military got a dishonorable discharge, making it impossible to find work or enroll in school. Others were fired from their jobs. Many were forcibly outed, and some found their family and friends were not supportive.

Despite it all, the Initial Group activists agreed that they would not publicly denounce the FSLN, neither within Nicaragua nor internationally. They had been betrayed by the leaders of the revolution they loved, and yet, poignantly, they refused to betray them in return. They agreed not to denounce the FSLN for its failure to live up to the revolutionary values of social justice for all. Even though up to one hundred people knew what happened in 1987, they all remained quiet.[7] It was not until after the revolution had ended, in the 1990s, when this story became more widely known.

Ana Quirós was spared from the worst of the interrogations, possibly because she was a little older than most of the leaders, or because she was the founder and executive director of CISAS, a very valuable NGO that the FSLN did not want to lose, or because she had Sandinista friends in high places. Or perhaps she was spared because she was foreign-born. Mainly she was warned, in a "friendly" way, to stay away from "those people."

I remember a conversation with a *gringa* friend regarding that situation and the persecution. She . . . insisted that we should denounce that persecu-

---

7. Such loyalty to the revolution was not unique to LGBTQ activists. Many grassroots Sandinistas, including women's movement activists, felt they had to censor themselves at times to avoid threatening the revolutionary project that they also loved (on the journalist Carlos Fernando Chamorro and self-censorship see Rosenberg 2009).

tion. . . . She said we should denounce it internationally. . . . Many of us said that, on the one hand, that would be suicide, but on the other hand, at that moment we still had deeply internalized the revolutionary discourse, to do such a thing would have been helping the enemy. . . . Looking back on it, I don't know if we should have acted differently; I am not clear about it. I think that the disempowerment that we suffered was too great to feel that a protest would be possible without affecting the revolution, which for most of us was the most important thing (December 5, 2013).

Many lesbian and gay Sandinistas who retained their positions within the FSLN sought ways to protect themselves, by avoiding the house in the Cen-troamérica neighborhood, and by ceasing to speak with the leaders of Initial Group. Some lesbians "even tried to get pregnant at that time. It was a combination of factors, I am not going to say that it was automatic, but there was some combination of the desire to become mothers with the desire to change their gender identities [transvertirse], so to speak. I don't really know. I have never thought about whether it was the right thing to do. I don't think there were the conditions or tools in which to do anything different from what was done" (Ana Quirós, interview, December 5, 2013).

In the months following the interrogations, lots of Nicaraguans tried to distance themselves from Initial Group. Those who could not, because they had been identified as leaders, did what they could to provide support to each other, providing both mental and material support, as many had lost their jobs. Some foreigners, like Ana Quirós's U.S. citizen friend, even took it upon themselves to formally denounce what had happened. She took the complaint to the *Centro Nicaragüense de Derechos Humanos* (Nicaraguan Human Rights Center, or CENIDH) but, since none of the directly affected Nicaraguans were willing to testify, that case went nowhere.

Another solidarity activist, Tede Matthews,[8] tried a different strategy. Matthews had been involved in solidarity work with the Sandinista Revolution for a long time: in 1979 he had cofounded the San Francisco group "Gay People for the Nicaraguan Revolution," and as a member of the San Francisco bookstore collective, Modern Times, he regularly visited Nicaragua to buy and sell books. In July or early August 1987 Matthews was in Managua

---

8. Julieta Martínez remembered spending a lot of time with Matthews before and after 1987. "He came here a lot; he stayed in my house sometimes, and that was a great boost for us in the early years, to see ourselves with more pride, more strength" (interview, December 11, 2013).

to participate in a book fair when he attended a *Cara al Pueblo* (Face the People) meeting.

The Face the People meetings, which were held regularly during the revolution, and irregularly after the FSLN lost the 1990 election, were informed by the transmission belt theory: FSLN leaders would present news of their policies, challenges, and accomplishments. In turn, members of the audience would ask questions and, theoretically, change the minds of the leadership. Matthews attended that meeting with Jeremy Grainger, a friend and fellow solidarity activist, who was also involved with gay rights work. Both Matthews (who died in 1993) and Grainger knew what had happened to Initial Group, just months before.

Based on her reading of a letter Matthews wrote at the time, dated August 8, 1987, the historian Emily Hobson told me:

> He wrote that first his friend Jeremy Grainger . . . asked a question about AIDS that was passed from [President Daniel] Ortega to [Minister of Health] Dora María Téllez. The audience was "buzzing," and she "gave a very pragmatic answer" but he didn't note the details. Then, Tede asked a question about the inclusion of gay people in the revolutionary process and efforts against homophobia. Ortega said that there was no official anti-gay repression, that there were more pressing issues, and that inclusion was just a question of every individual involving himself in the Revolution. Tede didn't describe any audience reaction here. He did note that Jeremy Grainger's question and [Téllez]'s answer were televised, but his question to Ortega and Ortega's answer were not. Later he was glad about this, because Grainger was later recognized on the street due to the TV appearance and while most reactions were friendly, there was an instance of teenagers chanting *SIDA* [AIDS] at him (Emily Hobson, email communication, March 24, 2013; Jeremy Grainger, personal communication by Facebook Messenger, May 11, 2013).

So publicly, President Daniel Ortega supported the presence of gay people within the revolution. Publicly, he denied that there was any antigay repression, possibly because he was unaware of what the Ministry of the Interior had done, more likely because he was not proud of that repression, or because he knew it had to be denied, especially to foreigners. It seems like a small thing, but different versions of that story came up in interviews with many people. It was not a small thing to them: that Grainger and Matthews had the nerve to ask these questions, and that, despite everything, the revolution was on record as including them.

Initial Group was forcibly shut down in March 1987 and the Face the People meeting, where President Ortega stated that the revolution did not have an antigay policy, was in July or August of that year. While Ortega's response was heartening, it did not really change anything for the activists whose lives had been turned upside down in March. But then international and domestic politics changed again, this time in a practical way.

In October 1987, the *Primer Encuentro de Lesbianas Feministas Latinoamericanas y Caribenas* (First Gathering of Latin American and Caribbean Lesbian Feminists) was held in Cuernavaca Mexico. Of the 250–300 women who attended the lesbian feminist conference, forty-two were Nicaraguan; Nicaragua was far better represented than any other Central American country (Miller 1991). It was an indication that many Nicaraguans remained committed to gay and lesbian rights, despite the end of Initial Group a few months earlier.

Early in November 1987, the V Annual North America Nicaragua Colloquium on Health was held in Managua (CHRICA 1987?). In 1987, the first case of HIV was identified in Nicaragua (Banco Mundial 2006, 4), and one of the themes of the colloquium was the issue of HIV/AIDS and how to avoid an epidemic. Lupita Sequeira explained how she and others (who were very quietly doing HIV/AIDS prevention work under the name CEP-SIDA) were invited to the colloquium, and their entrance fees were paid by the visiting health workers.

> I am still am very grateful to them, because they said, we are not going to talk about our experience there [in the U.S.;] we want you to talk about your experience here. It was lovely, in front of the authorities . . . that was the first time when they listened to us. . . . At that moment the Vice Minister of Health was there, Doctor Leonel Argüello, and he communicated all of that to the Minister of Health, who at that moment was the Commander Dora María Téllez. (Interview, December 2, 2012; Aráuz 1994, 274)

Later that same month, Joel Zúñiga was at the house in the Centroamérica neighborhood where he lived when the phone rang. His roommate Julie answered the phone and called to him: "Joel, there is a call for you from the Minister of Health, Dora María Téllez." Of course, he was very surprised: though he did not know her personally, she was one of the most famous political figures in the country. Years later, he still seemed a little surprised: "So I got a call from a commander" (interview, June 18, 2014).

When he got to the phone, Téllez explained, "Look, I understand that you have a gay-lesbian group and I want us to work together." She asked him to meet with her the following week—Wednesday at 6:00 pm—and he said he would. "I said that there is one condition: I do not want to go alone" (interview, June 18, 2014). His friends who were gathered around the phone listening in—Mayra, Lupita, Marta—were afraid for him to go to the meeting alone after they had been threatened at the Ministry of the Interior and told never to do political work again.

Over the course of the next few days, they tried to convince friends to overcome their fear and to join them at the Ministry of Health. When the group of some fifteen activists arrived for the 6:00 p.m. meeting, they found Dora María Téllez by herself. She had chosen a time when they could talk in peace, without fear, as all other ministry employees had left for home by that time.

> We spoke with the Commander. . . . We explained that we had big problems. This meeting [was] illegal for us. We explained that if we started meeting again [there would be even worse problems for them]. She told us, "You are with the Minister of Health." All the women were in love with her. (Joel Zúñiga, interview, June 18, 2014)

All the women were in love with her since Téllez was a hero of the guerrilla struggle, a former guerrilla commander. She was one of the few people who was powerful enough to confront state security. Certainly, she was the only person who was inclined to use her power to promote HIV-AIDS education and to protect the frightened activists who had gathered in her office.

It did not hurt that she was beautiful—short curly hair, big brown eyes, straight teeth—and only thirty-two years old in November 1987. Emily Hobson described a famous shadowy photo of hers from the early 1980s, published in Margaret Randall's *Sandino's Daughters*, as "undeniably romantic" (2012, 7).

She was also really smart. Rather than just starting an HIV-AIDS education project within the Ministry of Health, which she would have had the authority to do, she took her time, knowing that the activists she was asking to help her would need political cover. According to Joel Zúñiga, she first spoke with the head of state security, Tomás Borge, the head of the very Ministry of the Interior that had persecuted the group in March. After gaining his agreement that he would leave her people alone, she spoke individually with all nine commanders within the National Directorate (interview, June 18, 2014).

So in February of 1988, CEP-SIDA was officially formed. About ninety people were associated with CEP-SIDA, though perhaps twenty people were active members. CEP-SIDA was Initial Group with two differences: it had a narrower focus, on HIV-AIDS prevention rather than rights more generally, and it enjoyed the ongoing support of the Minister of Health. Martha Sacasa explained that

> the help of MINSA [the Ministry of Health] allowed us to go to parks—where you would find prostitutes—to give out condoms, talk about AIDS transmission and all of that. That was where the police grabbed us when we were going around giving out condoms. . . . Dora María called and explained that we were working with the Ministry, and they let us go. (Martha Sacasa, interview, December 5, 2012)

According to Zúñiga the police would sometimes pick up CEP-SIDA activists, and the activists would call "the Commander [Dora María Téllez]. She was like [their] godmother. She provided the protection of the state. She was the only person that [they] could call" (interview, June 18, 2014).

But even with a godmother, it was hard to promote HIV-AIDS education. Activists were harassed by the police, and some politicians were unhappy with their work. Yet Téllez held her ground. For instance, when Minister of the Interior Tomás Borge asked her for a list of all the HIV-positive people in the country she refused, telling him, "It is not available." When she told that story years later, she followed the observation that it was "not available" with a pause and a huge smile. Besides, she said, she saw no reason to give it to him, as it had nothing to do with state security (personal communication, October 9, 2010).[9]

---

9. Ironically, during the same time that Nicaraguan HIV-AIDS educators were treated with suspicion by the Sandinista state, they were also treated with suspicion by the Reagan-era State Department. Marcos Guevara, Mayra Guillén, and Joel Zúñiga had been invited "to address the Second International Lesbian and Gay Health Conference and AIDS Forum on July 21 [1988] in Boston [but] were unable to attend the meeting because the U.S. State Department denied their visa requests. . . ." The US government denied the visas under an immigration law that requires visitors to prove "compelling reason" to return home. According to the State Department,

Long-time activist Mario Gutiérrez disputed that version of events: "I never saw Dora María playing any role" (interview, November 30, 2012). Gutiérrez's point is important. When analyzing state-civil society relations it is easy to overemphasize the role of state actors, as they are usually more visible than civil society actors, even though people in civil society typically do most of the work and face greater personal risks. Nonetheless, there are many accounts of Téllez's behind the scenes role supporting CEP-SIDA (Martha Sacasa, interview, December 12, 2012; Joel Zúñiga, interview, June 18, 2014; Lupita Sequeira, interviews, July 5,1994, and December 2, 2012; Silvia Martínez, interview, June 8, 2011; Babb 2003, 308; Howe 2002, 244; Mogrovejo 2000, 335–37; Randall 1993, 914).

There were a few other examples of gay and lesbian organizing during the late 1980s. For instance, in 1989, the gay rights group *Somos Homosexuales* (SHOMOS, or We Are Homosexuals) was founded by a group of men including Alfonso González and Mario Gutiérrez. Gutiérrez explained, "The group was not very big, small, because our activism in that moment was dedicated to the prevention of HIV. Perhaps it was a group of 12 at that time" (interview, December 5, 2013; email communication, July 29, 2013).

On July 19, 1989, a group of activists wore black t-shirts decorated with pink triangles (a gift from solidarity activist Tede Matthews) to a parade marking the tenth anniversary of the revolution. The crowd of some fifty gay and lesbian Sandinistas and their allies marched behind an outstretched FSLN flag. They were joined in their march by about thirty foreigners: some who were visiting the country, some who lived there. The marchers sang the Sandinista anthem, danced to the salsa and reggae that blared from loudspeakers along the parade route, and chanted, "Without the participation of lesbians and gays, there is no revolution," making sure that the members of the National Directorate would note their presence (Matthews 1989, 8; Randall, 1993, 914; Hazel Fonseca, interview, December 10, 2013; Rigoberto Pérez Acuña, interview, December 7, 2015).

Another group of maybe ten to thirteen gay men and lesbians met for Bible study in the house that Mario Gutiérrez shared with his mother in the

---

"compelling reasons" include "'family, property or professional commitment.' It uses this law to discriminate against single people, including most lesbians and gay men. . . . The Department of State also refused to recognize the title 'AIDS educator' as a professional commitment, despite affidavits of support from physicians, health workers and at least five U.S. members of Congress" (San Francisco Sentinel 1988, 8).

Los Robles neighborhood of Managua in the late 1980s, moving to a center run by U.S. solidarity activists once their numbers grew too large to be accommodated by the house.

> We made contact with some North Americans from the Benjamin Linder House, in '89, '90, before the FSLN lost the [February 1990] election we had already begun to meet at the Benjamin Linder house, with the support of those North American missionaries who were very open-minded, progressive, and they were delighted [to help us]. That is where we began the first gay parties. It was a lovely time that has left many beautiful memories. For the first time trans people arrived dressed as trans, because up until then we were just gay and lesbian, but then we realized that there were some people—we did not say transgender at that time, we just said transvestite—that was where they began their own parades at the Benjamin Linder house. It is historical that a group of North American Christians played a role supporting the beginning of part of the gay movement. (Mario Gutiérrez, interview, December 5, 2013; Rigoberto Pérez Acuña, interview, December 7, 2015)

Until 1990, they continued to meet in Gutiérrez's house and to have larger events at the Benjamin Linder House, some of which were "white parties" in which all the party goers wore white (Bismarck Moraga, interview, December 1, 2015). In February of that year, President Daniel Ortega lost his reelection bid to Violeta Barrios de Chamorro. With that, the Sandinista revolution came to its formal end. Many of those who had been mobilized during the 1980s continued their work during the decade of the 1990s, but the world in which they organized was never the same. In April 1990 when Mrs. Chamorro became president, "Nicaragua changed completely. That was the beginning of the NGO world" (Mario Gutiérrez, interview, December 5, 2013). And just as Nicaragua changed, the lives of Nicaragua's gay men and lesbians changed, for better and for worse.

CHAPTER THREE

After the Revolution

1990–2006

1990 was a year of transition, starting in February when FSLN president Daniel Ortega was defeated by Violeta Barrios de Chamorro of the *Unión Nacional Opositora* (National Opposition Union, or UNO) coalition. That election, widely known as "the loss" for years to come, marked the end of the revolution. Also in 1990, "Sex and the Sandinistas," a BBC documentary directed by Lucinda Broadbent, was filmed in Managua, capturing a time of upheaval: the inauguration of Chamorro in April, and massive protests—with torn-up streets and burning tires—in July. It was a year of transition from socialism to neoliberal capitalism, from "people's revolution" to "governing from below" and "not one step backwards."

In the documentary, some participants in Initial Group and CEP-SIDA hinted at what happened in the 1980s, which was probably the first time the history of Initial Group and CEP-SIDA was told publicly. But it also reflected activists' hesitation to tell everything. Any of them could have clearly explained what had happened to Initial Group, had the time been right. In fact, the time was still wrong enough that the film was not for a Nicaraguan audience. Parts of the film were in English without Spanish subtitles, making them unintelligible to most Nicaraguans. Moreover, the film was unavailable in Nicaragua.

"Sex and the Sandinistas" told a somewhat simplified story of revolutionaries who supported gays and lesbians (despite some misunderstandings) and counterrevolutionaries who were hostile to gays and lesbians. Former president Daniel Ortega spoke in what appeared to be the office of the FSLN, his bright blue shirt contrasting with a sepia-toned photo of the nationalist hero Sandino, peering over his shoulder.

> It is important to be conscious and committed to addressing this real problem. The FSLN takes the position that this struggle [for LGBTQ rights] has to be incorporated into the whole society and that way we are making substantive changes. In the meantime, there is a struggle [of which] there will be manifestations, there is discrimination. This struggle does not just pertain to women, it does not just pertain to lesbians, it does not just pertain to homosexuals; rather it is a struggle that pertains to the whole Nicaraguan society. Why? So as to be able to overcome the sexist mentality that weighs down within ourselves. We are all marked by sexism and even when we are consciously against it, there will be manifestations of sexism that beat down women, that beat down lesbians, that beat down homosexuals, and we must make a greater effort at the level of Nicaraguan society. (Quoted in Broadbent 1991)

When Ortega spoke philosophically about sexism and discrimination, he did not know that in 1998 his stepdaughter Zoilamérica would denounce him for sexually abusing her from the age of eleven, a sexual scandal that would hang over his career, but without ending it. With the benefit of hindsight, his words rang sadly true regarding the difficulty of overcoming "the sexist mentality that weighs down within us."

In contrast with Ortega's supportive comments, the Catholic Church seemed unambivalently hostile. The Archbishop of Managua, Cardinal Obando y Bravo, argued that "the Church advises . . . that the generative potential of human beings may only be used within matrimony. The Catholic Church does not permit any sexual relations outside of matrimony." The film then switched to Marcos Guevara who said that he "first had sex" as an eight- or nine-year-old seminary student [that is, he was a victim of statutory rape] with the man he called his "confessor," arguing that "the majority [of priests] are homosexuals."

Later in the film, Obando y Bravo discussed the revolution. "During the Sandinista regime there was an excess of immorality; there was failure in the family. One has to keep in mind that when man is guided by an absolutist ideology, he walks along illicit paths of pleasure. It is logical that a man who has left God to the side, or for whom God is dead, will anxiously search out pleasures of the flesh, or every type of hedonism." Obando y Bravo's observations were followed with a headline from *La Prensa* (the newspaper owned by the Chamorro family): "Corruption in the Ruins: 18 Years After the Earthquake, a Sodom." The article was illustrated with photos of men sitting and talking in the ruins of the old cathedral, one of the main cruising locations in Managua, their eyes disguised with black rectangles.

Guevara noted that the government had threatened "that it would clean-up all the homosexuals in the park." One day those promises were fulfilled when the police arrived. But the men who hung out in the park by the cathedral had been tipped off, and so nobody was there on the day of the raid. They were safe then, though two or three years later, all entrances to the ruins of the cathedral were sealed off with iron bars, making it impossible to use the cathedral for hanging out, or anything else.

Despite suggesting that the end of the revolution threatened gay and lesbian Nicaraguans, the documentary ended on a joyous note. Norma Helena Gadea's rendition of *"Pajarita de la Paz"* (Little Bird of Peace) played as activists constructed a mural out of plywood and then painted in its theme of gay and lesbian relationships in preconquest Nicaragua, linked (in the mural at least) to the triumphant Sandinista Revolution. Lupita Sequeira explained that the mural would be placed in their soon-to-open gay and lesbian rights center.

Two Autonomous Movements Are Born

Sex and the Sandinistas portrayed an FSLN loss that was also a loss for Nicaragua's gay and lesbian community. The activists who were featured in the film all identified with the revolution to some extent. Most had devoted years of their lives to *Sandinismo*, and they mourned the electoral loss in 1990, particularly those who had been attacked by the Ministry of the Interior.[1]

---

1. Despite everything, as late as the 1990 election, many LGBTQ activists remained loyal to the FSLN. A story told by Lupita Sequeira and Joel Zúñiga, both leaders of Initial Group—both of whom were made to suffer by Ministry of the Interior—was illustrative. The night of the election, Lupita and Joel were out (separately), intending to celebrate the election results, Lupita carrying a Sandinista flag. When they met up late in the evening, once the loss was apparent, both were very upset. But Joel told her of a phone conversation he had that evening with Mayra, another Initial Group activist. He called to ask her how she was and was surprised because "she said she was fine." She explained, "That is because we lost on March 13th [1987, when the crackdown on Initial Group began]" (personal communication, June 18, 2014).

From the perspective of state policy, the early 1990s were generally bad for the gay and lesbian community. Under Violeta Chamorro, the state turned neoliberal, that is, many public sector jobs were eliminated, and many services that had previously been provided by the state (like day care centers, health care, and educational opportunities) were cut. Moreover, the state promoted policies that were far more conservative regarding gender and sexuality than had been the case in the 1980s (Kampwirth 2004, 47–54). But the Chamorro administration was also less inclined to try to control civil society than the Sandinistas had been.

The combination of those factors—neoliberal cuts, policies promoting gender and sexual hierarchies, and the state's fairly laissez-faire attitude toward social movements—meant that there were both new needs and new opportunities in the early 1990s. That combination gave rise to many autonomous feminist groups, as well as some gay and lesbian groups. Though a detailed history of the emergence of second wave feminism is beyond the scope of this book, it is impossible to tell the story of one movement without referring to the other. The two movements ran parallel during the 1980s and then became intertwined in the 1990s.

In the early 1990s, feminist activists, like gay and lesbian activists, were overwhelmingly people who first mobilized through *Sandinismo*, either through the struggle against the Somoza dictatorship in the 1960s and 1970s, or through the revolution in the 1980s. During the 1980s, activists in the women's movement faced some of the same issues that had faced gay and lesbian activists who were encouraged to organize for the revolution while discouraged from prioritizing work toward gender equality. But the problems they faced were not identical. Women were never repressed for publicly identifying as women, or even for promoting gender equality in limited ways, but rather for identifying as feminists, and for prioritizing the struggle against patriarchy over support for the FSLN. Even seeing pro-gender equality work as *equally* important to supporting the FSLN was treated by most leaders of the revolution as a deviation from the real struggle against imperialism and for class justice.

Despite tensions with the leaders of the FSLN, women's groups sometimes promoted feminist goals during the decade of the revolution. This was clear in the case of the official Sandinista women's association, AMNLAE, in the early 1980s, though that became less true over the course of the Contra War. In the mid-1980s, *Secretarías de la Mujer* (Women's Secretariats) were formed within a number of the Sandinista labor unions starting with the rural wageworker's union, the ATC, which made several successful demands for improvements in women's working conditions, including day care centers, paid maternity leaves, paid time off for the care of sick children, and better representation of women in leadership positions. Before the revolution had ended, there were similar Women's Secretariats in the peasant farmers' union, the health workers' union, the government workers' union, the urban union confederation, and the urban professionals' union (Kampwirth 2004, 19–35, 1998).

During the final years of the revolution, around the time of the Initial Group and CEP-SIDA, a number of autonomous feminist groups emerged. Being autonomous meant that, unlike AMNLAE, they did not promote the FSLN's party line, though most, if not all, of their members identified with *Sandinismo*. Unlike the Women's Secretariats, they were not even associated with a Sandinista popular organization. Those groups provided a variety of services to the community including theater and radio productions, psychological counseling, and medical exams, all without being endorsed by, or controlled by, the FSLN (Kampwirth 2004, 35–46). The independent women's groups that formed in the late 1980s formed the basis for what would be an explosion of autonomous feminist organizing in the years 1990 to 1992 (Kampwirth 1996, 144–53).

Another major change in the late 1980s and early 1990s was that a weekly feminist supplement, called *Gente* (People), was added to *Barricada*, the widely read Sandinista newspaper. Directed by Sofía Montenegro from 1989 to 1994, *Gente* played a critical role in pushing Nicaraguan culture toward a more open view of a variety of social topics including sexuality, women's rights, and LGBTQ rights. Because it was well-researched, lively, and often funny, many Nicaraguans, including many socially conservative people that I knew, eagerly awaited the new issue of *Gente* that came out every Friday.

The story of the gay and lesbian rights movement ran parallel to the story of the feminist movement. Both were movements that addressed personal politics; both were movements that were too often accused of deviating from the real agenda of the revolution. For the feminists, and the gay and lesbian activists, organizing work during the years of the revolution bore fruit in the early 1990s as their movements grew in size and independence.

CEP-SIDA, founded in 1988, continued its HIV-AIDS prevention work in 1990, but as it lost all support from the Ministry of Health once Violeta

Chamorro took power, it ceased to exist around 1991. Norman Gutiérrez, who coordinated CEP-SIDA in late 1990 and early 1991, explained that "along with the famous democratization discourse many groups emerged out of CEP-SIDA and earlier initiatives" (interview, June 11, 2011). Marvin Mayorga was one of the activists who helped found those new groups. Returning from several years of university study in Cuba in 1990, he joined CEP-SIDA during its waning days. He noted that the group had both public health and psychological goals.

> In 1991, either the end of '90 or the beginning of '91, in that group there were twelve of us, young males who at that time were not clear if we were gay [or] trans women, but we were seen as gay; there was a lot of confusion as to whether gays were feminine or masculine and that whole story. But at that time, we began to talk about including rights for ourselves as young people who were different in ways that we could not yet name, and that space . . . helped us to reflect upon our experiences and our rights. (Interview, June 3, 2011)

Despite losing support from the Ministry of Health, CEP-SIDA activists did not just go home. Instead, they founded a number of new organizations, including *Fundación Nimehuatzin* (Nimehuatzin Foundation), an HIV-AIDS prevention organization founded by a group including Rita Aráuz in 1990, and *Nosotras* (We Women), a lesbian-feminist collective of fifteen to thirty women, founded by a group including Hazel Fonseca in 1990.

Fundación Xochiquetzal (Xochiquetzal Foundation) was founded in 1991 by Mary Bolt, Elena Drémova, Hazel Fonseca, Alfonso González, Mario Gutiérrez, Martha Sacasa, and Lupita Sequeira. It provided gynecological services and HIV-AIDS treatment, organized support groups for lesbians, ran a telephone hotline, and lobbied for gay and lesbian rights. Beginning in 1993 and continuing through this writing, Xochiquetzal Foundation (hereafter referred to as Xochiquetzal) has published an important magazine, *Fuera del Closet* (Out of the Closet). The magazine, which focuses on issues of sexuality and health, aims at a general audience and publishes four times a year, with a print run of five thousand (Howe 2013; La Boletina 1993, 39; Fundación Xochiquetzal 2015; Fundación Xochiquetzal 1993, 3).

In July 1991, two regional networks, the *Red de Lesbianas Feministas Latinoamericas* (Latin American Lesbian Feminist Network) and the *Red de Lesbianas y Homosexuales Latinoamericanos* (Latin American Lesbian and Homosexual Network) were created at the conference of *Asociación Internacional de Lesbianas, Gays, Bisexuales, Trans e Intersex* (International Association of Lesbians, Gays, Bisexuals, Trans and Intersex people, or ILGA), held in Acapulco. At that conference Nicaragua was unanimously elected as managing member (*miembro propietario*), in charge of overseeing those networks. Finally, in the early 1990s, the lesbian organizations *Entre Amigas* (Among Women Friends), *Amigas Juntas* (Women Friends Together), and *Grupo por la Visibilidad Lésbica* (Group for Lesbian Visibility) were formed (Hazel Fonseca, interview, December 10, 2013; Martha Sacasa, interview, December 5, 2012; Mario Gutiérrez, interview, December 5, 2013; Marvin Mayorga, interview, June 3, 2011; Baldwin 1990, 18–20; *La Boletina* 1991b, 21; Sequeira Malespín and Berríos Cruz 1993, 13–15; Thayer 1997, 393).

The above-mentioned groups were all based in Managua, though many of them also worked in other cities or in the countryside. Additionally, there were some organizations based in small cities and towns. The group *AGAGAY*, coordinated by Marlon Plazaola Ramírez, began working in approximately 1991 in the town of El Viejo, department of Chinandega. With support from Managua-based CISAS, the sixty-some members of the organization carried out "training workshops [and] distribution of condoms, posters, and pamphlets against AIDS [along with] some recreational activities" (Sequeira Malespín and Berríos Cruz 1993, 7). In the neighboring town of Corinto, a small group named *Grupo Gay de Corinto* (Gay Group of Corinto), coordinated by Hector Alonso, met in a bar on the beach and did HIV-AIDS prevention work. In the city of Chinandega, the twenty-two members of *Organización Gay de Chinandega* (Gay Organization of Chinandega or ORGAYCHI), coordinated by Ofilio Rosales, put on "an artistic drag show, called La MOVIDA. They lip synced while accompanied by dances" (Sequeira Malespín and Berríos Cruz 1993, 8). Sometimes the members of La MOVIDA, in collaboration with AGAGAY, participated in workshops.

While some people first organized around pride issues in the 1980s, the majority of gay and lesbian Sandinistas had devoted all their organizing energies to the revolution. But things changed for many of them after the election of February 1990. Mary Bolt explained how the electoral results led her to rethink her political goals. "Later, after the [1990] election, an emptiness opened up, and I think that happened to a large number of Nicaraguan men and women. It was a political emptiness. . . . [F]or us it was a powerful thing, a cause for grief. . . . So, for me, this emptiness was filled by the feminist movement" (interview, July 5, 1994).

From a young age, Mary Bolt did political work. From the early 1970s, she was an urban guerrilla. During the revolution from 1979 to 1990, she was a Sandinista party member and activist. Then after the Sandinistas' electoral defeat in 1990, she became an autonomous feminist. She was a founding member of Xochiquetzal, one of the feminist organizations that was most associated with lesbian rights work (Howe 2013, 63–74). Bolt's personal story nicely illustrated the intertwined stories of the feminist and gay/lesbian rights movements in the early 1990s, and how both movements were rooted in the revolutionary transformation of the 1980s. Without rejecting her own history, she moved from one sort of activism to another as circumstances changed: from guerrilla, to FSLN party member, to autonomous feminist and lesbian rights activist.

While most of the work of the emerging gay and lesbian rights movement took place within organizations, like Bolt's Xochiquetzal gatherings, there were also some important mass gatherings in the early 1990s. The first one—the coming-out party for both the autonomous feminist movement and the lesbian rights movement—took place on the weekend of International Women's Day, or March 8, 1991. The cracks within the women's movement, cracks that had deepened over the course of the decade of the revolution, finally broke through in a way that was visible to anyone who cared to look. In fact, people who had nothing to do with the women's movement could look, as the competing celebrations of International Women's Day were covered on the front pages of the daily newspapers.

On March 8, the official Sandinista women's organization, AMNLAE, held a national convention in Managua over the course of the weekend. Though most of the women in attendance remained loyal to AMNLAE and the FSLN, some soon-to-be autonomous feminists spoke up in the breakout sessions, criticizing what they saw as AMNLAE's submission to the FSLN, and encouraging activists to help them make the organization less hierarchical and more feminist. At the convention, former guerrilla commander Dora María Téllez addressed the delegates, and former guerrilla leader Gladys Baez was named secretary general by acclamation (even though other candidates had been suggested at some of the preconvention gatherings).

At the second celebration on the weekend of March 8, 1991, the style and tone were quite different. Held at Managua's Piñata fairgrounds, it was called the Festival of the 52 percent, recognizing that the majority of Nicaraguans are women. By pointedly holding a gathering at the same time as AMNLAE's gathering, but in the open air instead of behind closed doors, the leaders of the emerging autonomous movement suggested that AMNLAE and the FSLN no longer spoke for the women's movement. And while AMNLAE had been hesitant to promote lesbian rights (or even to admit that some of its members were lesbians), lesbians had their own booth at the 52 percent festival, from which they sold lemon meringue pie and provided information about their political work. "That evening, same-sex couples were among the women and men dancing to the beat of a local band" (Babb 2003, 309; Kampwirth 2004, 56–63).

In June 1991, the emerging gay and lesbian movement hosted another public event in Managua, celebrating gay pride day.

> Several hundred people came to a well-known cultural center, *Coro de Angeles*, for a showing of the gay-themed North American movie *Torch Song Trilogy*, selected as emblematic of gay lives globally, followed by a panel discussion of homosexuality and human rights. The audience responded with passionate testimonies of experiences suffered in families and in society, speaking out about injustice and personal pain. The diverse crowd that evening included well-known Nicaraguans who were both straight and gay and who were clearly hopeful and enthusiastic about the historic event taking place (Babb 2003, 309).

The event was open to the public and the press. Unlike some previous events, the idea was not just to provide entertainment and support to gays and lesbians, but, as the sociologist Millie Thayer noted, to reach out to the whole of Nicaraguan society. "Organizers were explicit about this aim, choosing to invite well-known straight intellectuals to make presentations, alongside gays and lesbians" (Thayer 1997, 394). Hazel Fonseca explained that it was the first time when the new movement "came out into the light to publicly identify ourselves, giving faces to the movement, because we had not had faces in that sense: I am who I am, I am Hazel" (interview, December 10, 2013).

Article 204: Criminalizing Sodomy and Free Speech

By 1992, Nicaragua's gay and lesbian community seemed to be benefitting in some ways from what was often called the transition to democracy. Though the government's neoliberal policies caused hardship for many working-class gays and lesbians, there were also opportunities to form organizations and hold events without state interference. But that window of opportunity was slammed shut by the National Assembly and the Chamorro administration in 1992. In response to what they perceived as a series of threats—the legacy of the revolution, the creation of feminist and LGBTQ rights organizations, the arrival of foreign NGOs—they cracked down on nonnormative sexuality, informed by a moral panic like that which had informed the 1964–85 military dictatorship in Brazil (Cowan 2016, 72–75).

Many politicians feared new visibility for Nicaragua's gays and lesbians, since, in addition to the organizations and events discussed above, several feminist organizations were putting sexuality front and center in their work. *La Boletina*, a bimonthly (sometimes quarterly) magazine, was launched in 1991 by the feminist NGO *Puntos de Encuentro* (Common Ground), becoming a significant national voice.[2] On page five of issue one, published July 1991, there was an article about the first gay and lesbian pride event, held in *Coro de Angeles* and sponsored by *Puntos*, the feminist health NGO CISAS and a group called *Movimiento de Lesbianas Feministas y Homosexuales Nicaragüenses* (Nicaraguan Lesbian Feminist and Homosexual Movement). A half-page article on page sixteen, called "Focus of the Month" was simply a list of terms and definitions: *homosexuality, homosexual, gay, lesbian bisexual, heterosexual, homophobia*. Finally, a three-page article entitled "International Day of Lesbian and Gay Pride" provided an international context to help understand what was happening in Nicaragua (*La Boletina* 1991a, 5, 16, 17–19).[3]

---

2. Though *Puntos* only published five hundred copies of the first issue (labeled issue # 0), by the March/April 1992 issue 3,500 copies were printed. By the December/January 1993/94 issue 10,000 copies were printed, and *La Boletina* had become the most widely read magazine in the country.

3. Some readers were unhappy to read articles on gay and lesbian issues along with analysis of gender politics and the women's movement. In a letter to the editor, published in issue #2 of *La Boletina*, Margarita Lorío from the *Programa Mujer y Medio Ambiente* of the *Movimiento Ambientalista Nicaragüense* (Women and Environment program of the Nicaraguan Environmental Movement), praised *La Boletina* but suggested that it should not cover gay issues and instead devote more attention to women and the environment. The editors at *La Boletina* promised more on the environment and other topics related to women's lives but insisted that they would continue to cover gay and lesbian issues, not only because gay and lesbian rights was a just cause but because the way in which society viewed gays and lesbians was intertwined with gender roles. "We live in a society that looks down upon that which is 'feminine,' where men cannot do anything that women do and if they do it, or try to do it, people say that 'will make

In the early 1990s, critics of the Sandinistas often explained that the revolution caused social upheaval, the loss of traditional values, and a situation where many "confused liberty with licentiousness." From their perspective, publications like *La Boletina*, the activities carried out by the feminist movement, and the emergence of gay and lesbian groups all were evidence to support their views. And they were ready to fight back.

It was in this context that, in 1992, the Women's Commission of the National Assembly, comprised of women from the FSLN and the UNO, set out to revise Nicaragua's sex crime legislation. The 1974 (Somoza-era) penal code was still in effect, and the 1974 law was quite similar to the penal code of 1839, so the code did not reflect the social and legal changes that had occurred over the course of more than a century. Reforms of the penal code were overdue, so a draft bill was presented to the National Assembly. That draft bill (the only one that was ever debated publicly) would have resulted in several changes to the 1974 Code: changing the definition of rape (including acknowledging that men could be rape victims), permitting abortion for victims of rape, and eliminating the antisodomy provision. The changes to the abortion and sodomy law turned out to be controversial (Kampwirth 1998, 60).

A series of public debates were held regarding the draft bill, but the version of the law voted upon in the National Assembly was dramatically different from the version that had been debated. No longer were rape victims to have the right to an abortion. No longer was the antisodomy provision to be removed from the code. In fact, the sodomy provision of the penal code was dramatically strengthened, penalizing even speech in favor of gay and lesbian rights.

Article 205 of the 1974 Code stated that sexual relations "between persons of the same sex or against nature constitutes sodomy and those who practice it in a manner that is scandalous or outraging modesty or public morality will suffer the penalty of one to three years in prison; but if one of those who practices it, even in private, had over the other disciplinary power or control, as superior, guard, teacher, boss, guardian or in whatever other form that implies influence or authority or moral direction, the penalty shall be for him,

---

them' homosexuals. This is a highly developed expression of homophobia that we women share, and we express it through fear of inculcating a 'perverted' sexual identity in our sons. Often, we try to avoid it by sending our daughters to the kitchen while our sons develop a masculinity that excludes 'feminine things'" (1991b, 29–30).

from two to four years, the same as when it is practiced with one less than 15 years old or with force or intimidation" (quoted in Morgan 1995, 459–46).

In contrast, the final version of the 1992 reform, called Article 204 (which was opposed unanimously by the Sandinista bloc in the Assembly but ultimately passed by a 43 to 42 vote) penalized speech as well as conduct:

> Anyone who induces, promotes, propagandizes, or practices sexual relations between people of the same sex commits the crime of sodomy. That individual will be punished with one to three years in prison. When one of those who practice sodomy, even in private, has disciplinary power or authority over the other, such as a relative, guardian, teacher, boss, protector, or any other role that would imply authoritative influence or moral direction, there will be a charge of being responsible for illegitimate seduction (Asamblea Nacional de la Republica de Nicaragua 1992, 4).

Sandinista Congresswoman Doris Tijerino, a member of the Women's Commission who had been involved in the whole process of debating the Code, explained that she was "surprised" when the final version of the Penal Code came up for a vote along lines that were not those of men vs. women, nor heterosexuals vs. homosexuals.

> In the Assembly there are homosexuals. I know they exist, but they voted for this article. It is hypocrisy that shapes conduct. . . . It was so extreme that two Congresspeople who expressed agreement with my positions ended up voting in favor of the article. They voted for it because they could never vote for a Sandinista position, never. That is one of the big sticking points we have that makes it hard to create good laws. (Interview, October 27, 1992)

It was not surprising that members of the National Opposition Union (UNO) coalition, whose name referred to no particular value except for opposition to the FSLN, would vote against a position that they associated with the Sandinistas. Given the complicated relationship of gays and lesbians with the FSLN in the 1980s, perhaps it was more surprising that the FSLN voted unanimously against the new sodomy provisions. In part, they voted no because the legislation was proposed by the UNO. Additionally, Tijerino suggested that the FSLN's vote against the sodomy law was rooted in a willingness to debate within the party, something that was not so true during the 1980s. "I think that is an advance, but I would not say that this change is generalized within the whole Sandinista party. It does not mean that most Sandinistas think it is fine to be a homosexual, but it is true that the majority think that discrimination is not right" (interview, October 27, 1992).

Article 204 meant a loss of rights, sometimes even before the law went into effect. Erick Blandón noted that, just days after the Assembly voted for Article 204, "in Sébaco the education administrators were trying to fire a teacher because he was a homosexual" (interview, October 23, 1992). But the debate over Article 204 also illustrated a cultural shift.

> The Sandinista bloc in the National Assembly fought against those articles in a very public way. And it was notable that the person who led the fight was Doris Tijerino—first, because she is a woman who served as chief of police and her arguments demonstrated sensitivity regarding this issue. On the other hand, another one of the Sandinistas who defended homosexual rights was the Congressman Danilo Aguirre Solís, the Assistant Director of *El Nuevo Diario*, a newspaper that has always discussed homosexuals, drug addicts, prostitutes, and delinquents as though they had the same social status. (Interview, October 23, 1992)

Similarly, *Barricada* editor-in-chief Carlos Fernando Chamorro was unwilling to sign the petition asking President Chamorro [his mother] to overturn Article 204, "because he said that it did not affect him. Nonetheless, *Barricada* was a great defender of homosexual rights in its opposition to this law" (Erick Blandón, interview, October 23, 1992).[4]

Article 204 represented a turning point, illustrating the superficiality of the transition to democracy and doing damage to Nicaragua's relationship with the outside world. For years to come, the Chamorro administration would be under pressure from international donors and human rights groups to overturn the law. Amnesty International, for example, protested 204, telling President Chamorro that it would consider anyone who was imprisoned under the terms of 204 to be a "prisoner of conscience" (quoted in *La Boletina* 1993, 3).

---

4. Though Carlos Fernando Chamorro seemed indifferent to LGBTQ rights in 1992, it is worth noting that he changed over time. In 2015, he forcefully defended LGBTQ rights, which he described as an important indicator of societal progress (e.g., *Esta Semana* 2015, 12:31–13:16).

The passage of Article 204 also brought about notable changes in civil society. In late 1992, a coalition of more than twenty-five organizations and individuals came together in the *Campaña Por Una Sexualidad Libre de Prejuicios* (Sexuality without Prejudice Campaign). The Sexuality without Prejudice Campaign had to come together quickly because Law 105 (which included Article 204) was passed by the National Assembly on June 5, 1992, signed by President Chamorro just three days later and published in *La Gaceta* no. 174 on October 31, but backdated to September 9, so the time to submit an appeal was reduced from sixty to nine days.

Still, leaders of the new Sexuality without Prejudice campaign managed to put together a twenty-page legal challenge, arguing that Article 204 violated over twenty articles of the Constitution. That legal challenge was signed by thirty-two individuals, including lawyers and activists in the feminist movement and the gay and lesbian rights movement (*Centro de Derechos Constitucionales* 1992, 20). Organizations that belonged to the Sexuality without Prejudice Campaign included *Puntos de Encuentro*, Xochiquetzal, CISAS, ITZA Women's Collective, *Grupo Venancia* (Venancia Group), *Grupo de Mujeres de Matagalpa* (Matagalpa Women's Group), SI Mujer, *Colectivo de Mujeres 8 de marzo* (March 8 Women's Collective), *Colectivo de Mujeres Isnim* (Isnim Women's Collective), *Colectivo de Mujeres Xochitl* (Xochitl Women's Collective), NOSOTRAS, SHOMOS, and *Centro de Derechos Constitucionales* (Center for Constitutional Rights) (*La Boletina* 1992a, 22–23; Sequeira Malespín and Berríos Cruz 1993, 15).

The importance of the feminist movement for the emerging gay and lesbian rights movement was already clear in 1992. Though I do not have a complete list of the members of the campaign, in the list I have been able to compile, three organizations had an explicitly gay and lesbian rights focus (Xochiquetzal, NOSOTRAS and SHOMOS); one was a legal rights organization (Center for Constitutional Rights) and the other nine were feminist organizations. In addition to mounting a legal challenge, the campaign lobbied President Chamorro, held public events, and collected over four thousand signatures opposing Article 204 (*Centro de Derechos Constitucionales* 1992; Kampwirth 1998, 61; Thayer 1997, 394).

In a 1997 document produced by the same campaign, the members of the *Comisión Por una sexualidad libre de prejuicios* (Commission for Sexuality without Prejudice) were listed on the front cover: Xochiquetzal, *Puntos de Encuentro, Colectivo Feminista "La Malinche,"* ("The Malinche" Feminist

Collective), March 8th Women's Collective, Venancia Group, *Colectivo de Mujeres Iztá* (Iztá Women's Collective), *Colectivo de Mujeres Hablemos de Nosotras* (Let's Talk About Ourselves Women's Collective),[5] AMNLAE, CISAS, *Red de Mujeres Contra la Violencia* (Women's Network Against Violence), *Red de Matagalpa* (Women's Network of Matagalpa), Sí Mujer (Fundación Xochiquetzal 1997). This list was like the 1992 list, with a few changes. It was shorter (not surprisingly, as it was the commission rather than a complete list of members), and it included a few groups that did not appear in the 1992 list: the Malinche Feminist Collective, which, in 1992, did not yet exist; the Women's Network Against Violence, which was brand-new in 1992; and AMNLAE, the Sandinista-affiliated women's organization. One notable difference between the 1992 and 1997 lists is that the 1997 list was comprised entirely of feminist or women's organizations (two of which had a lesbian-rights focus). That does not mean that men all favored Article 204, and in fact many men participated in the feminist movement, but it seems likely that the Sexuality without Prejudice Campaign would have ceased to exist had it not been for the feminists.

In some ways, the Sexuality without Prejudice campaign failed. The Supreme Court eventually dismissed the case and Article 204 would remain on the books until a new penal code was ratified in 2008, after the FSLN had returned to power. Lola Castillo, who was active in the Sexuality without Prejudice campaign from its beginnings in the 1991 event at *Coro de Angeles*, noted that Article 204 frightened activists.

> There was a lot of fear because the article forbid propaganda regarding lesbian and homosexual relations. At that time, I was working at *Puntos de Encuentro*; I worked on *La Boletina*, and I remember that we were afraid to publish things. For example, we published a story about the life of a lesbian, using a pseudonym, a fictitious name, because there was a lot of fear of going to jail, but we carried on anyway. I think it is important to say that Article 204 really limited access to information. Though, at a social level there was an opening. I think that is when there were more gay bars, nightclubs, parties, that sort of thing. There was a sensation of freedom even though everything in public was prohibited. (Interview, December 4, 2012)

---

5. NOSOTRAS (in the 1992 list) and *Colectivo de Mujeres Hablemos de Nosotras* (in the 1997 list) are probably the same organization.

One might think that the gay bars and clubs that were founded by middle class Nicaraguans, often known as the "Miami Boys" (because they had recently returned from exile in the north), would have been prohibited by Article 204. Perhaps they were left alone because they were capitalist spaces where individuals (a mostly gay male clientele) met for private socializing rather than to demand public rights. As activist Hazel Fonseca suggested, "No one will move a finger against a homosexual who has money" (quoted in Andersson 1993, 23). The ethos behind gay businesses—freedom through the market—was consistent with the neoliberal capitalism promoted by the Chamorro administration, and so those institutions were not targeted. In contrast, social movements, and NGOs that promoted gay and lesbian rights felt threatened by Article 204.

But despite the fear that social movement activists felt, if the point of Article 204 was to put an end to the emerging gay and lesbian rights movement, the supporters of 204 were the ones who failed. Many new organizations, public campaigns, and even television programs promoting gay and lesbian rights were to emerge after 1992. It took courage to organize under the shadow of 204, but clearly many Nicaraguans had courage.

Ultimately, 204 forced people to choose sides. Many people who had not taken the side of gay and lesbian rights in the 1980s (or who had even explicitly opposed such rights) decided to side with those who opposed 204 in the 1990s. That was one more way in which the age of postrevolution was truly a new age. Thinking about the conflict over Article 204, Erick Blandón noted that "at the hour of protest, homosexuals and lesbians were not alone" (interview, October 23, 1992).

Victims of Article 204

Feminist- and LGBTQ-rights activists felt threatened by Article 204, but those threats were rarely carried out. I found no evidence of any NGO or social activist being accused or imprisoned due to 204 (though it is impossible to measure the chilling effect it had upon speech and activism). But 204 did have direct victims. For instance, in "2001, two homosexual professors were incarcerated under Article 204 . . . after being seen romantically together by police. During the same year, another homosexual couple was also subject to criminal prosecution for violation of Article 204" (Global Rights et al. 2008, 9; Sequeira Malespín and Berríos Cruz 1993, 8, 28, 39).

Article 204 was sometimes used as a tool of family authoritarianism, generally wielded against rural and urban working-class people who were dependent upon their extended family networks for survival. For instance,

> In 2005, a 28-year-old lesbian woman was expelled from the home she shared with her mother and sister due to her sexual orientation. They denounced her to the Ministry of Family for a violation of Article 204 and broke into her room to confiscate pictures, cards, and gifts she had received as well as her daughter's birth certificate and vaccination records to give to the Ministry. They also attempted to kidnap her daughter. (Global Rights et al. 2008, 8)

Officials at the Ministry of the Family took the family's complaints seriously, interviewing the neighbors regarding the lesbian mother's life, making her take multiple psychological tests, "calling her a bad mother," and trying to get her to give up custody of her daughter (Global Rights et al. 2008, 9; Howe 2009, 376, n. 5).

The most well-known case of Article 204 being used within a familial dispute was that of an impoverished rural woman, Aura Rosa Pavón Pavón. Pavón was imprisoned for violating the antisodomy provisions of Article 204, though it seems that her real crime was being involved in a multiyear relationship with Karla Vanesa Muñoz, a young woman who was also the wife of Daniel Norori, one of the wealthiest and most powerful men in the village, and about four decades older than Muñoz. Norori wanted Pavón imprisoned for rather obvious reasons as she was humiliating him and trying to "steal" his wife; Karla's mother (Melba Rosa Muñoz Gutiérrez) apparently wanted Pavón imprisoned, because she feared that her apparent agreement with Norori (that he would help support her if he could marry her teenaged daughter) could fall apart if her daughter were to leave Norori.

Norori and Pavón succeeded, and in 1999, Pavón was imprisoned for several months for the crime of sodomy, serving some of that time in a men's prison. Shortly after a coalition of lawyers, human rights advocates, feminist, and LGBTQ activists managed to get her released early, she was tricked into going to a meeting late at night, where Daniel Norori shot her to death, dumping her body in a latrine where it was found months later. Though the husband and the mother were each sentenced to twenty years in prison for Pavón's murder, they were released after three years. Karla Muñoz (Rosa Pavón's lover, and Daniel Norori's wife) killed herself two weeks after her husband and mother were released from prison (Arias 2000; Howe 2009, 367–68; Sirias 2009, 239–40).

It would be wrong to claim that Article 204, alone, caused these tragedies. Governmental institutions sometimes intervened in family conflicts against LGBTQ people before Article 204 was signed into law in 1992 (Andersson 1993, 24). And after it was repealed in late 2007 (a repeal which went into effect in 2008), cases of discrimination by governmental institutions continued (Global Rights et al. 2008, 3).

Still, even though family and community authoritarianism did not end when Article 204 was repealed, the repeal of Article 204 made the playing field a bit more even. If discrimination happened, it was sometimes possible to successfully appeal to higher authorities, something that was not possible during the 204 years (Nacho 2008). Ultimately the law mattered, but it was not the only thing that mattered.

Worshiping in the Shadow of 204

Most of the gay and lesbian rights groups that emerged in the early 1990s emerged out of the Initial Group and CEP-SIDA experiences of the 1980s. But there were some organizations that were rooted in other experiences such as the gay men's group SHOMOS, and the gay and lesbian bible study group, both of which started in 1989. SHOMOS and the bible study group both evolved over the course of the 1990s, though in different ways.

SHOMOS faced economic difficulties in the 1990s, with its members unemployed—in part due to neoliberal spending cuts, in part due to discrimination against openly gay men—and its programs unfunded. Though the members of SHOMOS applied for grants, they had little luck in getting funding for their activities, unlike many organizations that were directly linked to the feminist movement. Its members continued to meet throughout the 1990s, collaborating with other groups on projects like AIDS prevention, but the group became more social and less political over the course of that decade. It may be that international funding agencies preferred to fund feminist organizations and lesbian projects within those organizations than to fund a gay men's group like SHOMOS. "In the competitive terrain of international funding, lesbians, who are seen as twice marginalized—as women and as sexual minorities—may constitute a more attractive constituency" (Howe 2013, 192, notes 27, 120).

In contrast to the fate of SHOMOS, the gay and lesbian bible study group became more of a public force over the course of the 1990s. That was largely due to the 1991 meeting of the ILGA in Acapulco, Mexico. Thanks to Tede Matthews, the U.S. solidarity activist who paid for transportation and other expenses, five or six activists, including Hazel Fonseca, Lupita Sequeira, Alfonso González, and Mario Gutiérrez, were able to attend the ILGA conference. Another Nicaraguan who joined their group, Marcos Guevara, was sent by the Nimehuatzin Foundation (Hazel Fonseca, interview, December 10, 2013; Mario Gutiérrez, interview, December 5, 2013). Mario Gutiérrez explained,

> That was the first time when we went to the ILGA [meeting], and for the first time we portrayed ourselves at a global level as a Nicaraguan gay-lesbian community. We were warriors both at the ILGA and afterwards. . . . It was in Acapulco, and that is where I met the reverend from the Metropolitan Church in Mexico. . . . They invited me to go to Mexico; you should come through your church [they told me,] because we would like you to found a church in Nicaragua. After the ILGA I returned to Nicaragua, but I went to Mexico again [to] Guadalajara [and] Mexico City, but this time through the Metropolitan Church. And due to the decision of all the young men and women, a large group, we had a large community of over 30 gay and lesbian people who decided to found our community under the name of the Metropolitan Church of the Community[,] and I was the one who gave [our congregation] the name "Peace and Joy"; . . . "joy" because [it is a synonym] of gay, and "peace" because we had really just ended a war, and we really thought that peace was a way to keep us going. That was in '93 (Mario Gutiérrez, interview, December 5, 2013).

About the same time that the bible study group gained a name—Peace and Joy congregation of the Metropolitan Community Church (*Iglesia Metropolitana de la Comunidad "Paz y Alegría"*)—and an affiliation with the international Metropolitan Community Church, it changed its location and broadened its mission.

Through 1992, the church met in the house in the Managua neighborhood Los Robles that Mario Gutierrez shared with his mother, just as it had in the late 1980s. After Gutierrez's mother died in January 1993, he moved in with his sister who lived in the San Judas neighborhood of Managua. "We continued to meet as the Metropolitan Church in San Judas, but they were no longer just meetings of gay youth or gay men [and] lesbians; we were doing or living Christian faith from a gay perspective" (interview, December 5, 2013). In coalition with several local groups (the neighborhood health center, the feminist NGO SI Mujer, and the Sandinista Heroes and Martyrs House), the Peace and Joy congregation of the Metropolitan Community Church campaigned for the prevention of HIV in the San Judas neighborhood, celebrated gay pride, and held religious services (Mario Gutiérrez, email communication, July 2013; *La Boletina* 1992b, 35). Article 204 clearly made that work illegal, yet the church held services and did community work for many years anyway. Indeed, over the course of the decade of the 1990s, it was to become "one of the major organizations serving the gay community" (Babb 2003, 311).

When I asked him about his first political experience, Ebén Díaz, born in March of 1973, talked about attending a service at the Metropolitan Community Church in 1993. At the time of the interview, he was very experienced as an activist, but of course he was not always an activist. "I was invited by a lesbian friend who was from Holland, and who was studying here in Nicaragua. She opened up with me and told me she was a lesbian, and she suspected that I was a gay man, and she invited me to the [church], at that moment to explore my identity and sexuality. I went with her because she told me that besides being a church, a lot of homosexuals went there" (interview, December 3, 2012).

Díaz only returned a few times, instead joining a group called Neconi, where he felt he fit in better. Nonetheless, the few services he attended made an impression. He described what it was like to arrive with his Dutch friend.

> We arrived and Mario [Gutiérrez] was talking about the message of the word [of God,] and also there was something like a political discourse; it was more or less trying to relate the experience of faith, and the message of the word of God, with the situation of Nicaragua at that time. Great, I am talking about 1993 when the government of Violeta Barrios de Chamorro had been in power for more or less three years, and in this country it was a serious matter to be gay. (Interview, December 3, 2012)

Only twenty years old and still coming to accept his sexual orientation, Díaz was startled by the whole experience, including Gutiérrez's hour-and-a-half-long sermon criticizing Nicaraguan politics in the light of the Gospel, and especially the social atmosphere after formal services were over. "There was a dynamic in the faith community that I did not like very much; it was not something to which I was accustomed. For example, maybe after the end of the sermon someone would take out a little bottle of liquor, and some of the girls, who I think were transvestites or trans, began to put on make-up. Those sort of things at first, maybe because I was not sufficiently identified as gay, I did not like them much. Later I realized that is nothing wrong with that, obviously, but at first, I did not like it. I only went three Sundays and then I never went again" (interview, December 3, 2012). Nonetheless, the experience of those early services—of entering a surprising world—remained vivid many years later.

In the early years the church moved around a lot. It was hard to find an appropriate space to meet, as their numbers were often too large to fit easily into anyone's house. At one point in 1998, having run out of good options, they met for a few weeks in the garden in front of the Managua's Catholic Cathedral.

> Nobody had ever seen such a crazy thing: a group of some 25 people of all sexual orientations praising God in front of the hierarchy that condemned them through its unconditional support for the recently endorsed Article 204 of the Penal Code, the very one that denied [the benefits of] Nicaraguan citizenship to anyone who practiced, promoted, or even spoke in favor of homosexuality. (*Iglesias de la Comunidad Metropolitana* 2012[?], 10)

Later, the church met in the *Centro Ecuménico Antonio Valdivieso* (Antonio Valdivieso Ecumenical Center), thanks to the support of the Catholic theologian Michelle Najlis, and after that in the Ave Maria House, thanks to the support of Episcopal Reverend Grant Mauricio Gallup.

For a number of years, the church was led by Armando Sánchez (a former Catholic priest) and Mario Gutiérrez, both of whom were eventually ordained as ministers of the Universal Fellowship of the ICM in a ceremony at the Antonio Valdivieso Ecumenical Center in September 1999. In 2003, Sánchez was elected bishop of the international church and left Nicaragua, and a new pastor, Alberto Nájera, took over. He led the church until 2011 when, for personal reasons, he had to leave Nicaragua for Panama and, at that point, the church ceased to meet regularly. Nonetheless, the small gay and lesbian bible study group, founded in 1989, had a long run as an important cultural force (Iglesias de la Comunidad Metropolitana 2012[?], 10–11; Other Sheep 2000; Mario Gutiérrez, email communication, July 2013; Sequeira Malespín and Berríos Cruz 1993, 52–58).

Pride Within the Feminist Movement: 1992–2006

The passage of Article 204 practically guaranteed that the gay and lesbian rights movement would be closely intertwined with the feminist movement. By 1992, when President Chamorro signed Article 204, the autonomous feminist movement was already much larger than the gay and lesbian rights movement, and it had more resources. Additionally, feminists were not directly targeted by Article 204, so they could offer some protection to gays and lesbians. And of course, feminists cared deeply about sexual autonomy. Azahálea Solís of the Autonomous Women's Movement (MAM) noted that "the Nicaraguan women's movement was a great promoter of rights in all dimensions but also in particular of lesbian groups, of LGBTQ issues. . . . It is unthinkable that a Nicaraguan feminist group would not have LGBTQ rights as part of its Ten Commandments" (interview, June 9, 2011).

During the years when 204 was in effect, what many Nicaraguans call "the neoliberal years" (the administrations of Violeta Chamorro, 1990–1997, Arnoldo Alemán 1997–2002, and Enrique Bolaños, 2002–2007), new gay and lesbian rights projects emerged regularly, typically, but not always, under the umbrella of feminist organizations. It is not surprising that many lesbian activists first became politicized through the feminist movement but that was also true for many male activists (especially those who were not involved in Initial Group or CEP-SIDA in the 1980s). So gay and lesbian rights work in Nicaragua had more of a feminist flavor than in many other countries.

Bismarck Moraga, director of the *Iniciativa desde la Diversidad Sexual por los Derechos Humanos* (Sexual Diversity Initiative for Human Rights or IDSDH) at the time of the interview, was a feminist long before he was a gay-rights activist. Born in October of 1970, he was of the same generation as many who were revolutionary activists as children and adolescents. But when asked about his first political experience, Moraga did not mention Sandinista children's groups. Instead, he explained that his childhood was sheltered, perhaps because his family was evangelical. He spoke with pride of his single mother who raised him, the second of five children, despite huge sacrifices.

I was raised and educated with my Mom's guidance, and I am very proud of that. My mom is a poor woman from a peasant background, from Diriomo, a town that is famous because it is the town of the witches. . . . From a very young age I was very close to my mom . . . even though for a large part of our childhoods we lived alone, because my mom worked all day long, which is typical of Nicaraguan families. . . . I recognize the sacrifices my mom made; . . . there was a moment when she had to start working as a live-in maid, because that was the only work she could find (Bismarck Moraga, interview, June 7, 2011).

As his mother was away working to feed her children, the one who did the day-to-day work of raising the children was Moraga's older brother, who was fourteen or fifteen years old when his mother took the job as a live-in-maid.

I thank God that he took care of us, and I cared for my other smaller siblings, using the same guidance and advice that my mom provided. We did not choose the wrong path even though we lived in a community where we were surrounded by alcoholics, by people who fought a lot. I always thought about my mom's guidance and advice, which allowed us to grow up to be decent men. . . . We have never intentionally hurt anyone. We have never used drugs. We have never robbed. Thanks to God we were raised with that healthy spirit. (Interview, June 7, 2011)

To prove that all his mother's children turned out well, Moraga proudly described the stable lives his siblings led: all but the youngest girl married, and with a child or two each. He finished the story with himself: "And from the age of 20 I have had a partner and I currently have lived with him for the last 14 years" (interview, June 7, 2011).

In 1995, Moraga was hired as a night watchman at the *Colectivo Feminista La Corriente* ("The Current" Feminist Collective), his first contact with the feminist movement. A couple of years later he worked with the *Movimiento Comunal* (Communal Movement) in his neighborhood, leaving *La Corriente* for a while.

My mom was a member of the Communal Movement. She worked for and gave a lot of support to that community so people would have better conditions, especially the most defenseless ones. And I joined her effort, and I learned, and I became a volunteer teacher. I was there for a long time. But also, in that process I became more conscientious; I was part of the life of my community. (Interview, June 7, 2011)

Moraga returned to *La Corriente* in 2000, but this time he oversaw the documentation center. That is, officially he was the librarian, but it was a small organization, so he carried out many tasks. While there, he said, "I was a part of some political situations, and I became more conscientious."

Thanks to the human-rights advocacy work skills he acquired working for *La Corriente*, Moraga got a job working for the Women's Network Against Violence, where he worked from 2002–04. While there, as he said, "I came to be conscientious regarding women's right to decide about abortion," a new belief that he illustrated with a long and harrowing story about his teenaged niece who nearly bled to death because of a pregnancy that went wrong, "a fetus never formed, just a number of fibroids," and who was only saved because of a therapeutic abortion that she received thanks to activists in the feminist movement. But while his work for the Women's Network against Violence was profoundly meaningful, it was also difficult. He sometimes faced

situations in which being in the Women's Network I had to work hard because I was very stigmatized due to my being gay, and because I was the only man who worked at the Women's Network. [I suffered] attacks from my co-workers, professional jealousy, and I never intended what they thought, which was to take away their work. . . . That caused professional problems for me, within the organization, and they banned me from providing help to women. (Interview, June 7, 2011)

Though that prohibition was eventually lifted (once the director found out what was happening), Moraga still found the atmosphere at the Women's Network against Violence challenging. Eventually Moraga returned to *La Corriente*, where he was working as the 2006 election approached, the election that would return Sandinista Daniel Ortega to power. During the campaign, a new LGBTQ rights group, the IDSDH, was founded by a group including Moraga. I will pick up the story of the IDSDH and the 2006 election later in this chapter.

Eventually Moraga left the feminist movement, but feminism never left him. "I was very interested in learning, acquiring experience, knowledge about things that were new to me: speaking about violence, sexual abuse. . . . At a certain point in my life, I considered it important to analyze and assimilate the whole experience with *La Corriente*, with the Women's Network [against Violence], finding out how they did political analysis, their political debates and all of that, to see how they made proposals to development agencies, how they proposed things. It was a great school for me" (interview, June 7, 2011). Other gay and trans-rights activists like Marvin Mayorga, Juan Carlos Martínez, Joel Zúñiga, Silvia Martínez, Ebén Diaz, and Aldrín Torrez also were politicized within the feminist movement in the 1990s and early 2000s (Juan Carlos Martínez, interview, December 6, 2012; Silvia Martínez, interview, June 8, 2011; Marvin Mayorga, interview, June 3, 2011; Aldrín Torrez, interview, November 30, 2012; Ebén Díaz, interview, December 3, 2012; Joel Zúñiga, interview, June 18, 2014).

Regarding the impact that feminism had on his thinking as a gay man, Elvis Salvatierra wrote,

It is a fallacy to think that the LGBTI struggle is unrelated to the feminist struggle given that it was the feminists themselves who were the first in history to identify sexuality as part of life, and part of the human rights of all people. Thanks to feminisms we realize that sexualities are diverse rather than static, and that heterosexuality is a system of oppression that crushes all expressions that deviate from heteronormativity, and it is exactly there [in feminism] where we LGBTI people all find a place. (Salvatierra 2015a)

During the 204 years, many feminist groups had a profound impact on the lives of thousands of LGBTQ people, far more than ever worked directly for one of those organizations, both for the theoretical reasons noted by Salvatierra and for very practical reasons. Feminist groups that played key roles in promoting gay and lesbian rights—hosting support groups, running public education campaigns, lobbying, and protesting—included the health collectives CISAS, SI Mujer, and Xochiquetzal; the popular education NGOs CANTERA, Venancia Group, *La Corriente*, and *Puntos*; the theater collective *Hijas de la Luna* (Daughters of the Moon); as well as the multiservice feminist organizations Matagalpa Women's Network, 8th of March Women's Group, and *Asociación de Mujeres Acahual* (Acahual Women's Association) (*La Boletina* 1992b, 34–35; Ebén Diaz, interview, December 3, 2012; Julieta Martínez, interview, December 11, 2013; Aldrín Torrez, interview, November 30, 2012; Elizabeth Torres, interview, December 12, 2013).

One coalition that played a crucial role in supporting LGBTQ organizing during the 204 years was *Coordinadora Civil* (Civil Coordinator). That coalition was founded in 1998 in response to the crisis created by Hurricane Mitch, uniting more than three hundred organizations in 1998, and more than six hundred by 2013 (Coordinadora Civil 2013[?], 5). Though not exclusively feminist, it counted many feminist organizations among its members, and its first national liaison, Ana Quirós, was a well-known feminist. In fact, President Arnoldo Alemán threatened to deport Quirós and others—all female allies of the feminist movement—in an openly antifeminist and antiforeigner campaign (Kampwirth 2003, 140–42, 146–48).

Civil Coordinator was one of the networks that supported the gay and lesbian community through a *"Red Temática de la Diversidad Sexual LGBTIQ"* (LGBTIQ Sexual Diversity Theme Network) beginning in 2002 (Facebook page of the *Red*, consulted February 14, 2017). According to Ebén Díaz, though some members of the Coordinadora were not pleased to host LGBTQ activists, many of the leaders of the Coordinadora at the time, like Georgina Muñoz, were quite helpful. "They treated us very well. When we asked for funds to do some workshops, they helped us; they had a meeting room that they always lent whenever we requested it. . . . When the Civil Coordinator hosts activities or marches we always attend. When we invite them to activities sponsored by gay groups here in Managua they always attend. There is always a relationship of one sort or another" (Ebén Díaz, interview, December 3, 2012; Alvarenga López 2013).

While it would take another book to trace all the interconnections between the autonomous feminist movement and the emerging LGBTQ movement during the 204 years, in the following pages, I consider two feminist organizations that played especially important roles in promoting the lesbian, gay, and trans rights movement: *Puntos de Encuentro* (Common Ground) and the Acahual Women's Association.

Puntos de Encuentro

Puntos was founded in 1991 by a collective including Amy Bank, Vilma Castillo, Ana Criquillion, Helen Dixon, Olga Espinoza, Colette Fine, and Ana Quirós. It launched the magazine *La Boletina* that same year, which soon became the most read magazine in the country: by 2015, twenty-six thousand issues were distributed for free at least three times a year, in all seventeeen departments of the country, in tiny towns and big cities (*Puntos de Encuentro*

2015). Even after Article 204 was ratified, the editors of *La Boletina* continued to promote gay and lesbian rights. They did this fully aware that through
their words, they were taking the risk of being prosecuted: "given the way
the law is written, even this article that you are reading in *La Boletina* could
be grounds for indictment if anyone said that with writings like this one we
are 'promoting' or propagandizing' homosexuality or lesbianism. . . . The
purpose [of the law] seems to be to make people afraid" (*La Boletina* 1992a,
25–26). The editors of *La Boletina* (whose full names appeared on the back
cover of every issue) were afraid, but they spoke out anyway.

From early on *La Boletina* featured articles on masculinity, including
masculinity and violence (e.g., Montoya 1992a, 1992b). So it was not surprising when *Puntos* sponsored an organization called *Grupo de Hombres
Contra la Violencia* (Men's Group against Violence), founded in 1993 by
about twenty men. Its early members included Rubén Reyes, Osvaldo Montoya, Edgar Amador, Patrick Welsh, Joel Zúñiga, and Ariel Morales de Oca.
The Men's Group against Violence held discussion groups, presented workshops to interested men, published articles and books, and lobbied for legal
changes. From their first year, the members of the Men's Group against Violence worked closely with the feminist NGOs CANTERA and CISAS, and
the Network of Women against Violence, in addition to *Puntos* (Reyes 1994,
40; EuroPROFEM, n.d.).

Although the Men's Group against Violence was not a gay men's group,
typically about half of its members were gay, and it played a role in the emerging lesbian and gay movement, because addressing the complicated and
deep-seated relationship between masculinity and violence required confronting sexual insecurity and homophobia. Members of the Men's Group
against Violence wrote:

> Masculine identity is associated with the act of possessing, taking, pene-
> trating, dominating, and affirming oneself, if necessary, through violence.
> Feminine identity [is associated with] the act of being possessed, docile,
> passive, submissive. So "normality" and sexual identity is represented in
> the domination of men over women. Seen through this optic, homosex-
> uality is unacceptable as . . . a homosexual is not a man who has sexual
> relations with another man, rather he is the one who takes on the passive
> role: in reality a homosexual is the *marica*, the *loca*. . . . Ultimately [he] is a
> woman. In its active form, homosexuality may be considered a means for

a man to affirm his power; under its "passive" form, it is a symbol of decadence. Heterosexuality is the proof of masculinity. The "true man" should prove that he is not a homosexual, that he does not want to desire other men, nor to be desired by them. . . . To the extent that gender continues to be defined by sexual orientation, opposing masculinity to femininity, it is inevitable that homophobia, just like misogyny, plays an important role in the feeling of masculine identity. (Grupo de Hombres Contra la Violencia de Managua 2013)

During its first decade, in addition to the group in Managua, new groups were created in "Ciudad Sandino, Mateare, Jinotega, Ocotal, Jalapa, Nueva Guinea, Matagalpa, León and Mulukukú" (Cañada n.d.). Later, groups were founded in more towns, including Chichigalpa.

Jorge Lozano was one of the members of the Chichigalpa group. Born in Chichigalpa in 1989, he lost his mother early, when he was only fourteen. After her death, he lived with one grandmother, and then with his other grandmother, until he set out on his own, along with his sister, a transwoman. But despite the instability of his family life, he never got involved with gangs or drugs, instead filling his time with political activities: as an environmental activist from the age of twelve, working with the Liberal Party on elections from the age of fourteen, as a member of a sexual diversity group (without a name) from about the age of fifteen, and then as a member of the local chapter of the Men's Group against Violence.

[Within the Men's Group against Violence I] learned a lot, because before I didn't know; I thought that speaking about violence, violence was just hitting. Here one realizes that there are huge numbers of types of violence. I began to recognize my sexual identity. I came to understand the difference between sexual identity [and] sexual orientation. . . . At that moment in my adolescence I was quite confused, because I did not understand specific concepts. It was here that I finally came to differentiate between concepts, to define them. They taught me a lot about sexual diversity and such things that I liked very much. (Interview, November 28, 2012)

About a decade after the Men's Group against Violence was founded, the Managua group decided to set up an NGO with a similar name, *Asociación de Hombres Contra la Violencia* (Men's Association against Violence, or AHCV). The purpose of the AHCV was "to guarantee the continuity of the work that had been carried out by NGOS in the 1990s, given that their capacity was limited, and to further develop strategies and methodologies for work with men" (Welsh 2010, 7). By 2010, hundreds of men participated in AHCV activities in thirty different municipalities. None of this would have happened, or at least it would have been very different, if not for the LGBTQ and feminist relationship in the 1990s and early 2000s.

While *Puntos'* support for the Men's Group against Violence was important, the focus of that feminist NGO was influencing culture through the mass media, including the magazine *La Boletina. Puntos* also promoted youth radio programs and multimedia campaigns (including tv and radio ads, posters, stickers, flyers, and rock concerts) on themes related to violence, gender, and sexuality. Those included the 1990 campaign "*Rompiendo el silencio*" (Breaking the silence) on sexual abuse within families; the 1992 campaign "*Mi cuerpo es mío: no a la violencia sexual*" (My body is mine: no to sexual violence); the 1993 campaign "*Seamos diferentes: no más violencia en la calle, en la casa, en la cama*" (Let's be different: no more violence in the street, at home, in bed); the 1996 campaign "*La próxima vez te levanten la voz . . . que sea para felicitarte*" (Next time he raises his voice . . . may it be to congratulate you); and the 1999 campaign "*La violencia contra las mujeres es un desastre que los hombres sí podemos evitar*" (Violence against women is a disaster that men can prevent). Those campaigns reached many people. "For example, in a national opinion poll (1996), with a sample of 3,000 adult women and 3,200 young people, between 25 and 30% of people who were polled correctly explained the campaigns 'My body is mine,' and 'Let's be different' even three and four years after the implementation [of the campaigns]" (*Puntos de Encuentro* 2015).

Puntos made its biggest national and international impact through the television programs *Sexto Sentido* (Sixth Sense) and *Contracorriente* (Against the Current).[6] Both programs built on the soap opera model, but with several twists. Instead of setting their stories in luxurious settings, their episodes unfolded in modest houses. Instead of featuring light-skinned actors wearing

---

6. Eighty episodes of *Sexto Sentido* were broadcast during the years 2001–05; sixteen episodes of *Contracorriente* were broadcast during 2011 and 2012. Both were later broadcast in reruns in Nicaragua and as well as in Bolivia, Costa Rica, El Salvador, and Guatemala (Facebook pages of *Sexto Sentido* and *Contracorriente*, consulted June 11, 2015; Agüero 2014; Howe 2013, 128; *La Boletina* 2011, 45).

expensive clothing, which is the norm in Latin American soap operas, the actors had the range of skin colors that were common in Nicaragua, and they wore ordinary clothing. Instead of reinforcing the dominant class, racial, and gender dynamics of the societies in which they were produced, they challenged those dynamics: addressing issues such as domestic violence, rape, abortion, friendship, families, commercial sex, human trafficking, and sexuality. *Sexto Sentido* was also notable for including sympathetic gay and lesbian characters within its regular cast, characters whose sexuality was just one aspect of their personalities. Plus, the shows were often funny. That was a winning combination.

> After six months of Sunday afternoon screenings, prime time for family viewing, *Sexto Sentido* was rated the most popular TV program among Nicaraguan youth, its target audience. According to polling data, 80 percent of thirteen- to seventeen-year-olds tuned in to watch the show. The program also had some of the highest television ratings in the overall national market, claiming 70 percent of the *entire* Nicaraguan viewing audience (more than double the percentage of Super Bowl Sunday viewership in the United States). (Howe 2013, 129)

The makers of *Sexto Sentido* regularly tried out new story lines through focus groups, and the actors traveled throughout the country talking to groups of adolescents and preteens (often organized in *Sexto Sentido* fan clubs) about the show and the issues it raised (Howe 2013, 138–47; Miller 2004).

As a result of these conversations, characters and story lines sometimes evolved. Cymene Howe noted that there were benefits and costs to that interaction.

> Partly in response to the antisodomy law [Article 204] that was in place at the time, and partly because of their goal to create more tolerance for sexual diversity, the advocates who produced *Sexto Sentido* opted for a particular kind of homosexual subjectivity. . . . Gay men and lesbians are crafted to meet ideal types of monogamy, gender conformity, and social success, even if obtaining these successes may be out of reach for many Nicaraguans, both gay and straight. The strategy behind *Sexto Sentido* relied heavily on 'normalizing' . . . rather than 'queering' sexual subjectivity. (Howe 2013, 145–46)

Sexto Sentido presented a world that was simultaneously "very Nicaraguan" and "not very Nicaraguan." There were no characters who fit traditional Nicaraguan stereotypes of the feminine "*cochón*" or the masculine "*cochona*." Instead, Vicki, the lesbian character, with her lipstick and feminine spaghetti strap tops, and Angel, the simultaneously masculine and angelic gay guy, emerged from a series of decisions made by *Puntos* activists, who saw those characters as "the most politically efficacious way to circulate ideas of tolerance and create opportunities to promote sexual rights. The cost of these decisions, however, [was] the continued erasure of the *cochona* and the *cochón*" (Howe 2013, 147).

In the end, of course, there were no perfect options. Certainly, the choices made by the producers of the TV series were understandable given the social climate of the time and, even in retrospect, it is not clear what other choices would have been possible. Despite the constraints within which they were created, *Sexto Sentido* and *Contracorriente* were real successes, presenting entertaining and egalitarian ideas to millions of people.

Asociación de Mujeres Acahual

Along the shores of Lake Managua sits the impoverished neighborhood of Acahualinca, famous for prehistoric footprints that reside in a small museum, famous for *La Chureca* (the largest garbage dump in the country), famous also for "The Earth Is a Satellite of the Moon," the poem by Leonel Rugama, with which I opened chapter 1. Acahualinca is also the home of the Acahual Women's Association, founded in 1993. When the women of *Acahual* began organizing, death rates in the community were so high, some sadly joked that they should provide free coffins. But of course, they preferred to address the multiple health problems that community residents faced, including respiratory infections and skin diseases from working at the garbage dump, along with sexually transmitted diseases and cervical-uterine cancer.

By 1996, they had a large building, complete with a patio, out of which to work. By that year, Norma Villalta explained, "We have trained 300 women in workshops on gender, self-esteem, human rights, and violence. At this point we have 48 youth promoters who help us present workshops with community youth. We did a reforestation project in our zone and that was a way to employ 21 women. We also got a hold of loans so 50 women could improve their small businesses" (quoted in *La Boletina* 1996).

Acahual director María Elena Bonilla noted that the more they did, especially in the area of health, the more they realized that they needed to reach out to the LGBTQ community. She explained that in 2002,[7] *Acahual* "started with a group named UNE [that] looks at LGBTQ issues, *Una Nueva Esperanza* [A New Hope] is its name, that group is with Acahual" (interview, June 3, 2011). Ricardo Rios, who was president of UNE at the time of the interview, was one of the young men who was contacted by the *Acahual* women. "They contacted me, we built connections, they said that they wanted to form an LGBTQ group, it was their idea, that they were going to provide us with documents for preventing [STDs], they would guide us a little. We decided to do it. I met up with other friends of mine, and my *compañeros* accepted [the offer]" (interview, June 8, 2011).

Rios, who was born in 1974, already had some organizing experience when he was contacted by the women from Acahual. "I worked for CEPRESI; from then I was a leader until the present day, [and] we connected, and later I brought a network of my friends to them. . . . I am talking about maybe '95 or '96 in which I was trained with them. Later we met PASMO [Pan American Social Marketing Organization;] we made connections with the Nicaraguan branch of PASMO. They gave us talks; they are the ones who make Live condoms [*condones Vive*]. We had a relationship with them. They gave us talks about LGBTQ issues, STDs, how to use condoms well and such things" (interview, June 8, 2011).

So, with the help of Acahual, Rios and his network of friends formed their own group, UNE. As an established NGO, Acahual had the ability to get grants from foreign donors: in the case of the UNE project, they obtained a grant from an NGO in Spain. Also, having UNE work under the umbrella of Acahual might also have offered some political protection, as Article 204 remained in effect until 2008. On the other hand, as gay men with experience doing HIV-AIDS prevention work, Rios and his friends had experience that the Acahual women did not have.

In short, they were a good team. "We got together with them for workshops. They give workshops to us because there is a small fund which we obtained from them, from . . . [a group] from Spain that is called *Paso*

---

7. In an earlier publication (Kampwirth 2012, 145), I said that *Una Nueva Esperanza* or UNE was founded in 1992. Since that chapter was written I have determined that 2002 is the correct date.

Cooperación . . . an NGO that helps [Acahual] and sometimes it helps us if we ask for money to print up a banner, [or] for snacks for a meeting[;] the women [of Acahual] help us to get support" (Ricardo Rios, interview, June 8, 2011).

Nine years later, the ties between UNE and Acahual remained strong because they shared the goal of preventing sexually transmitted diseases but also because Acahual continued to provide access to some funds from foreign donors (which UNE, as a small organization without legal standing, could not get on its own). Plus UNE sometimes needed space for big meetings, something that Acahual could provide. When the UNE meetings were not too big, activists met in the small living room of Rios's wooden house, decorated in an eclectic mix of gay rights and Catholic themes: images of the Virgin Mary and Pope John Paul II observed the rainbow banners and safe sex posters that shared their space. "Here is our small office: we have a small desk, a typewriter and there you have it. We have not fallen apart, our group continues. . . . There are six of us in the leadership, and forty people belong to the group" (interview, June 8, 2011).

UNE was a success, but it was a group of and for gay men. So along with UNE, the women of *Acahual* promoted a series of other groups, including *Grupo Lésbico Artemisa* (Artemisa Lesbian Group), founded in 2006. Imara Largaespada, born in Managua in 1984 but living in the department of Chinandega at the time of the interview, explained that the women who first joined were all young, mostly eighteen to twenty years old, and most of them lived in the western departments. It was difficult to travel to Managua all the time for events, plus the organized women in the group in Managua tended to be older than the women from the western departments.

> Our priority was to work with young lesbians to promote LGBTQ and reproductive rights from a lesbian perspective. . . . We are working on issues that are important in the western part of the country, which are violence [and] discrimination, and today we have overcome a lot. And we have experienced discrimination in a different way, because when we began the group, discrimination was a problem in our own homes, and today we are fighting against political actions. When we started, we were four young women; now there are more than 50 of us who are organized in the western part of the country. (Interview, June 7, 2011; *Movimiento Feminista de Nicaragua* 2011)

On the one hand, they felt the need to work as young lesbians in the western departments, without older women from the capital. On the other hand, Largaespada recognized the critical support they had received from the larger feminist movement.

For about the past year, we have received financial help from the Central American Women's Fund. . . . Before we [tried to] work with our own funds, but we did not have sufficient funds to carry out our empowerment work, workshops, trainings, talks; and now the Fund helps us so we have covered various issues: about lesbian maternity, about sexual and reproductive rights of lesbians, HIV-ADS in lesbians, lesbian empowerment and leadership. Additionally, we are in contact with other allied groups in Managua like SAFO Group, MOVFEMD, which is the Feminist Movement, the IDSDH, and there are some LGBTQ groups of lesbians in Boaco that is called Young Bisexual Women, which works on bisexual identity, and today we receive help from the FED, the Fund for Equity and Development. The FED, which supports us . . . in one-time activities, and we have already done two forums that were organized just by lesbians and 100 lesbians met in an auditorium here in Managua. . . . The speaker was María Teresa Blandón from *La Corriente*— she was the speaker and she helped facilitate [the forum]. *Artemisa* works on lesbian empowerment and fulfillment and also on political action. (Interview, June 7, 2011)

Those political actions included a paid announcement that ran in *El Nuevo Diario* on May 17, 2011 (less than a month before the interview), which Artemisa ran in conjunction with other groups called "Lesbian Manifesto," a similar announcement that they published in the newspapers and presented to the FSLN in 2010, and their regular participation in LGBTQ protests and celebrations, including a lesbian-only march organized by *Artemisa* along with other groups. Cristina Arévalo from *La Corriente* noted, "What they did was really wonderful because lesbians tend to disappear within the LGBTQ community. Gay men are almost always there; they are the ones who take the lead in the marches; they are the ones who are present in the demonstrations. The lesbians disappear, and the trans put on the show" (interview, June 9, 2011).

So even though *Artemisa* largely broke with Acahual as it turned to focus on the western departments, it continued to be supported by a number of other feminist organizations. In the credits to a video produced by the group in 2013, the women of *Artemisa* acknowledged the support of the feminist organizations *La Corriente* and *Puntos*, the Central American Women's Fund, along with the international NGOs FED/HIVOS, Doctors of the World/Chinandega and TRUST Fund, and the technical help from RDS, an NGO that counted LGBTQ rights among its central programs (Artemisa 2013). Largaespada emphasized that the women of *Artemisa* identified simultaneously with the LGBTQ and feminist movements.

When *Artemisa* broke from the Managua-based group, the lesbians who stayed in Managua changed their name to *Movimiento Feminista por la Diversidad* (Feminist Movement for [Sexual] Diversity, or MOVFEMD)[8] in 2007. MOVFEMD retained its close ties to *Acahual*, among other things, holding some meetings in the *Acahual* building. For instance, María Elena Bonilla noted that just days before the interview, on "Saturday we did a lovely workshop on identity, and it went very well. We have also had leadership workshops for ourselves, to recognize and know how to be a leader" (interview, June 3, 2011). Karina Porras, who was the president of MOVFEMD, said that about fifty young women volunteered with the organization in the cities of León, Masaya, Matagalpa, and Managua. As Porras states, the work involved

> holistic support for all members: psychological, medical, and legal. We provide support and medicine, we have an agreement . . . with the public health center, because we have seen that there are a lot of needs . . . because when we lesbians go to have a PAP smear in a private clinic, sometimes the doctor thinks one is heterosexual or something like a sex worker, they don't even ask what your sexual orientation is. . . . Before that happens I say that I am LGBTQ so that they treat me a bit differently. They are very rough; when it is time for the exam they just arrive and boom, it is very painful. That is a demand that we have, that we should have a holistic clinic for lesbians in Nicaragua. (Interview, June 3, 2011)

While self-help activities were important, MOVFEMD was also a political actor: lobbying, demonstrating, and participating in social events in favor of abortion rights, the recognition of all families, and civil rights for all Nica-

---

8. The acronym MOVFEMD appeared in many lists of organizations as MOFEM. The two acronyms referred to the same organization.

raguans, especially those belonging to the LGBT community (CCEN 2014). For instance, on May 17, 2011, two weeks before our interview, they had marched from the *Parque las Madres* (Mothers Park) to the governmental *Procuraduría de los Derechos Humanos* (Human Rights Office) along with representatives from several other groups (IDSDH, ADESENIC, RDS, and *Camenas Trans*), demanding that gay conversion clinics be closed. They demanded "that clinics that kill should not be acceptable; instead of supporting them they should take away their licenses. We had many demands; we made many demands in that document" (Karina Porras, interview, June 3, 2011; also, María Elena Bonilla, interview, June 3, 2011).

Finally, along with the gay health group UNE, and the lesbian rights groups ARTEMISA and MOVFEMD, the women's NGO *Acahual* was involved in the creation of two other groups. According to María Elena Bonilla, "Before MOVFEMD came into being, we also founded another group that emerged out of UNE. *Camenas Trans* (Trans Goddesses) was founded [as] a trans group. Also out of UNE, two years ago the *Movimiento Trans Gay de Managua* [Trans Gay Movement of Managua] was founded. All of these groups were created after the foundation of UNE. . . . That does not mean that we at Acahual separated ourselves from them, rather Acahual supported their initiatives; we are always supporting them, so that they do not feel alone. We are always right by their sides in their struggle, the building is here, the space; they can come to do their workshops here" (interview, June 3, 2011).

Trans Goddesses was founded in about 2005. Paholy Alvarado, who was the general coordinator of the organization at the time of the interview, was born in August 1982, in the Acahualinca neighborhood, explaining that she still lived very close to the office of the Acahual women's center. But even though she already had some political experience—first attending a protest against Article 204 at age fifteen and later doing popular education with CEPRESI—she hesitated to join the new group that Acahual was organizing. "They called various young women from the LGBTQ community. I was not interested in working with any group, my position was that I only wanted to be autonomous." But María Elena Bonilla convinced her. It helped that she already knew Alvarado who had been "an LGBTQ beauty queen" (Paholy Alvarado, interview, November 30, 2012).

My first time participating was in 2000. I was Miss Top Model. I participated in a beauty contest, [and] at that time it was called a gay [contest;]

we were not trans. [It was] very well known as a gay group, Miss Gay Top Model. . . . Now I am the Producer of the beauty contest that was founded through Acahual. . . . It is called Miss Managua, the queen of Managua, Miss Managua Trans, [and] it has been going on for six years now. I am the General Producer of the pageant, and the coordinator of the group. (Interview, November 30, 2012)

Alvarado identified *Miss Managua Trans* as a separate organization, though it could also be seen as one of the cultural activities carried out by *Camenas Trans*, as the two groups seemed to be different aspects of one organization: both directed by Alvarado and sharing a Facebook page (under the name *Camenas Trans*). *Miss Managua Trans* contests were held at least every year, often in bars, though, on August 18, 2012, the contest was held in the Ministry of Culture thanks to the Minister of Culture Luis Morales Alonso, who Alvarado described as "a friend of the diversity community."

In addition to promoting cultural events, *Camenas Trans* did a lot of political work. Like UNE and MOVFEMD, it remained economically dependent upon *Acahual*, because it had no independent source of funding. "Right now, we do not have funds. We struggle with whatever help the Women's House [Acahual] is able to give to us; we are hanging on by our fingernails." So the *Acahual* office was their office: "We have use of the auditorium. We have it right now, whenever possible, [and] they offer HIV workshops; they provide check-ups without charging anything at all, [and] they help us with part of the costs of medicine, but we don't have any funds of our own. We have projects but we haven't applied for funds [and cannot apply, because we do not have legal standing]" (interview, November 30, 2012). Despite their own economic limitations as individuals (Alvarado earned a living by cutting hair, a skill she learned at Acahual) and as an organization, the twenty-four members (twelve of whom were very active) of *Camenas Trans* were genuinely involved.

We participate in demonstrations; we organize marches; we offer workshops; we do focus groups; we work on HIV/AIDS prevention, on STDs and other sorts of illnesses; we support the community—we don't just work for ourselves, nor just for the LGBTQ community, [rather] we support the whole community. We promote and defend the human rights of the LGBTQ community, and not just that. We also support people, children, young peo-

ple, older women, especially women since, as the coordinator of Trans Goddesses we provide psychological attention to women who are victims of sexist and patriarchal violence. We help the community; we go to the *Chureca*
[garbage dump] to do workshops, give advice. Within our group six of us
are HIV prevention counselors. If we are invited to a fair, we put up a stand
[and] Trans Goddesses along with Acahual give out condoms, lubricants.
(Interview, November 30, 2012)

Alvarado emphasized that their work mainly took place in the streets, for
that was where their people could be found, noting that *Camenas Trans* was
becoming known outside of Managua and internationally. "Tomorrow I have
to travel to the city of León. I will be going to a beauty contest and at the same
time [we in the] the contest we will promote prevention. . . . We were at the
National Gathering for Public Health that took place at the Crowne Plaza Hotel near the end of October. I was a presenter, speaking about Central American countries and to the general population about what is sexual diversity,
[sharing] that there are more than gays and lesbians . . . because even today
the general public thinks that trans women are [the same as] gay guys, so we
were explaining about transgender issues" (interview, November 30, 2012).

The final group that was founded (indirectly) by the *Acahual* Women's
Association, was "*Movimiento Trans Gay de Managua*" (Trans Gay Movement of Managua, or MTGM). Founded in 2006 by several gay men and
trans women who had participated in UNE, they had no formal office at the
time of the interview, so the interview was to be, apparently, at the house of
Trans Gay of Managua president Franklin González. Following the directions, it took a long time to find González: though the neighbors all knew
him, nobody was sure where he was. The confusion, as it turned out, was
that we were to meet at a lumberyard, which was the informal office of *Trans
Gay de Managua*. Complete with a stage in the corner, the partially shaded
lumberyard was a pleasant place to meet, except for the loud power saws.

González, born in 1988, explained that he was an accidental activist. He
had never belonged to a group before *Trans Gay de Managua*, and he had
not sought out a leadership position.

I did not used to be the coordinator, that was another person called Pedro
Pablo Orochena. He was involved in another group that was called [UNE]. . . .
They had some quarrels, arguments, problems [so] Pedro left and decided

to meet with another person who is called Alberto Mayorga [who is] a gay guy and [with] a trans who is named Rachel Frixiones. They formed a little group, Trans/Gay Movement, [and] later on Rachel . . . left and joined ANIT, [and] now she is in ANIT. Alberto Mayorga is not in the group either; he is in another one . . . called Two Generations [*Dos Generaciones*]. Pedro stayed and one day he spoke to me, he said we were in a meeting, before I was timid, he spoke to me and asked if I wanted to belong to the group. I told him yes, no problem, I would like to. I knew that he was the coordinator, and they put me in that job. . . . Pedro is no longer in the country, and he left me in charge of the group. [Now] I am the coordinator of the group, he is in the United States. (Interview, November 29, 2012)

Like Trans Goddesses, Trans Gay Movement's main activities were a combination of drag shows, HIV-AIDS prevention, and political protest. "46 people belong to our group including trans people, gay guys and men who have sex with men. For the past six years we have been defending our human rights by preventing HIV and STDs; we have hosted events every year, including last October when we hosted an event called 'Queen of the Gay Night'—something that we do every year so that people become more sensitive and so they understand that we are equal within society." He explained that just about every neighborhood has groups like theirs that put on shows, "gay guys who put on drag shows to compete amongst themselves, and we give out a prize." They were fortunate to have the use of the lumberyard with its stage: "it belongs to a friend of ours. His name is don Víctor; he is easy going and he always supports us" (interview, November 29, 2012).

A Growing Movement: 1992–2006

In 1993, Lupita Sequeira and Javier Berríos visited cities and small towns in fourteen departments in the western and central regions of Nicaragua, for what to my knowledge was the first study written by Nicaraguans on Nicaragua's LGBTQ community. They were on the lookout for gay and lesbian rights groups and found some in the departments of Managua and Chinandega (Sequeira Malespín and Berríos Cruz 1993, 7–8, 12–17). They also found people who had participated in support groups and safe sex workshops offered by the Managua-based NGOs CISAS and *Nimehuatzin*. But even though they did not find organized groups in most departments, they found that gay and lesbian (and sometimes trans) people were present everywhere, holding jobs such as waiting tables in restaurants and bars, selling food in the market, cutting hair, teaching, or working in health care. In their pioneering study, they drew a map of key social groups and meeting spaces, naming the specific parks, bars, restaurants, and annual festivals where members of the LGBTQ community gathered.

In 1993, there clearly was an LGBTQ community in Nicaragua, even in many of its smallest towns. But just as clearly, it was hard to convert community into a social movement due to fear of the antisodomy law Article 204, as well as long-term problems of poverty and homophobia. Sequeira and Berríos's study, funded by a Dutch solidarity group, was informed by activist goals, and they offered to provide their informants with written information and contacts to help them create organizations, but they often had a hard time getting people to accept their offer. A comment on their visit to Jinotepe reflected the tone of many interactions: "There was a lot of interest in receiving informative documents related to lesbian-gay issues, though there was not much enthusiasm about doing anything" (1993, 18). Nonetheless, some expressed interest in mutual support groups, and a number liked the idea of gay economic collectives such as a chicken farm in Juigalpa, or a tailoring shop in Somoto (1993, 27, 32).

In the final pages of their study, Sequeira and Berríos described five organizations, sometimes with biographies of the organizations' leaders, along with proposals for projects that their members hoped to carry out as well as budgets for those projects, with the hope that one of the readers of the study would be able to help. Of the five organizations, only one, the Metropolitan Church of the Community in Nicaragua (discussed previously) was not brand-new. The second organization, Managua-based Neconi, founded by Lupita Sequeira, Javier Berríos, and Patricia Cuadra in June 1993, had quite an ambitious agenda, perhaps because, though the organization was new, none of the founders were new to grassroots politics: all three had been active in Sandinista activities in the 1980s. Additionally, Berríos had participated in Initial Group and CEP-SIDA. They proposed to buy a house and materials to permit them to reach out to the LGBTQ community nationwide:

> We will work to form Mutual Support Groups in the places that request them. . . . We will promote a systematic and planned education focusing on the following issues: Lesbian-Homosexual Identity, Human Sexuality (in-

cluding sexual health), Gender and Human Rights. To accomplish this, we will need the support of some human and media resources which we will put together in the future: * A team to carry out gay socio-economic research * A lawyer * A psychoanalyst * A theater group * A library * An audiovisual team * Pamphlets * A magazine * A radio program (Sequeira Malespín and Berríos Cruz 1993, 43; *La Boletina* 1994).

Neconi was only to last two or three years. Nonetheless, during those years, they were willing to dream big.

Three other brand-new organizations—Grupo *"Liberación"* ("Liberation" Group) of Jinotega, *Proyecto Lésbico Homosexual "Renovación"* ("Renovation" Lesbian Homosexual Project) of Estelí, and *Colectivo Homosexual "Sol Naciente"* ("Rising Sun" Homosexual Collective) of Juigalpa—were described in the final pages of the study (1993, 58–66). Although the overviews of those three organizations did not offer founding dates, it is reasonable to think that they were new in 1993, given that the organizations were not mentioned earlier in the study. In fact, it seems likely that they were inspired to form a formal group and to propose a project and a budget (either renting a space or constructing a room) by Sequeira and Berríos themselves. As the author of the description of Renovation said: "It is important to note that the visit of the Neconi collective to our region has inspired our social group to think about our just demands, [and] the struggle for Lesbian-Homosexual dignity" (1993, 62). I do not know if Liberation of Jinotega, Rising Sun of Juigalpa, or Renovation of Estelí continued to offer emotional support and political work after 1993. But their very existence, even if it was brief, spoke to the failure of Article 204 to put an end to the emerging gay and lesbian movement.

CEPRESI

Some gay and lesbian rights groups that were founded in the early 1990s were far from ephemeral. I already mentioned the Foundations *Nimehuatzin* (founded in 1990) and *Xochiquetzal* (founded in 1991). Both still exist as of this writing. Norman Gutiérrez, who was a member of Initial Group and CEP-SIDA, explained that many early activists participated in all these organizations, plus the organization he founded: CEPRESI (*Centro para la Educación y Prevención de SIDA*, or Center for Education and Prevention of AIDS).

At the time of the electoral loss is when the *Nimehuatzin* Foundation was created with Rita [Aráuz]. . . . I began to work with *Nimehuatzin* in 1990, near the end of 1990. Later I was the coordinator of CEP-SIDA, between late 1990 and 1991. I was coordinating the CEP-SIDA collective and then there was an impasse, because in 1992 *Nimehuatzin* had to close [temporarily] . . . due to budget problems. . . . Since *Nimehuatzin* was gone at that time we looked into creating another group, and new ones emerged like the Metropolitan Community Church . . . also Lupita [Sequeira]'s group Neconi, the group SHOMOS . . . *Grupo de Educadores en la Lucha contra el SIDA*, GESIDA [Group of Educators against AIDS], and the Xochiquetzal Foundation. . . . The group SHOMOS was always bringing together the other small groups, but there arrived a moment when each group preferred autonomy. At that time the lesbians had their own issues and demands, and they came together in the *Xochiquetzal* Foundation. Some of the gay men came together in our group which was formally founded on the 19th of May of 1993, which today is known as CEPRESI. We have been around for 18 years. (Interview, June 8, 2011)

During those early years, the members of CEPRESI did grassroots HIV/ AIDS education, participated in campaigns to eliminate Article 204, and sought outside help to pay for an office and other projects. In 1999, the Dutch NGO HIVOS gave them a grant that permitted them to purchase a spacious building in Managua.

By 2011, CEPRESI had five offices and forty employees nationwide. Additionally, about two hundred people did volunteer work with the gay population, and they gave presentations to adolescents on reproductive health with adolescents, in the public schools. CEPRESI also continued to participate in various political campaigns: against homophobia, Article 204, and the total ban on abortion (even to save the life of the woman), which was passed by the National Assembly in 2006 (interview, June 8, 2011).

RDS

Like most of the groups I have discussed, the *Red de Desarrollo Sostenible* (Network for Sustainable Development, or RDS) traced its roots to the political changes of the early 1990s, but it arrived at LGBTQ rights activism very differently from those other organizations. José Ignacio López Silva, coordinator of the RDS at the time of the interview, explained that he became an LGBTQ activist through a circuitous route. H explained that he was born in 1968, in Managua

> within a poor family that had a long history of community work regarding health, because my grandmother was a nurse's assistant and my mother also worked as a nurse from the age of 18. I mention that because it explains a lot about social activism and some of the values that informed the activism. Also, on my paternal side . . . my father was a community activist. My grand-mother, my father's mother, was a messenger in the times of the revolution, before the revolution, during the Somoza dictatorship. She was a historic collaborator of the Sandinista Front. That made a big impression, that [and the fact that] in the decade of the 1980s my family had been very involved in volunteer [and] party activism in Managua in the area where we lived. (Interview, December 7, 2012)

López Silva's family was Catholic, but as the local Baptist school was a good school, various generations of his family, going back to his grandmother, had studied there.

Studying at the Baptist school during the revolution was complicated. School officials were obliged to let the Sandinista Youth organize within the school, as "a way to keep control." In 1983 or 1984,

> a movement emerged in reaction to that, within the school, and I was part of that movement. I ended up promoting my candidacy as student presi-dent of the school, explicitly against the platform of the Sandinista Youth. That happened also because . . . my school was attacked a couple of times. A crowd of 700, 800 young people from the Sandinista Youth arrived that made the Sandinista Youth students from the school go out and help them. Rocks rained down upon those of us who were inside. I used the school bus, and when we tried to leave with the school bus, they broke the windows of the bus, attacking it with sticks [and] pipes. They entered the bus to look for people, because they knew who they were looking for. . . . It was terrifying. (Interview, December 7, 2012)

Similar things happened at about the same time to students at other schools, "at *La Salle Pedagógico*, at *la Asunción, Pureza de María*, all of those private schools, at [López Silva's] school [they] were attacked that way two or three times" (interview, December 7, 2012).

The strategy ended up backfiring, not surprisingly. The Sandinista Youth tried to pressure private school students to participate in health and coffee harvesting campaigns and to identify boys who had reached the age for military service, but considering these aggressive tactics almost none of his fellow students volunteered to participate in any Sandinista activities. So the Sandinista Youth gave up and stopped pressuring people, creating relative peace at the school.

Of course, military service was still obligatory. By the age of seventeen, López Silva had been called up twice, but they never took him.

> I was not taken either of the two times, because I was always small, thin, [and] I never looked my age, and also, I was color-blind. In the woods a color-blind person can't defend himself. Color-blind people confuse greens and reds [like] camouflage . . . and at night [color-blind people] lose depth perception, vision. For all those reasons they never took me for military service. (Interview, December 7, 2012)

It was good not to have to fight in the Contra War, of course, but it had its downside. Without proof of military service young men could not enroll in college, and it was extremely hard for them to get work. One day, with nothing else to do, he accompanied a friend who was applying for a scholarship to study in the Soviet Union. To his surprise, he won a scholarship, and in 1986 he left for what would be six years in the Soviet Union.

Those were years of great changes. He learned to speak Russian fluently, received a college degree in oceanography, came to accept himself as gay, and had long-term boyfriends. Ironically, given his earlier experiences, he joined the Sandinista Youth (which was obligatory) and was elected to a leadership position in the youth group. During that time the Soviets tried to control foreign students in general, and the Sandinistas tried to control Nicaraguan students in particular. But neither the Soviets nor the Sandinistas could control everybody all the time, and there were many enchanting aspects to being a foreign student.

> Odessa, the place where I lived, was a port city. It was marvelous. It was even founded by the Romans; it was a mix of things, that city Odessa. It also

had a lot of culture, because it was the place where, in the times of the tsars, where they sent poets, writers, politicians, people from the upper classes, into exile. It is a very pretty city in terms of architecture, culture, it remains dynamic. . . . In 1991, I met a Cuban, that was the one with whom I had the most serious relationship. He also lived in Moscow. In 1991, I went to Nicaragua for vacation for a month. When I returned, I stayed in Moscow a while, and I had found my place. It was a different atmosphere . . . more relaxed. There were gay discos in Moscow . . . rather, there were gay parties, [not] discos. They rented theaters—the foreigners who lived there did those sort of things. . . . There was even a newspaper, a gay newspaper, about places where one could meet-up, with stories, and one already knew which were the meeting places, near the theater and the ballet, the town square, the park of peace, in the museum [*exposición permanente*] on the inventions and ac-complishments of the Soviet Union. There were a ton of places in Moscow, [and] life was structured, organized. . . . I saw life differently. They lived freely, . . . parties, cultural events, but in a really opulent [and] interesting way. That was where I opened my eyes. I thought that there could be something like that in Nicaragua. (Interview, December 7, 2012)

Best of all, after completing his bachelor's degree he was offered a partial schol-arship to study for a doctorate in oceanography in Russia. So, he returned to Nicaragua in 1992 to get money to cover the remaining costs of graduate school. That was when his plans ended abruptly. "I began collecting money at home, and the house was burglarized. They stole everything I had, all the money. I lost my chance to return [to Russia]" (interview, December 7, 2012).

It was not easy to live in Nicaragua in 1992. That was the year when Ar-ticle 204 was signed by President Chamorro. Additionally, the state's neo-liberal policies created a lot of unemployment, and there was tremendous discrimination against people with degrees from the Soviet Union or any socialist country. Of course, that discrimination was political (assuming that those who had studied in a socialist country were Sandinista supporters), but it also had a class content as people who studied in socialist countries usually were from working-class or lower-middle-class backgrounds.

Unable to find work, López Silva went to Costa Rica in 1993, but that did not go too well either. By 1994, he was back home in Managua. "I was depressed for about six months. I didn't leave my room. My Mom said why don't you go out and do this or that. Then she saw an announcement looking for young environmental volunteers, and that is what rescued me from my depression. My Mom made a great effort, and she gave me bus fare, lunch, so that I could participate in the activities of that environmental youth group" (interview, December 7, 2012).

Jovenes Ambientalistas (Environmentalist Youth, or JA!) was a somewhat radical group along the lines of Greenpeace, whose members did things like chaining themselves to the entrances of oil refineries to protect sources of drinking water, planting trees, and moving turtles (Morales 2015). JA! gave López Silva a reason to leave his room, and his depression ended. Within a year he had been chosen to help found the RDS, originally a project of the United Nations Development Program (UNDP). In the RDS, his academic training and his organizing experience came together.

Founded in 1994 or 1995, the RDS had an ecological focus but a broad understanding of sustainable development. In 1998, RDS members participated in workshops (provided by the *Nimehuatzin* Foundation) on HIV-AIDS prevention and what were then called "sexual preferences." Those workshops had a big impact, and so they put respect for sexual preference into the by-laws of the RDS. Beginning in 2006, LGBTQ rights were one of the RDS's major goals (Juan Carlos Martínez, Facebook Messenger, June 19, 2015).

José Ignacio López Silva served as general coordinator of the RDS for about a decade, stepping down in 2014 and becoming president of the board of directors. At that point, Juan Carlos Martínez became the new general coordinator of the RDS, which had its office in Managua. From that office five employees, six volunteers, and the five members of the board of directors also worked in Boaco, the Autonomous Regions of the South and North Caribbean Coast, Chontales, León, and Chinandega (Juan Carlos Martínez, Facebook Messenger, June 19, 2015). By 2015 the RDS had evolved into an NGO (despite the word "network" in its name), which worked on a series of interrelated issues: promotion of cultural identity among Indigenous groups, promotion of human rights, training of community communicators, training in audio and video, youth participation, audio production, and information services (RDS 2015a, 2015b). It continued to work in all these areas, but eventually it focused on LGBTQ rights (Facebook page and YouTube page of RDS Nicaragua, both consulted June 19, 2015; Comunidad Homosexual de Nicaragua 2014).

AMGLIM and ADESENI

The *Asociación Movimiento Gay Lésbico Trans Inter Municipal* (Gay Lesbian Trans Intermunicipal Association Movement, or AMGLIM) was founded in 1998, the first group, to my knowledge, that openly advocated for trans rights. According to its president, Marlene Vivas, it originally had thirty-five members who worked within "the municipalities of Mateares, Nagarote, La Paz Centro and Ciudad Sandino. Why these four municipalities? Because they were places where there was a lot of discrimination and social-cultural exclusion in the areas of education and health" (interview, June 4, 2011).

Marlene Vivas was born in January 1981, and she was only seventeen years old when AMGLIM was founded. She was a small child during the days of Initial Group and CEP-SIDA and was also too young to have participated in the early protests against Article 204. So it is not surprising that she had not participated in politics prior to the founding of AMGLIM. Nonetheless, AMGLIM did not emerge by itself. From the beginning it was supported by a broad network of organizations that promoted women's rights, LGBTQ rights, and human rights, including *Puntos de Encuentro, Xochiquetzal*, CEPRESI, *Nimehuatzin*, CEPS (*Centro de Estudios y Promoción Social*), and the Movement of Autonomous Women. As Vivas noted,

> [all these groups are] our allies, among other organizations here in Nicaragua, [the human rights organization] CENIDH also. They started to offer workshops on our rights as people, as citizens who contribute to the development of this country. I became empowered. I was the one who recruited new people in 1998 and '99. In 2005 AMGLIM had 76 members. We continued to grow over the years . . . so that in 2007, we came to receive funds from the Dutch Embassy, from Christian Aid, which is from Norway, [from] the UNDP; [also if] you know the Central American Women's Fund, FCAM, they helped us. I was talking to them, and FCAM was the [first] one that believed in us, that gave us opportunities. (Interview, June 4, 2011)

Of all the organizations that played an important role in making AMGLIM possible, Vivas singled out the Fondo Centroamericano de Mujeres (Central American Women's Fund, or FCAM), and she was not alone. Many activists in groups of trans women, lesbians, or bisexual women identified FCAM's help as critical, since FCAM prioritized grants to new organizations of in-experienced young women (people who usually have a hard time getting funding), and it then provided guidance in budgeting and in raising funds from other sources (interview, June 4, 2011).

In 2006 AMGLIM broke into two groups. Those who kept the name, AMGLIM, continued to advocate for gay, lesbian, and trans rights. Speaking at an International Women's Day demonstration in 2010, Rubi Paiz Linarte, vice president of AMGLIM, told a reporter that the organization "counts 2,000 transgender people among its affiliates at a national level" (*El Nuevo Diario* 2010). The offshoot of AMGLIM took a new name: *Asociación por los Derechos de la Diversidad Sexual Nicaragüense* (Association for the Rights of Sexually Diverse Nicaraguans, or ADESENI). Under the new name it sought legal standing (*personería jurídica*), something that would permit ADESENI to fundraise as an independent NGO.

The process of getting legal standing is often quite drawn out, and some have suggested that it is political. Arguably it is easier for a conservative or-ganization, such as an evangelical church, to get legal standing, than it is for a trans-rights organization. The fact that ADESENI spent several years trying to get recognized suggests that is true, but eventually, in 2009, it was granted legal standing, a decade after its founding (as AMGLIM) and without having to disguise its identity too much.

Unlike AMGLIM, ADESENI's name did not explicitly include the word "trans," but rather the somewhat more generic term *sexual diversity*. More-over, in the paperwork for requesting legal standing, the ADESENI officers who were trans had to use their birth names, rather than the names that reflected the gender with which they identified, undercutting the logic of the new group, which sought to promote the right of all Nicaraguans to choose their gender identities. Nonetheless, the sort of work that ADESENI proposed to do should have been obvious. A December 11, 2007, letter to René Núñez Téllez, the president of the National Assembly, explained that ADESENI's goals included:

1. Working to improve the quality of life and human rights with a focus on universal access to prevention of, and treatments for, HIV-AIDS.
2. Supporting training in issues like violence, gender, sexual and reproduc-tive health.
3. Promoting the insertion of the population in education and work.

4. Promoting a framework of respect and tolerance of the human rights of the LGBTQ population.

5. Promoting and strengthening cooperative ties at a national, regional, and superregional level in the areas of gender, violence, HIV-AIDS, sexual health, and reproductive health (Asamblea Nacional 2007–09).

In 2010, the members of ADESENI wrote, "It is extraordinary that we are the first NGO with legal standing in all of Nicaragua that is directed by TRANS people. [W]hen this change happened going from being a group that forms a movement to being an NGO, it was a great step, as though we had jumped across a ditch, a chasm with no bridge; now they cannot knock us around [*bolear*] legally, the way they knocked us around before, because we are legally speaking as an NGO" (ADESENI 2010, 51).

After legal recognition in 2009, ADESENI continued to grow. Marlene Vivas estimated that, by late 2013, three hundred people belonged to ADESENI, and the organization had grown in terms of the territory in which it worked, and it had received some very large grants as well. It was able to do this in part due to legal recognition, in part because powerful international interests were looking for local partners to work on HIV/AIDS and LGBTQ rights work. "In 2012 the embassy of the United States . . . and the current government of Obama, started a new program for the issue of LGBT rights and gender violence, not just in Nicaragua but rather . . . worldwide. As a sexual diversity organization, ADESENI is the counterpart of the new program of USAID in HIV-AIDS prevention combined with the issue of citizen participation and democracy" (interview, December 9, 2013).

In addition to preventative health care, ADESENI's work involved training human rights activists and pressuring local governments to protect the rights of the LGBTQ community, especially the rights of trans people. An example that particularly pleased her was a declaration from the government of the city of Mateares (Vivas's hometown) against "discrimination due to sexual orientation and gender identity, which was signed by the Mayor and City Council people [in June 2013]. This is a very big achievement" (interview, December 9, 2013).

A Cell Is Formed

The U.S.-based anthropologist Florence Babb made several trips to Managua in the 1990s and early 2000s, doing research on, among other things, the

evolution of the LGBTQ-rights movement. By the turn of the century, she
found few indicators of a robust movement.

> In contrast to what I found in the early to mid-1990s when a fledgling move-
> ment was celebrated, my revisits to Managua in June 2000 and June 2002
> produced contradictory responses to the question. Whereas some individ-
> uals were still confident that a young movement was in the making, others,
> including some of the pioneers in political groups and NGOs, were reluctant
> to say that any unified social movement could be identified. Instead, they
> asserted, there were activities undertaken by a number of smaller groups
> that addressed issues of concern to lesbians and gay men. Although my trips
> were scheduled to coincide with Gay Pride, I had trouble learning in 2000,
> despite much questioning, what major activities were planned that would
> draw people together as in past years. I finally heard of and attended several
> events . . . but they did not bring out the large crowds that were typical a few
> years earlier. (Babb 2003, 315)

Babb went on to note that there were more Gay Pride activities the next year,
and they were well attended. But in a later article she returned to this theme,
reporting that in response to a 2003 talk on her research, the people who
were present launched into a "lively conversation . . . about whether there is
truly something that can be called a 'movement' in the country" (Babb 2004,
27–28). One could argue that Article 204 was succeeding as planned. It was
not that there was no organizing, but it was never easy, and activists carried
a heavy burden for reasons including the fear of Article 204, the hostility of
the Alemán administration to feminists and their allies, the poverty of most
activists, and the inevitable tensions created by the need to compete for
limited funds from foreign donors.

It was in that context that a cell was formed. In June 2002, a group of equal
numbers of lesbians and gay men[9] came together at the Managua bar Tabú
to plan for the future. Samira Montiel was a participant in one of the lesbian
discussion groups that the *Xochiquetzal* Foundation sponsored over a period
of many years,[10] and it was *Xochiquetzal* that organized the meeting of the

---

9. According to Samira Montiel there were fifteen lesbians and fifteen gay men at the founding of the cell; according to Florence Babb there were thirteen of each (Babb 2003, 316; Samira
Montiel, interview, May 31, 2011).

10. On *Xochiquetzal*'s discussion groups see Howe 2013, 63–74.

cell, inviting approximately thirty people to think about their work as part of a movement, rather than as isolated organizations. There was a

> day-long meeting held at a lesbian-owned bar, Tabú, to form a Managua "cell" that would be a model for other cells and help build a national lesbian and gay movement. Among the principles established were those to endorse lesbian and gay rights, to support other Nicaraguans to "come out," and to move cautiously toward forming alliances at the international level. (Babb 2003, 316)

Samira Montiel identified that meeting as a precursor to the formation of the lesbian rights organization, Safo Group. In terms of creating a broader movement, the cell did not lead to immediate changes, but it laid the groundwork for what would be an explosion of organizing after the 2006 election.

Samira Montiel herself would find her life changed dramatically after 2006 as she was named the first national Special Ombudsperson for Sexual Diversity, a key position within the governmental human rights agency. Many of the people who participated in that meeting played central roles in the transformation of the movement after 2006. As Montiel noted, speaking from her new role as an LGBTQ rights bureaucrat, those people "still keep me busy" (personal communication by Facebook private message, June 23, 2015).

Grupo Safo

Group Safo was founded in February of 2004 by "three lesbians, all of [whom] came from different groups that worked in different NGOs" (Marta Villanueva, interview, June 2, 2011). Marta Villanueva, president at the time of the interview and one of the founding members of Safo Group, explained that they hoped to do something different than the other NGOs.

> We definitely wanted to make ourselves visible as lesbians; from our very beginning, our first objective was to make Nicaraguan lesbians visible. . . . We are the first group to speak out in any place, any space, and say, 'I am Martha,' for instance, 'I belong to the Safo Lesbian Group.' . . . The group does political work, through video groups, film festivals, through discussion groups. [W]e have done demonstrations, [and] we have done marches. (Interview, June 2, 2011)

Samira Montiel, who had participated in Xochiquetzal activities and in the meeting of the gay and lesbian cell in 2002, was another founding member. Like many others who were involved in LGBTQ organizing around the turn of the century, she and her cofounders had some organizing experience, but they had neither money nor fundraising experience. The support of the Central American Women's Fund was critical at the beginning.

> We did not get any funding until 2005, [and] it was very direct through the Central American Women's Fund, with the help of Aníbal Martínez who was with the *Puntos de Encuentro* Foundation. I remember that he called me and said to me: there is a fund for young women; they are going to finance lesbian groups; they are going to finance feminist women. [I said] but look we don't have legal standing, and he said: It does not matter; you do not need it. I remember that Aníbal sent us an email with absolutely everything we needed, and he told me, look they asked me if I knew of a group and I said yes. They asked me for the name of the group, and I told them that the group is called "Safo." From now on you are Safo because that is the name, I said. . . . Later we received our first grant, [and] I remember that it was barely $2,000 [US dollars]. For us that was a large amount of money. (Interview, May 31, 2011)

By 2011, Safo Group had around fifty members, and it worked in Masaya, Estelí, Malpaisillo, and Somotillo in addition to Managua, where it had an office. By 2015, according to its website, the organization (whose slogan was "*doblemente mujer*" [doubly women]) dedicated itself to

> the defense of human rights in society, including women who are housewives, professionals, technical experts, women who are urban and rural and of different ethnic groups. . . . We promote sexual and reproductive rights, lesbian sexual health, family rights. With[in] our main areas of work are psychological and legal support for lesbian mothers and relatives of lesbians, sexual and reproductive health, political work, and prevention of STDs [and] HIV. (Grupo Safo 2015)

Marta Villanueva explained that Safo also sought to represent lesbians and bisexual women at an international level. "Currently we are members of the ILGA, currently we run the lesbian subsecretariat in Central America, which is part of ILGA. It is my responsibility" (interview, June 2, 2011).

Colectivo NAHOMY

NAHOMY CLUB TT&TT (also known as *NAHOMY Club Colectivo Nacional de Homosexuales, Lesbianas Unidos con los Bisexuales, Travesti, Transgénero, Transsexuales y Transformes*, or NAHOMY Collective National Club of Homosexuals, Lesbians, United with Bisexuals, Transvestites, Transgender People, Transexual People, and Those Who Transform) was founded by a group led by Rigoberto Pérez Acuña in 2006 (MSM GF n.d.). In 2006, Pérez Acuña, who was born in May 1970, was not new to activism, or even to LGBTQ activism. As a child and adolescent during the 1980s, he was involved in politics in various senses of that word: "in artistic culture, [and] also during those years [he] participated in the CDS, in the revolutionary vigilance, [and in] neighborhood activities" (interview, December 7, 2015).

Starting in 1985, Pérez Acuña was a professional dancer, participating in the *Grupo Danza Nacional Güegüense* (Güegüense National Dance Group) in the 1980s. "I did not do military service, because the requirement was waived since we were artists, dancers" (interview, December 7, 2015). By the late 1980s, he began to participate in a number of the LGBTQ activities I discussed in chapter 2: he went to parties at the Benjamin Linder House, he marched with the LGBTQ contingent in the July 19, 1989, parade celebrating the tenth anniversary of the Sandinista Revolution, and he was active in the HIV-AIDS education collective CEP-SIDA, continuing to be active when that group was reformulated as the *Fundación Nimehuatzin* in the 1990s.

So NAHOMY Collective grew out of those earlier activities. Pérez Acuña estimated that twenty to twenty-five people participated in NAHOMY Collective, often meeting at the *Nimehuatzin* Foundation, later participating in events sponsored by the trans rights organization ANIT. In addition to promoting rights, they worked on HIV-AIDS prevention with a focus on dance and theater performance (interview, December 7, 2015).

Out in Public

Simultaneously in and out, in public but behind closed doors, much of the organizing during the 204 years took place in that liminal space, not fully in nor out. As one gay man noted, "*Yo no soy closet, ni soy balcón*" (I am neither a closet nor a balcony) (quoted in Babb 2003, 314). In many ways, the *Jorna-*

das de Sexualidad (Sexuality Workshops) were in-between events. Evelyn Flores of *Puntos* explained,

> The first gay and lesbian pride festival was in June 1991, and *Puntos de Encuentro* . . . was one of the organizers along with a bunch of other people. It was a collective of gay men and lesbians with the CISAS collective, [and] there were two or three organizations and some groups that no longer exist. . . . For many years we held the Sexuality without Prejudice Workshops along with *Xochiquetzal* and others at the end of the last week of June . . . to do sensitivity activities, to distribute educational materials or position papers to the mass media. We always had a slogan so that slogan could work into people's heads and reduce the stigma that existed against homosexuals and lesbians, and that happened . . . until . . . 2007 more or less, because after that we broadened into other sexual identities and we had only been working with gays, lesbians, bisexuals, and then the trans began to organize and have a much stronger presence. (Interview, June 6, 2011)

The Sexuality without Prejudice Workshops were very important for the people who attended. But while the events were generally open to the public, and while they received some press coverage, they were also usually held within closed spaces that one had to seek out, and so most members of the public did not see them.

Certainly there were momentary exceptions. For instance, in late June 2001, a group of twenty young men marched toward the National Assembly arguing through their banners and chants that they, like all people, had a right to sexuality and to human rights. They released yellow balloons printed with the slogan "No to Article 204" at the National Assembly, then continued down the main road that slopes toward the lake, stopping at the enormous statue of the unknown soldier, also known ironically as Rambo, a symbol of Sandinista resistance to violent imperialism. The marchers appropriated that symbol for their own resistance, plastering its base with "No to Article 204" stickers (Howe 2013, 94–96).

But that sort of demonstration was unusual. Most events—whether the inclusive Sexuality Free of Prejudices campaign or the more lesbian and gay specific pride events—happened behind closed doors (Howe 2013, 98–116). On June 24, 2005, that changed. Norman Gutiérrez explained that the *Fes-*

tival Cultural por la Diversidad Sexual (Sexual Diversity Cultural Festival), organized by CEPRESI, was innovative, because it was

> the first LGBTQ march in the country. It was very hard because of fear, because Article 204 was in effect, and people were very afraid. I had to travel across the whole country to convince groups that were organized with us that they should participate in the march. Finally, that march was a big success. We started at the Sandino hill of the Monimbó neighborhood in the town of Masaya. . . . There were more than 400 of us—gays, lesbians, transgender people—and . . . we were afraid, first, that people were going to demonstrate against us and, second, that we would not have support from the police. Nonetheless, we completed all the legal requisites to get police protection, [and] the police supported us—they accompanied us during the march. But the most surprising part of that march, and it still is so vivid to me, is how the people exceeded our expectations. The people of Masaya overflowed into the streets to support the march. We started with 400 when we began the march, and when we looked the streets were full of people. . . . There were women carrying children; there were older people. (Interview, June 8, 2011)

The first march, held in Masaya in 2005, was followed by a second in Managua in 2006 (in which approximately eight hundred people participated) and a third in Granada in 2007 (in which more than two thousand people participated). (*La Boletina* 2005, 59; 2006, 81; 2007, 66).

The marches were different from the *Jornadas* that began in 1991, breaking with what Evelyn Flores called the old "collective imaginary."

> It is not just [the same as] taking a position for the media, creating a sticker, rather it is walking in the streets. . . . Obviously, many people passed by the march and applauded us, others whistled at us, others said vulgar things, because they said we were good-for-nothings, whores, degenerates, abnormal, and other people said that [it was] a good thing, [to] keep it up. The truth is that we never had realized that there were so many of us. (Interview, June 6, 2011)

Those marches represented a qualitative change in the movement. It no longer was a gay and lesbian pride movement; instead, it was a movement for gay, lesbian, bisexual, and trans pride, or as it began to be called by the turn of the century, a movement for sexual diversity. It had ceased to be a movement in which intellectuals gave presentations behind closed doors. Rather it had become a movement that took to the streets, with some support from the international solidarity community (*La Boletina* 2006, 81; Mock 2005).

Out in Poetry

Light is a loving relationship
between the object and the eye.
We only see that which we love (Avellán 2002, 24).

FIGURE 4   LGBTQ rights activists participate in the public celebration "Joy of Life" in Managua, 2010. The banner reads: "Sexual Diversity, Cultural Diversity: Cultural Commission LGBTTTI." Courtesy of Bismarck Moraga Peña.

Important collective action took place during the neoliberal years (1990–2006) within organizations, public events, the media, even in the streets. But not all the transformation of those years was collective. Much of it was individual, sometimes with important implications for cultural life. That was certainly true for the work of the prize-winning poet Héctor Avellán. In a commentary that was printed on the jacket of Avellán's collection *Las ciruelas que guardé en la hielera: poemas 1994–1996* (The plums that I saved in the refrigerator: poems 1994–1996), Marco Morelli notes that Avellán "has set himself apart as the first openly gay Nicaraguan poet, in a culture in which there thrives a sexism that is stubborn and intolerant of sexual diversity" (Avellán 2002).[11]

Born in Managua in October 1973, Avellán described his childhood as different from many of his generation, a childhood that was

11. According to the researcher and poet Helena Ramos, the first collection of lesbian poems was written by the screenwriter and poet Erika Castillo, born in 1977. The book, which was entitled *Te desnudas como si estuvieras sola* (You undress as though you were alone) won a prize in the María Teresa Sánchez poetry contest, sponsored by the *Banco Central de Nicaragua* (Central Bank of Nicaragua) in 2014. Castillo is a member of the *Asociación Nicaragüense de Escritoras* (Nicaraguan Women Writers Association, or ANIDE) (personal communication by Facebook Messenger between Victoria González-Rivera and Helena Ramos, January 20, 2021).

very happy, very protected, perhaps a bit too much, due to my mother. . . . [I]t was very peaceful because of my understanding and protective mother. I should say that I never felt that I suffered from discrimination until I realized that some social norms kept me from many things, but before that I never felt discriminated against because of who I was. I always was who I wanted to be. I come from a poor [and] intellectual family, with a lot of appreciation for education. (Interview, December 9, 2013)

Like so many people of his generation, his early years were marked by revolutionary politics; unlike many of those who went on to become LGBTQ activists, his relationship with the revolution was always ambivalent.

I belong to a family that did not support the guerrillas; rather it supported Somoza's government. My father [and] my grandfather had positions in Somoza's army. My family was affiliated with that [political] current like many people. . . . When the revolution came to power, we had to leave the place where we lived. We were not able to leave the country, but our social class changed, [and] we turned to another political color. . . . We had lived in a suburb where the National Guardsmen lived and [so we] had to go to another place in Managua. I think that was my first political experience, at the age of six. I was a child, I remember. . . . Everything that we experienced during the time of the revolution also affected me politically. . . . With respect to my experience as a gay man, one key experience would have been . . . when I began to write and felt the need to speak using the gender words that came naturally to me. If I wanted to write a poem about a love relationship between two men, I felt the need to say so and not to cover up things, not to clean them up; that also is a political experience, because it made me make a decision. (Interview, December 9, 2013)

As far as Avellán could remember, he had always been a poet and always gay. "I did not realize one day that I was gay. I don't think that happens; one is who one is from the beginning." Moreover, he rejected the trope of "coming out" as foreign to Nicaragua. "I think that is due to a foreign influence; it has been influenced a bit by television, by [international] culture." He noted that the *cochón* had existed for centuries. But "the *cochón* does not come out" (*el cochón no se declara*).

Without rejecting the idea of politics, he rejected the idea of collective politics, at least for himself. "I have a very personal position with respect to politics. For me the revolution is a personal thing—it is not a collective thing. For that reason I hardly belong to anything, other than to myself. That is a political position" (interview, December 9, 2013). His work during the 204 years walked this line: highly personal and yet political, advocating for gay rights, and human rights more generally, from an individual perspective.

GOD KILLS PEOPLE WHO ARE ALONE
23 year old man.
Of mixed race, 135 lbs, approximately,
(on a diet due to the orders of the World Bank)
wishes to meet a person
of any age, sex,
race and
nationality.
For a loving relationship
at a prudent distance
Write to HECTORAVELLAN@HOTMAIL.COM
Do not include a photo.
nor a metaphor (Avellán 2002, 60).

A New Initiative

2006 was an electoral year in Nicaragua. Elections are always a time of opportunity and risk as candidates make promises in the hopes of getting their supporters to the polls, demobilizing their opponents, and attracting new voters. Marvin Mayorga was part of a group of gay and lesbian activists who seized the opportunity presented by the electoral year, ultimately deciding that the only way to promote their rights was to participate directly in politics. Their efforts came together in an organization known as the IDSDH or the Initiative, founded in 2006. Mayorga explained,

The idea of the Initiative was born before the 2006 election. . . . The first public activity that we decided to do was to invite the presidential candidates—who never responded—to have a debate with us, but we did get a response from some of the candidates for Congress. We had our first electoral forum in . . . the auditorium of the University of Managua with Mónica Baltodano representing the *Movimiento de Renovación Sandinista* [Movement of Sandinista Renewal or MRS, and], FSLN was not there, Norman Gutiérrez representing the *Partido Alternativa por el Cambio* [Alternative for Change Party, or PAC], which was Edén Pastora's party. . . . At that time, we proposed the need for politicians to talk about human rights, and nobody knew what we meant, because in Nicaragua . . . there is a lot of political clientelism just like elsewhere. They told us at that time, in the forum, that gay and lesbian groups were not very numerous and that we made up five percent of the population. (Interview, June 3, 2011)

The results of the LGBTQ electoral forum were not encouraging. None of the three parties that ended up getting the most votes—the FSLN, ALN (*Alianza Liberal Nicaragüense*, or Liberal Nicaraguan Alliance), and the PLC (*Partido Liberal Constitucionalista*, or Liberal Constitutionalist Party)—sent representatives of any sort.

The candidates at the forum were from two small leftist parties: the PAC and the MRS. The PAC's candidate at the forum, Norman Gutiérrez—a gay-rights activist from the days of Initial Group in the 1980s—attended the electoral forum as an individual citizen, not as a representative of his party. While he ran for the National Assembly, he was also director of the HIV-AIDS prevention organization, CEPRESI, and he ran as an openly gay candidate. He did not win (nor did any of the other candidates from the PAC), but he was a pioneer as the first openly gay candidate for a national office in Nicaraguan history (interview, June 8, 2011; Córdoba 2006).

The MRS was represented at the forum by National Assembly candidates Vidaluz Meneses, Violeta Delgado, Azahálea Solís, and Mónica Baltodano. The MRS, comprised largely of Sandinistas who had broken with the FSLN in 1995, was the party that was most closely identified with the feminist movement, especially with the *Movimiento Autónomo de Mujeres* (Autonomous Women's Movement, or MAM), which was the official sponsor of the forum (Juanita Jiménez, interview, December 4, 2012). Unlike the other parties, the MRS included LGBTQ issues in its platform,[12] and it tried to organize gays and lesbians as part of the campaign.

12. Journalist Sofía Montenegro explained, "The Autonomous Women's Movement made an alliance with the MRS [in June 2006] based upon five programmatic points that involve demands regarding: 1) Secular state and secular public policies, 2) Institutional reform of the state, 3) Social justice, 4) National population policy and 5) Gender democracy. In point 4 it is clear that the demands made by the Movement include leaving the right to therapeutic abortion in the new Penal Code, that will be approved by the National Assembly, as well as the demand to respect sexual diversity and to eliminate the crime of sodomy from the new [Penal] Code" (Montenegro 2006, 1–2).

Juan Carlos Martínez, who at the time worked as an administrator for the feminist organization SI Mujer, explained: "Beginning in 2006 I began to work more directly on the issue of sexual diversity . . . thanks to some feminist *compañeras* who invited various gay men who were committed to working together, [and] to affiliate ourselves with the MRS Alliance that was headed by Herty Lewites. . . . We gay men were called in with the goal of working together, and so our group could make concrete proposals to the MRS, that was our main ally at that time, but the idea was to promote changes and proposals in the platforms of the candidates running in the forthcoming election" (interview, December 6, 2012; also, Bismarck Moraga, interview, June 7, 2011).

While the presence of people from those two parties was a good thing, the party representatives who attended the forum were not encouraging. They made no promises, and they implied (though they did not directly state) that political parties were uninterested in the sexual diversity community, because they believed that LGBTQ Nicaraguans made up a tiny percentage of the population. If they wanted their rights to be addressed, the members of the audience were told, they would have to become better organized, and they would have to increase their visibility. They could not ask for respect on the grounds of human rights, a concept that did not resonate in Nicaragua as well as the idea of social justice. Instead, they would have to "earn" their rights by proving that they were a numerous, and therefore politically valuable, sector of society.

So the people who founded the IDSDH got together to discuss how to make their community more visible. They needed to make it clear that their problems were not just anecdotes, rather, their problems were systematic, facing LGBTQ Nicaraguans across the country and class structure. Following meetings with activists in Managua, Matagalpa, and Estelí in 2006 (IDSDH 2009), they decided that their first tactic would be a national study, to prove that they were everywhere, that LGBTQ issues were not simply a concern of a few middle-class people who lived in the capital. In theory, conducting such a study was a great idea. In practice, it was not going to be easy.

Living in the Shadow of Article 204

The end of the Sandinista Revolution brought real changes to Nicaragua's LGBTQ community. On the one hand, the FSLN's electoral loss in 1990 meant that gay and lesbian Nicaraguans who identified with the revolution often felt cast adrift, the movement that gave meaning to many of their lives battered, though not destroyed. Violeta Barrios de Chamorro's inauguration as president in April 1990 ushered in the age of neoliberalism. That is, it was an age when the state shrunk and the market expanded, an age of major hardships for LGBTQ Nicaraguans who on average were more impoverished, and therefore more dependent on state services, than heterosexual Nicaraguans.

But 1990 also was the beginning of a hopeful period for gays and lesbians. Compared to the Sandinista state, the neoliberal state was simultaneously less interested in providing for the well-being of average Nicaraguans and less interested in controlling their political actions. The relative political freedom of the first two years of the 1990s allowed for the emergence and growth of a number of new organizations that built on the legacy of Initial Group and CEP-SIDA. It was a time when there was a virtual explosion of autonomous feminist organizing, and many of the new gay and lesbian rights organizations benefitted from that cultural shift.

Then, in 1992, the National Assembly passed Article 204, trying to close the brief cultural opening that followed the FSLN's electoral defeat. In the long run, despite the intentions of the supporters of Article 204, the antisodomy law did not silence all speech in favor of the rights of LGBTQ Nicaraguans; it just made the speakers afraid. Nonetheless, many of them continued to speak, worship, organize, protest, and hold parties.

The years between Sandinista President Daniel Ortega's loss in 1990, and his reelection as president in late 2006, were years of cultural change and of political organizing, often with the direct support of feminist organizations. Politics during that period began with a focus on sexual health and ended with a focus on visibility and political rights. During the 204 years, trans Nicaraguans began to organize politically. While in 1990 activists spoke of an incipient gay and lesbian rights movement, by 2006 that movement was broader based and was called the sexual diversity movement. By 2006, when the Daniel Ortega was reelected, ushering in what some called the second Sandinista revolution, the FSLN was very different than it had been in 1990.

CHAPTER FOUR

The Return of Daniel Ortega

In the months leading up to the November 2006 election, the FSLN seemed to reinvent itself, becoming Christian rather than secular, antifeminist rather than feminist, and incorporating LGBTQ people into its coalition rather than rejecting them. On the billboards that sprang up all over Managua, the FSLN's traditional red and black was replaced with an array of brilliant colors, especially hot pink. Daniel Ortega, the Marxist-Leninist in military uniform, was replaced by Daniel the practicing Catholic in a collarless white shirt and jeans. On the billboards, the rhetoric of anti-imperialism and class struggle was replaced with the language of peace and reconciliation. In fact, many historic enemies of the FSLN joined the Sandinistas' electoral coalition, most prominently the vice-presidential candidate and former Contra commander Jaime Morales Carazo.

The FSLN's religious discourse was one of the most striking novelties of the campaign. Speaking about his opponents' campaigns against him, Ortega even compared himself to Jesus Christ.

> They defamed Christ, they slandered him, they whipped him. They put a crown of thorns on Christ and mocked him and, finally, when they were crucifying him, that was when He said: "Forgive them Father for they know not what they do." And these people who are full of bitterness and who carry out those dirty campaigns are the ones we should pardon[,] because they themselves do not realize what damage they are doing in their hearts. (Quoted in González Siles 2006)

The colors, the clothing, the new alliances, and the religious rhetoric of the 2006 campaign signaled that the FSLN had changed from its guerrilla days. Daniel Ortega had also changed, supposedly, and one of the many signs of that change was his marriage to Rosario Murillo in a Catholic ceremony presided over by former Archbishop Miguel Obando y Bravo, a little over a year before the 2006 election (Ríos 2007). By the time of the wedding, they had been together for 27 years, having raised nine children together: six from their marriage, and three from her earlier marriages, whom he later adopted (Medina and González 2016).

During the 2006 campaign, Daniel often remained silent, allowing his long-term companion and new wife—who also headed his electoral campaign—to speak for him. Among other things, she promoted the abolition of therapeutic abortion, the Penal Code's Article 165, a late-nineteenth-century reform that permitted doctors to legally perform abortions in extreme circumstances, as in the case of rape, danger to the pregnant woman's life, or severe damage to the fetus. In condemning therapeutic abortion, Murillo allied herself, and her party, with the Catholic Church. Rosario Murillo explained in an interview on *Radio Ya*,

> Precisely because we have faith, because we have religion; because we are believers, because we love God above all things. . . . For those reasons we also defend, and we agree completely with the Church and the churches that abortion is something that affects women fundamentally, because we never get over the pain and the trauma that an abortion leaves us! When people have had, or have had to resort to that, they never get over it. And this pain is something that we don't want for anyone. . . . The [Sandinista] Front, the Great Nicaragua Unified Triumphs [coalition], says "No to abortion, yes to life!" (Murillo 2006)

And so, Murillo cemented the pact with the Catholic Church in general, and with former Archbishop Obando y Bravo (whom she praised elsewhere in the interview) in particular. Those words represented a real shift in the position of the FSLN, that had not legalized abortion when it was in power but that had never opposed therapeutic abortion (Wessel 1991, 541–44).

Daniel Ortega was elected president in late 2006 with only 38 percent of the vote, thanks to a decade of pact making with the historic leader of the other major political force in the country: Arnoldo Alemán of the PLC. The pact, as it was called (even though it was really a series of agreements worked out over a number of years), was the result of surprising negotiations between historic enemies: Arnoldo Alemán and Daniel Ortega. Through those negotiations, the FSLN and PLC made third party challenges extremely difficult and divided the spoils of government between themselves. Furthermore, the pact helped ensure that Alemán and Ortega would be protected from prosecution for crimes committed while in office, something that was of concern to both of them (Hoyt 2004, 17–42; Lacombe 2010, 100–102).

Among other things, the pact shifted the electoral rules in favor of the FSLN: because of these changes a presidential candidate could win outright with just 40 percent of the vote, avoiding a second round (or even with as little as 35 percent of the vote if the next runner up trailed by at least 5 percent). In exchange for the electoral rules that he wanted, Ortega arranged for former president Alemán's release from prison (where he was serving twenty years for embezzlement) to house arrest, later extended to "arrest" within the borders of the country (Torres-Rivas 2007, 7).

When Ortega was inaugurated as president in January of 2007, the FSLN ended nearly seventeen years in the opposition. Though Sandinistas sometimes called this new period the second Sandinista revolution, or the return of the revolution, in reality much had changed. The Contra War was long over, the old FSLN had broken apart, and new coalitions were formed.

Nobody would have expected the new FSLN and the new Daniel Ortega to be exactly the same as the old ones. But few could have expected the gender paradox that marked the return of the Sandinistas. During the last weeks of the campaign, the FSLN promised to strip many women of civil liberties through the abolition of therapeutic abortion at the same time as it promised to restore some civil liberties to the LGBTQ community by eliminating the antisodomy law Article 204. And it was to keep both promises.

As the Penal Code was revised in 2007, Article 204 was eliminated, and a series of articles (36, 427, 428, and 315) were added, all of which banned discrimination based on sexual orientation in some way (Moraga Peña et al. 2010, 8). After the abolition of 204, LGBTQ groups participated in a long series of workshops with various state agencies (Moraga Peña et al. 2010, 7–79). That sort of consciousness-raising work would not have been possible during the 1980s.

Another indicator of the changes in the relationship between the LGBTQ community and the FSLN was the fact that an LGBTQ group was created within each office of the Sandinista Youth, in both big cities and small towns (Harim Sánchez, interview, June 8, 2011). Moreover, in 2009 the Ortega administration named a Special Ombudsperson for Sexual Diversity within the *Procuraduría para la Defensa de los Derechos Humanos* (Legal Office for the Defense of Human rights or PDDH), the first time that such a thing existed in Central America.

The Special Ombudsperson for Sexual Diversity, Samira Montiel, emphasized that her position was part of the state—not part of the government—which was true (interview, May 31, 2011). Nonetheless, given the difficulties in separating the state and the party that characterized the Sandinista Revolution from 1979 to 1990, and the difficulty in separating the state, the party, and the Ortega-Murillo family that characterized the period from 2007 until this writing (Chaguaceda 2012, 166–69, 173; Martí i Puig 2016, 255), it was hard to believe that any of these changes in the politics of sexuality would have happened without the endorsement of the Ortega-Murillo family.

Gender Paradoxes and the FSLN

When scholars, journalists, and political activists wrote about the abolition of therapeutic abortion, just two weeks before the November 2006 election, they always noted that the ban was a way for FSLN to get the support of the Catholic Church and the evangelical churches (e.g., Aizenman 2006; Human Rights Watch 2007; Reuterswärd et al. 2011, 820–22). That argument was true up to a point, but it did not do a great job of explaining what happened.

At most, painting the party with a veneer of religiosity, and voting to ban therapeutic abortion, might have helped neutralize the power of the Catholic Church (which had campaigned against the FSLN in the past). But that strategy did not help the FSLN to win new votes. Analysts from the journal *Envío* argued that the FSLN "won without growing." In other words, it won thanks to its traditional base of support, and would have lost if not for the fact that the electoral rules had been changed by the pact between Daniel Ortega and Arnoldo Alemán. Even with electoral rules that highly favored the FSLN, the party would have lost had the Right not been divided into two parties. "Ortega won [in 2006] with 38% of the vote. In the three earlier elections he got similar or higher percentages: in 1990, against Violeta de Chamorro, 41%; in 1996, against Arnoldo Alemán, 38%; and in 2001, against Enrique Bolaños, 42%" (*Envío* 2006, 4).

So why did the FSLN turn its back on its traditional allies in the women's movement by supporting the total ban on abortion—with no exceptions even to save a woman's life—at the same time as sought to incorporate LGBTQ people into the new Sandinista coalition? I will argue that there are two reasons that better explain what happened in 2006—one which can be generalized to much of Latin America; one which requires that I consider the story of Ortega's stepdaughter Zoilamérica.

The first explanation for why the Sandinistas reversed their historic commitment to therapeutic abortion rights draws on Jocelyn Viterna's work on El Salvador. Noting that the first decade of the twenty-first century in Latin America was marked by a dramatic swing to the electoral left—including the election of former guerrillas to the presidency in El Salvador, Brazil, Uruguay, and Nicaragua—Viterna first asked a common question regarding this trend, and then a very uncommon question. "Does the rise of the Left promote women's equality? Or in contrast, could women's continued subordination be an important factor promoting the rise of the Left?" (2012, 248).

Viterna contested the common assumption that leftist parties, with their rhetoric of social justice and equality, necessarily promote gender equality once in power. Instead, she argued that the electoral success of El Salvador's FMLN rested in part on its role in the ban on therapeutic abortion. By withdrawing its opposition to the ban (which then passed) in 1999, and by not restoring therapeutic abortion rights despite controlling the presidency between 2009 and 2019, the FMLN moderated its radical guerrilla image and made itself an electorally viable party, at the cost of the lives and freedom of many Salvadoran women.

> This transformation appears critical to the solidification of the party's image as political mainstream rather than radical fringe. Similarly, in Nicaragua, Daniel Ortega's return to power was accompanied by his rebirth into the Catholic Church and his support for the total criminalization of abortion. In Brazil, Dilma Rousseff, the nation's first woman president, has self-reported a transition away from pro-choice Marxism to pro-life "pragmatic capitalism" prior to her presidential success. Cases like these suggest that the political Left in Latin America, in order to gain power, has made conciliatory moves toward the Catholic Church and conservative religious values. (Viterna 2012, 253–54; Friedman 2018; Webber 2016)

In El Salvador, the FMLN's promotion of women's sexual subordination made the party more acceptable to the Catholic Church, and to the socially conservative elements of the electorate. That argument helps make sense of politics in Nicaragua too.

But neither the Sandinistas' desire to reach out to the Catholic Church and evangelical churches, nor their wish to deradicalize their image, can completely explain why the FSLN promised to implement a sexually reactionary law (banning therapeutic abortion) and a sexually progressive law (eliminating antigay Article 204). Making both promises was contradictory from a religious perspective, as the Catholic and evangelical churches strongly supported one change and strongly opposed the other. But it was not contradictory if seen in the light of Zoilamérica's story and the role of the feminist movement within it.

Zoilamérica Ortega Murillo is the first-born daughter of Rosario Murillo and the stepdaughter (later adopted daughter) of President Daniel Ortega. According to her testimony, in the form of a letter that was published by the newspaper *Bolsa de Noticias* on March 3, 1998, she was sexually abused by Daniel Ortega from the age of eleven, raped repeatedly from the age of fifteen, and harassed by Ortega long after she had married and left his house. With that letter, she said, "I assert my right to be the owner of my own future, though I have not been the owner of my own past" (quoted in Lacombe 2010, 81).

At noon that same day her mother and Daniel Ortega held a press conference surrounded by most of their children and some political supporters. Daniel was almost silent, just saying "that it was a 'very sensitive' subject" (Equipo Nitlápan-Envío 1998). He then listened as his wife Rosario read a statement in which she denied everything, going on to say that "we want this to be treated as a family matter" (quoted in *Equipo Envío* 1998).

Later that afternoon, Zoilamérica herself held a press conference. Though Zoilamérica had not been personally involved with the feminist movement up until that point, representatives of the Women's Network against Violence were by her side. She was also accompanied by her Aunt Violeta and her estranged husband, Alejandro Bendaña, both of whom corroborated her version of the story. A week after that press conference, Bendaña wrote her an open letter in which he said, "Today as a man I ask you for forgiveness, Zoilamérica, because I did not do enough to stop Daniel Ortega's aggression against you, aggression that I came to witness from years before we were married. . . . How many times did he call me in the morning to collaborate politically, [only to] dial the same number at night to insinuate all sorts of things to my wife" (quoted in *Equipo Envío* 1998).

A rather different voice supporting Zoilamérica came from Margaret Randall, a U.S.-born author of a number of books on Nicaragua. Randall was a sympathizer of the Sandinista Revolution who lived in Nicaragua from 1980 to 1984, but she did not live in the Ortega-Murillo household, nor did she have special access to the details of the first family's life. Yet it had been an open secret, at least within her social circle, that Ortega had a sexual relationship with his stepdaughter. In an open letter dated April 11, 1998, she apologized for having been complicit through her silence. "We knew about it, and we stayed quiet because we wanted to support the Sandinista Revolution, because we were afraid, and [because of] our view that this was Zoilamérica's story, to be told or not told by her. I am ashamed of our silence, but perhaps the time and place did not allow any alternative" (quoted in Lacombe 2010, 91–92; also see Belli 1998; Morris 2010; Narváez 1998; Roberts 2016).

Feminist Disloyalty and the FSLN

Almost all the second wave feminists were former comrades in arms of the FSLN as the feminist movement emerged in an indirect and unintended way out of the revolutionary mobilization of the 1970s and 1980s. Though some Sandinista feminists challenged the FSLN's hegemony in the 1980s, the real boom in autonomous feminism came after the FSLN's electoral loss in 1990, as I discussed in chapter 3. Most of the leaders of the autonomous feminist movement were Sandinista activists, often party members, who reached the point where they felt they had to reject the FSLN's control so as to promote the egalitarian values that, ironically, the FSLN had inspired in many of them. Though most of them deeply mourned the FSLN's 1990 electoral loss, that loss also represented a sort of opportunity for feminists, as the FSLN no longer had the power to control their actions.

From the perspective of the FSLN, seeking autonomy was unacceptable. As a party that had been a clandestine guerrilla organization, the FSLN's central value was loyalty. Throughout the early and mid-1990s, the disloyalty of the autonomous feminist movement was something that FSLN leaders could barely tolerate. But when the feminists took Zoilamérica's side in 1998, that was absolutely intolerable.

Zoilamérica's story explains a great deal of contemporary Nicaraguan politics. In large part, it explains the enmity between the FSLN and the feminist movement. It helps explain the rise to power of her mother, Rosario Murillo, who—by denouncing her daughter and proclaiming her husband's innocence in 1998—saved Daniel Ortega's political future, and perhaps that of his party. It explains the pact between historic enemies Daniel Ortega and Arnoldo Alemán, for without his fear of prosecution for sexual abuse, Ortega would have had less incentive to negotiate with Alemán.

Most important for this book on LGBTQ politics, Zoilamérica's story makes sense of the simultaneous abolition of therapeutic abortion and antisodomy Article 204. While apparently contradictory when seen from the perspective of Catholic Church preferences, the simultaneous abolition of therapeutic abortion and Article 204 was not contradictory, it was complementary. Both acts served to undermine the feminists. Banning abortion under all circumstances was a rather obvious attack on feminist interests in women's right to control their own bodies and to protect their own lives. In fact, eliminating therapeutic abortion endangered many women's lives and health, and it was to lead to the deaths of over a hundred women (Newman 2011).

Eliminating Article 204 was not as obviously linked to the FSLN's conflict with the feminists (especially as many feminist organizations had helped lead efforts to eliminate the Article). But the elimination of Article 204 (accompanied by other legal changes, and efforts to incorporate elements of the LGBTQ movement into the FSLN's clientelistic networks) was a way to undermine the feminist movement by trying to separate feminists from their natural allies in the LGBTQ community.

The Sexual Diversity Boom: 2007–2017

When Daniel Ortega became president in January 2007, many of the LGBTQ organizations that were founded in the 1990s and early 2000s were still active. Those included Xochiquetzal, Nimehuatzin, Association of Men Against Violence, UNE, Artemisa, MOVFEMD, Trans Goddesses, CEPRESI, RDS, AMGLIM, ADESENI, Safo, NAHOMY CLUB TT&TT, Trans Gay Movement of Managua, and IDSDH. The years following the Sandinista's 1990 electoral defeat had been years of growth for Nicaragua's LGBTQ movement, despite the long shadow cast by Article 204. But there was an even more notable expansion in LGBTQ groups and coalitions during the decade that coincided with the return of Daniel Ortega's FSLN to power.

In the following pages, I present an overview of the organizational activities of what I call the decade of the boom. No doubt readers will think there are too many acronyms: a perennial problem when writing about Nicaraguan politics, and one that has no solution as that is what the groups call themselves. In this section I write of large and small groups; both are important. Certainly, the large groups had a more significant social presence and were more likely to capture media attention. On the other hand, small town and neighborhood groups had the advantage of intimacy and of providing leadership opportunities to less experienced activists. Those are both powerful things, especially for young people in the process of coming out to themselves or others.

2007

Red Trans (Trans Network) was founded in 2007, with support from Xochiquetzal, to focus on the issue of health and the trans community. President Silvia Martínez (whose involvement with LGBTQ politics dated back to CEP-SIDA in the late 1980s) explained that, given the abuse that young trans people often endured in school, many dropped out, finding themselves without degrees or opportunities.

> The issue of sex work is proposed as a right or . . . perhaps not as a right. If there are no opportunities, it is the only thing available for a certain part of the population. It is not the same to be gay as to be a trans person. Because if a gay person can get access to education that is fantastic, but trans people don't have access to education, because everything is about men [and] women. Very few [trans] girls finish their educations. (Interview, June 8, 2011)

At the time of the interview, Trans Network had an office within the public health school at the Managua campus of the public Autonomous University (UNAN Managua), where it trained activists and tried to educate politicians and the public in the issues that faced trans people.

> In this sense we think that our contribution is for people to see us, so that we are visible, so they see that we are not the problem, that we are part of

the solution for the issue of HIV, for the issue of health. That places us in an interesting position, because my *compañeras* are also invited by mayors within the departments where they live. We have a network comprised of 25, we graduated 22 people—including trans people and sex workers—from that school. Now we have 10 health educators who are working with our program or project. And thinking back, I see that one is working with the mayor's office in her municipality, another one is working with the Sandinista Youth, another with other movements like the Communal Associations, and we can see there is interest in this issue. We signed an agreement with the State Human Rights Office, and that helped us because regarding human rights in Nicaragua, even though it is true that there have been big changes, there is still a long way to go. As a result of that agreement, and the fact that the first Sexual Diversity Ombudsperson was named, who . . . is an open lesbian, that all shows that change is possible as long as we think about what it is that we want. (Interview, June 8, 2011)

The public health program had support from the World Bank, though as Martínez noted, there was often a disconnect between resources at the macrolevel and the lack of resources at the microlevel, that is, in the hands of trans people themselves.

There is a cultural problem. [In the clinics] they call out the name that was given to us [at birth], the one on the governmental identification card. If I am not that person, I am not going to answer, [and] I am certainly not going to go to get an HIV test. We have seen all these things and even with the regulations [requiring health workers to use people's chosen names] that Nicaragua has, unfortunately many health professionals are not aware of our regulations[,] and that is why the office of Trans Network is located here in the School of Public Health[,] and we have worked in coordination with the [Public Health] School, to train the first group of health care advocates comprised of sex workers and trans girls supported by the university. Nowhere else in the world is there support like this. Trans people and trans sex workers have always been the topic of studies, of opinion polls, but we never are in charge of programs or projects regarding our own lives. (Interview, June 8, 2011)

Ultimately, health concerns could not be separated from political concerns. The fact that trans people were forced to use identification cards with names that did not correspond with their gender identities meant that many were effectively denied health services. So as part of promoting access to health care, the members of Trans Network sought an identity law. "If I am going to be Silvia Martínez I need my gender identity law so that I don't have trouble in getting access to the legal system. If it happens someday that a police officer does not want to help me after I have been beaten up or something, I could say to the officer, this is my identity, you must respect it" (interview, June 8, 2011). In its work, Trans Network was supported by the *Red Latino Americana y del Caribe de Personas Trans* (Latin American and Caribbean Network of Trans People, or REDLACTRANS), of which Silvia Martínez was the national contact (*referente*) for Nicaragua.

The *Asociación Diversidad Sexual Carazo* (Carazo Sexual Diversity Association) emerged from a coincidence of transportation: the founding members met because they all lived in the city of Jinotepe and took the same hour-long bus ride to Managua for work or school. In 2007, those young men, including Mario Vásquez López, decided to form an association advocating for issues of rights and health in their hometown. For three years they worked with the support of the United Nations Development Programs and the Ministry of Health through Silvia Martínez of the Trans Network. Although the association never was affiliated with the state, they benefitted from the shift in the state's position regarding the LGBTQ community upon the return of the FSLN to power in 2007.

> For example, the mayor of Jinotepe, who was a Sandinista, helped us because I knew him, I had worked in the Jinotepe mayor's office, and I had access to the mayor's secretary. She was the connection who helped us to get a meeting place, who helped us with permission; [she also helped] with the Initiative, with Marvin, Bismarck, as they were very associated with the *Club de Cultura* [Culture Club], and . . . at that time Luis Alonso was a man of influence in the government. He is the director or assistant director of Culture, so through him, with a letter from Luis Alonso, we had access to meeting places, help with those sorts of things. (Interview, June 6, 2011)

At the time of the 2011 interview, the association had ceased to exist, as each of its members had become too busy with other activities. In the case of Mario Vásquez the activity that used up so much of his time was creating the two most detailed LGBTQ blogs in the history of the country up until this writing, blogs that I discussed in the introduction.

Finally, 2007 was the year in which the *Colectivo Feminista TransDeseo* (TransDesire Feminist Collective) was founded by a small group of young people in Managua, including Aldrín Torrez (born in 1988) and Dámaso Vargas (born in 1993). Both credited activists within the feminist movement with inspiring them. Torrez explained that

> from 2001 onwards I had contact with feminist movements which for me have provided a great tool for the construction of my knowledge. I have always participated in a variety of activities. . . . The March 8th [Women's Collective] was a big door for me as a person. The 8th of March movement has been a great support in my life, because it always got rid of things like questioning myself as a person, fears, myths and those sorts of things. (Interview, November 30, 2012)

Other feminist groups that provided critical support to TransDesire were *La Corriente*, Catholics for Choice, and Central American Women's Fund. Additionally, Athiany Larios of the trans rights organization ANIT gave advice and support to the ten members of TransDesire, and they participated in workshops organized by IDSDH and the RDS.

For trans-rights activists, basic physical survival was often a major goal. Torrez shared a house with her brother and sister, along with two members of TransDesire who were no longer welcome to live in their families' homes. Sometimes, even if their relatives accepted them as gay people, they were not willing to accept them as trans women. Like so many trans people, both Torrez and Vargas had faced difficulties completing school, and more difficulties getting a job.

On top of that, they always lived in fear of violence. Just six weeks before the interview, one of the members of TransDesire, a trans woman named Juli, was murdered. "At night she was found in a house, the body of our friend was found, her skull was totally destroyed because they hit her on the head multiple times with cement blocks. We never expected that" (Aldrín Torrez, interview, November 30, 2012). Vargas noted that, following the tragedy, the activists of Transdesire had received legal support. "RDS accomplished a great thing, a project of access to justice. . . . They made the connection and affiliation . . . with the legal clinic at the UCA of Managua. . . . That has helped us a great deal. The UCA supported us in the case of the atrocious murder of [Juli] a trans *compañera*" (Dámaso Vargas, interview, November 30, 2012).

They thought that violence against trans people was on the rise. "We think that now LGBTQ movements are beginning to be publicly known, we no longer are afraid when walking in the street, [and] we now demand rights. . . . It seems that people with established patriarchal ideas, those well-developed machos, they don't accept us . . . that has led to the increase in the number of hate crimes in Nicaragua" (Dámaso Vargas, interview, November 30, 2012).

It was possible that the greater visibility of trans people led to more hate crimes, or perhaps Nicaragua's trans community was in a better position to denounce violence than it had been. Either way, violence was a terrible problem and each new murder was devastating (*Esta Semana* 2015; CEJIL 2013, 176, 192–205, 209–21; Córdoba 2014; Murguialday 2017, 48–49; Romero 2015). For example, on November 18, 2017, Ludwika Ruby Vega wrote on ANIT's Facebook page: "The Nicaraguan Trans Association is in mourning for the *compañera* who because of her disability was known by everyone as the mute girl. Pain affects all of us in the community because we know [her death] was a vivid example of the violence and discrimination that we Nicaraguan trans women endure. She made and sold piñatas to support herself. May you rest in peace. My girl."

A related Facebook post was written by David Rocha on December 8, 2017:

Ronaldinho died. Just like that, while my barber cut my hair he told me the story, or at least the version people are telling in the neighborhood. I was left stone-faced, watching my hair fall while her image and that story resonated in my head.

Would that it were a fictional story but tragically it is not fiction. The last time I saw her I was leaving work. She walked along the dark streets of [the neighborhood] Batahola. For this murderous society *Ronaldinho* was four times a lumpen: a *loca*, a transvestite, mute, and a sex worker.

The barber told me she was doing her work. She went to work with some guys, to give them pleasure. One of them drank too much, he hit her, and she died from the beating. The murderer got away like so many others on the list. The invisible list that the dead seem to take with them.

The social system in which we live kills all of those that it considers feminine and therefore weak. Many hate crimes, many murders of homosexuals

FIGURE 5 ANIT president Ludwika Vega (left) with Ronaldinho, also known as the mute girl (*la Muda*), celebrating the festival of Santo Domingo, Managua, August 2016. Courtesy of Ludwika Vega.

happen because of misogyny. It may seem exaggerated but at the end of the day homophobia is a variant of that fear of the feminine that turns into violence against bodies that deviate from the 'norm.' . . . The mute *loca*, the disabled *loca* could not say anything in response to the murder, in response to the hate crime, in response to the violent misogynistic fists that exploded until they silenced her forever. (David Rocha, Facebook post, December 8, 2017; for more on the life and death of the 41-year-old called *la Ronaldinho* and *la Muda*, known for her devotion to Managua's patron saint, see *La Nueva Radio Ya* 2017)

2008

2008 was the year when Róger Antonio Larios Zúniga became Roxanne Athiany Larios Zúniga. It was also the year when she helped found a new group of trans women, ANIT, the *Asociación Nicaragüense de Trans* (Nicaraguan Trans Association), which grew out of a division within AMGLIM. Those who wished to do more social work remained in AMGLIM; those that wished to do more political work founded ANIT in December 2008, though the distinction between social and political demands was never clear-cut, even after the creation of two separate organizations.

In October of 2008, Larios had participated in the Social Forum of the Americas as a representative of AMGLIM, and she identified that event as her first political experience.

In October I went to the Social Forum of the Americas in Guatemala. I had only recently come out. I had only escaped the claws of the sexist patriarchal system five months earlier, and I had to live in a double closet: feminine at night and masculine during the day. When I went to Guatemala to participate in that Social Forum of the Americas, to talk about LGBTQ issues, I threw all my masculine clothing down a ravine [and] I began to buy feminine clothing and accessories. That was how I presented myself throughout the whole Forum. I began to shine during that October. . . . From the 4th to the 12th of October I shined as Athiany. . . . I even participated in the conclusion to the Forum. I went up on stage to read a proclamation . . . where I explained my vision of human beings with all our differences, all our nuances, and the varied ways in which we behave to express ourselves. And that at the same time, the things that would hurt heterosexuals hurt those of us who are not heterosexual, or those of us who do not act like men, rather like women. (Interview, June 1, 2011)

Upon her return from Guatemala, Larios helped found ANIT, participated in the team that conducted research for the study, *Una Mirada Hacia la Diversidad Sexual*, attended monthly demonstrations, and participated in workshops conducted by LGBTQ and feminist groups. That was not always easy.

There was tension between trans women and organized cisgender[1] women [*mujer biológica*] . . . due to the problem that we were born as men, and we were taking on the identity of women. . . . We recycle these things . . . [these] issues of gender inequality. That is one of the big sources of hurt feelings between two groups who have different bodies but the same gender expressions. . . . María Teresa Blandón [of *La Corriente*] and I began . . . to see how we could sit down with trans women and . . . talk to them about their sexual and reproductive rights, but with a gender focus. (Interview, June 1, 2011)

Larios explained that thanks to her work with *La Corriente*, her ideas regarding what it meant to be a woman had changed.

If you wish to wear excessively high heeled shoes, or to wear an excessive amount of make-up, there are moments and spaces for such things, but you are not necessarily going to walk around in broad daylight with those huge high heels, you are not going to walk around in broad daylight with that sort of make-up. . . . Rather it is best to go around like many cisgender women, in a pair of blue jeans, flip-flops, or a t-shirt, with your hair pulled back or maybe without make-up, that is the typical Nicaraguan woman. . . . She is

---

1. Cisgender women are women whose gender identity conforms with their biological sex, people who are known to almost all Nicaraguans as biological women. In contrast, trans women or gender non-conforming individuals are people whose gender identity does not (or does not always) conform with their sex. According to *Una Mirada Hacia la Diversidad Sexual*, "Biological sex is determined by the anatomy of each person at birth. We think it is important to emphasize that [sex] is only determined by anatomy, that is, it does not take into account feelings, lived experiences, and culture. . . . From our perspective gender identity is a cultural and social construction. The ways of being, types of behavior, ways of dressing, aspirations, in short, one's way of life, is in large part trained, inculcated, in people according to their sex. . . . Gender Identity . . . refers to internal experiences, that which every person feels deeply, which may or may not correspond with their sex at birth" (Moraga et al. 2010, 9–10).

more concerned with looking out for her own well-being and that of her family, with meeting her basic economic needs, . . . [than] with walking down a catwalk (interview, June 1, 2011; for more on Athiany Larios see Benavides 2011; Garay 2014; García 2011).

By 2017, more than fifty trans women identified as members of ANIT, of whom about fifteen were very actively involved. ANIT continued to do political work, lobbying for political changes such as incorporating trans people into the Family Code and the Law against Hate Crimes and passing a Gender Identity Law. Additionally, they visited schools and other organizations to talk about trans rights, conducted workshops, appeared on television talk shows, and helped their members finish high school or college, though none of the people who got degrees were able to get formal-sector jobs, apparently due to their being trans women.

ANIT also worked on HIV-AIDS prevention, at times with support from foreign donors (USAID 2015). Doing such work often meant taking to the streets at night and providing for people's immediate needs along with disease prevention. According to ANIT president Ludwika Vega,

> as part of the night-time visits, we bring informative material on prevention, but we also bring a little snack to the *compañeras*, a sandwich and juice, and then we can visit with the girls who sometimes are in poor health, who have not eaten anything, who have problems, some of them are sick. Also, we try to distribute medicine like for pain, fever, diarrhea, vomiting, sanitary pads for the cisgender [*mujeres biológicas*] sex workers. (Interview, December 1, 2015)

ANIT sometimes found itself working with cisgender female sex workers, since when they went out to help trans sex workers, they often would find two or three trans women amid a group of cisgender women.

In cases when a trans women was seriously ill or injured, they accompanied her to one of the clinics specializing in the LGBTQ population or to a hospital, "because often they are afraid to go to a hospital and be discriminated against, [because] they stick out if they are there by themselves, but if there are two or three of us they feel more secure" (interview, December 1, 2015; on clinics that serve the LGBTQ population see Unidad de VIH 2017 and Murguialday 2017, 46).

The organization known as *La Corriente* was far from new in 2008. In 1994 it had been founded as a coalition of feminist organizations from all the countries of Central America, with its headquarters in Managua. But over the years, it evolved into a Nicaraguan, rather than Central American, feminist organization, while keeping its coalitional ethos. Starting in 2008, according to director María Teresa Blandón, the organization

> began to do a lot of work on sexual and reproductive rights and, of course, the issue of gender identities [which] is central to this discussion, just like the issue of sexual diversity is central, to recognize the many ways to live, sexuality in its emotional dimension but also in its erotic dimension. But as we found that gender identity is deeply rooted in men and women, and to move those gender identities, to question that monolithic thing that it is imagined to be, one had to look for other ways and we hit upon the need to recognize the fact of transgenderism. Transgenderism itself is evidence of the fallacy of gender essentialism. We decided to do two things: one, to work directly with trans women and, two, to promote exchanges between trans women and cisgender women [*mujeres biológicas*]. (Interview, December 12, 2012)

Those exchanges were eye-openers. "On the one hand, the trans women had never reflected in feminist ways . . . and on the other hand, the young women with whom we worked, the cis-gender women, had not confronted the reality of transgenderism so as to also question their own gender identities" (interview, December 12, 2012).

In the years following 2008, *La Corriente* did a series of workshops with various groups: Transdesire, ANIT, *Colectivo de mujeres bisexuales y trans del distrito VI* (Collective of bisexual and trans women of district VI [of Managua]), ARTEMISA, Safo, and with lesbians who formed part of other organizations in the cities of Matagalpa, Jinotega, Estelí, and León. Moreover, *La Corriente*, itself a long-term member of the autonomous feminist movement, sought to change the feminist movement from within.

> We have done a lot of work to get those of us in the feminist movement to make the demonstration of June 28th [LGBTQ pride] our own, and so that has been an important advance in the past few years. . . . Last year the feminist movement promoted a campaign with the slogan "their love does not hurt, your rejection does [hurt]," [and] that was the first public campaign

that we did, and . . . it seems to me that it had a very positive impact. That is, we made efforts, not just in our workshops, but also by making sure that lesbian and trans demands are on the agenda of the feminist organizations. We weren't the only ones who did that, but we were collaborators. I think that work has been very important. (Interview, December 12, 2012)

In 2011, as part of this focus on the intersections between sexual orientation, gender identity, and feminism, *La Corriente* (in collaboration with ANIT) published a forty-two-page book called *Ser mujer más allá del cuerpo* (To be a Woman Beyond the Body). That book told the stories of four trans women—including Aldrín Torrez from Transdesire—with words and photos (Arévalo Contreras 2011). "In 2013 [*La Corriente*] published 'Cuando las lesbianas hablamos' (When We Lesbians Speak). . . . Also, in 2012 *La Corriente* produced a series called '*Transitar por el Género*' (To Move through Gender), which was a tool to raise consciousness so as to question gender binaries" (Blandón and Medal Salaverry 2015, 63).

Finally, *La Corriente*'s radio program, "*Cuerpos Sin-Vergüenzas*" (Bodies without Shame), could be heard every Thursday from June 5, 2013, through this writing on University Radio, and all the episodes were available at www .ivoox.com. Cristina Arévalo and Elvis Salvatierra[2] usually cohosted the hour-long program of music and interviews addressing topics like "Bisexuality: Orientation or Indecision?" (October 28, 2013); "Gays and Lesbians in the Revolution" (July 24, 2014); "There Is No Pride without Feminism" (June 29, 2015); "Women Who Write: A Threat to Patriarchy" (April 22, 2016); and "Lesbians, Gays and Trans Are Also Devoted to the Virgin Mary" (December 7, 2017).

In June 2008, the *Asociación Movimiento de la Diversidad Sexual Costeña* (Association Movement of Coastal Sexual Diversity, AMODISEC), was founded by three young Indigenous people including Natty González. González, who

---

2. Prior to the creation of Cuerpos Sin-Vergüenzas, in 2009 and 2010, Elvis Salvatierra hosted his own radio program, "*En Ambiente*" (In the Environment) which was also broadcast on *Radio Universidad* (University Radio), the radio station of the Jesuit-affiliated UCA. Like others, Salvatierra noted that the UCA was a supportive place in the early 2000s, and he had many gay friends on campus. "That is the way the UCA was, a place of diversity and a place of respect in which one wanted to work. In the case of almost all my academic work they let me focus on promoting mass media for development, LGBTQ issues, transgenderism, lesbianism, bisexualism, and anything else you could imagine" (interview, December 6, 2013).

was just seventeen when she helped to found AMODISEC, the first such organization in Nicaragua's Caribbean Coast region, explained that doing the sort of work she does in the northern Caribbean Coast is somewhat different than it would be in the Pacific Coast and central regions of the country, because "the northern region is known for being a multiethnic [and] multicultural region, it is known as the capital of Miskitu people, a group that until today have maintained their culture, their beliefs, their religion, and their native language, Miskitu" (interview, November 28, 2012).

By 2017, eighty people belonged to AMODISEC, and they had accomplished a substantial amount, such as

> regional and national authorities recognizing [their] work, endorsement and recognition on the part of the regional government and council, [and] creation of an area of special attention to sexual diversity concerns within the regional government. Membership in the National GLBTI Roundtable of Nicaragua. First vice president of the World Bank's mechanism for coordinating representation of the trans community within the region. Oversight of grants for various issues regarding the GLBT population. Creation of alliances with local and national offices. Recognition received from the U.S. Ambassador for our work regarding HIV and STD prevention. (Personal communication by email, February 13, 2017)

Their successes pointed to the importance of building alliances with other groups. AMODISEC had no office of its own, but the *Clínica Bilwi* (Bilwi Clinic) provided a space for them to meet. They also were allied with the Nidia White Women's Movement, the "Black movement people," and the *Centro de Derechos Humanos, Ciudadanos y Autonómicos Centro de Derechos Humanos Autonómicos de la Región Norte de Nicaragua* (Center for Human, Citizenship and Autonomous Rights or CEDEHCA). They worked with USAID's AIDS prevention program, and with CEPRESI, based in Managua. Though they did not have a regular source of funding, they sponsored fundraisers like "Miss Costa Caribe Gay" pageants (interview, November 28, 2012).

2009

AMODISEC was not the only LGBTQ-rights organization on the Caribbean Coast for long. The very next year, the *Movimiento de la Diversidad Sexual*

Alexis Montiel Alfaro, also known as the Movimiento de la Diversidad de la RAAS (Alexis Montiel Alfaro Sexual Diversity Movement, also known as the RAAS Diversity Movement, or MDS RAAS) was founded in the city of Bluefields by Alexis Montiel Alfaro, Saul Lira, Tyrone Aburto, Juaquin García, Oel Cuadra, and Selena Valle (Yellow-Place n.d.). President Tyrone Aburto explained,

> We found ourselves with needs and realized that it was time to form a group to represent the LGBTI community, because that community has been pretty beaten up . . . in different social areas: health, education, security. . . . We have been working with different organizations that work on the issue of human rights and HIV prevention. We have also been working on political lobbying directed at decision-makers in our community. At the same time, we have been working on consciousness-raising with the population, organizing various activities like the Miss Gay Caribbean Coast [and] Miss Trans Caribbean Coast pageants. We have been participating on December 1st [World AIDS Day] activities. . . . We have also been working on activities like the Day Against Homophobia, Transphobia [and] Lesbophobia. At the same time, we are working on Gay Pride Day. (Interview, November 28, 2012; also see *El Nuevo Diario* 2011a)

By 2018, leaders of the RAAS Diversity Movement estimated that it had more than one thousand affiliates, though the growth of the organization had not changed the problems they continued to face; they still needed access to justice, employment, health care, and basic respect. According to Tyrone Aburto, "We have been the target of mockery, discrimination, different forms of violence against our sexual identity, with grave psycho-emotional, social, physical, and economic consequences" (*La Costeñísima* 2018).

In 2009, *Agentes de Cambio* (Agents of Change) was founded in the northern city of Matagalpa by a group of young people including Christopher Mendoza, Jary López, and Alfredo Ocampos Ortega, with support from the feminist organization Venancia. "The group came to life as a space to express opinions and chat about issues that affect LGBTI people. Eventually the coordinators looked for . . . financing to do education projects, including a radio program, a television program, and street murals to raise consciousness about LGBT people. There are also educational projects about HIV, and projects along with the Ombudsperson for Sexual Diversity so as to educate the police and clinic workers about discrimination" (Crane 2015, 41; Mugen Gainetik n.d. [2017?], 29; Ocampos Ortega 2013).

The *Alternativa Nicaragüense de Diversidad Sexual* (Nicaraguan Sexual Diversity Alternative, or ANDISEX) was founded on July 1, 2009, by a coalition including Luis Torres and Danilo Sebastian González, in the city of Jinotepe. According to its website, "Our organization works on promoting and defending the human rights of the sexually diverse population in Nicaragua. We seek to contribute to the construction of robust citizenship through the empowerment of the BGLTTTI population in exercising its rights, and through actions to prevent STDs/HIV/AIDS" (ANDISEX n.d.; for an interview with Luis Torres see *Cuerpos Sin-Vergüenzas* 2017a).

As was true for many of the other organizations in the LGBTQ movement, ANDISEX activists had deep roots in several other feminist and LGBTQ organizations. For instance, between 2007 and 2017, Danilo González either worked for or volunteered with the feminist organization *Puntos*, the *Red de Diversidad Sexual de Nicaragua* (Sexual Diversity Network of Nicaragua), the Carazo Sexual Diversity Association, *Panteras Rosas* (Pink Panthers), and Two Generations. During that decade he also spent three years in Mexico as an employee of the NGO *Elige* (interview, July 18, 2017).

In 2009, the *Asociación Diversidad Sexual Nicaragüense* (Nicaraguan Sexual Diversity Association, or ADISNIC) was founded in the northern department of Chinandega.[3] According to ADISNIC's General Coordinator, Harvey Vladimir Maradiaga, "[The association was created] due to the National Police of Chichigalpa increasingly using violence against LGBTI people, attacking us verbally and physically, [and] we lived in fear of the National Police and were afraid to file complaints against the Police who had attacked us or another person. Among our goals was to educate the local government employees so that the reality of what we were going through would change" (personal communication via email, June 16, 2017).

The activists of ADISNIC were successful in several ways. Maradiaga noted, "[They had] around 25 people collaborating with us including LGBTI men and women from the 13 townships of the state of Chinandega, Quezalguaque and León, [and] at the same time we [had] a Board of Directors comprised of five LGBT people" (personal communication via email, June 16,

---

3. ADISNIC built on the earlier experiences of a group that used the name *Asociación Diversidad Sexual de Occidente* (Western Sexual Diversity Association, or ADSO) in 2004.

2017). Starting in 2012, ADISNIC activists organized a series of workshops with the National Police, including "three dialogues with the National Police in the state of Chinandega" with the participation of "the state delegation from Chinandega and municipal delegations from Chichigalpa, Somotillo, Corinto and El Viejo." Those workshops addressed the ways in which LGBT people had been treated by the police.

The following year, in 2013, ADISNIC built on its earlier work with new workshops addressing the themes of human rights, gender identity, and sexual orientation, this time with financial support from the Spanish organization *Médicos del Mundo* (Doctors of the World). They included "3 dialogues with officials from the National Police of the state of Chinandega [in which] 35 police officers from the 13 municipalities of the state of Chinandega were trained, [leading to the]" "signing of an agreement [*convenio*] with the head of the Chinandega state branch of the National Police." Finally, in 2014 and 2015, ADENESIC organized "eight dialogues with officials of the PN [National Police] in the state of Chinandega: 120 officers who worked in the municipalities of Chinandega, Chichigalpa, Somotillo, Corinto, La Paz Centro, Nagarote and León" (slide show provided by Harvey Vladimir Maradiaga, June 16, 2017).

ADISNIC sometimes collaborated with Managua-based LGBTQ organizations including CEPRESI and *Xochiquetzal*. Moreover, the organization belonged to several national and international networks, such as the Mesa Nacional LGBTI, the *Comisión Nicaragüense del SIDA* (Nicaraguan AIDS Commission or CONISIDA) in the departments of León and Chinandega, and the international association ILGA. But despite the organization's national and international ties, Maradiaga sometimes faced difficulties working on the periphery of Nicaragua, wishing that "donors could separate themselves from the NGO clientelism and Managua-centrism that one lives in the current context of the country, and that they would take a financial and technical chance with LGBTI organizations that are outside of the capital, since there is no real support for the experiences of people who live in different parts of the country" (personal communication by email, June 16, 2017).

2010

The *Colectivo Feminista Panteras Rosas* (Pink Panthers Feminist Collective) was founded in March or April of 2010 by a group of young people including Katya Acuña (born February 1989) who explained,

What we do in the collective is to fuse feminist activism with our identity as young people. So it is a mixed [gender] collective. We are self-organized, [and] we promote reflection spaces, spaces for the participation of young people. We do workshops . . . a little while ago we had what was basically a communication workshop. We always try to do street activism, with ordinary people. . . . We have ties with the Feminist Movement of Nicaragua, also with the Latin American and Caribbean Network for Sexual and Reproductive Rights, with *La Corriente*, which also supports us a lot. . . . We meet in a space at the *Corriente*, [and] they provide all the conditions we need, the auditorium and everything. (Interview, June 9, 2011)

Acuña and the other thirteen members of the Pink Panthers worked to make themselves visible (a strategy common to most LGBTQ groups, in Nicaragua and elsewhere), but they did not think visibility was enough. "It also has to do with work within our group. . . . I am not going to repeat the heterosexual model within a homosexual relationship" (interview, June 9, 2011; for an interview with Katya Acuña see *Cuerpos Sin-vergüenzas* 2017b; also, Movimiento Feminista de Nicaragua 2010b).

In 2010, Mario Gutierrez, whose work as a gay-rights activist dated back to the 1980s, was one of the founders of the *Grupo Gay de Actores Sociales para la Incidencia Municipal y la Integracion Centroamericana* (Group of Gay Social Actors for Municipal Politics and Central American Integration or GAY GAS). That small NGO engaged in political lobbying and alliance-making, both in Nicaragua and in the Central American region, along with work against violence and preventing HIV-AIDS. In 2012, the members of GAY GAS obtained legal status from the National Assembly under the name Asociación FIATPAX, HAGAMOS LA PAZ (personal communication by email, July 2013; Portalsida n.d.).

The largest LGBTQ organization in Nicaragua was founded in June 2010. Harím Sánchez, the coordinator of the *Movimiento de Diversidad Sexual de la Juventud Sandinista* (Sandinista Youth Sexual Diversity Movement) explained that from a young age he had been an FSLN supporter. Born in September of 1989, from the age of fourteen or fifteen he volunteered with the Sandinista Youth in Managua's Monseñor Lezcano neighborhood. By the age of sixteen he was the coordinator of the Sandinista Youth for the entire neighborhood, and at age twenty he helped found the Sandinista Youth Sexual Diversity Movement for the entire country.

Our sexual diversity movement was created a year ago [in 2010], on the 25th of this month we will be celebrating our first anniversary. The movement was created in response to a proposal made by organizations [that] came up with a concrete proposal . . . so that we from the sexual diversity community could propose laws and government policies that would benefit us and that would restore our rights. (Interview, June 8, 2011)

In contrast with Sánchez's description of a movement arising from the grassroots, Clara Murguialday argued that the creation of the LGBTQ section within the Sandinista Youth was the result of a decision from above.

In 2010 the *Instituto Nicaragüense de la Juventud* (Nicaraguan Youth Institute or INJUVE) created the Youth Movement for Sexual Diversity within the Sandinista Youth. This movement, that says it works in all 153 municipalities of the country "to continue on the path of restoration of rights that was initiated by the Sandinista government and to promote our Christian, Socialist, and Caring [Solidario] model, seems to exist in a different country than the rest of the LGBTI organizations." In 2013 its national coordinator said: "This June 28th is a very special day since we proudly emphasize the improvements attained by the trans and lesbian movements. . . . The rights that we have been gaining [include] mutual respect within all our institutions, additionally homosexual people are no longer discriminated against in the street, it is not like it used to be, rather they recognize our grace, our hard work, our dedication . . . In the Sandinista government's seven years the face of the country has changed slowly regarding infrastructure and restitution of rights, that change can also be seen in the LGBTQ community, which is now more understood and respected by Nicaraguans, who are diverse in many ways" (Murguialday 2017, 51–52).

Of course, both versions of the story could be true. The LGBTQ movement of the Sandinista Youth could have been created in response to grassroots concerns, and also in response to an order from above. In fact, in a later interview, Harím Sánchez himself explained that the LGBTQ section of the Sandinista Youth was an idea that arose from the grassroots but that had to be proposed to the head of the party "to the Secretary General of the Party, to Daniel himself" (interview, July 17, 2017). As Daniel Ortega supported their proposal, they were able to go ahead, despite the opposition of some labor union leaders.

But regardless of whether the main goal was to co-opt LGBTQ youth as some have suggested (Comunidad Homosexual de Nicaragua 2010c; Murguialday 2017) or to promote their rights, the Sandinista Youth's LGBTQ movement was significant, if only due to its size. According to Sánchez, the Sandinista Youth LGBTQ section incorporated 7,500 young Sandinistas nationwide just one year after its founding (interview, July 8, 2011).

As an organization that was integrated into the ruling party, activists within the Sandinista Youth had access to state actors that autonomous activists might not have. For instance, they worked with the Ministry of Health (MINSA) to defend the interests of LGBTQ people. "Since 2009, as a result of a Ministry of Health resolution, MINSA requires that people get quality attention without discrimination, regardless of the sexual option or gender identity of the person" (interview, June 8, 2011). The resolution was a significant step forward though Sánchez admitted that it was not always put into practice. "In the most far-flung clinics it is very hard. We have received complaints, but we have overcome them in coordination with the Ministry of Health" (interview, June 8, 2011).

Another way in which the Sandinista Youth's access to the state was helpful was regarding education. "In the Ministry of Education, we have implemented a guidebook on sexuality. It is for the teachers to consult to speak about sexual diversity issues, sexual health, reproductive health, so they might orient young people, because young people and adolescents spend most of their days with teachers and [the teachers] are the ones who could give them guidance. If not, the issue is everywhere, so we really needed that guidebook. It was already launched, and it is soon to be distributed nationally" (interview, June 8, 2011).

In Nicaragua, the majority of second wave feminists and LGBTQ activists have seen autonomy from political parties as a prerequisite for their work. But Sánchez saw his organization's lack of autonomy (in other words, its forming part of the FSLN) as an advantage: "A big accomplishment is that the organization runs parallel to the Sandinista Youth structure. The Sandinista Youth is in every corner of the community, in all neighborhoods, in all communities, and wherever you find the Sandinista Youth, there is [also] a coordinator of the LGBTQ organization" (interview, June 8, 2011). The LGBTQ section of the Sandinista Youth sometimes worked with nonpartisan LGBTQ groups—Sánchez mentioned the IDSDH, Safo, and CEPRESI— but he complained that many autonomous activists looked down upon our movement because they said that it was a partisan organization. I explained that as sexually diverse people we also have a right to choose a political ideology. . . . We may be homosexuals, lesbians, but also, we may form part of the Sandinista Front, and [the Sandinistas] have given us a place in the teams, in the decision-making structures, and we have both voice and vote. We may present proposals, and they are discussed at the departmental, municipal, and neighborhood-level. (Interview, June 8, 2011)

For Sánchez, working with other LGBTQ groups was mutually beneficial. On the one hand, groups like IDSDH, Safo, and CEPRESI had years of experience behind them. On the other hand, the Sandinista Youth had "party structures in the entire country, which is something that no other organization has done" (Interview, June 8, 2011).

A year after its creation, the LGBTQ movement within the Sandinista Youth was huge and quite visible. But in the following years, the status of that movement became unclear. Harím Sánchez explained that in 2012 he ceased to coordinate the LGBTQ movement within the Sandinista Youth and moved on to other work. At some point after he left, the movement became a secretariat, which he thought was less important than a movement, and then "at the end of 2013 the LGBTQ movement of the Sandinista Youth completely disappeared, and young people were supposed to join other groups, that is, other groups, like the *Movimiento Cultural Leonel Rugama* (Leonel Rugama Cultural Movement) were supposed to address sexual diversity issues" (Interview, July 17, 2017). Many autonomous activists also told me that the LGBTQ movement within the Sandinista Youth no longer existed.

Nonetheless, the LGBTQ movement of the Sandinista Youth did not disappear completely. One LGBTQ Sandinista Youth activist said the movement still existed, though it had made "few advances. The government [was] not reaching out much to the diversity community" (Vanesa interview, 2014). As a Sandinista, she and other LGBTQ activists within the Sandinista Youth found it difficult to maintain both loyalties: to the party and to the LGBTQ community. For instance, they sometimes coordinated with groups like Agents of Change from Matagalpa and AMGLIM and ANDISEX from Mateare, but in some ways they were ambivalent about those alliances. In Vanesa's view, those groups were "against the government. We cannot be against the government because we are part of the government" (interview, 2014).

Other members of the LGBTQ community told me that, at least in some places, the LGBTQ movement of the Sandinista Youth continued its activities. In 2013, Helen Alfaro said that she and other activists in the House of Colors Collective (in the city of León) sometimes worked in coalition with LGBTQ Sandinista Youth activists (interview, December 11, 2013). In 2017, David Rocha told me that the LGBTQ movement within the Sandinista Youth continued to carry out activities in Managua's Bello Horizonte and Colonia Salvadorita neighborhoods (interview, July 11, 2017). Additionally, the sexual diversity movement of the Sandinista Youth had an ongoing presence in the Sandinista press (Cerón Méndez 2014; Chávez 2016; Zeledón 2013).

The debate over whether the largest LGBTQ movement in the country even existed nicely illustrated the contradictions of civil rights advocacy within a hierarchical political party. It was not even possible for me to contact the Sandinista Youth and ask if the LGBTQ movement continued to exist. When I tried, I was told that the people from the Sandinista Youth could not speak to me without asking the first lady, Rosario Murillo, for permission, and that the answer would be no.

2011

The *Colectivo Casa de los Colores* (House of Colors Collective) was created in 2011 in the city of León. Helen Alfaro explained that she has been an independent lesbian rights activist for six years prior to the founding of the collective, during the years that she studied social work at the National University of Nicaragua or UNAN. After graduating she and other women founded the House of Colors collective. With a team of approximately thirty sexually diverse young people ("we have heterosexuals, bisexuals, gays, lesbians, transgender people, some of everything") including Ana Lucía Guerrero, Massiel Moreno, and Jennifer Corea, they carried out a wide variety of activities, with support from the Norwegian Embassy.

> In the House we do a bit of everything; the focus of the space is to work on legal complaints [*denuncia*], for example. . . . We [also] facilitate educational processes on themes that have to do with sexual diversity in general [including] . . . identity, self-esteem, self-care, self-awareness, self-acceptance. We work on nonviolence, gender violence, [and] we promote life skills among which are decision-making, self-recognition also. We . . . promote develop-

ment and skills. . . . Let me mention some: we offer English classes, we do *biodanza*, we have dance classes that are part of biodanza, we do arts and crafts, we have film festivals, [and] for a year we have been showing educational films every Friday afternoon. . . . We also . . . have a sports program where the girls play soccer. . . . Before the soccer game what we do is to have educational talks about issues that have to do with women, a little feminism. We talk a bit about the history of feminism, which is part of self-care. As the girls have their experiences with people of their own sex, lesbians or bisexual women should know about sexual and reproductive health . . . like how two lesbians can protect themselves. . . . In León we are the only group that addresses these issues in such a deep way. (Interview, December 11, 2013; Wikipedia 2017)

In 2014, Alfaro participated in the radio talk show *Cuerpos Sin-Vergüenzas* addressing the theme of unity (or disunity) within Nicaragua's LGBTQ rights movement. She argued that the divisions with the movement were significant enough that it was not always possible to talk about an LGBTQ movement: "just regarding lesbian groups, there is incredible segregation [and] divisions. There is a lot of struggles for leadership, a lot of struggles for power" (*Cuerpos Sin-Vergüenzas* 2014a).

Those divisions were also due to the very different experiences of members of the LGBTQ community: gay men, trans people, bisexual people, and lesbians all faced somewhat different issues, issues that were further shaped by factors like class, ethnicity, and region of the country. For example, while there were other LGBTQ groups in the city of León, "the House of Colors is the first group in which lesbians are very prominent" (*Cuerpos Sin-Vergüenzas* 2014a; Wikipedia 2017; for another interview with Helen Alfaro see *Cuerpos Sin-Vergüenzas* 2015).

The organization *Grupo Lésbico Somos Tribadistas* (We are Tribadists Lesbian Group) was founded in late 2011 or early 2012 in Managua. It evolved out of the lesbian group of IDSDH, which had been founded in 2006. Jaika Gradiz, the vice-coordinator, explained that the twelve to fifteen young women who founded the organization "decided that we were going to change the name of the group which had been 'Lesbians of the Iniciative' [IDSDH], and then to make ourselves more independent and autonomous, and to not be part of the Initiative anymore. Basically, we wanted to finally decide for ourselves as autonomous lesbian women" (interview, December 4, 2015).

Under the coordination of Evelyn Peña and Jaika Gradiz, members of the organization participated in activities like protests and gay pride parades. Additionally, they lobbied for greater rights for lesbians and the LGBTQ community more generally. According to its Facebook page the women of We are Tribadists continued to participate in some activities as late as 2014, but it is no longer an active organization (RDS n.d. [2013?]; EFE 2013; Carolina Gallard, interview, May 31, 2011).

2012

The year 2012 opened with coalition building. According to a Facebook post, a press conference was held on January 9 at the Managua office of the Association of Men against Violence to announce the new coalition of fifteen organizations that belonged to the *Movimiento Nacional de la Diversidad Sexual, Por Los Derechos Sexuales y Reproductivos* (National Movement for Sexual Diversity, Sexual Rights, and Reproductive Rights, or MNACXDSSRR).[4]

According to the press release, "We organized so as to have influence in public, civil, and political ways, so that the LGBTI population could enjoy better human development and the establishment of just and equitable relations, along with the prevention of STDs, HIV-AIDS, gender violence, other types of violence, the promotion and defense of human rights, sexual rights, reproductive rights, demands for respect, and that the state guarantee the security of citizens who belong to Nicaragua's LGBTI population" (*Movimiento Nacional Mnacxdssrr and Fondo Centroamericano de Mujeres* 2012). The coalition, comprised of organizations based in Managua, León, and Chinandega, continued to be quite active as of this writing, as indicated by its Facebook presence.

Just a month later, on February 29, 2012, a twenty-one member coalition, the *Mesa Nacional LGBTI* (National LGBTI Roundtable), was presented to the public at an event held at the Managua office of the RDS (RDS 2012c). By 2017, the National LGBTI Roundtable had shrunk a bit (from twenty-one

---

4. Fifteen organizations belonged to the MNACXDSSRR alliance: 1. ORGANIZACIÓN VIDA INTEGRAL (Wholistic Life Organization, or OVI); 2. TEATRO NUEVA GENERACION (New Generation Theater, or TNG); 3. Trans Goddeses; 4. MTGM; 5. JOV JOV (Youth to Youth); 6. ASOCIACIÓN NOVA ODISEA (New Odyssey Association); 7. AHCV; 8. GRUPO 8 (Group 8); 9. CODISEX; 10. MOJUDS; 11. RED X UNIDAD SOCIAL (Network for Social Unity); 12. Artemisa; 13. ADISNIC; 14. Acahual Women's Center; 15. AVETRANS.

Las familias DIVERSAS exigimos IGUALES derechos

PLANTÓN SEMANAL

Jueves 14 de Junio 2012   Hora: 9 – 11 AM
Frente Asamblea Nacional, Managua

Lleva algo con lo que hacer BULLA: pailas, matracas, megáfono, pitos, tambores, platillos...

FIGURE 8   A poster by a coalition of fifteen feminist, human rights, and LGBTQ organizations for a fair Family Code, which reads: "DIVERSE families demand EQUAL rights. / Weekly Protest. / Thursday June 14, 2012. Time: 9:00–11:00 am. / In front of the National Assembly, Managua. / Bring something with which to make a RACKET: pans, rattles, megaphones, whistles, drums, cymbals. . . . "

to eighteen members), but it remained regionally diverse and active in collectively demanding civil rights for the LGBTQ community.[5] Acting in coalition, the members of the National LGBTI Roundtable were more effective than they would have been had each organization simply acted individually, organizing public events like gay pride marches, denouncing violence, and lobbying for civil rights. It pushed to include hate crimes in the Penal Code,

5. The groups that made up the LGBTI Roundtable were geographically diverse. They came from the West: ASOTRACHI, CODISEX, House of Colors Collective, and *Diversidad Sexual Nangrandana, Nagorte* (Sexual Diversity Group of Nangrandana, Nagarote); from Managua: MOJUDS, MOVFEMD, RDS, AMTC, Trans Network, UNE, MTG, and Transdesire Feminist Collective; from the East: Metamorphosis Club; from the North: *Grupo Ideas por una Cultura de Paz, Matagalpa* (Matagalpa Group of Ideas for a Peace Culture), DEIGEORSEX; and they came from the Autonomous Regions of the Caribbean Coast: MDS RAAS and AMODISEC, RACS (Facebook, consulted February 10, 2017).

and to recognize LGBTQ families in the Family Code. Perhaps most significantly, it created LGBTQ legal clinics in the cities of Managua and Bluefields, something that no other group had done (Vásquez López 2017a).

Two of the members of the LGBTI National Roundtable—Metamorphosis Club and ASONIDHJO—were brand-new in 2012. Metamorphosis Club was founded in 2012 by a group of young people, including Chester Córtez, in the city of Jinotepe. Córtez, who directed the Club, was born in July 1987 and was twenty-five years old when it was created. At that point, he already had many years of political experience behind him. In 2003, when Córtez was still in high school, he became a member of the *Consejo Juvenil de Jinotepe* (Youth Council of Jinotepe) as well as a dancer, participating for seven years in the folkloric ballet in the municipality of Diriamba. An essay on Córtez noted that

> he began working in the Association of Men Against Violence in 2009, where he coordinated the area of Political Affairs; in 2012 he held the same position in the *Movimiento de Jovenes Contra la Violencia en Nicaragua* [Movement of Nicaraguan Youth Against Violence]. Currently he is the National Assistant Coordinator of the PREVIOS network (*Red de Prevención de Violencia Sociales* [Network for Prevention of Social Violence]), a member of the Coordinating Committee of the National LGBTI Roundtable and part of the Youth Network of the MRS political party (Ciudadanía Regional de la Juventud Centroamericana 2015).

Cortéz's work in Metamorphosis Club clearly built on his earlier work. He and the other fifteen participants in the Club focused their energies on violence prevention, the depenalization of therapeutic abortion, and promoting the rights of the LGBTQ community (interview, June 19, 2014).

Miguel Ángel Gómez, the coordinator of the *Asociación Nicaragüense por los Derechos Humanos de los Jovenes LGBTI* (Nicaraguan Association for the Human Rights of LGBTI Youth, or ASONIDHJO) was born in August 1993. His first political experience happened when he was eighteen years old.

> It was in 2012 when I first went to a meeting of the National LGBTI Roundtable, [and] . . . that was where my activism began; it was like it filled a hole in my life. . . . I did not know anything about it just that some other people said to me, there is going to be a meeting, please come as we have to fill the

space. . . . I did not know anything, but I liked the exchanges, I said wow, there are people who have gone through more than I have. I no longer felt like the only one in the world . . . As a result of that, I decided to do something, and that was the idea that came to me: I am going to organize the young men and women of my community first, and that is how the organization ASONIDHJO began . . . on the 23rd of September of 2012. (Interview, December 8, 2015)

The twenty members of the group, mainly from district V of Managua, carried out "activities in other districts like video viewing meetings. In the neighborhoods, [they] also do HIV prevention with the kids, workshops, and training with the young people. . . . [They] let them know about their rights and we tell them about any new things, like for example, there was a recent ministerial resolution 641, 2014, from the Ministry of Health [which] is a resolution that benefits the community in the sense that . . . [it] forbids discrimination in a public or private health clinic."

Gómez noted that many young LGBTQ people did not know they had rights regarding health care. Even when they learned of those rights, they often were unwilling to demand them, because they were uncomfortable with their own sexuality. So ASONIDHJO also worked on psychological well-being. As Gómez commented, "Personally I think one has to love oneself the way one is" (interview, December 8, 2015).

2013

Bismarck Moraga Peña and Vladimir Reyes García formally founded the *Asociación Nuevos Horizontes* (New Horizons Association, or ANH) in 2013, but that was hardly their first political experience. Their activism dated back to the 1990s, including their work as founding members of the Initiative (IDSDH) in 2006, where Moraga served as director for several years. Among other activities, he and Reyes were both deeply involved in the research and writing of the landmark study, *A Glance at Sexual Diversity* (Moraga Peña et al. 2010).

The new nongovernmental organization, ANH, worked in close alliance with the trans rights group ANIT, first sharing office space in Managua's Benjamin Linder House and then moving together to the house across the street. ANH was active in a range of activities, including lobbying and protesting for political rights, facilitating workshops, promoting HIV-AIDS pre-vention, and visiting trans women and gay men in prison (Bismarck Moraga Peña, interview, December 3, 2015; TeleSUR TV 2014).

The *Organización de Personas Trans* (Organization of Trans People, or ODETRANS) was founded in 2013, as some members of Trans Network decided to set off on their own. According to ODETRANS president, Mística Guerrero, the seventy-nine members of ODETRANS came from nine of the fifteen departments of the country. Guerrero, a professional hairdresser, owned her own salon, giving me a business card complete with her photo. She and her boyfriend lived in their own place, and as she explained, "my mom and my nephew live right next door" (interview, December 11, 2013).

Though she personally had done well as a hairdresser (one of the few em-ployment options traditionally open to trans women), she noted that many wanted to challenge their limited options, rather than focusing on issues like HIV prevention.

> They should be included in the educational system so that they may get good jobs, not the sorts of jobs that we have always done like haircutting, [rather] real jobs. They should be able to study to have a chance at good work, not the same old thing. The majority of trans women work in the markets, in the beauty parlors, they are wherever people accept them or exploit them. Be-cause if a family accepts you, it is because you are the employee or the maid, and they make you do absolutely everything in the house. They accept you as a woman because they know it benefits them. They give you 50 córdobas a week, and here in Nicaragua 50 córdobas is practically nothing[, but] to avoid being on the street, many prefer to be there [working as maids]. (In-terview, December 11, 2013)

An ongoing problem was that funding agencies (especially foreign agencies) were interested in funding disease prevention programs, but they were less interested in efforts to address the kind of problems that Guerrero identified. So ODETRANS tackled those issues through a campaign that Venus Cabal-lero López (the Executive Director of ODETRANS in 2016) discussed in an article in the daily newspaper *El Nuevo Diario*:

> This message was promoted through the Facebook page of the *"Somos ig-uales a vos"* ("We are the same as you") campaign, where the videos may be

viewed. Additionally, the campaign appeared on both radio and television, an important first step in "beginning the process of thinking about an issue that is rarely addressed from the perspective of human rights." (Caballero López 2016)

In 2013, Operation Queer collective (later renamed Operation Queer/ *cochona*) was founded by six people—Camilo Antillón, Elyla, Jilma Estrada, John Petrus, Ana Victoria Portocarrero, and Guillermo Sáenz—who were joined by Alejandro Belli in 2015. It was very different than the other groups I have discussed so far, as it was devoted to the arts rather than lobbying or service provision (Bienal Centroamericana 2016).

The idea for the collective began at least a year or two before it was founded, when Elyla said, "[I] began to write about those concerns that I did not fit within what I could see I was supposed to be. . . . I began to go out into the street, to do little unofficial actions in the street, without recording myself, nothing[.] I just did it because I needed to go out into the street" (interview, July 14, 2017). Discussing these issues with the group of friends who eventually created Operation Queer/*cochona*, Elyla explained that they felt "at that moment something like the need to open up spaces to reflect and criticize, which would be related to activism, art, culture, and that would be, that would speak, about another experience, about different experiences, with bodies that are not taken into account, and with experiences that are not taken into account. That was our first slogan as Operation Queer: the need for a complete alphabet, a sexuality with a complete alphabet, we wanted to think about thousands of different ways to feel" (interview, July 14, 2017).

In the following years, Operation Queer/*cochona* sponsored a series of often provocative events. For instance, Javier Poveda of the newspaper *El Nuevo Diario* wrote of an upcoming event at Managua's Tabú Discoteque:

It will be another gathering of the Operation Queer artist collective, that for four consecutive years has convened [events] and partaken with participants in distinct ways (performances and conferences) regarding themes of gender and sexuality. Operation Queer member Guillermo Sáenz pointed out that as part of the party they would be presenting a performative conference that "was born of a series of workshops called *Cochona* memoir, which we have been working on in the collective for a whole year, in this conference, through our personal memories, we will address themes like sexual awakening from childhood and the construction of our identities as a result of abuse, what it means to be outside of heteronormativity, new ways to have affectionate relations with others, being political within sexual and gender dissidence, how memory has helped us to construct the community in which we live, among other things" (Poveda 2016).

Not everyone loved their work, as was evident when the management of *El Centro Cultural Pablo Antonio Cuadra* (the Pablo Antonio Cuadra Cultural Center) "censored four works at the Operation Queer 2015 art exhibition. According to [Ana Victoria] Portocarrero, [it was censored] because some of the works show nudity, mix religious and LGBTQ elements, and show men having sex. 'I understand that many people may be offended by it, but it is a valid form of art. Aside from the content of the work, even though we accept art shows on sexual diversity, we continue to define what is acceptable and what is not'" (López Chavarría 2015).

The members of the collective decided they preferred to close the exhibit rather than to leave it up in a partial way. After a lot of media coverage, the management at *Galerías Códice* (Manuscript Gallery) volunteered its space for the entire show, including the controversial parts. So, in the end, the show got more attention than it would have otherwise, and the Operation Queer/ *cochona* collective probably benefitted from the censorship, as so often occurs with censorship (*Esta Noche* 2015; https://www.operacionqueer.com/).

2014

In 2014 a group of people from the town of Jalapa and the surrounding countryside in the far northern department of *Nueva Segovia* founded *Grupo Fabiola* (Fabiola Group) "with the goal of defending human rights, and increasing the visibility of the lesbian, gay, bisexual, and trans community" (Calero Sequeira 2015). Digmari Gómez, born in 1985, and president of Fabiola Group, explained that the forty members of the organization were inspired to come together in response to the 2013 murder of a trans woman named Fabiola, who was originally from the town of Somoto. Though members of the community, with the help of Marvin Mayorga of Managua's IDHDS, denounced the crime to the national human rights agency as well as to the local police, the crime remained unsolved.

One of the strategies that they used to prevent future tragedies, and to seek justice for their community, was a radio program called "*Atrévete a aprender*" (Dare to learn), which could be heard on Radio Voz de Mujer 90.5 FM. Gómez explained that "our mission is to send out messages so that our rights are respected; we talk about the meaning of trans so as to make people more conscientious, and to eliminate violence once and for all" (quoted in Calero Sequeira 2015; personal communication with Digmari Gómez by Facebook Messenger March 13, 2018).

2014 was also the year when the first organization devoted exclusively to trans men—called *Transmen Nicaragua*—was founded. According to Tyler Moreno, "TRANSMEN was founded on October 21, 2014, by two trans guys from the Southern Caribbean Coast region, Tristán Downs and Tyler Moreno. TRANSMEN works to make masculine trans people more visible in Nicaragua, for holistic health care for the [trans] population, [and] support for a law of gender identity in Nicaragua. Currently TRANSMEN is made up of more than 22 young people from 11 of the departments of the country, with its greatest number coming from Chinandega, Managua, Masaya, and the two autonomous regions [on the Caribbean Coast]. . . . We are the first group of trans men in Nicaragua, and we form part of the *Red Centroamericana de Hombres Trans* [Central American Network of Trans Men]" (personal communication through Facebook Messenger, November 29, 2017; for a short video of Tyler Moreno see La Costeñísima 2018).

The MRS was the first political party to create an LGBTQ network within its party structures, a project that was initiated by a small group including Joel Zúñiga in June 2014. At this writing it remains the only political party with such a network within the structure of the party. It was also the only party in which an open trans woman (Athiany Larios) held an elected position (Navas 2017; Vilchez 2017). Other parties, like the FSLN and the Sandinista Youth, organized LGBTQ people sometimes, but as Joel Zúñiga noted, without incorporating them into a permanent structure.

The FSLN uses invitations a lot. . . . One of the guys saved his invitation from the mayor of Estelí. . . . It reads: "Sexual diversity day for respect," [and then you] read below, "contests in cooking, the best hairstyles, beauty." So then the kids say, that is not promotion of rights, that is a circus. . . . We have a lot of . . . trans *compañeras* who tell you that they get tired of participating in street festivals, or in beauty contests, that is the only thing they use them for, like a kind of circus. When did they talk rights, about the right to a law about gender identity, a law for access to education without discrimination? Never. (Interview, July 20, 2017)

Many of the founders of the network built on years of experience. Joel Zúñiga, for instance, could trace his political life back to the 1980s, as a veteran of Sandinista Army, and a founder of Initial Group. But the majority of the over one hundred and fifty members of the network (in eleven of the seventeen departments of the country) had come to politics more recently.

Believe me it fills me with pride . . . that 95% of them are between the ages of 19 and 25. . . . Their main demand is for education: [they say] we want education; we want information; we want to understand the history of this country; we want to know how the political parties work; we want to learn about the laws. I think all this enthusiasm and interest in learning is funda- mental for the growth of an LGBTI community. (Interview, July 20, 2017)

It was challenging to work within an opposition party during the first de- cade after Daniel Ortega's return to power. During that period, power in all four branches of government[6] became increasingly concentrated in the hands of Daniel Ortega's allies until the point when many of the political parties, including the MRS, were stripped of their right to participate in elections, and the main opposition strategy was a purely symbolic election boycott (Mirando Aburto and Cerda 2016; Álvarez 2018; Chavarría 2008; Cruz 2016).

That concentration of political power and weakening of democratic in- stitutions had serious consequences for the LGBTQ community. According to Joel Zúñiga, while the decade of the boom was a good time for LGBTQ visibility as indicated by ever larger crowds at events like gay pride marches, being visible was not the same as having rights. Many who were happy to march for pride were afraid to demand rights, and those who had the courage to seek legal changes were repeatedly disappointed. He offered the example of gender identity laws in Nicaragua and neighboring Costa Rica.

---

6. As in many Latin American countries, the Electoral branch is the fourth branch of gov- ernment, alongside the Executive, Legislative, and Judicial branches.

To demand rights is not very easy in a country where democratic institutions are not functioning at all. Now under the will of such an absolutist government there are few possibilities to open up space to even pass a law. Look, the gender identity law . . . [is] the most accessible thing that one can imagine, because it is so simple: if you wish to change your name [you may], it is as basic as could be. That law has gone through proposal after proposal; it has been going on for something like ten years [but] they don't want to talk about it and it is not going to be passed. And in the neighboring country, Costa Rica, the law passed last year, so see the difference between one state and the other. (Interview, July 20, 2017)

Zúñiga insisted that the difference in the two countries was institutional rather than cultural. "Don't think that Costa Ricans are very open-minded, or that [Costa Rica] is a liberal society. No, Costa Rican society is more conservative than Nicaraguan society. But it has democratic institutions [and] a great deal of respect for individual rights. For me, that is the great difference" (interview, July 20, 2017).

2015

In 2015 Nicaragua became the only Latin American country with a labor union for trans women who do domestic work and other informal sector work, such as cutting hair and performing manicures, when the *Sindicato de Trabajadoras Domésticas y Oficios Varios Transgénero* (Union for Transgender People Who Work in Domestic Service and Other Jobs, or SITRA-DOVTRANS) was founded. Yadira Gomes, the executive secretary of the union, arrived in that position after a long history as a domestic worker and political activist. Born in December 1987, the fourth child of a woman who cleaned houses for a living, Gomes was only seven when her family reacted badly to her gender identity.

I began to dress in a feminine way, and to take on feminine mannerisms at the age of seven. . . . I had trouble with my mother and siblings, because my mother decided to force me into the street at the age of seven just because I wanted to be a woman. At that time nobody knew what was a trans women, a gay person, a transvestite, [but] she chose to throw me into the street at the age of seven. And because I was the way I still am, I decided that I would go, because I did not want her to tell me, while you are under my roof, that she would tell me what to do with my body, my way of being, my attitudes [and] virtues. I decided to go. (Interview, July 20, 2017)

A neighbor took her in, and that was when she became a domestic worker. "Today people say that really, she exploited me, but at that time I don't know that I would have called it exploitation. . . . That was a house where I was welcomed for many years and [the women] taught me to clean, sweep, cook. They raised me as a woman. . . . They practically domesticated me like any other girl. . . . We are the submissive ones; we are the ones who have to take care of things while men are out working. . . . Her slogan, that she would say to me, was that if I wanted to be a woman, I had to know what all women [know,] starting with cooking, cleaning, ironing" (interview, July 20, 2017).

Eventually, the husband of the woman with whom she lived objected to Gomes's presence. So when Gomes was a teenager, she spent time living on the street, negotiating a world of drugs, prostitution, and violence. Once she was attacked with a machete and nearly killed. While she was still recovering and selling Coca-Cola on the street with her aunt, some LGBTQ activists invited her to the Giordano Bruno House. There she met activists in the LGBTQ rights group IDSDH, the trans rights group ANIT, and the lesbian group Safo.

With the support of her new friends, she learned to read and write. She volunteered with ANIT and Trans Network for five years, largely working on HIV-AIDS prevention, until the "30th of May in 2015 [when] I was invited to a LGBTI community workshop at . . . the Acahual Women's Center . . . and that is where they talked about the issue of labor rights for the LGBTI population. . . . That was the way that I . . . began to immerse myself in the issue of labor rights, and I met a person who taught me, who told me, work on it, this issue is very important. Her name is Andrea Morales, she is the secretary [general] of the *[Federación de] Mujeres Trabajadoras Domésticas, Julia Herrera de Pomares* [Julia Herrera de Pomares Federation of Women Domestic Workers]. That was where we began" (interview, July 20, 2017).

The problem was that trans women were easily exploited because they had so few opportunities. "When we work as domestic workers, we don't get paid what the law requires. Right now, in the current month and year, a domestic worker should be paid 5,080 córdobas and [next month] in the month of August the amount will go up to 5,200 córdobas, a little more is coming. But they do not pay us what they are required to pay to us, the trans women; they don't pay us much. They pay 70, 80, 90 córdobas per day in a lunch stand, or a bar. For domestic work we are paid 100 córdobas per day or 80 [córdobas]. . . . We survive on a dollar or a dollar and a half per day" (interview, July 20, 2017).

With support from the Julia Herrera de Pomares Federation of Women Domestic Workers (FETRADOMOV), an affiliate of the Sandinista labor confederation, the *Central Sandinista de Trajabadores* (Sandinista Workers' Central or CST), and from the Central American Women's Fund, SITRADOVTRANS was created in August 2015 with 106 members (SITRADOVTRANS 2016, 6). The following year it received legal standing, and it was acknowledged publicly: "Our first accomplishment as a labor union was to go to the National Assembly. . . . We were invited to celebrate December 10th [2016], the National Day of Domestic Workers in Nicaragua, and where the National Assembly recognized trans women who are domestic workers" (interview, July 20, 2017).

SITRADOTRANS was also innovative internationally. To my knowledge it is the only union of its sort in Latin America. Gomes explained SITRADOTRANS was invited to the "third international gathering of domestic workers in Colombia. . . . I had the opportunity to go to give a presentation for the first time, on trans women. . . . There were women from 30 countries there, all [cisgender] domestic workers. . . . I was the only [trans woman] there" (interview, July 20, 2017).

By 2015, LGBTQ organizations had spent years lobbying for a gender identity law that "would permit [transgender people] to be registered in the civil registry with the name and sex they choose, as well as having personal documents that are consistent with their decisions" (EFE 2016a). Given its importance (it would save trans people from being harassed, or denied public services when they had to present identification in which the photo and name did not match their appearance and identity), many decided it was time for a new strategy, and so forty-nine organizations joined forces in the *Grupo por la Ley de Identidad de Género* (Group for a Gender Identity Law).[7] The very

---

7. The Group for a Gender Identity Law was comprised of: AEDSN, AMTC, ASOTRACHI, Fabiola Group, DEIGEORSEX, Movimiento de la Diversidad Sexual de San Carlos, Río San Juan (San Carlos Sexual Diversity Movement, or MODIVERSEX), ANDISEX, ADISEX, ADMUTRANS, ADISNIC, AMODISEC, ASONIDHJO LGBTI, Metamorphosis Club, House of Colors Collective, CODISEX, TransDesire Feminist Collective, INDS VIH+, MDS RAAS, MESC LGBTI, MOJUDS, MNACXDSSRR, MTGM, ODETRANS, Grupo Ideas por una Cultura de Paz Casa Matagalpa

existence of a coalition of forty-nine organizations from across the country was an important measure of the size and scope of the LGBTQ movement.

Due at least in part to the efforts of the members of the Group for a Gender Identity Law, Nicaraguan public opinion was warming up to trans rights. According to polls carried out by CID-Gallup in 2013, 32 percent said they would not be comfortable working alongside a trans person. By the time new polls were conducted in 2016, only 20 percent said they would be uncomfortable working with a trans person, while 65 percent would be comfortable. In 2013, 64.3 percent of Nicaraguans "rejected the idea that trans people should have an ID card that would identify them as they would wish, while in 2016 that rejection dropped to 47%" (Velásquez 2017c). That represented a rapid change in public opinion: over the course of four years, opposition to a gender identity law had dropped by 17.3 percent.

2016

In January 2016 a new organization, *Comunidades Diversas* (Diverse Communities), was founded by Harím Sánchez, the former coordinator of the LGBTQ movement within the Sandinista Youth. Diverse Communities—which often worked with Trans Network and Miss Gay—was not affiliated with the FSLN, though its members "sympathize with the FSLN. Diverse Communities is not within the structure of the FSLN, but some of the kids are coordinators within the [FSLN's] cultural movement, [and] some of them are neighborhood coordinators [for the FSLN]" (interview, July 17, 2017).

Like the Sandinista Youth movement, Diverse Communities was quite large. By October 2016, in the department of Managua alone, 1,749 people participated in the new organization (Harím Sánchez, personal communication by Facebook messenger, October 22, 2016). Among the activities sponsored by Diverse Communities was a campaign event for the FSLN in late October 2016. Luis Carlos Estrada, one of the participants in the event, explained,

---

(Group of Ideas for a Culture of Peace, Matagalpa House), TNG, UNE, RDS, AVETRANS, MDS-MANAGUA, ANJODISEX, Agents of Change, ADESENI, ANIT, MOVFEMD, Artemisa, GAY GAS, We are Tribadists Lesbian Group, Safo, IDSDH, ANICHTRANS, GAO, Grupo 8 (Group 8), MOVIDERSEX, Trans Goddesses, Joven a Joven (Youth to Youth, or JOV JOV), NOVA ODISEA, Grupo Drugo*s (Drugo*s Group), Transmen of Nicaragua (Excel document, sent by email by José Ignacio López Silva, December 3, 2015).

> We are here in support of the presidential ticket comprised of Commander Daniel Ortega and *Compañera* Rosario Murillo, [and] thanks to them there have been great changes and we want that to continue. . . . We want to continue forward, now we have access to health care with dignity, we can go to clinics that used to reject us . . . that gave us the chance to be able to develop ourselves even in our studies, they no longer reject us and in our sexually diverse spaces we need to follow them so as to become more empowered and with Daniel and Rosario we are always going to move forward (quoted in Areas Esquivel 2016).

Other activities that the members of Diverse Communities participated in included the LGBTQ pride parade in June 2017; according to Sánchez, 650 of them marched. They also worked to promote citizenship, human rights, and to prevent sexually transmitted diseases in coordination with the Ministry of Health.

While they did not have a formal budget for their activities, the government provided them with support. "They help us out with meeting places, auditoriums, they might provide a snack for the activities, for the meetings, but we don't have a budget as such. We are working on a proposal for employment and self-employment. . . . We are working on this project for entrepreneurial LGBTQ youth. We are going to present it to the government to see if it could be financed through the Ministry of the Family Economy" (interview, July 17, 2017).

On July 27, 2016, a coalition of three LGBTQ groups (IDSDH, Grupo Lésbico Safo, and ODETRANS) came together in a campaign named *En la Viña del Señor, Todas y todos somos sus hijos* (In the Lord's Vineyard, We Are All His Children). Unlike earlier campaigns, in which LGBTQ people spoke of their experiences, this campaign featured heterosexuals from all walks of life—television celebrities, evangelical ministers, musicians, and business owners—who supported equality for everyone, regardless of sexual orientation or gender identity. With support from the Human Rights Campaign (HRC) and the National Democratic Institute (or NDI), both NGOs based in the United States, and funding from the United States Agency for International Development (USAID), the Nicaraguan groups hoped that this campaign would reach a broad audience of young heterosexual people.

The campaign, which was partially inspired by a successful HRC campaign in socially conservative and highly religious areas of the southern

United States (HRC 2017), started with a video clip in which Eveling Lambert, the producer and presenter of the television show *Esta Mañana* (This Morning), talked about her support for the LGBTQ community. That video was followed by many more video clips and posters, which were shown on television and social media. Some of those videos and posters featured parents and other relatives of LGBTQ people, asserting their love for their children, just as God loves all his children.

As the campaign drew attention, several business owners became interested, inspiring the second phase of the campaign. If a business owner declared support for the LGBTQ community, "We would put up a sign that said, 'Discrimination Free Zone.' . . . So we came up with the idea for this heart, it is a circle containing a multi-color heart, and above that it says, 'Discrimination Free Zone.' So that was the second phase of the campaign, to seek out businesses; we already have 22 businesses" (Marvin Mayorga, interview, July 17, 2017).[8] The third phase of the campaign was to propose a municipal ordinance that would make the city of Managua a "Discrimination Free Zone." As of January, 2018, thirteen thousand people had signed petitions supporting that proposed municipal ordinance (Garay 2018; Velásquez 2017a).

2017

In June 2017, members of Nicaragua's LGBTQ community welcomed their counterparts from across the region to try to tackle the problem of unemployment. During the conference, which was planned by a coalition formed by members of "Safo, SITRADOTRANS, IDSDH [and] the Federation of Domestic Workers FETRADOMOV 'Julia Herrera de Pomares' of the José Benito Escobar Sandinista Worker's Federation" (Sequeira 2017, 2), more than 120 activists from Central America, South America, and the United States studied the problem and made plans to address it.

Since the "Primer Encuentro Latinoamericano y del Caribe LGBTI: Inclusión Laboral" (First Latin American and Caribbean LGBTI Gathering: Labor Inclusion) took place in Managua, many Nicaraguans attended, in-

---

8. The establishments that were "Discrimination Free Zones" included La Hora del Taco (Taco Time), Maura & Simón, Ruta Maya (Mayan Route), Radio Universidad (University Radio), Layha Bistro, Art Burger, Chocolate Momotombo (Momotombo Chocolates), UNAN-Managua (Autonomous University of Nicaragua–Managua campus), El Garabato (The Doodle), La Selva (The Jungle), Ron Kon Rolas (Kon Rolas Rum), Holiday Inn, and Walmart.

cluding members of twenty-one LGBTQ organizations. It was no surprise that the first such labor conference in the hemisphere was held in Managua, as the Nicaraguan movement stood out in the region.

But despite its size and national scope, the LGBTQ rights movement had not yet accomplished its goals regarding the right to work, and many LGBTQ people found that they could only get work if they hid their identities (Jarquín 2017). By 2017, many LGBTQ Nicaraguans had been organizing for thirty-some years, as I have detailed in this book. They sought a series of cultural opportunities and political reforms, all of which were important. But the right to safe and decently paid work was probably the most fundamental of those rights, a right that as of 2017 was far from being won.

CHAPTER FIVE

A Sexually Diverse Decade

2007–2017

As I documented in chapter 4, the early twenty-first century was a time of great growth for the LGBTQ movement. Others have made the same observation. According to Ana Quirós, "the decade from 2010 onward is like the decade of the 1990s for the [women's] NGOs" (personal communication, June 17, 2014). Similarly, Clara Murguialday notes, "LGBTI collectives and associations emerged so rapidly that in barely a decade (2006–2016) they went from 10 to 52" (2017, 50). What caused those changes during what I call the decade of the boom?

First, that decade began with Daniel Ortega's return to the presidency in 2007. In 2008, the FSLN ratified a new Penal Code (already many years in the making) that banned discrimination based on sexual orientation through several articles, specifically 36, 427, 428, and 315 (Moraga Peña et al. 2010, 8). Critically, the 2008 Penal Code eliminated the infamous anti-LGBTQ Article 204, in effect since 1992. Though the anti-discriminatory articles in the Penal Code were not generally codified into anti-discriminatory laws, the new legal regime might have given members of Nicaragua's LGBTQ community the confidence to organize without fear of breaking the law.

A second factor is that the FSLN—which had crushed the first efforts to organize a gay and lesbian rights movement in the 1980s—treated the LGBTQ community differently during its second time in power. Some individuals and organizations received economic assistance from the party; all benefitted from the fact that the party no longer persecuted LGBTQ groups simply for seeking rights. The FSLN itself may have had more to gain from that pro-diversity policy than did members of the LGBTQ community, as I will address in the concluding chapter. But even if the changes were mostly symbolic, symbols matter. It mattered that the pro-Sandinista press sometimes gave a great deal of positive coverage to the LGBTQ community (especially regarding activities that seemed more cultural than political, such as Miss Gay pageants or gay pride parades).

A third factor was that, in the twenty-first century, more funding was available to support LGBTQ activities than ever before. That is not to say that any of the organizations were ever well-funded. But just as the autonomous feminist movement that emerged after 1990 benefitted from a shift in the priorities of international development organizations (as they recognized that meaningful development needed to incorporate women), the LGBTQ movement benefitted, in the 2000s, from the development agencies' realization that development also needed to incorporate LGBTQ people. Foreign organizations that provided significant funds to some Nicaraguan groups included the United Nations Fund for Gender Equality, World Bank Country Coordinating Mechanisms, the U.S. Agency for International Development (USAID), the U.S. Embassy, and the Norwegian Embassy.

Foreign grants, while helpful in many ways, could also be problematic. Far more money was available for HIV-AIDS prevention than for cultural or political projects, and so some groups that might have devoted their energies to promoting rights found themselves doing medical work. The preference for HIV-AIDS projects tended to skew funding toward organizations comprised mainly of gay men (and to a lesser extent, trans women) and away from lesbian groups. Emphasizing HIV-AIDS projects continued to stigmatize the LGBTQ community by identifying its members with a disease (even though HIV-AIDS was hardly exclusive to LGBTQ people). And as is always the case, groups led by highly literate middle-class people, especially if they are proficient in English, have a better chance of getting resources than groups led by less-privileged people.

Nicaragua-based funding agencies were better than agencies based in other countries regarding the overemphasis on HIV-AIDS and the skewing of funds toward the relatively privileged within the LGBTQ community. For new organizations, no funding agency was more supportive than the Central American Women's Fund (FCAM). Founded in 2003 in Managua as a project of the autonomous feminist movement, by 2011 FCAM had "given financial support to more than 117 organizations" (Lina Morales, interview,

June 9, 2011).[1] FCAM prioritized organizations of young people who identified as women, the sort of groups that often have the most trouble raising
funds. Moreover, small grants—usually $5,000, occasionally more—came
accompanied with training in budgeting and program development, a critical thing for first time grant recipients, many of whom were teenagers or
young adults.

The other Managua-based funding agency that played a critical role in
supporting the growing LGBTQ movement was the *Fondo para la Equidad de Género y los Derechos Sexuales y Derechos Reproductivos* (Fund for
Gender Equality and Sexual and Reproductive Rights, or FED). Founded in
2009, it was supported by the governments of several countries, mainly in
Western Europe. The FED worked with civil society organizations, running
programs that fit into three categories according to the FED's coordinator,
Lola Castillo:

> The first, which is the most important in terms of our budget, is our contri-
> bution to projects. Once a year, we call for project proposals from 15 to 50
> thousand dollars, for one or two years of funding for the organizations. . . .
> There are usually around 16 to 19 projects every year. . . . Then we support
> small projects that cost up to 15 thousand dollars: six months, eight months,
> a year. We also support short term activities like marches, fairs . . . participa-
> tion in national and international events. And our second component is skill
> development. . . . We accompany them in their work; we advise organizations
> in specific issues and administration. We also organize thematic forums that
> are a place for dialogue between civil society and governments. . . . The third
> component of our work is knowledge building; we either conduct research
> projects of our own, or we support the research of others, and we promote
> exchanges of ideas. (Interview, December 4, 2012)

New laws, a new relationship between the FSLN and the LGBTQ community, and greater funding opportunities all contributed to make the decade

---

1. Up until 2011, the Nicaraguan groups that received grants from the Central American
Women's Fund included Safo Group, ARTEMISA, Agents of Change, the Lesbian group of the
IDSDH, ANIT, and ADESENI (Lina Morales, interview, June 9, 2011). Later grant recipients
included the TransDesire Feminist Collective, the National Movement for Sexual Diversity,
Sexual Rights, and Reproductive Rights (MNACXDSSRR), House of Colors, Trans Women and
Cultural Association (AMTC), and the trans labor union SITRADOVTRANS (FCAM 2018).

from 2007 to 2017 one of growth, creativity, and visibility. A final and critical factor was the role played by Zoilamérica Ortega Murillo, daughter of first lady Rosario Murillo, and stepdaughter of President Daniel Ortega.

How did Zoilamérica end up as a supporter of LGBTQ activism? Activism itself was not new for her. Indeed, from a young age, political activism helped Zoilamérica take some control over her life. During the years that she lived under Daniel Ortega's roof, participation in the 1980 Literacy Crusade, followed by coffee harvesting brigades and the Sandinista Youth, got her out of the house and gave her work that she found meaningful. For example, she explained that "the [Literacy] Crusade made me more conscientious as was true for many young people, and that was where my political life began. . . . It began with an unwavering moral training" (quoted in Belli 1998). In 1987, she began a new sort of political work when she was hired by Alejandro Bendaña, the secretary of state, whom she later married.

Shortly after April 1990, when Daniel Ortega passed the presidential sash to president-elect Violeta Barrios de Chamorro, thousands of Sandinistas lost their government jobs, to be replaced with supporters of the new government. A common response to that crisis, for those with sufficient resources and connections, was to create NGOs, allowing them to continue their previous work or to begin new projects. Alejandro Bendaña was one of many who founded an organization, the *Centro de Estudios Internacionales* (Center for International Studies, or CEI) in 1990. Zoilamérica joined him as a member of the CEI's staff.

The end of the revolution and the end of the Contra War largely coincided as, once Violeta Barrios de Chamorro took power, the administration of George H. W. Bush cut off funding to the *Contras*, forcing them to demobilize. But of course, demobilizing was not enough to heal the pain of the war. Reconciling former combatants from the Sandinista and Resistance armies took great effort, and the CEI was devoted to that cause for years. In 1996, Zoilamérica Ortega wrote a book about that experience, in which she noted that working with demobilized Nicaraguans "embodied the last five years of my life and it was the synthesis of three things that . . . made it possible for me to do this work accompanying them: The confirmation of my Sandinista values from the perspective of reconciliatory justice, the experience of being a mother, and having come to understand the reality of the demobilized [soldiers]. Those were some of the real privileges of my life" (Ortega 1996, v).

Despite the important reconciliation work she did through the CEI, and despite the satisfaction of raising a family, the 1990s were difficult for Zoilamérica. Even after she married and had children, Daniel Ortega continued to pursue her on the telephone, and her mental and physical health was often fragile. In 1998, two years after publishing her book on postwar reconciliation, she went public with her own story and spent the next several years occupied with court cases, both within Nicaragua and internationally, as she pursued her day in court, and attempted to reclaim the last name—Narváez—that she had been given to her by her biological father.[2]

Zoilamérica had taken over the leadership of the CEI by 2007 when her life intersected with new groups: an LGBTQ rights group (IDSDH), a lesbian rights group (Safo), and a trans women's group called AMGLIM.[3] They had big plans but little money. Samira Montiel, one of the founders of Safo, explained,

> When we formed this alliance, we had nothing between us, no money at all, [and] the alliance that we made was with what resources Safo and IDSDH had. We were a group of dreamers . . . for saying let's try to do something that has never been done in this country . . . from holding demonstrations to inventing completely new things that were not [drag] shows. We did not want another show; we had a political vision for what the demonstrations should be. . . . But as neither IDSDH nor Safo had legal standing, we did not have the right to administer money. Then one of the guys from IDSDH said, I know some people [and] he began to knock on doors. (Interview, December 9, 2015)

When the activist knocked on the CEI's door, Zoilamérica let him in. More remarkably, she agreed to help.

---

2. For many years after denouncing her stepfather's abuse, she used her birth name: Zoilamérica Narváez. But eventually she went back to Ortega (which had been her legal name since Daniel Ortega adopted her in 1986), since she was unable to change her name legally, and so was obliged to use her legal name for work purposes. Moreover, it was the name she shared with her siblings (Medina 2013a). As her first name is unusual and she is a well-known figure, most people, including those who do not know her, simply refer to her as "Zoilamérica." Others alternate between calling her Zoilamérica Narváez and Zoilamérica Ortega, sometimes at the same event.

3. In 2008, AMGLIM split and the activists who continued to work with IDSDH and Safo formed a trans group called ANIT.

It must have been a surprise when Zoilamérica said yes. She was married to a man and had never worked on LGBTQ issues prior to that knock on her door. But there were many reasons why she would identify with socially excluded people. According to Aynn Setright, "Her collaboration with the Sexual Diversity movement in Managua, which dates back to 2007, was born from her militancy in the Sandinista Revolution, that her training as a peacemaker began the day she first heard the testimony of a contra—but mainly because she had lived violence '*en carne propia*' or in her own flesh" (2013, 3). Zoilamérica explained,

> My own history of violence links me to other survivors. Together we discovered that we could promote collective healing through political advocacy. When I told my story of sexual abuse publicly I suffered a social stigma; the individuals in the sexual diversity groups also live with social stigmas and discrimination. I learned to negotiate with my family, with the State of Nicaragua, and with all those who had offended me. I learned to look for solutions, not just for myself but for others. I have learned to find justice in the love, solidarity and acceptance of those who work with me. (Quoted in Setright 2013, 5)

She emphasized that her successes in collaborating with LGBTQ groups and helping to raise money for their activities (which the CEI then administered as the other organizations lacked legal status), did "NOT come from her familial ties with the President and First Lady" (Setright 2013, 3–4).

A Big Push for Activism

In 2007, even before LGBTQ activists met Zoilamérica, they had been organizing demonstrations that featured music, dancing, and poetry reading along with political speeches. But it cost money to organize the demonstrations. Once they started collaborating with Zoilamérica she was able to utilize the status of the CEI, plus her own resources as an educated and socially prominent person, to raise funds for future demonstrations from the Norwegian Embassy and the FED.

The location of their demonstrations—the Metrocentro traffic circle (right next to the Metrocentro shopping center)—was chosen carefully. It was a good location, because it saw a lot of car and pedestrian traffic, and it had been used by demonstrators with a very different message.

We decided that we would hold our demonstrations in the same place where the evangelical pastors met to tell us that we were condemned people, and that we were going to go to hell. It was a carefully considered thing; it took us like fifteen days to decide, because we debated whether to hold it in the same place as the pastors from HOSSANA [church]. . . . If we set up there, they will call the police, they will throw stones at us, they will say tons of things [but] we decided to do it. Against all odds we are going to do it. We began the demonstrations on June 26, 2007. . . . Our intention was to set up there and see if the police arrested us. The police did arrive to prevent disturbances, [and] we thought that they were there to keep an eye on us because of our relationship with Zoilamérica. This has been like a school since that moment, the demonstrations went on for about two years every month. (Marvin Mayorga, interview, June 3, 2011)

In a video created by activists in the Initiative or IDSDH, they explained that their goal was to build alliances, especially with the women's movement, to do political work. Without naming names, the men and women of the Initiative criticized the "passive role" that earlier groups had maintained with respect to the state and society, the focus on social (rather than political) events, with a particular criticism for the Miss Gay contests, which they argued had the effect of reproducing "roles and stereotypes" (IDSDH 2009, 1:05). They also criticized previous antagonism between gay men and lesbians. In the video they described Article 204, noting that its elimination was the first, but not the only, priority for the Iniciative.

Most of the video was devoted to demonstrating what IDSDH (in coordination with the lesbian organization, Safo, and the Youth Network) did during its first years, illustrated with photos. In 2007 they organized four demonstrations in the Metrocentro traffic circle: one for pride day in June, one called "demonstration of pride" in September, one called "demonstration of masks" in October, and finally a November "demonstration in solidarity with people who live with HIV/AIDS." Members of UNE and Trans Goddesses participated in the demonstrations as well. On September 28, 2007, IDSDH signed "a political accord with the Autonomous Women's Movement and *la Campaña 28 de Septiembre—Capítulo Nicaragua* [the 28th of September Campaign—Nicaragua Chapter]" (IDSDH 2009, 1:12–1:30).

A January 25 demonstration marked the beginning of 2008, advertised with a poster exclaiming: "In January . . . *a calzón quitado!*" [boldly, without shame]. February was marked with another demonstration: "Through thick and thin, love and friendship continue." At the March demonstration, which celebrated women's struggles, Déborah Grandison, the *Procuradora Especial de la Mujer* (Special Ombudsperson for Women, from the state human rights institute) spoke, and singer-songwriter Gaby Baca sang for the crowd. The poster advertising the April demonstration read "Since Jesus said: 'Love One Another' Why Does Your Church Persecute Us?"

During those same months, the Iniciative and Safo members presented five different video forums on university campuses and participated in International Women's Day festivities at the UCA. In May they distributed posters that read: "The Sexual Diversity Initiative for Human Rights and Safo Group Invite You to Our Press Conference in Honor of the International Day against Homo/Lesbo/Transphobia," directing reporters to the Giordano Bruno House where the press conference was held, and where the IDSDH and ANIT had their offices. Also in 2008, they participated in demonstrations in the northern city of Estelí and outside the offices of the FED.

All these activities responded to the concerns that had led to the founding of IDSDH during the electoral campaign of 2006: most politicians were reluctant to take the risk of supporting LGBTQ rights as long as they saw those issues as anecdotal and only relevant to a tiny minority. The demonstrations, university visits, and press conferences all responded to the reluctant politicians, but the most important way to address them would be by documenting LGBTQ concerns, proving that they were not just a miniscule group of affluent urban people. Such a study required resources that IDSDH did not have in 2006.

A Much Higher Profile

In 2008, when they finally had those resources—space to work in the Giordano Bruno House, plus funding to carry out the research—the team, which was now named *Grupo Estratégico por los Derechos Humanos de la Diversidad Sexual* [Sexual Diversity Strategic Group for Human Rights, or GEDDS] began the study. Researching and writing turned out to be a challenge given the different backgrounds of the team members: "Before we did the study we realized . . . that there were real differences [among us] because of discrimination. . . . Almost none of [the trans women] knew more than how to read and write" (Marvin Mayorga, interview, June 3, 2011). While all had certain things in common, the experiences of gay men were not identical to those of lesbians or bisexual men and women. And none of them had faced as much discrimination as the trans women who were usually less educated than their colleagues, because the hostility they faced—from other children and even their teachers—had led many of them to drop out of school. Nonetheless, despite those challenges, a number of trans women made significant contributions to the research team.

Since the goal of the study was to prove to politicians and the public that their issues were not just anecdotes, the study had to be based on a large sample. Additionally, it had to cover all regions of the country, small towns, and big cities. Such a study was not going to be cheap.

> We did a pilot study in Managua with eight hundred some interviews, in almost all the districts of Managua, including *Ciudad Sandino* and *Tipitapa*, but we did not have the cash for a nationwide study. We thought that if we left it there it would be valuable but not as much. . . . Finally, we decided to do it at a national level [since] we could count on the support of the Center for International Studies of Zoilamérica Narváez. (Marvin Mayorga, interview, June 3, 2011)

The final study, entitled *Una mirada a la diversidad sexual en Nicaragua* (A Glance at Sexual Diversity in Nicaragua) was very impressive, by far the most extensive study on the topic up until that point. In its eighty-nine pages, the GEDDS team[4] presented a overview of the LGBTQ community in Nicaragua. Drawing on a sample of 1,295 interviews, the study covered themes such as violence, education, family life, health care, work, the legal system, human rights, religion, gender identity, and relations between LGBTQ Nicaraguans and governmental institutions (Moraga Peña et al. 2010). As it was posted online in PDF form, it was a critical resource for LGBTQ organizing and education.

---

4. Bismarck Moraga Peña coordinated the team and Ricardo López provided statistical support. The other members of the team who worked on *Una mirada a la diversidad sexual en Nicaragua* were Alberto Araica, Tracy Boniche, Marta Cuarezma, Jorge A. Fiedler, Jairo Dávila Flores, Carol Fonseca, Athiany Larios Zúniga, Manoly López, Marvin Mayorga Norari, William Mayorquín Flores, Jairo Mejía Largaespada, Zoilamérica Narváez, Antonio Parajón Loredo, Marilié Reyes, Vladimir Reyes García, Rosa Salgado, Samy Sierra Sandoval, Martha Villanueva, and Marcela Zúniga Lara.

Thanks to the relationship between the CEI and several LGBTQ organizations, 2008 was a year of demonstrations, lobbying, press conferences,
and research. As though that were not enough, the year closed with an international event. In December the "First Central American Seminar, 2008"
was held in Managua and attended by some 75 people. At that first Central
American seminar, the initial results of the research project, *Una mirada a
la diversidad sexual en Nicaragua*, were presented, and speeches were given
by Zoilamérica Narváez and "Ole Oveaas, Advisory Counselor of the Royal
Embassy of Norway in Nicaragua" (*El Nuevo Diario* 2008; IDSDH 2009,
1:36–3:03).

According to Carolina Gallard, the coordinator of the lesbian group within
the IDSDH, the three Central American Sexual Diversity Seminars (called
Encuentros in 2009 and 2010) were the most ambitious activities that they
organized. All of them were well attended: "Maybe 300 people at each one.
Many people stayed at the hotel and from there they came from the whole
country, from the greater Managua area, journalists were in attendance . . .
people were there from Panama, Costa Rica[, and] Guatemala. Last year we
had major figures from Cuba. They gave a wide-ranging presentation on
Cuban activism, led by Mariela Castro, who is the main supporter of the
LGBTQ community" (Carolina Gallard, interview, May 31, 2011; CEI 2008,
4–5; *El Nuevo Diario* 2008; Lara 2009a; Vásquez 2010).

In 2009, the activists of the Iniciative, Safo, ANIT, and the CEI (with economic support from the Norwegian embassy) continued to sponsor public
demonstrations, including the March "Feathers with Pride" demonstration.
They also launched a poster campaign on a range of subjects including sex
abuse, therapeutic abortion, young people, religion, and the love of mothers for their LGBTQ children. One poster series portrayed happy gay and
lesbian couples outdoors at recognizable spots in Managua (IDSDH 2009,
3:09–3:47).

Yet another innovation of 2009 was the inauguration of a series of leadership schools, which involved

the training of 47 leaders within the sexual diversity movement through 18
workshops covering topics of leadership, identity, negotiation, gender, and
research skills over 48 course hours. Additionally, [there was training] for
95 representatives from the movement for sexual diversity from Matagalpa,
Masaya, Carazo, and Jinotega and 161 persons identifying as transgender

from Managua, Nagarote, Mateare. Trainings served the dual purposes of transmitting skills to monitor cases of discrimination and violence against this population and taking initial steps to develop a national network to monitor the abuse of human rights within this population (CEI 2009, 16).

Those projects (leadership schools, demonstrations, posters, university presentations, press conferences, international conferences, and the nationwide research project) were mutually reinforcing. As Marvin Mayorga explained: "We began to be visible everywhere, they began to call us from all places to learn more about us, so as to get training. We went to give trainings in León, Chinandega[, and] to the *Asociación de Mujeres Constructoras de Condega* [Association of Women Construction Workers of Condega.] . . . We were beginning to have a larger presence, more responsibility, and more of a political vision" (interview, June 3, 2011).

By November 2009, the increasingly high profile of the LGBTQ community was clear when Omar Cabezas, the director of the Office of the Attorney General for Human Rights named María Samira Montiel Sandino special ombudsperson for sexual diversity (Lara 2009b). Samira Montiel, as she was called, was the first state advocate for the LGBTQ community in Nicaragua and initially the only one in Central America[5] (interview, May 31, 2011). As it turned out, Zoilamérica had a hand in that turn of events as well.

Samira Montiel explained how it came about. Montiel was one of the organizers of the First and Second Central American Diversity Gatherings, which took place in 2008 and 2009, and with preparation for the second gathering in mind, she stated,

We invited the Attorney General, Doctor Omar Cabezas Lacayo, and to the great surprise of all of us who were organizing the event, the man arrived. We had just invited him for the sake of inviting him; we invited the police, the Minister of Health, but nobody showed up. But then he arrived and when we saw him the first thing we said was, now what do we do, because we had

---

5. Four and a half years later, in April 2014, a similar office, the *Defensoría de la Diversidad Sexual adscrita a la Procuraduría de los Derechos Humanos* (Ombudsperson for Sexual Diversity within the Office of the Attorney General for Human Rights) was created in Guatemala (CIDH 2015, 247). In May of 2018, Luis Eduardo Salazar became the first "Comisionado Presidencial para Asuntos de la Población LGBTI" (Presidential Commissioner for LGBTI Affairs) in Costa Rica (EFE 2018).

not thought that he might come. Okay then, we are going to welcome him, and effectively that is what we did, we welcomed him: sit up here [on the stage] preside together with the rest of the organizations, and he joined us and said: It seems to me that it is necessary to address this issue as one of human rights. I admit that I am ignorant regarding this issue. I know nothing about it. I think it is very late for you to find me, [but] I would like to support this struggle, and I promise to support you. (Interview, May 31, 2011)

According to Montiel, when he heard Cabezas's surprising suggestion, the Norwegian Ambassador said, "If the Attorney General's office, or the Attorney General is really interested in that, we will provide the money so that it works out." Montiel and her collaborators realized that they would have to be involved: "The third point of the triangle is the organizations, and we said, okay, are we prepared to make a leap of that sort?" (Interview, May 31, 2011).

After a long process of debate and reflection they decided to accept the challenge. At that point, according to Montiel, "My understanding is that Zoilamérica went to the Attorney General [of Human Rights]'s office and met with the Attorney General [of Human Rights] and he said . . . I would like to name a Special Ombudsperson, but know what, I want an Ombudswoman, not an Ombudsman. I trust women more" (interview, December 9, 2015). After meeting with Omar Cabezas, Zoilamérica returned to the CEI and met with the coalition of LGBTQ groups known as GEDDS. After much deliberation they chose Samira Montiel, who said of her selection, "[It was] because I was the only lawyer [in the group]. That was something that worked in my favor, and the other was that my Sandinista affiliation was well known" (interview, December 9, 2015).[6]

As Ombudsperson, Montiel's duties included advising the head of the human rights agency, Omar Cabezas, on LGBTQ issues, educating state employees, and defending individuals who suffered violence or other forms of

---

6. The account in the CEI's 2009 annual report was consistent with Montiel's version of events. The report identified the creation of the office of the Ombudsperson for Sexual Diversity as one of the major accomplishments of the organization, directed by Zoilamérica. "As a result of CEI's direct negotiations with the Human Rights Office, the need to monitor and defend the rights of the sexual diversity community were recognized and the office of a special Ombudsperson was established with a clear mission to defend and protect sexual diversity rights. This was the culmination of an ambitious research and advocacy agenda carried out by CEI and its partners that form the Strategic Group for Sexual Diversity" (CEI 2009, 5).

discrimination. Additionally, her role was to educate the general population. She was so frequently quoted in newspaper articles on LGBTQ issues that she called herself "the most public lesbian in Nicaragua" (Brenes 2014).

Costs of the Higher Profile

Almost all the LGBTQ people who spoke of the changes in the early twenty-first century identified the creation of the office of the Ombudsperson for Sexual Diversity as a major advance. But complaints were also common. Many were not convinced that the existence of the Special Ombudsperson's office was evidence of the FSLN's support for the LGBTQ community. According to an activist who I call "Miguel,"

> I don't think the government supports [LGBTQ rights.] If it supported them it would speak publicly through a greater authority than Samira Montiel: in Cuba, the one who speaks of such things is the daughter of [President] Raúl Castro. I think [LGBTQ rights] is not a policy of the Ministry of Health as such, it is not a policy of the Ministry of the Interior, nor of the Ministry of the Family. It is not, [and] that is how I see it. [They say] since we have all these things on the table: children, youth, LGBTQ, women, what can we do to shut them up? Okay, let's create an Ombudsperson for Sexual Diversity, and then we will go out telling the whole world that we are the first Central American country to have an Ombudsperson for Sexual Diversity? What does the Ombudsperson do? Nothing. ("Miguel," interview, June 6, 2011)[7]

Miguel immediately qualified his comments, noting that Samira Montiel was a good person who was doing the best she could. But in his opinion, the real purpose of her appointment was not to promote LGBTQ rights. Rather, the point was to buy off, or shut up, an LGBTQ movement that was ever more prominent by late 2009. Even worse, some began to accuse the LGBTQ

---

7. Samira Montiel volunteered that she had heard such complaints. "Many people have the tendency to think that, well, the Ombudsperson [for Sexual Diversity] does not do anything. What happens is that our work is not so visible, [and] it is not possible to say, okay, let's have a public presence every five minutes. No, because we should remember that the Ombudsperson's office has a target population with whom we do specific work. And in the case of political office holders, we have spent years providing evidence about all the needs of the LGBTI community, which we then provide to the State" (interview, December 9, 2015).

groups that were involved in the creation of the office of Ombudsman for Sexual Diversity with having sold out to the FSLN in exchange for very little (*Comunidad Homosexual de Nicaragua* 2010a, 2010b).

Other activists thought that Samira Montiel's office was important, and not just symbolically. While discussing a meeting of LGBTQ groups, Evelyn Flores from the feminist NGO *Puntos* brought up Samira Montiel's role.

> If the meeting were today, since now we have an Ombudsperson for Sexual Diversity and as you know, Karen, here in Nicaragua lesbian, trans and gay groups do not have many resources, what the Ombudsperson's Office has done is to provide a few minimal conditions like a meeting place, water, coffee, the sort of thing that the NGOs have provided. But in this case [Montiel] as Ombudsperson is playing an active role. She is not just waiting until things happen; rather she is one more within the group who is organizing things. (Interview, June 6, 2011)

By the end of 2009, the LGBTQ rights groups that were allied with Zoilamérica's CEI had accomplished a great deal. Zoilamérica was able to use her social contacts to raise significant amounts of money, helping her less powerful LGBTQ allies to budget and manage that money, negotiating with the office of the Ombudsman of Human Rights on their behalf, and meeting with them weekly to help guide their work.[8] But some LGBTQ activists thought there was sometimes too much guidance. Or put another way, guidance could sometimes feel like control.

In 2010, when a coalition of feminist organizations launched the social acceptance campaign entitled "Their love DOES NOT hurt, your rejection DOES [hurt]," Miguel thought that an opportunity was lost. "When . . . the feminist movement put out banners that said 'I love Juan'[9] and on Channel

---

8. "Throughout 2009, CEI has convened the organizations and networks that form part of . . . GEDDS . . . weekly to aid in the planning and implementation of all of their activities. The 41 planning meetings held between January and November 2009 have enabled all members of the group to construct a common agenda to strengthen the sexual diversity movement in Nicaragua. Meetings have also been used to strengthen members' capacity in specific areas such as research design and implementation, communications and advocacy" (CEI 2009, 8).

9. For an overview of the campaign called "Su amor NO daña, tu rechazo SÍ" that used the slogan "Juan loves Carlos" posted in public places such as the sides of buses, see *Movimiento Feminista de Nicaragua* 2010a.

12 they started to talk about it, making a scandal about it, and people from the very [LGBTQ] associations came out saying that now is not the time to talk about matrimony since we are focused on other things. But for years we have focused on health, on education, and so? Until they give us health and education, we will not ask for another thing?" (Interview, June 6, 2011).

The feminist campaign was not about marriage. It was simply about visibility and tolerance. But in response to the campaign, several religious figures who were against such tolerance "accused" LGBTQ people of requesting marriage rights (Chamorro 2010). According to "Danilo" some of the responses to the social tolerance campaign were nasty, with some people saying that if there were marriage equality, "that a [male] pig could marry another [male] pig, a hen could marry another hen, they compared us to animals" (interview, June 8, 2011). Danilo explained that, in February 2011,

> All the sexual diversity organizations met with Zoilamérica and we had a debate with all of us from organizations who would be affected by gay marriage. And we all raised our hands and said we do not agree with that. Because we knew that that issue was not promoted by us, rather it was promoted by the fathers of the fatherland, by the PLC [the Liberal Constitutionalist Party], which was addressing this issue to counterattack. (Interview, June 8, 2011)

Representatives of fifteen organizations attended the meeting, and, according to Danilo, all organizations except for one (which one he did not remember) voted to reject marriage rights. He thought that in a country where some people compared sexually diverse individuals to animals, it was not possible to even ask for such rights.

> We are asking that you accept us as we are, that you do not compare us to animals. First, we have to begin from below so that in the future you accept us, then we would agree; but we are not bringing it up. We held a press conference where we agreed, and we put out a statement in which we proclaimed that we ourselves are not in agreement with gay marriage. What we were asking for is that you accept us just as we are. (Interview, June 8, 2011)

Finally, they sent a message to the National Assembly signed by all the organizations. Danilo said, "We asked Daniel Ortega, we asked the government to help us in that . . . he was not addressing the issue, but through him we asked for people to speak in the Assembly in favor of respect for us" (interview, June 8, 2011).

It was an odd thing for a group of LGBTQ activists to proclaim, in writing, that they were against greater rights for themselves. Some people, like Miguel, were unhappy to read

> in the government affiliated newspapers [that] "Sexual diversity associations say no to gay marriage." . . . This is not the time, that is what they said. My criticism is, then, when is it going to be the right time? Argentina did not have so many things ready when [gay marriage] was approved, nor did Spain. I am reading a book now about the activism in Spain and the history of Spain is an incredible history of rupture and rejection, and then to arrive at that triumph [the passage of marriage equality] in 2000 for me is very good. Because they didn't know how to do it either. . . . Also, I think that Nicaraguan society is [a] society that adapts to change rapidly. (Interview, June 6, 2011)

Maybe it was a lost opportunity. Or perhaps it would have been a disaster to pursue marriage rights at a time when powerful forces in society were lined up against them, and when public opinion was not on their side.[10]

LGBTQ Houses

In 2011, most of the activists who attended the meeting led by Zoilamérica decided that they had to pick their battles carefully, to continue to quietly expand their social presence, as with the CEI's creation, in 2012, of three new regional *Casas de Diversidad Sexual* (Sexual Diversity Houses). Those houses—in Masaya, León, and Matagalpa—joined Managua's Giordano Bruno House (*Comunidad Homosexual de Nicaragua* 2013a; CEI 2008, 3). According to the CEI's Ebén Díaz (who supervised the house project), the idea was that those houses would promote LGBTQ rights in each community. He

---

10. According to a 2010 opinion poll, only 15.6% of Nicaraguans supported same-sex marriage (Lodola and Corral 2010, 2). But there was evidence to support Miguel's suggestion that Nicaraguans were inherently tolerant and would come to accept marriage equality with time. By 2015, the percentage of Nicaraguans supporting marriage equality had increased a bit, to 19.2%. Respondents were far more supportive of LGBTQ rights when it came to economic concerns: 57.1% believed that "an established gay couple should have the right to use INSS services," that is, the right to social security benefits (Córdoba 2015).

noted that, so far, "the major accomplishment has been . . . the creation of four municipal ordinances against discrimination against sexually diverse people. . . . Manoly, who is a trans woman, already got the ordinance passed and everything by the city council [in Masaya]. And that has probably been the jewel in the crown of this project, having succeeded with the first ordinance" (interview, December 3, 2012).[11] In addition to lobbying for better laws, the houses provided a range of services:

> Psychological attention is offered, they are sent to allied groups that can offer this sort of attention to LGBTQ people who need it. Support is provided in cases of discrimination, cases of violence, cases of rape, violence of any sort, [and] we offer follow-up, we offer legal support. We have a team of lawyers, [so] if a case arrives, for example, of a rape, as happened to a gay guy in Matagalpa less than three months ago . . . we followed up with his case going to court, et cetera, until there is a conviction, that is what we are working on. Also, services are offered in education and leadership training. For example, in Masaya, we have a trans group . . . [who] frequently visit the house, and they get advice about their identity, leadership training workshops, political support. (Interview, December 3, 2012)

The plan was to open more houses; Díaz was hopeful that there would be ten houses across the country by the end of 2013.

The idea of the house itself being the project (rather than quantifiable services that donors often prefer) was a powerful one. Having spaces where people were free to socialize and organize was critical, especially given the lack of privacy in the multigenerational households in which most Nicaraguans lived. I had the opportunity to spend time in three of the houses (Giordano Bruno House in Managua, the House of Colors in León, and the House of the Butterflies in Masaya). All were large, cheery places with areas for large group activities and where multiple small groups could meet in private. They were also safe spaces that were available to members of the LGBTQ community, even if they did not have offices in the houses.

One experience was particularly instructive. I first interviewed Mario Gutiérrez in the large back patio of the Giordano Bruno house. To my sur-

---

11. On Manoly Massiel López (1968–2015) see Masaya para todxs 2015 and Vásquez López 2017d.

prise, that same afternoon the Miss Nicaragua Gay organization was using the house for the casting of the 2013 competition. And so, the sidewalk that ran along the side of the patio where we talked was a makeshift catwalk where beauty contest hopefuls paraded in evening gowns, high heels, and heavy makeup, accompanied by booming dance music. At one point, Gutiérrez commented upon the scene, "If these kids did not have this space, they would be enduring family abuse, sexual harassment from their own cousins [and] brothers, sexual harassment from their neighbors, within their schools, and on top of that the huge danger of being thrown out of the house by their parents due to their being gay. And to allow them a space for coexistence, that is enormous, huge" (interview, November 30, 2012).

Miss Gay Nicaragua

In April 2012, the Miss Gay Nicaragua pageant was held in Nicaragua's most prestigious venue, the Rubén Darío theater.[12] Zoilamérica Ortega Murillo served as a juror, and the event was sponsored by the Norwegian embassy, private donors, as well as the office of the president of the Republic. Even though neither President Daniel Ortega nor first lady Rosario Murillo attended, their party was acknowledged. Melodie Dicaprio, identified as one of the "transsexual dancers," told a reporter "We are grateful for the support of the Sandinista Front" (Agence France Presse 2012). Miss Gay Nicaragua captured many of the contradictions of LGBTQ organizing in the twenty-first century. Despite a long history of activism dating back to 1993, Ebén Díaz of the CEI was surprised by the way in which the national Miss Gay competition came together. Near the end of 2011,

three young people showed up here [in Managua], three kids from Granada looking for support from sexual diversity groups, because they wanted to

---

12. In 2012, Miss Gay Nicaragua was presented for the first time in the Rubén Darío theater, but that was not the first Miss Gay pageant in Nicaraguan history. According to Miss Gay organizer Luis Ojeda, the first pageants were held in Managua in the 1970s. "They were no longer held for political reasons [in the 1980s] . . . They started up again in the 1990s . . . and the pageant has gone through a significant transition process because now the [Miss Gay] pageant is seen as one of the most important ones in the country" (interview, December 4, 2013). For analysis of similar performances, part of the "Sexuality without Prejudice" campaign in the 1990s, see Howe 2013, 111–18.

celebrate the national Miss Gay Nicaragua pageant for the first time in the Rubén Darío theater. It was a group of three: two gay men who are a couple and the sister of one of them who is not a lesbian but who loves them very much. . . . They have been celebrating Miss Gay Nicaragua for about . . . 10 or 12 years, but they have always held it in Granada. Last year they came here and asked for interviews with activists, [with] LGBTQ groups, because they wanted to hold the pageant here in Managua. Some LGBTQ groups agreed, others said they were not interested. They said that they were going to do it with or without the support of the groups and they came here [to the CEI office] to ask for Zoilamérica's support. . . . Apparently, they fell under the good graces of Zoilamérica, and she said yes, that she thought it was a good idea and that we would help them. (Interview, December 3, 2012)

Díaz himself was not so sure, having always thought that gay beauty contests were "a waste of time." But Zoilamérica was taken with the idea, so it went forward. Her mother Rosario Murillo even offered some material support.

The first lady was the one who lent them the theater. She authorized the use of the theater, [and] she covered a good part of the expenses. In more than 30 years of activism we have never gotten anything from any government authority. Obviously, those kids [from Granada] have taught us an enormous lesson, that there are other ways of doing activism, that there are other trenches in which one can do activism, and that we are not the most capable [*mamacita de tarzán*;] there are others who can do it and who know how to do it. That is a very big lesson. (Interview, December 3, 2012)

Díaz described it as a beauty contest with a human rights focus, and in a certain sense that was true.

The event opened with contestants dressed in matching turquoise, white, and black outfits performing a dance to a medley including Lady Gaga's "Born This Way" and Christian Chávez and Anahí's "Libertad" (Liberty) (Martínez 2012). In the costume segment, the contestants marched on the stage, one by one in their elaborate dresses and headsets, asserting through their images that they too were daughters of Nicaragua. The contestant from Masaya, clad in yellow and black, adorned with feathers, mirrors, and masks, turned around on the stage as the announcer mentioned the Indigenous neighborhood of Monimbó, noting the elegance of its women. Managua's representative wore a gold and silver costume that extended far over her head and past her arms. Adorned with peacock feathers and what appeared to be images of saints, she was introduced with praise for the hospitality of the residents of Managua. Matagalpa's contestant, in her role as Corn Goddess, clad in green, yellow, and gold feathers, claimed to "reflect the arrival of Europeans to the American continent, for their encounter with our Central [American] culture." Chinandega's contestant wore a gown in the Virgin Mary's trademark white and blue entitled "fervor and faith, the mysticism of a people." She seemed to cross herself as she greeted the cheering crowd (missgaynic nicaragua 2013). And they went on and on, thirteen contestants, each equally fabulous.

Throughout the event, the masters of ceremonies emphasized that the lesson of the evening was that we are all equal. It was a human rights pageant and yet, the performance was also profoundly conservative. If they had been cisgender women many would have seen their portrayal of Nicaraguan culture—usually drawing on religious themes—as a reinforcement of traditional roles. If they had been cisgender women, the emphasis on appearance would have been a conservative message. Moreover, the Miss Gay candidates were not gay men nor lesbians—they were trans women. Many LGBTQ activists noted that the event should have been named Miss Trans Nicaragua, but that such a name might have been too daring.

Shortly after the pageant, the winner, Ladieska Diedrick, was interviewed by Xiomara Blandino on her morning talk show, First Hour, on channel two. That was hardly the first time that a member of the LGBTQ community appeared on Nicaraguan television, but it was notable for its respect and warmth. Blandino introduced Ms. Diedrick—fully made up in evening gown, high heels, and crown despite the early hour—explaining how important she was for Nicaragua, given all the changes that have occurred. Ms. Deidrick stated, "I think that people are a little more tolerant, that we respect each other a little more. And the fact that there is a Miss Gay in our country, that it has been televised, that it has been in the Rubén Darío theater, that they did it with the respect it deserves, that all [people] deserve, because we all are equal." Blandino then welcomed Ms. Diedrick, noting how beautiful she was, and how she loved the pageant, and how she loved Diedrick's answer: "You gave a Gandhi message, a message of peace."

The newly crowned Miss Gay said that "it was a triumph for the gay community" and that it had been an honor to be on the stage of the Rubén Darío theater, like so many great artists before her. Blandino agreed that it was an honor, explaining that she too had had that opportunity. As she mentioned her time on the stage of the Rubén Darío, viewers saw a photo of her in a bathing suit, performing in the Miss Nicaragua 2007 contest, which she won.

Of course, it was not exactly the same. Blandino asked what barriers she had to overcome to get to the pageant, and Diedrick explained, "Look, in fact families are the biggest barrier," sharing that she had faced difficulties with her own family. Her family recognized that she was gay but not that she performed in drag. "I can say that today my family accepts me, just the way I am. I think they support me to one extent or another, but maybe not like I would wish. But I think that it is always an ongoing process."

Blandino responded that parents are often unprepared for the news that a child is gay, or lesbian, or trans, asking Diedrick how she dealt with having to be the strong one even though she was the victim, "the person on whom all of that falls." Diedrick agreed, noting that coming out was not just a personal decision; it involved everyone. "Because at the end of the day, I think that we live in a community in which we have to learn to love each other, our neighbors, our *compañeros*, friends, despite the fact that often they exclude us from society." She noted that employment discrimination was an especially big problem, and that of all the members of the LGBTQ community, trans people were the ones who faced the greatest prejudice.

Near the end of the twelve-minute interview Blandino asked what Diedrick would recommend to families who learn that they have an LGBTQ loved one. "I think that the first thing is to learn to tolerate. Really, we don't want tolerance, but it is the first step. Because tolerance is like saying 'ok that is the way you are, whatever.' We don't want that, we want respect from society, and especially from the family" (Canal2Nicaragua 2012).

Xiomara Blandino's interview was one of many examples of positive press coverage of the Miss Gay Nicaragua pageant. Ebén Díaz, who had been a skeptic regarding the pageant, noted that Miss Gay Nicaragua 2012 represented a series of "firsts." It was the first time that the event was celebrated in Nicaragua's Rubén Darío theater. According to Díaz, it was also the first time a Miss Gay pageant had been held in such a setting anywhere in Latin America, and it was the first time the pageant had been televised.

On that day 64 representatives from the worldwide press got accreditation to be in the theater . . . from Deutsche Welle, from AFP, from CNN, from the BBC, from Univisión; that is, because it was an historic occurrence in which for the first time the LGBTQ community of this country celebrated an event in the most emblematic cultural building of the country. . . . The next day we did a review of some LGBTQ media and it had been the most viewed LGBTQ news in the history of Nicaragua. (Interview, December 3, 2012)

Despite his 20 years of experience in LGBTQ rights organizing, three young people from Granada, whose experience had been in "beauty contests, glamour, sequins, [and] feathers," taught him a new way of doing politics.

Díaz and his allies had previously sent letters to the first lady, but she did not respond. It took three young people who were not even FSLN party members (though they did identify with the party) to get a response from the first lady "authorizing the use of the theater. She gave an order to the Ministry of Culture so that they would help them. She did not attend, Zoilamérica did, but . . . she authorized the use of the theater, [and] she authorized the Ministry of Culture which got involved due to the order from the first lady, [and] she financed part of the expenses. And now that the event was such a success, she promised the use of the theater for next year—it is already guaranteed. I think it was an enormous accomplishment" (interview, December 3, 2012).

After 2012, Miss Gay Nicaragua pageants were never quite the same. In 2013 Miss Gay Nicaragua returned to the prestigious Rubén Darío theater, but funding was less accessible and there was much less press coverage. The 2013 theme was equality and inclusion, tied together with the slogan: Nicaragua Somos Tod@s. The winner that year, identified in the press as both Dallas Hernández and Elizabeth Ríos, took her political responsibilities seriously. "During my reign I am going to fight for LGBTQ rights because there is still a lot of discrimination." She also promised

that she would lobby Congress for the right of gay people to adopt children. She also would ask them to permit transvestites to change their names to coincide with their sexual orientation, through legal reforms that the union [*gremio*] would promote. The recently crowned one affirmed that the gay community—which is estimated to include 15% of the six million Nicaraguans—does not reject the possibility of fighting in the future for the legalization of gay marriage. (Agence France Presse 2013)

Zoilamérica Ortega Murillo continued to play a central role in the pageant (serving as a juror) and in LGBTQ rights activism more generally. One example of that role was a photo that was posted on the Miss Nicaragua GAY Facebook page on April 30, 2013. Zoilamérica, dressed in professional clothing (small gold earrings and chain, red print blouse, black pants), and Elizabeth Ríos, dressed in beauty queen attire (rhinestone necklace, earrings, and tiara, multicolor dress), smiled as they stood together in the front yard of the CEI. The caption explained: "Elizabeth Rios, Miss Gay Nicaragua 2013, will travel tomorrow to San José Costa Rica for the *Cumbre Centroamericana de Diversidad Sexual* [Central American LGBT Summit,] which coincides with the *Cumbre de Mandatarios Centroamericanos* (Central American Presidential Summit)" (Miss Nicaragua GAY 2013). Twenty organizations from across the region met on May 2 through May 4 in what was officially known as the *I Cumbre Centroamericana de Organizaciones LGBTI* (First Central American Summit of LGBTI Organizations). Zoilamérica explained that her goals included that the LGBTQ community "make advances in legislative changes so that the good will that there seems to be, is recorded in law, guaranteeing that rights are more visible" (ACAN-EFE 2013).

There were many ways to become more visible. As had been the case in 2012, the winner of the Miss Gay pageant was interviewed by Xiomara Blandino during her morning talk show. The eighteen-year-old beauty queen from Granada told Blandino that she entered the contest to "fight for the gay community" and because her family encouraged her to do it. She went on to say, "everything has been wonderful with my family." When fifteen-year-old Dallas Hernández told his grandmother that he was gay, she told him that she would always love him. She explained to him, "One doesn't place conditions on love, one just gives it" (Canal2Nicaragua 2013).

Visibility without Rights

Social and political integration could be contradictory, especially for trans women like "Martina" who explained,

> Trans women have always been utilized for a show. For example, where I live, *compañeras* come by to say there will be . . . caravans, that they will supply the gowns, that there will be floats. They go in their gowns, dancing, and all of that. They go on that the mayor is recognizing us and giving us

the opportunity to be visible, but when they need something and they go to the mayor's office, they deny their request. (Interview, December 7, 2012)

At one point Martina participated in a group doing a study that required information from the office of the mayor who was a Sandinista. "We went eight times, and of the eight times, we were seen once, by his secretary. . . . [Another time] the mayor saw me on the street and [said] 'look we are go- ing to have an event and we know that you are a well-known person who has appeared elsewhere, we would like you to honor us with your presence, blah, blah,' but when you really need them they are not around. . . . They sent me an official invitation from the mayor's office asking me to be the official representative of LGBTQ issues in [my town]. I said no way . . . because it was like . . . using me in all their events, that [Martina] is coming to dance, to provide decoration, [to provide] a show" (interview, December 7, 2012).

Another frequent complaint was that years after the Ministry of Health had promised to treat members of the LGBTQ community with the same re- spect as heterosexuals, that did not always happen. Either employees of local clinics were unaware of the agreement signed by the Ministry and LGBTQ groups, or they chose to ignore it. FED director Lola Castillo even objected to my referring to the 2007 elimination of the anti-LGBTQ Article 204 as an example of returning civil rights to the sexual diversity community.

> I don't see it as returning civil rights because the sexual diversity community does not have civil rights. I would [just] say that they decriminalized [homo- sexuality]. . . . That is, I see it as an advance because they opened more space for [the free exchange of] information, but that is it. . . . There is no right to adoption, marriage, social security. . . . Health is a problem; trans women do not have access to health, education, [and] the majority [of trans women] don't even . . . complete grade school. And for the lesbians, when they are found to be lesbians they fire them, when a lesbian goes to the gynecologist the first thing they ask is what contraceptive they use. They cannot image that a woman could have a partner and not have to do family planning. . . . There are problems with the issue of the parental rights of lesbians with threats from their families to take their sons and daughters away from them. (Interview, December 4, 2012)

Promised improvements had been only slowly put into practice, or not at all. Many state employees were rude to trans people; LGBTQ couples still could not marry and adopt children; lesbians still were not protected from job discrimination. Those were serious issues that had a huge impact on the quality of life of many Nicaraguans although they could comfort themselves with the thought that change was moving in the right direction, if much too slowly. But then the direction seemed to shift.

Pressures on the Norwegians

The Norwegian Embassy was a very important force behind the new wave of LGBTQ activism. So many panicked in April 2013 when Valdrack Jaentschke, Deputy Foreign Minister for Cooperation, told the Norwegians that they no longer could fund the many programs administered by the CEI. The reason? Because the director of the CEI was Zoilamérica Ortega Murillo (Vásquez 2013a). Matters of the state were never just matters of the state. In fact, there was little effort to disguise the confluence of family and state. When Guatemalan activist Aldo Dávila tried to lobby the Nicaraguan Embassy to permit the Norwegians to restore the funds, the ambassador told him that "he did not get involved in family affairs" (Vásquez 2013b; Comunidad Homosexual de Nicaragua 2013c).

Some outside observers guessed that Zoilamérica was able to do her work in support of the LGBTQ movement because she apparently reconciled with her mother in 2004, and because in 2008 she withdrew her lawsuit in the Interamerican Commission for Human Rights against the Nicaraguan state. Indeed, some hypothesized that she was quietly serving the interests of the FSLN, her mother the first lady, and her stepfather the president by patronizing the LGBTQ movement, and thus drawing a new social sector into the clientelistic networks of the party.

But in a rare interview with Fabián Medina of *La Prensa*, Zoilámerica explained that it only seemed that she and her family had reconciled. In fact, there never was a significant reconciliation with her mother, much less with her stepfather. Furthermore, she never repudiated her original accusation against her stepfather, President Daniel Ortega, that he sexually abused her for years, starting from the age of eleven. She had withdrawn the CIDH case because ten years of pursuing justice was taking its toll, but she always maintained the truth of her story.

Her explanation as to why the state, through the figure of Deputy Foreign Minister for Cooperation Valdrack Jaentschke, had made efforts to cut off funds to the CEI, had to do with her increasing international prominence as an antiviolence and pro-LGBTQ rights leader.

> The fact that since last year I began to get job offers from other Central American countries, I was elected president of the Central American platform for violence prevention, I think that intensified a series of actions that ended up affecting me. . . . [F]rom the time when I took on those responsibilities since last October, I began to get calls from [Nicaraguan] government officials letting me know that I did not have authorization to work. Nonetheless, that became worse in the month of January, when I was coordinating with the System for Central American Integration to work with [the] mayor's offices in Central America and for the first time, in a clear way, the Deputy Foreign Minister Valdrack Jaentschke made phone calls to say that Nicaragua had not authorized that they do this sort of work with me. Finally, and the most surprising thing had to do with the call that the same Foreign Minister Jaentschke made to the Norwegian ambassador to let him know about the government's concerns and to pressure him to suspend all the agreements he had signed with our organization. That practice makes it clear that there is a sort of bullying in diplomatic activities because they were using cooperation agreements as a way of intimidating or eliminating social actions that they may undermine in some way. (Quoted in Medina 2013a)

Medina concluded by asking if she had ever thought about leaving the country. It was a solution she rejected. "That is the sentence that I have heard more than any other during the past two or three weeks. I am going to struggle to be in my country. Much of my calling to struggle is something that I inherited from the revolution. I am a daughter of the revolution" (Medina 2013a). Clearly there were many ways to be a daughter, or a son, of the revolution. At the same time as the party of the revolution sought to cut off her attempts to carry out the values of the revolution, as she understood them, she tried to stay and fight.

The CEI Stands Alone, Almost

It was not surprising that the FSLN pressured the Norwegian Embassy to cut ties to the CEI as that pressure was consistent with previous efforts to constrain and control (when it could not simply co-opt) civil society. According to one prominent feminist, who had been one of the targets of an earlier effort to repress civil society, the efforts to cut off funding to the CEI had more to do with the Ortega administration's campaign to contain the threat of independent civil society than with conflicts within the first family. "At one point they wanted to exploit the struggle of sexual diversity groups and now that those groups have managed to organize and to have an important social presence, I think they dislike that" (quoted in Vásquez 2013c). Another social movement activist agreed, though he thought the conflict within the Ortega-Murillo-Narváez family was also important.

> The FSLN is taking advantage of the moment in which a new cooperation agreement is being signed by the CEI, the different LGBTI groups that are allied with this project, and the Norwegian Embassy to kill various birds with one stone: to eliminate the CEI's financing, to place conditions upon the donors (not just Norway), so as to eliminate the civil society organizations and incidentally to exhaust the LGBTI groups because for the great majority of them, they're dead without financing. Of course, they are taking away a number of our rights: the right to organize and ally ourselves with whomever we like (including NGOs), the right to work and liberty. They are absolutely declaring a policy of state homophobia, not just against these four LGBTI groups that benefitted from this project, rather it is a real blow against many other LGBTI groups that receive funds from other donors. (Personal communication by email, April 11, 2013)

He clarified that the state did not have the right to "condition" aid. Legally the state was not authorized to tell the Norwegian Embassy and other donors which organizations to fund and which to cut off. But of course the law was one thing, practice often quite another.

That activist, who had previously been employed by the CEI, was willing to speak out in defense of that organization. The only other LGBTQ organization that publicly defended the organization's right to raise funds without state interference was the Initiative, or IDSDH, which issued a communique condemning the pressures on the Norwegian Embassy and calling on the Norwegians to resist those pressures (Vásquez 2013d).

Two meetings were held on April 5 and 9, 2013, in the office of the Attorney General for Human Rights to come up with a collective response from the at least nine LGBTQ-rights organizations that were represented. It was ironic, to say the least, that a meeting to discuss, and possibly condemn, state pressures to defund an LGBTQ-ally organization was held at a state agency. As it turned out, the press conference scheduled for April 12 had to be cancelled, as the activists were unable to agree upon a response to the FSLN's pressure on the Norwegians (Comunidad Homosexual de Nicaragua 2013b and 2013d). Arguably efforts to undermine organizations like the CEI hurt the movement as a whole, but many were understandably afraid to publicly denounce the pressures on the Norwegian Embassy.

In the end, the Norwegians could not, or would not, resist those pressures. Not only did they cut off their funding of the CEI's LGBTQ-rights programming, but they turned around and signed an agreement with the state human rights institute. In that new agreement, the Norwegians promised to continue to fund LGBTQ rights work, but this time their work would be directly overseen by the Nicaraguan state. According to a press release dated May 13, 2013, "The agreement establishes as its goal that the community of lesbians, gays, bisexuals, transexuals, and intersex people (LGBTI) enjoy full respect, protection, and defense of all of their human rights, as active members of an inclusive and progressive society, and that such labor will continue to develop 'in alliance with the organized population and public institutions of Nicaragua, under the guidance of the Special Ombudsperson for Sexual Diversity'" (*Procuraduría para la Defensa de Derechos Humanos* 2013).

Clearly one goal of the campaign—to reduce the autonomy of civil society— was met as the state successfully pressured the Norwegian embassy to cut off an old ally in civil society and to sign an agreement to carry out its work with guidance (*asesoría*) from a state agency. If another goal of the campaign was to divide and weaken the LGBTQ movement, that seemed to be accomplished too. Many activists had told me what an important role the CEI, and Zoilámerica in particular, had played. And yet only two organizations—the CEI itself and the IDSDH—were willing to publicly criticize the state's efforts to cut off the CEI's funding.

Then it got worse. Early in the morning of May 10, 2013, several activists from the trans rights organization ANIT and the lesbian rights organization We are Tribadists walked the half block from their offices in the Giordano Bruno house to the office of the CEI. They were there "to 'demand' the handing over of computers that were donated by the government of Norway, that until a little less than two months ago financed a project defending the human rights of [trans people] in Nicaragua" (Comunidad Homosexual de Nicaragua 2013e).

Members of ANIT and We are Tribadists contacted personnel from the human rights organization CENIDH, which had been supportive of those former allies, and threatened to call the television stations. Since the CEI was no longer the recipient of Norwegian funding, the members of ANIT and We are Tribadists wanted computers and other material that had been purchased with the grant to be handed over at once, presumably to be carried down the street to their offices. The representative of the CEI explained that

> there is no problem in transferring ownership of the computers, but there is a legal process, established by the laws of this country, that must be followed in handing them over: the transfer should be notarized by a lawyer and once there is proof of the inventory to be donated, the transfer document must be confirmed by all the parties that are involved, and then the handing over of the computers will proceed. The laws of Nicaragua do not permit that donations be handed over to private individuals, and as ANIT does not possess legal standing [*personería jurídica*][13] the paperwork is somewhat more complicated, but it is not impossible. (Comunidad Homosexual de Nicaragua 2013e)

The author of the blog post, who clearly sympathized with the CEI's position, concluded with the proverb, "If you raise crows, they will gouge out your eyes" (Comunidad Homosexual de Nicaragua 2013e).

Later that week, ANIT activists filed a police report, accusing CEI personnel of having stolen their computers, other goods, and outstanding funds for salaries. "They allege that those materials were purchased with funds provided by Norway, so they claim that they belong to them. . . . In a communique they point out that there is no political goal. They clarify that, because they have been accused of acting on behalf of the Government" (Alvarado

---

13. Since the CEI possessed legal standing, something that was difficult for small or new organizations to obtain, it had "lent" that status to small, allied LGBTQ groups, giving them access to large grants that the CEI administered. This was a common solution to the problem of legal standing in Nicaragua: established organizations often lend their status to smaller ones. Of course that meant that the smaller organizations were dependent on the larger ones, which they might resent, though the other option was to have no chance of requesting grants.

2013). According to the members of the trans organization ANIT, "Norway sent an email which tells the CEI to hand over the computers. They explained that initially there were five organizations in the project, and some 28 people who earned salaries, while the CEI 'was the umbrella [organization]' for international aid and it administered and executed the funds," since as they noted, the CEI had legal standing and ANIT did not (Alvarado 2013).

Was it true that ANIT members acted with no political end? Did they act independently from the government as they claimed? It is certainly possible that they were panicked at the thought of losing access to the Norwegian grant money that had been dispensed by the CEI for several years and were doing what they could to recuperate something. Without legal standing, and without the educational and material resources that people associated with the CEI tended to enjoy, they had reason to feel vulnerable. Given the discrimination they faced, many trans women in Nicaragua found that the only way to earn money was through sex work. On the other hand, that very vulnerability would have made it easy for government officials to pressure them into a public confrontation with Zoilamérica's CEI.[14]

In contrast, the staff of the Norwegian Embassy was not personally vulnerable at all. They were educated, wealthy in comparison to most Nicaraguans, and did not even live in Nicaragua (rather, working out of the Norwegian Embassy in Guatemala). They would have seemed impossible to push around, and yet apparently it was easy to pressure the Norwegian Embassy to

---

14. According to Samira Montiel, the conflict had nothing to do with the government, rather the Norwegian Embassy would have withdrawn its support on its own. "The girls of ANIT came to me because CEI gave orders that they could not take their things out of the Giordano Bruno House and that is when they looked for me. They asked me to talk to Zoilamérica to ask her to give them their things back [they said] we are not asking for anything more than what belongs to us. It fell to me to go back and look for a solution to the conflict, but the conflict was irreparable, [the relationship] was broken. A few days later we had a scandal in the press that supposedly the government had ordered Norway to cut CEI's financing for its LGBTQ projects, but that is not true, it never was true. . . . What happened is that the project itself collapsed, logically that was going to come to an end. . . . Norway withdrew but it withdrew its cooperation from all Latin America, not because of a political question, rather because they definitely were rethinking their cooperation policies and that is valid. They withdrew and they are not going to continue to finance the Office of the Attorney General for Human Rights, nor any of the organizations. But it never was a question of the government [or] Mrs. Rosario [Murillo engaging in] persecution, not at all. The tensions were due to other things, and at no time was the government involved in this issue. That is something that was not the case" (interview, December 9, 2015).

cut off the CEI and to sign an agreement with the state Office of the Attorney General for Human Rights.

For trans women who were citizens and residents of Nicaragua, the calculus was totally different. Given the sort of educational and workplace discrimination that they faced, they had few economic options outside of their activist work. And since the value of their ties to Zoilamérica had just evaporated, it made sense that they would be open to a new patron. Whether or not FSLN officials were that new patron, the logic is the same. ANIT and We Are Tribadists might have acted on their own, or they might have acted on behalf of a new patron. Either way, the LGBTQ movement was weakened.

Despite the attacks on the CEI in April and May of 2013, Zoilámerica insisted on her right to live and work in Nicaragua. But the last straw came a few weeks later. In mid-June, she and her partner, the Bolivian Carlos Ariñez Castel (who had been a legal resident of Nicaragua for four years), joined a group of retirees protesting for pensions, a sit-in known as OcupaINSS. According to Wilfredo Miranda Aburto and Octavio Enríquez, "the persecution against [Ariñez Castel] . . . began . . . when the couple expressed their solidarity with the grandparents who [asked] the government for a pension" (Miranda Aburto and Enríquez 2013). At 2:30 in the afternoon of June 25, a patrol from the state immigration agency stopped the couple in the parking lot of a bank.

> Four officials, who traveled in a patrol, surrounded the vehicle in which Ortega Murillo was traveling with the Bolivian Ariñez Castel, who works as an adviser for projects and communications at the Center for International Studies (CEI). . . . "They told me to show them my documents, as I don't carry my passport every day, I gave them my driver's license, I returned [to the car] and they wanted to open the back [doors] of the car and get in," maintained Ariñez. According to his testimony, three of the four officials wore uniforms, the other was wearing civilian clothes when he got into their car, at that point the couple was getting ready to start their car when they saw the officers arrive. Ariñez recalled that one of the uniformed officers wore a Sandinista Youth shirt. (Miranda Aburto and Enríquez 2013)

Carlos Ariñez and his partner, Zoilámerica Ortega Murillo, were taken into custody, where they were separated. Zoilámerica explained to a reporter that while waiting for him, "I received a call from my mother telling me that these were the consequences for my actions and [so] I hold her responsible [for what happened to Carlos]" (Miranda Aburto and Enríquez 2013; also, Romero and Vásquez 2013). Within an hour or so Carlos Ariñez had been deported to Costa Rica. A few days later, Zoilamérica Ortega finally gave up, moving to Costa Rica to join Ariñez, along with her youngest child.

For Zoilamérica it was ironic to find herself in Costa Rica. She considered it "her second exile, in the same country, and in similar circumstances. In 1978 she arrived in Costa Rica holding the hand of her mother, Mrs. Rosario Murillo, fleeing from the Somoza dictatorship. [In 2013] she returned to Costa Rica, holding the hand of her nine-year-old son, and fleeing the powerful group that was headed by her own mother" (Medina 2015). In Costa Rica she supported herself by teaching occasional university courses and working with *Casabierta* (Open House), an organization for refugees, mainly LGBTQ people, from neighboring countries. "While in exile, she says, she has learned to live without the privileges that she had, for a time, as a member of a powerful family, and without the advantages that she had as a professional and director of a non-governmental organization in her own country. Now she lives like any other immigrant, and enduring harassment from the government of Nicaragua, [harassment] that did not end with her abrupt exit from the country on June 29, 2013" (Medina 2015; also, Miranda Aburto 2014). She hoped to return to her country someday, once the time was right.

After the Fall

Zoilamérica's flight to Costa Rica had an immediate impact on LGBTQ politics. The CEI closed its doors in July (*Comunidad Homosexual de Nicaragua* 2013f). Masaya's Butterfly House, and Managua's Giordano Bruno House closed shortly thereafter (Ebén Díaz, interview, December 5, 2013). For a time, the organizations that had offices in the Giordano Bruno House were effectively homeless. Eventually, the IDSDH was given a space within the long-established feminist health organization CISAS. ANIT and ANH rented space together in the Benjamin Linder House,[15] then later in a building

---

15. The U.S. citizens who ran the Benjamin Linder house (named after a U.S. citizen who was murdered by the *Contras* while providing electricity to small towns in the north of Nicaragua) had provided space for some LGBTQ gatherings in the late 1980s, the so-called "white parties" (in which partygoers wore white) at a time when it was still quite difficult for LGBTQ people to meet in large numbers. So there was a certain irony in the return of LGBTQ organizations to the Benjamin Linder house a generation later.

directly across the street from the house, in Managua's Monseñor Lezcano neighborhood. The lesbian organization We are Tribadists broke up around that time. Miss Gay pageants never returned to the prestigious Ruben Dario theater, and they were never again televised, though they did continue on an annual basis, typically in hotels. Even though Miss Gay never had an office in one of the LGBTQ houses, like many organizations and individuals it had benefitted from access to those spaces and from the support the pageant received from Zoilamérica.

After she fled into exile, resources were always harder to come by for those groups that had been closest to the CEI. Additionally, some felt that the movement was less energetic in Zoilamérica's absence, because as one activist noted, she is "a woman with vision; she is a woman who was raised with power; she was educated for power, and she knows how to attack power" (interview, December 2015). Nonetheless, in some ways activists were better off than they had been before the "Zoilamérica years." Many of them had made international connections, learning how to budget and how to do research. While many of them were experienced organizers when they originally knocked on Zoilamérica's door in 2007, their organizing went through multiple innovations in the years between 2007 and 2013. After she was gone, they were sadder, perhaps, but wiser too.

If any LGBTQ organization benefitted from that turn of events, it was the RDS, directed by José Ignacio López Silva and Juan Carlos Martínez. The RDS, which had been working on LGBTQ issues since 1998, was well-established by 2013, allowing it to successfully apply for grant money that became available when the CEI closed. One could argue that when the CEI's alliance collapsed, the center of gravity of the LGBTQ movement in Managua shifted to the RDS, which was instrumental in providing resources such as computers and meeting space to some of the more impoverished LGBTQ groups (e.g., Acevedo 2014), producing powerful videos (e.g., RDS 2012a), organizing and hosting events, and promoting innovations in LGBTQ organizing, including the formation of the LGBTI National Roundtable, the recording of local history (RDS 2012b), and the planning of the *Primer Conversatorio sobre Aportes LGBTI a la Cultura Nacional* (First Dialogue about LGBTI Contributions to National Culture). I now turn to that first dialogue, which was held at the UCA as part of gay pride festivities in 2017.

Cultural Pride

Who made you, witch
you emerged among the stars and moon
a paradise touched your feet
and thanks to God you were born a woman
—from *"Mujeres Brujas"* (Witchy Women) lyrics and music by Gaby Baca
    (Baca n.d.).

On June 26, 2017, singer-songwriter Gaby Baca participated in the panel entitled "First Dialogue about LGBTI Contributions to National Culture" along with the journalist and college professor Silvio Sirias, the novelist Carlos Luna, the performance artist Elyla, and the scholar, poet, and puppet artist David Rocha. The panel was moderated by José Ignacio López, who noted that "we also contribute to the country's development, for example, the *baile de negra* (dance of the black woman), which characterized the cradle of Nicaraguan mestizo folklore, is a transvestite dance; it is the symbol of Masaya. Today it is [danced by] a group of gay dancers who play an important role in preserving traditions and defining the aesthetic of fashion and dance. We have examples in theater, with [Alberto Ycaza], one of the principal playwrights in the country; we have prize-winning novelists; we have singer-songwriters, and all of that is unknown" (quoted in Mendoza 2017).

As far as she knew, Gaby Baca was the only open lesbian singer-songwriter in Nicaragua. Born in 1969, her childhood and adolescence were shaped by revolutionary politics—vaccination brigades, coffee picking brigades, literacy brigades—both the horrors of war and the cultural richness of the revolution. After the revolution ended in 1990, she spent time working in communications and was offered the chance to perform with groups that were patronized by big corporations. But she rejected communications, and corporate-supported music, so as to travel the world singing about the topics that mattered most to her, including street harassment, animal rights, single mothers, and love in Managua. An important figure at community events, Baca had participated in (and often performed at) gay pride events starting with the 2006 pride parade. "I feel like a real pioneer. I was remembering how in the first gay pride marches in Nicaragua there were about twenty of us" (interview, July 22, 2017).

In the most recent march [in June 2017] there were so many people that Gaby went unnoticed. It made me laugh because thinking back on previous years, I was always like the focus—there is Gaby!—but now there are so many of us that I can go about happily unnoticed in the middle of the crowd and that makes me very happy, because there are many young people. This year a lot of people even brought their families with them, which seems very important to me, the involvement and acceptance of families with a view to doing the same thing I do with my music. That is the spearhead to getting people to change their attitudes; still, we have a long way to go, a very long way. (Interview, July 22, 2017; for an interview with Baca see Arévalo Contreras 2013, 66–88)

Though she did not belong to an organization, both the feminist and LGBTQ-rights movements would have been poorer without her presence.

Carlos Luna Garay wrote what some called the first gay novel in Nicaragua: *Debajo de la Cama* ("Under the Bed," published by Centro Nicaragüense de Escritores in 2013). If it was not the first novel of its sort, it was certainly part of a select category, that is, Nicaraguan fiction that explored LGBTQ themes. Other works in this genre included Lizandro Chávez Alfaro's book, *Trágame tierra* ("Swallow Me Up," published by Editorial Diógenes in 1969), the collection of erotic short stories, *Misterios gozosos* by Erick Blandón ("Joyful Mysteries," published by Editorial Vanguardia in 1994), and the erotic novel *Cecilia Barbarosa* by José Román ("Barbarous Cecilia," published by Dilesa in 1997).

Luna was not a professional writer; rather, he worked in the tourist industry. But he had been a boy who loved to read and who wrote his own stories from the age of twelve. All that time reading and writing paid off, as his first novel, which he completed at age nineteen, won him a jury prize from the *Centro Nicaragüense de Escritores* (Nicaraguan Writer's Center). In some ways, the novel was autobiographical: the parents in the novel resembled his own parents, the beautiful Apoyo Lagoon was the backdrop for the early stages of the romance between the main characters in the novel—Alec and Eduardo—and the Apoyo Lagoon played a role in Carlos Luna's own life as he administered a hostel and a vacation house there (interview, July 21, 2017).

"Under the Bed" offered a powerful critique of sex and romance among middle class Nicaraguans. In one scene Alec complained about high school classmates who had sex with him in private yet disparaged homosexuality in public. "'They have the nerve to leave my house talking about their girl-

FIGURE 7 Singer-songwriter Gaby Baca passes out balloons at the 2017 LGBTI pride celebration in Managua. Courtesy of Jaika Gradiz.

friends like a couple of very macho guys after having penetrated each other repeatedly,' he laughingly told his friend Gabriela. . . . 'But of course, I am the only faggot, unless they are with me, they do not do anything together'" (Luna Garay 2013, 13).

Elyla also participated in the cultural panel. They were a cofounder of the group Operation Queer and a performance artist whose work reimagined gender binaries, political memories, and cultural traditions. Born in Villa Sandino (Chontales) in 1989, their work had been shown in "Spain, Holland, Nicaragua, Canada, United States, China, Cuba, Costa Rica, Guatemala, and Chile" (Elyla n.d.). It would be impossible to present an overview of their massive body of work, which is available online. Instead, here is an excerpt from Camilo Antillón's powerful analysis of one of Elyla's most famous performances, entitled "Sólo fantasía" (Just a fantasy).

Late in the afternoon of March 14 of [2015], at the time in which the sun is setting and the trees of life are illuminated, [Elyla], dressed in a costume gown of the sort that Misses wear in beauty contests, paraded down Bolivar Avenue, from the Hugo Chávez traffic circle, previously named the [Christopher] Columbus traffic circle, down to John Paul II square, previously named Carlos Fonseca square. The bottom of the gown made references to the Sandinista insurrection and revolution: olive green cloth, bullet casings, the silhouette of [nationalist hero] Sandino in black against a red background. Going up to the waist of the dress one sees a white dove surrounded with flowers, and in the bodice, costume jewelry stones and fragments of broken güegüense y el macho ratón masks (symbols of the national mestizo identity) adorned with cloth in pastel colors. The headdress, bracelets, and the walking stick that accompanied the gown are golden and their designs allude to the trees of life (sculptures of metal and yellow lights that are inspired by similar work of Gustav Klimt) that were recently erected along Bolivar Avenue and many other points in the capital city. On the back of the gown, one may view the same multi-colored sun that adorns the Chávez monument and the now gone bandshell at Faith Square, the points of the beginning and the end of [Elyla]'s march. [Elyla]'s heavily made-up face is white, and their beard is golden. Despite their efforts to hide their emotions, there are moments when one can see the pain of this two-kilometer march along the streets of Managua, caused by the high heels and the weight of the gown. At points they hide their face behind a wire mask painted with a white face with feminine features; a mask like those used by the men in drag who perform in the "dance of the black women" of Masaya and also how the guerrilla fighters of the indigenous neighborhood of Monimbó [in the 1970s] hid their faces, those that were captured by Susan Meiselas' lens as they practiced throwing contact bombs. . . .

[Elyla]'s route during the performance is also significant because it is a space that they understand to be "a sacred historical place" and which refers us to key people and moments in the narrative of the formation of the Nicaraguan nation. They walked close to two kilometers along Bolivar Avenue, recently rebaptized Route from Bolivar to Chávez, going by the ALBA Park, the monument to Pedro Joaquín Chamorro, the National Assembly, the Luis Alfonso Velásquez Flores Park, the monument to the unknown soldier, Revolution Square, Managua's old cathedral, Carlos Fonseca's mausoleum, and the monument to Rubén Darío. Watching [Elyla] walk down that avenue, walking past sites that are full of significance, wearing that gown of fantasy/memory/history, seeing their exhausted face, the pain that the high heels cause, seeing them trip and fall, we cannot fail to think of the suffering that the narrative of the nation disguises, of all the victims that are made invisible by that narrative. (Antillón 2015, 3–6)

Though Elyla did not speak during their performance, they expressed themselves in writing on the invitation to "Just fantasy." Antillón concluded his analysis with a reference to that invitation in which Elyla quoted the satirical writer Laurent Tailhade: "Why do the victims matter if the gesture is beautiful?" (Antillón 2015, 6).

The final panelist, David Rocha, wrote poetry, creative nonfiction, studies of the history of LGBTQ Managua (e.g., Rocha Córtez 2015), and he performed with the *Teatro de Títeres Guachipilín* (*Guachipilín* Puppet Theater). Rocha was born "on October 26, 1990, the same day when [then Managua Mayor] Arnoldo Alemán began to paint over the murals of the revolution. So I was marked by revolutionary forgetting at my birth, and it is very metaphorical because I always say that things don't happen by chance. And perhaps we could say that is one of the reasons . . . why I have so much interest in the past. As I say I am a *loca* who is tied to the past" (interview, July 11, 2017).

Rocha's extensive work was informed by memories of the Managua that existed before the 1972 earthquake. "In '34 my great-grandmother migrated from Granada to Managua with her two older daughters. My grandmother was born in Managua in 1945 and let's say that has marked me a lot. . . . That is why I like this city—crazy, chaotic, disordered, with all that implies—with

FIGURE 8 Operation Queer cofounder and performance artist Elyla performing in "Just Fantasy," Managua, March 14, 2015. Courtesy of Elyla.

all its eccentricity, I like Managua" (interview, July 11, 2017). Though his work was very different than that of Elyla, writing about it presented the same problem: no short summary could do it justice. With no way to resolve that dilemma I offer part of one of his poems, entitled "I have arranged my books."

I have arranged my books and I have put one next to the other, I have seen my life summarized in their vast pages lined up on the bookcase. I have seen my life and your kisses. . . .

I have arranged my books and I wrote in one of them the fleeting idea of our love in the past: I will kiss you in front of the Variedades Theater, I will kiss you in 1931 before the Holy Tuesday earthquake destroys the echoes of Raquel Meller singing "La Violetera," I will kiss you amidst the tears of Managua . . . and then you will know how much I love you.

And the books are still there, immobile, indifferent, and they accompany me in my memories this evening, the hugs that I did not give you, the words that I did not say to you, they accompany my shoes that are wet with the water of this city that I do not recognize as mine, wet with the desire to have you . . . here. (Rocha Córtez 2013)

Rocha did not identify as an activist: "Even though many people see me as an activist, I always say that my political trenches are the stage and letters" (interview, July 11, 2017).

Conclusion

Nicaragua's Family Regime in Comparative Perspective

In many countries in the Global North, and in some of the wealthier countries of the Global South, LGBTQ people have made remarkable political gains in the past generation. Legal successes include the right to marry, the right to legally change one's gender, and protection from housing and employment discrimination. Moreover, in some cases LGBTQ groups have had significant influence as a lobbying force.

As I argued in the introduction, those accomplishments would have been unlikely if not for a series of long-term social and political changes. In many countries, over the course of centuries, sexuality evolved from a practice rooted in community concerns for reproduction, to a practice rooted in individual concerns for freedom, pleasure, and identity. Central drivers in that transition were migration, changes in capitalism that led to the creation of urban gay and lesbian neighborhoods and businesses, along with liberal democratic institutions or democratization processes. Those factors, in combination, made often successful LGBTQ politics possible, although even where conditions were propitious, political gains nearly always were the result of long-fought battles by LGBTQ people and their allies.

In many countries, including Nicaragua, political leaders have found that they may benefit from extending rights to LGBTQ citizens and thus increase their own legitimacy through LGBTQ incorporation. So the concept of legitimacy is central to my arguments in this concluding chapter. Though the word "legitimacy" is often used as a synonym for "popularity," legitimacy is not just popularity, or even mostly popularity. It means that citizens believe that a ruler has the right to rule. So, one could dislike an elected president but still recognize the legitimacy of her administration, because one believes that electoral democracy is a fair way of choosing rulers. In electoral democracies, legitimacy resides in the system (the regime) rather than in the individual. In personalistic authoritarian or semi-authoritarian regimes, leaders must put much more energy into generating legitimacy than they would in an electoral regime as, in effect, they are the system.

Backlash Politics

Unfortunately, I cannot end this book with a happy story of ever-expanding rights. While in some places, urbanization, capitalist development, and increasing LGBTQ visibility provided opportunities for those who sought greater rights for LGBTQ people, in other places politicians found that those same factors provided opportunities to scapegoat LGBTQ people as foreign agents, or threats to traditional family values, or both. In doing so, some politicians consolidated their power at the cost of the rights—and sometimes the lives—of LGBTQ people.

As I discussed in chapter 3, LGBTQ Nicaraguans were victims of a political backlash starting in 1992, in the form of the antisodomy Article 204, the worse anti-LGBTQ legislation in the Americas at that time. The backlash was caused by what some saw as the threats of the revolutionary legacy, the emergence of the autonomous feminist movement, and the apparent encroachment of global gay culture, as indicated by the beginnings of the autonomous LGBTQ rights movement. Article 204, which was not overturned until 2008, did not prevent the growth of that movement, but it clearly had a chilling effect, and it was sometimes utilized as a tool against LGBTQ people by their own relatives.

Across the globe, backlashes against improvements in LGBTQ rights, or even greater LGBTQ visibility, were all too common. In the United States, the forces of backlash could be seen in 2018 opinion polls conducted by GLAAD and Harris Poll, which found increasing discomfort with LGBTQ people, a reversal of the trends of previous years. "GLAAD President Sarah Kate Ellis said that President Trump's policies, including his announced ban on trans military members and the appointment of Neil M. Gorsuch to the Supreme Court, were partially responsible. So was his rhetoric" (Curry 2018). In the United States, the increased visibility of LGBTQ couples engaging in homonormative behavior, like planning a wedding, did not always lead to their easy incorporation into mainstream society, as bakers sometimes refused to sell them wedding cakes, a refusal that was upheld by the Supreme Court (Liptak 2018).

In Indonesia, some politicians responded to international pressures to expand LGBTQ rights by attacking their fellow Indonesians. In 2016, "Indonesia's Defense Minister, Ryamizard Ryacudu . . . labelled the emergence of the lesbian, gay, bisexual, and transgendered (LGBT) movement in Indonesia as a form of a proxy war to subtly undermine the sovereignty of a state—without the need to deploy a military force" (Tempo.co 2016). The rhetoric of the "enemy from within" was accompanied by concrete policies: banning LGBTQ groups from university campuses, conducting raids on gay nightclubs, bathhouses, and even private apartments (followed with prison terms for some who were caught in those raids), and prohibiting the portrayal of LGBTQ people on television. That backlash was framed as a defense of traditional Indonesian values even though in "Indonesia, the world's largest Muslim-majority country, homosexuality has generally been tolerated, if marginalized" (Hutton 2017).

How do we explain those backlashes? Homophobic politics was often justified as a defense of religious values. But there was no common religious tradition that informed the scapegoating of LGBTQ people by Catholics in Nicaragua, evangelical Christians in the United States, and Islamists in Indonesia (and in fact, some of the people they attacked were themselves Catholics, Evangelicals, and Muslims). Another hypothesis would be that globalization was at the root of the backlash, though of course globalization also contributed to the expansion of LGBTQ rights.

Whether globalization ended up being a force for expanded LGBTQ rights, or a threat that justified crackdowns on LGBTQ people or their allies, was ultimately a political choice, one that often had little to do with reality on the ground. Noting that, in 2011, Muslim Brotherhood supporters suggested that Egyptians should support a series of Constitutional Amendments to stave off the threat of men marrying other men (even though very few LGBTQ Egyptians were organized, and none of them had requested marriage rights), Meredith Weiss and Michael Bosia wrote,

> The invocation of such incongruous marriage fears demonstrates the particular power of homophobia, not as some deep-rooted, perhaps religiously

inflected sentiment, nor as everywhere a response to overt provocation, but as a conscious political strategy often unrelated to substantial local demands for political rights. (Weiss and Bosia 2013, 2)

So we should expect waves of homophobic backlash to return periodically, as long as some politicians think they have something to gain through such politics.

Russia's Vladimir Putin may be the clearest example of a politician who has mobilized patriarchal and homophobic sentiments as part of an effective strategy to consolidate power. According to Valerie Sperling,

> Putin's numerous masculinity-displaying feats have included his "saving" a crew of journalists from a Siberian tiger (by shooting it with a tranquilizing dart), zooming around a track in a Formula-One racecar, braving rough seas to garner a skin sample collected with a crossbow from a gray whale, and showing off his martial arts skills . . . a "masculine posturing" that coexists with real failures of governance and an increasingly nondemocratic political system. (2015, 29)

Of course, Putin's remarkable popularity, with approval ratings as high as 88 percent in September 2008, "slipping to 55 percent" in 2005, and quickly recovering to hover in the range of 67–71 percent (Sperling 2015, 45–47) was not due to his image alone. "It is impossible to disaggregate the impact of Putin's masculine aura on his generally high approval ratings from that of rising oil prices and their positive effect on Russia's economy and standards of living during his first two terms. Yet, citizens certainly take seriously the overall image of their political leaders, and it is not purely economics that determine regime legitimacy" (Sperling 2015, 47).

Putin claimed that he would protect Russians from threats that were both internal and external. According to Sean Guillory, Putin needed to "create an 'other'—gays, immigrants, multiculturalism, the West, Fascism. . . . By exclusion and demonization of the 'other,' you consolidate society against threats. . . . It defines who is a friend and who is an enemy; who we are and who are the 'others'" (quoted in Newsweek Global 2014, 3–4). Those efforts to create an excluded "other" had serious consequences for many people.

In March 2012, a homophobic law banning promotion of homosexuality to minors was passed in St. Petersburg; this joined previous laws passed in multiple Russian cities, in effect outlawing gay rights rallies and the distribution of literature about homosexuality. In January 2013 a nationwide ban on homosexual 'propaganda' . . . [passed] by a vote of 436 to zero, with one abstention, before Putin signed it into law. It outlawed the distribution or expression of information that portrayed "nontraditional" sexual relationships in a positive light or that equated them in value with heterosexual relationships and that did so in such a way that minors could be exposed to this information. (Sperling 2015, 73–74)

Just as had been the case regarding Article 204 in Nicaragua, the anti-LGBTQ laws passed under Putin were sometimes utilized as a weapon in intra-family conflicts, such as those regarding child custody. More generally, the laws had the effect of making LGBTQ people more vulnerable to discrimination and violence than they would have been otherwise (Gevisser 2013).

The most extreme manifestation of the Putin administration's homophobic policies occurred in the Russian republic of Chechnya, in a campaign led by Putin ally Ramzan Kadyrov. In 2013, more than one hundred gay men were detained by police and held in secret prisons where they were tortured. "At least three of them were killed" (Sokirianskaia 2017). When a group protested the treatment of Chechen gay men near the May Day parade in St. Petersburg in 2017, twenty of them were arrested. "'They even deny they exist and deny the problem exists,' Andrei Potapov, one of the protesters, told Euronews of Chechen officials. A spokesman for the regional leader, Ramzan A. Kadyrov, [said] . . . that Chechnya had no gay men" (Kramer 2017). In 2018, the Chechen human rights organization "Memorial" confirmed that twenty-seven people had been disappeared (Rainsford 2018), including pop-singer Zelim Bakaev, who was grabbed on the street on August 8, 2017, and forced into a car, never to be seen again (Lobanov 2017).

Another way in which the Putin government built legitimacy was by promising a return to Soviet-era greatness, to Russian leadership on the world stage. Here again, patriarchy and homophobia became tools in the restoration of empire. U.S. theologian R. R. Reno endorsed Putin's homophobic and patriarchal policies, calling them "moralism." He argued that those policies were not just aimed at a domestic Russian audience but also at international social conservatives such as Reno himself.

> Putin is thinking internationally . . . positioning Russia to lead an anti-Western coalition along moral as well as geopolitical lines. In a speech last December, [Putin] pledged to defend "family values" and reject moral relativism, pointedly observing that this message appeals to "more and more people across the world who support our [Putin's] position." . . . For a long time, [the U.S. government and Western NGOs have] been promoting contraception and abortion throughout the world. More recently, we've promoted gay rights as well. The U.S. Department of State's Global Equality Fund, dedicated to advancing LGBT rights, is one among many initiatives, some government sponsored, others carried forward by international organizations. (Reno 2014)

Reno argued that many westerners' repudiation of homophobia and sexism, challenging what he called "traditional culture," is a new type of imperialism. "Reproductive rights, gay rights—they're the new White Man's Burden." Citing pressures on the Vatican, Uganda, Nigeria, and Middle Eastern countries, Reno argued that this "new imperialism, like the old imperialism, is bound to create ill will. . . . For every LGBTQ move we [in the U.S.] make, Putin makes a countermove, positioning himself as the global leader of traditional values over and against the moral nihilism that, sadly, is becoming the American brand. The goal of true patriots should be to deprive Putin of this easy anti-Americanism by restoring the moral dimension of our vision of freedom" (Reno 2014). Clearly Reno's equation of LGBTQ rights and reproductive rights with moral relativity runs counter to the arguments I have made in this book. Nonetheless, his insight that Putin's policies spoke to an international as well as a domestic audience was an important one.

Putin paid a price for his mobilization of homophobia, especially the violent homophobia in Chechnya, in the form of pressure from human rights proponents in powerful countries. For instance, the *New York Times* editorial board forcefully condemned what it called "Putin's war on gays" (New York Times 2013). In separate meetings with Putin in 2017, French president Emmanuel Macron and German chancellor Angela Merkel pressured Vladimir Putin to address a range of human rights violations including violence against LGBTQ people. Similarly, international human rights organizations, including Amnesty International and Human Rights Watch, condemned homophobic policies in Russia. In a ruling "in favor of three gay activists, the European Court of Human Rights found that 'the very purpose of the laws [prohibiting the 'promotion' of homosexuality] and the way they were formulated and applied' was 'discriminatory and, overall, served no legitimate public interest.' It ordered Russia to pay the men a total of 43,000 euros, or $48,000, in damages" (Chan 2017).

For the president of an oil-rich and powerful country like Russia, those sorts of outside pressures were fairly easily brushed aside. Indeed, pressures to respect human rights might have backfired, reinforcing Putin's antihomosexual "nationalist message, one that has positioned Russia as a defender of Christian and traditional values, and the West as decadent and godless" (Chan 2017). But for politicians in the poorer and less powerful countries of the Global South, outside pressures were often a real concern. For leaders of countries that could be hurt if their access to markets or development aid were cut off, harnessing sexism and homophobia as tools for consolidating power was more complicated than for a leader like Putin.

Like Putin, President Daniel Ortega and his wife, Rosario Murillo, concentrated power in their own hands over the course of more than a decade at the head of government. Like Putin, they invoked gender and sexuality to lend legitimacy to their rule but not by attacking the LGBTQ community. Instead, they sought to incorporate members of that community into their clientelistic networks rather than ceding to their demands for full civil rights, or outright repressing them.

From Revolution to the Family Regime

Looking back to the founding of the FSLN in 1961, it would have been hard to imagine the twists and turns of Sandinista politics through 2017 and even harder to foretell the role that LGBTQ people would play in that story. In the previous chapters of this book, I told that story largely from the perspective of LGBTQ people. In this concluding chapter, I consider that same story from the perspective of the government of Daniel Ortega and Rosario Murillo. As is often the case, the story is different when seen from another angle.

Ortega's return to the presidency in 2007 would not have been easy to predict: after all, he lost the presidential election of 1990 to Violeta Barrios de Chamorro, who was representing the UNO coalition, and he lost again in

1996, this time to the candidate of the PLC, Arnoldo Alemán. At that point, it seemed that Ortega's presidential career might have reached its end. But he retained considerable power as leader of the largest opposition party, and the best organized political force in the country, one that had the ability to mobilize people in the streets. "The question for President Alemán was how to incorporate Daniel Ortega and the FSLN into a new political regime without putting his Liberals' control of the state at risk" (Close 2016, 107). As I explained in chapter 4, the solution was to make a pact between Alemán and Ortega.

Ortega and the FSLN joined the pact as junior partners and probably would have remained that way except for events in the early 2000s. As the Constitution did not permit two presidential terms in succession, Alemán's vice president, Enrique Bolaños, successfully ran for president on the PLC ticket in 2001. According to the terms of the pact both Arnoldo Alemán (as the former president) and Daniel Ortega (as the second-place finisher) were seated in the National Assembly, guaranteeing them some formal power, along with immunity from prosecution. But then Alemán was elected president of the Assembly and began "to act as a de facto prime minister . . . [so] President Bolaños clearly had to defend himself and his presidency, and he did so by bringing charges of corruption against Alemán" (Close 2016, 123). Once a coalition of Sandinistas and dissident Liberals in the National Assembly voted to strip Alemán of his parliamentary immunity, Sandinista appointee Judge Juana Méndez (who had dismissed the sexual assault charges against Daniel Ortega in 2001) sentenced Alemán to twenty years in prison in December 2002.

At that point, Ortega and the FSLN used their control over the judiciary to alternately reward and punish Alemán and the PLC. "When the PLC cooperated with the FSLN, the conditions of Alemán's confinement were relaxed, usually house arrests in his *finca* (ranch) near Managua. If, on the contrary, the PLC was proving recalcitrant the Sandinistas could threaten to return Alemán to jail. This cat-and-mouse game continued until 2009, when Alemán was finally freed" (Close 2016, 125). By that time, Daniel Ortega's power was well consolidated, and the power of Arnoldo Alemán and the PLC had diminished to almost nothing: when Alemán ran for president in 2011 he received 5.9 percent of the vote, while Ortega easily won the election with 62.5 percent of the vote (Close 2016, 150).

Without the pact, it would be hard to imagine Ortega's reelection in 2006, or the consolidation of power in the hands of Ortega and his family over the following decade. Then his wife, Rosario Murillo, consolidated her many sources of formal and informal power when Ortega chose her as his vice-presidential running mate. She was second in power only to Ortega, and perhaps not even to him, in the opinion of many Nicaraguans. In 2017, pollsters from CID-Gallup reported that "Rosario Murillo, the first lady and vice-president, who also serves as the government's spokesperson, with daily reports in the governmental media, is the one who really 'rules' in Nicaragua, according to 53% of respondents to a national survey" (Cerda 2017).[1]

Ortega and Murillo governed with the help of a small group of loyal followers, most important, many of their own children (BBC Mundo 2017; Close 2016, 135, 137–38, 145; Esta Noche 2016a; Salinas Maldonado 2016b; Univisión 2011). The result was a regime that observers have classified with terms including "semi-democratic," "hybrid," "authoritarian," "strongman politics with amoral family-ism," and "modern authoritarianism" (Close 2016, 174–80; Martí i Puig 2016, 255–56; Salinas Maldonado 2016a; Flores 2017). Their efforts to consolidate power worked well. In fact, even though power was increasingly concentrated in the hands of the family of Daniel Ortega, the government tended to become more popular over time, as indicated by opinion polls.

In early 2018, according to Adolfo Pastrán Arancibia, CID-Gallop polls showed that "by those indicators the popularity of President Daniel Ortega was up to 50% [in 2007], while between 2014 and 2018 it was up to about 72% and between September [2017] to January [2018] which was the last time it was measured, the approval of the President [was] around 65%" (Ortega Ramírez 2018). Opinion polls carried out by Latinobarómetro, M&R, and CID-Gallop all showed similar patterns. Nicaraguans were sometimes displeased about the state of Nicaraguan democracy, political parties, and state institutions, yet they tended to approve of Ortega and Murillo (Carranza 2015; Carranza Mena 2015; Hispantv 2018; La Voz del Sandinismo 2018; Miranda Aburto 2016, 2017). There were many ways in which Ortega and Murillo consolidated their own power and legitimacy, starting with questionable legal changes, along with some electoral fraud.

---

1. Few people had knowledge of the inner workings of the state, and they could not know whether Ortega or his wife, the vice president, made most decisions. So, the confidence with which so many ordinary citizens asserted that Rosario Murillo was really the one who ruled the roost had a misogynistic element. It was the old trope of the henpecked husband.

Legal Changes and Electoral Fraud

In 2006, Daniel Ortega was elected president with only 38 percent of the vote, thanks to the electoral rules that had been created through the pact. But if those rules had remained in place, Daniel Ortega would have truly reached the end of his career with the 2007–2011 presidential term, since according to the Constitution, an individual was permitted to serve no more than two nonconsecutive terms. Fortunately for Ortega, he found ample opportunities to change inconvenient rules. Regarding those rule changes, the editorial board of the daily newspaper *La Prensa* wrote,

> Daniel Ortega's first blow against rule of law in Nicaragua was in September of 2010, when he utilized the judges of the Supreme Court to illegally reform Article 147 of the Constitution, permitting his reelection in 2011. In this way the Court spuriously declared that Article 147, which prohibits presidential reelection, was inapplicable. In 2010, with the desire to concentrate power more, the National Assembly, which was dominated by Ortega, approved a package of laws (Security Law, Border Law, and Judicial Border Regime Law) where significant powers were given to the Executive and to the Police, above the Constitutional rights held by Nicaraguans. . . . In addition, during those 10 years [Ortega] has used the judicial branch to eliminate political parties, to reject appeals of unconstitutional laws, to utilize penal processes to stop those who oppose his political projects . . . to penalize worker's protests, among other violations of rights (La Prensa 2017).

Once Ortega was elected president, he was able to use his power as president to appoint officials to the judiciary and the electoral branch. Then his appointees oversaw elections that—according to the media, outside observers, and even a Sandinista insider who spoke to me off the record—were increasingly fraudulent (Close 2016, 38–39, 145–51; Peraza 2016, 124–40).[2] Those elections allowed the administration to take control of the National Assembly, which changed a number of laws so as to extend Executive branch control over the police, army, and municipalities, and to protect insiders from corruption charges. Once the Sandinista appointees chose a day when no Liberal Party appointees were present to overturn the Constitutional pro-

---

2. For an astonishingly detailed first-person account of electoral fraud, see Bosworth 2012.

hibition on presidential reelection (Close 2016, 128), there were few institutional limits on the concentration of power in the hands of the executive.

Mass Media

The steady concentration of power in the hands of Daniel Ortega and his family was duly noted by many observers. One might think that the mass media would have served as an effective check on the government, but the media was increasingly owned or controlled by the Ortega-Murillo family and its close associates, as Julie Cupples and Kevin Glynn writes.

> The Nicaraguan television broadcasting system is now in duopoly. . . . The Ortega-Murillo family owns [channels] 4, 6, 8, 13, and 22, while Mexican media entrepreneur, Angel González [an Ortega ally], controls channels 2, 9, 10, and 11. . . . These channels make up 90 per cent of the terrestrial broadcasters in the country. Furthermore, the Ortega-Murillo family and González own more than 100 Nicaraguan radio stations. There is now only one nationwide terrestrial TV broadcaster in Nicaragua that does not belong to the duopoly: Channel 12. . . . Until recently, Nicaragua had two independent daily newspapers, the centre left *El Nuevo Diario*, established in 1980, and the centre right *La Prensa*, which was established in 1926 and belongs to the Chamorro family. In 2011, *El Nuevo Diario* was purchased by Banpro (a private banking group) and is now widely considered to be a co-opted publication that does not challenge the Sandinista party line (Cupples and Glynn 2018, 26–27; Close 2016, 138, 168, 182; López 2017; Miranda Aburto 2018).

Nonetheless, online sources like the newsmagazine *Confidencial* were good sources of investigative journalism so those people who had access to the internet, or who could afford to purchase *La Prensa*, could read independent journalism. Moreover, the investigative news shows *Esta Noche* and *Esta Semana* were available to television viewers six evenings a week. In no sense was Nicaragua a totalitarian state. But access to information is always mediated by money. That was especially true as the Ortega-Murillo family and its associates took over most of the radio and television stations, in other words, those parts of the mass media that were most accessible to lower income people.

The Economy, Social Programs, and Clientelism

Even though the revision of the Constitution and other laws to favor Daniel Ortega, the well-documented electoral fraud, and the concentration of the mass media in the hands of the Ortega-Murillo family was infuriating to many Nicaraguans, that was probably not true for the majority. In Nicaragua, like every other country in the world, most people judge politicians on the economy, and especially on the well-being of their own families. During the first decade of the Ortega-Murillo government, economic policy

> was built on three seemingly incompatible bases: redistributing wealth to alleviate poverty (below the \$2.50/day threshold) and especially extreme poverty (under the \$1.25/day threshold); following IMF standards and cooperating with Nicaraguan capitalists; and joining ALBA (Alianza Bolivariana para los Pueblos de Nuestra América), the regional alliance built by Hugo Chávez.... [During the period 2007–2012] Nicaragua's economy shows the third highest growth in Central America and effectively matches the Latin American mean. (Close 2016, 141; Spalding 2017, 170–73)

Comparing figures from 2001 (during the government of Alemán) to 2012 (five years into Ortega's presidency), the percentage of the population that lived in poverty dropped from 69.4 percent to 42.7 percent. Even more important, the percentage of the population that lived in extreme poverty dropped from 42.5 percent to 7.6 percent (Close 2016, 142). "That only the much wealthier Costa Rica recorded a lower percentage of its population suffering from extreme poverty is truly impressive since Nicaragua is Central America's poorest country" (Close 2016, 142).

The drop in poverty rates following Ortega's return to the presidency were caused by several things, including macroeconomic stability, annual growth "rates between 2.9 and 6.2 percent between 2007 and 2016" (*La Prensa* 2017), and remittances (money sent home by Nicaraguans working abroad), what has been called "the 'social security' of the poor" (EFE 2018). Remittances were strong during the first decade of the Ortega-Murillo administration. "During 2016, the remittances that Nicaraguans who resided abroad sent to their families [in Nicaragua] reached 1.264 billion dollars, the greatest amount in the past two decades, according to official figures" (EFE 2018; Sáenz 2016, 231).

The final factor that helps explain the drop in poverty during those years was a series of social programs including *Usura Cero* (Zero Usury, a microcredit program), *Calles para el Pueblo* (Streets for the People, a program of paving roads), *Plan Techo* (Plan Roof, distribution of sheets of zinc for roofs), *Hambre Cero* (Zero Hunger, distribution of animals and seeds to women), *Bono Solidario* (Solidarity Bonus, bonuses for state employees), and *Casas para mi Pueblo* (Houses for my People, or low-income housing). Those programs had several benefits from the perspective of the Ortega administration. First, they were often quite visible. For instance, houses provided through Houses for my People were painted in distinct ways, and the recipients of various "bonuses," in the form of money, or food that was free or subsidized, could be seen standing outside in line to access those benefits. Being visible helped to bolster the legitimacy of Ortega's government, perhaps even in the case of some people who did not directly benefit from those programs, as it was evidence of the government doing something to address citizen's needs, especially those of the most impoverished citizens.

Second, those programs provided very concrete benefits to people who participated, including inexpensive or free food, improvements in their housing, support for productive projects like vegetable gardens and small businesses, and neighborhood improvements (Close 2016, 142–43, 145–46; Kampwirth 2010, 14–18). Starting in 2007, "the Ortega government froze bus fares and subsidized electricity for consumers who use less than 150 kilowatts/hour. In an inflationary context, that makes commuting and energy increasingly cheaper. The workers who have to take two or more buses to get between home and work find that the transportation subsidy is a significant benefit" (Rocha Cortez 2016). Such policies made it easier for many working-class people to make ends meet.

A final benefit, from the perspective of the state, was that those programs and policies provided multiple opportunities for clientelism (Close 2016, 142–43). None of those programs were openly clientelistic, that is, none of them were supposed to involve a direct exchange of political loyalty for a material benefit. Nonetheless, they were sometimes used as political tools. For example, the *Empresa Nicaragüense de Alimentos Básicos* (Nicaraguan Staple Food Enterprise, or ENABAS) ran a program for several years in which subsidized food was available periodically at very small neighborhood stores. When ENABAS subsidized food was available, store owners sold it at below market rates. At other times they tended ordinary corner stores, but access to such subsidized food was sometimes politicized. Former guerrilla commander Dora María Téllez (perhaps the most prominent critic of the FSLN) told me that "The young lady who works in my house cannot buy in the ENABAS store because she works in my house. They do not sell her beans. They do not sell her sugar" (interview, December 5, 2008).

It was not obvious that ENABAS distribution would be politicized, as the only formal prerequisite for buying subsidized food was supposed to be willingness to stand in a line. But other social programs required that recipients be selected for participation, creating many more opportunities for clientelism. One study of participants in the Zero Hunger program in the municipality of Matagalpa found "it was impossible to identify even a single Zero Hunger beneficiary who did not identify as a Sandinista" (Grupo Venancia 2015).

Similarly, a 2009 report from the *Ministerio del Trabajo* (Ministry of Labor) implied that to "get a public sector job one needs the endorsement of the *Consejos del Poder Ciudadano* (Councils of Citizens' Power, or CPC). Last year, a little more than four thousand people got a public sector job just with the recommendation that they got from those official organizations" (Romero 2010).

Employees of state institutions (even those who were hired long before Ortega's 2007 return to power) were often expected to participate in political activities in support of the FSLN. According to one participant in a demonstration in a traffic circle, "'They invite us to assemblies, they tell us what activities there will be. This year I have gone to four. Every time there is an invitation one has to respond, and if you are not going, you have to give a reason [for not going]' explained a government worker who preferred not to provide a name for fear of retaliation. 'I am ashamed to be involved in such things, one does it mainly to keep one's job' the worker acknowledged" (Mendoza 2014). Additionally, they had to pay for the opportunity to participate in those political events: "The transportation, sound system, and drinks for the activities are paid for out of a common fund to which employees contribute every month. 'They don't cover the expenses through the payroll, on payday there is someone in charge of collecting a cash contribution equivalent to ten percent of one's salary,' explained the worker" (Mendoza 2014).

Though some participants in Sandinista activities were coerced, large numbers of the poorest of the poor chose to participate. In December of

2008, Daniel Ortega, and Rosario Murillo, along with other members of their family, personally gave away almost 40,000 packages of food to people who were needy enough to stand for hours in the tropical sun, in a line that stretched for five blocks, to get a package that included "rice, beans, sugar, oil, tomato sauce, cereal, and some sort of pasta" (Marenco 2008). I asked a Sandinista union leader where the money came from for those gifts, and he replied: "From Uncle Chávez. Thanks to aid from Venezuela, we have had a fairly good year regarding electricity. This [next] year, that aid is not going to be as generous" (interview, December 8, 2008). The union leader's explanation reflected both the glee and caution with which many Nicaraguans viewed Ortega's close relationship with Venezuelan president Hugo Chávez (on the importance of support from Chávez, see Close 2016, 140–41, 143; Jarquín 2016, 33–36; Sáenz 2016, 217–28; Spalding 2017, 170–72).

Defending the Family Regime

Due to tight controls over the mass media, relatively good economic times, and often clientelistic social programs, many Nicaraguans supported the family regime. But Chávez's 2013 death, and the subsequent collapse of the Venezuelan economy under his successor Nicolás Maduro, threatened those programs, some of which were quietly downsized or eliminated. Additionally, the government faced the ongoing problem that some citizens objected to Ortega-Murillo's increasing control over the institutions of the state and the mass media, as well as to electoral fraud. So the Ortega-Murillo government responded to those threats to their power by co-opting opponents in civil society (if possible), along with violence against opponents in civil society (if "necessary").

Prior to 2007, two of the most powerful institutions in the country—the big business organization *Consejo Superior de la Empresa Privada* (Greater Council of Private Enterprise or COSEP) and the Catholic Church—had tense and sometimes hostile relations with the FSLN. After 2007, COSEP and the Church's dealings with the Ortega administration changed dramatically. Both COSEP and the Ortega-Murillo administration benefitted from this new relationship. Business leaders made money, and in exchange they said little about corruption and the concentration of power in the hands of Daniel Ortega and Rosario Murillo's inner circle, an arrangement that some compared to corporatism, a system "in which the leadership of the private sector stands as the only actor that represents the rest of society in negotiating economic issues with the government, and those agreements are later converted into laws, endorsed by a parliament that has no power to deliberate because it is completely subject to the Executive" (Chamorro 2018; Spalding 2017, 168).

Church-state relations also changed compared with the 1980s. The most obvious symbol of that new relationship was Ortega's alliance with former adversary Cardinal Obando y Bravo starting around 2005 (when he and Murillo were married by Obando y Bravo) and the central role of the FSLN in abolishing therapeutic abortion in 2006, something the Church had been seeking for years.

Moreover, Daniel Ortega and Rosario Murillo promoted themselves as defenders of Christian values through the t-shirts worn by party members proclaiming in bright colors that Nicaragua was "Christian, Socialist, and in Solidarity." Similarly, billboards all over Managua, and in some other cities and towns, featured photos of Ortega, and sometimes also Murillo, similarly proclaiming Nicaragua to be "Christian, Socialist, and Supportive." Starting in 2013, Murillo offered radio and television addresses to the nation, nearly every weekday. She always opened her address with remarks of this sort:

> Good afternoon, *Compañera*, good afternoon to the dear families of our Nicaragua: Blessed, United, Always Free! Affectionate greetings to you from our Commander Daniel, and from the whole team of the Presidency of the Republic, and from our whole government, our state—Christian, Socialist and Supportive—where we feel, each and every one of us, proud to serve you, and with a firm commitment to try to do better every day. That is the instruction from our President: To serve our people, just as we serve God, our Lord. (Murillo 2017)

Following her introduction, which tended to follow the pattern of praising Nicaragua and its hardworking people, and offering the people a hug or other affection from her husband the President, who she often referred to by his title from the days of the guerrilla movement—Commander—Murillo would then discuss the news of the day, sometimes including international events but usually national news, especially regarding the achievements of the government (often reporting in great detail how many houses were constructed, or roads repaired, or individuals vaccinated, during the past month). Her national reports sometimes included information regarding saints' days, and how many people had made a pilgrimage to a particular chapel.

Murillo's phone calls to the nation, averaging twenty minutes each, were broadcast "on at least four television stations and the same number of radio stations" (Cronio 2018). She often provided detailed accounts of even small earthquakes, or other weather events. Speaking in a soft voice, she frequently expressed concern for the victims of various sorts of disasters: shipwrecks, traffic accidents, deaths in childbirth. Often, she would identify the person who died by name, offering her condolences and prayers to the family of the victim.

The president and vice president's religious discourse was accompanied by occasional meetings with Church officials (La Nación 2014). Sometimes members of the clergy openly campaigned for Ortega (El Nuevo Diario 2011b; La Prensa 2011), though that was not true of all Church leaders, and there were times when they criticized the administration for things like electoral fraud and repression of peaceful protests (Chamorro and Romero 2016; Salinas Maldonado 2009). While many members of the clergy were not fully co-opted by the Ortega-Murillo government, there was no doubt that during the decade spanning 2007–17 the Church had ceased to pose the threat to the Sandinista project that it had posed in the 1980s.

David Close referred to the new relationship with big business and the Church as one "of the great surprises" of the Ortega-Murillo government. Yet there were differences between the administration's policy of "elite accommodation" and its relationship with nonelite social groups. One of those differences was that protests by nonelite groups were sometimes met by violence, something that never happened in response to disagreements with COSEP or the Catholic Church (Close 2016, 138, 183).

In its 2016 report, CENIDH documented state institutions' increasing use of violence and impunity (Salinas Maldonado 2016c). According to CENIDH president Vilma Núñez, in 2016 Nicaragua faced the worst human rights situation of the organization's twenty-five-year history (Esta Noche 2016b). In addition to police and military violence resulting in the deaths of some political dissidents, during the decade of the Ortega-Murillo government, "Sandinista supporters began responding violently to peaceful protest" (Close 2016, 138; Martí i Puig 2016, 247). Civil society groups that were sometimes violently repressed included peasants protesting plans to construct an interoceanic canal that would have cut through their communities, people demanding pensions for retired people, Indigenous people defending their land, young people calling for environmental protections, opposition party supporters, and feminists (CINCO 2016; Espinoza 2017; Pineda 2016, 160– 85; Salinas 2017).

The Feminist Threat

Ortega and Murillo's support for the therapeutic abortion ban in 2006 could be viewed as a sort of payback to the feminists for their disloyalty, as I argued in chapter 3. During the Ortega-Murillo administration's first decade in power (2007–17) there were many other examples of payback including a campaign of ransacking and attacking several (mainly feminist) NGOs in 2008. That campaign, which finally ended due to a lack of evidence, was described in the journal *Envío* in January of 2009.

> On January 22, the Office of Public Prosecutor General decided not to criminally indict eight NGOs it had been investigating since October, after having accused them of money laundering and "illegal triangulation of funds" for their activities, with no evidence. It had also called some of their activities— such as the struggle to overturn the criminalization of therapeutic abortion— "conniving against a criminal act." The attacks on the Center of Research for Communication (CINCO), the Autonomous Women's Movement (MAM), the Civil Coordinator, the Nicaraguan Network of Community Commerce, the Network of Municipalist Women, Venancia Group of Matagalpa, Forum Syd (a Swedish NGO) and Oxfam UK was officially orchestrated with great fury by the Ministry of Government and pro-government media, causing an international scandal. In January the Public Prosecutor's Office returned to these NGOs all the accounting information it had requested—or taken by force, in the case of CINCO and MAM. (Envío 2009b)

Though that particular campaign against the NGOs came to an end, the Ortega-Murillo administration's first decade in power was marked by repeated attempts to constrain independent civil society in general and feminist leaders and organizations in particular, using tactics that ranged from fiscal harassment to personal attacks in the Sandinista press, repression of feminist demonstrations, and physical attacks on individual feminist activists (Álvarez 2017; EFE 2008; Kampwirth 2010, 24–28; Lacombe 2010, 105; Murillo Zambrana 2008; Villavicencio 2017).

Nonetheless, despite the administration's campaign to repress the feminist movement—or perhaps because of that campaign—feminists continued to confront the Ortega-Murillo government, both in Nicaragua and elsewhere in Latin America, to the point where it sometimes was difficult for Ortega to travel throughout the region.

> The minister of women's affairs in Paraguay's new left-wing government, Gloria Rubin, whipped up a media storm in August by calling Ortega a "rapist" and protesting his invitation to President Fernando Lugo's inauguration—an event Ortega eventually skipped to avoid the heat. A week later in Honduras, Selma Estrada, minister of the National Institute of Women, resigned her government post in protest over the official invitation of Ortega to Tegucigalpa. And in El Salvador, feminist leaders are asking their government to declare Ortega persona non grata before he's scheduled to attend a presidential summit there at the end of the month. Throughout Latin America, the feminist movement has become Ortega's nemesis, challenging his efforts to restore his image as a progressive and revolutionary leader. (Rogers 2008; Oettler 2009, 179).

A decade into Ortega's second presidential term, Edmundo Jarquín wrote that the feminists "have become one of the principal forces of opposition to the government of Daniel Ortega" (Jarquín 2016, 59).

It was simply impossible for the Ortega-Murillo administration to silence or co-opt many of the feminist organizations because their leaders were too well established. Instead, the Sandinista government periodically and repeatedly reached out to members of the LGBTQ community, because reaching out to LGBTQ organizations and individuals, and trying to co-opt some of them, helped to weaken the long-standing feminist-LGBTQ alliance.

Alejandra, an LGBTQ activist who had worked with several feminist organizations in the 1990s and early 2000s, explained, "Friends from the feminist movement see us now and say: 'Seriously? And now we see you with the red and black flag participating in the FSLN's marches. . . .' For me, political struggle has been undermined by partisan clientelism, in one way or another, and that weakens [our] social movement." She noted that she would like to maintain good relations with everyone, but that was difficult: "You are with the FSLN or you are against the FSLN" (interview, 2011). This could be seen as an example of the classic clientelistic game of divide and conquer, pitting one group against another. And the FSLN was good at that game (on Sandinista efforts to co-opt, divide, or demobilize civil society organizations, see, e.g., Cannon and Hume 2012; Cuadra et al. 2013; Howard and Serra Vásquez 2010, 73–77; Rogers 2013; Romero 2013).

Co-opting the LGBTQ Community

The FSLN's policies toward LGBTQ Sandinistas during the 1960s, 1970s, and 1980s were inconsistent. At best, the party welcomed the contributions of LGBTQ people, and, at worst, it repressed efforts by LGBTQ people to meet with each other, even within private houses. Given that history, it could come as a surprise that the policies of the FSLN, during its second decade in power (2007–17), were dramatically different. The "second Sandinista revolution" was marked by some legal changes that benefitted the LGBTQ community, along with multiple instances of the FSLN offering benefits to LGBTQ individuals and groups.

Yet there were limits to those benefits. "Vanesa," an activist in the Sandinista Youth's sexual diversity project, complained that the party was increasingly stingy with benefits for members of the LGBTQ community. She was particularly dismayed that LGBTQ families were explicitly excluded from the Family Code, approved in 2013, and that no LGBTQ family had ever received a house through the Houses for my People program, though Vanesa may not have known that the famous trans food vendor and performer, *la Sebastiana*, was the recipient of such a house (González-Rivera, forthcoming). In fact, she rejected my use of the word "clientelism" for the relationship between LGBTQ groups and the FSLN since, in clientelistic relations, the clients get things in exchange for political loyalty (interview, 2014).

Similarly, "José," an LGBTQ activist, noted that in the small town where he lived there existed as "a commission for LGBTQ affairs, in the mayor's office. . . . I have gone to meetings that are supposedly about LGBTQ affairs, and you always have to hold up the red and black flag. I don't think I am there to talk about [partisan] politics. I go to talk about LGBTQ issues. . . . The only thing that [the FSLN] supports is if we want to go to a beauty contest held by LGBTQ people, they give us a bus to take us there. But as the government is implementing different things, like Plan Roof for poor families, Zero Usury for working single mothers, I think that if they really supported LGBTQ people, they would provide all these options. But

LGBTQ people have not been given access to Plan Roof, nor Houses for my People, nor have they been offered loans, nor housing, nothing" (interview, 2012).

Despite the limits to the material benefits to LGBTQ groups, the most important thing was what the FSLN did not do during its second decade in power: it did not repress efforts to create LGBTQ rights organizations. Partially because of that freedom from repression, the period from 2007 to 2017 can be called the decade of the LGBTQ boom, as dozens of new groups flourished in small towns as well as big cities.

As I noted above, trying to break apart the alliance between the feminists and the LGBTQ community that had been forged during the years when Article 204 was in effect (1990–07) was one benefit of the FSLN's attempts to reach out to the LGBTQ community, from the perspective of the FSLN. Another benefit that the FSLN received from its new LGBTQ policy related to international relations. The early twenty-first century was different from the world of the 1980s regarding LGBTQ issues. By that point, most expected that twenty-first century leftists would promote the rights of many people who did not fit into the project of the classic left, including members of the LGBTQ community.

It was even possible to use a relatively good record on LGBTQ rights to justify other policies, or at least to distract attention from them. This practice was called *pinkwashing*, a play on the term whitewashing. In the political sense, to whitewash something is to cover it up—to deliberately conceal it; whitewash is a solution of lime and water used for painting something white. Similarly, pinkwashing is using gay-related issues in positive ways in order to distract attention from negative actions—covering up a problem by painting over it with pro-LGBTQ actions (Schulman 2012, 2011; Grass 2011; Lind and Keating 2013, 519–20).

One way to see the FSLN's policies with respect to the LGBTQ community is as an example of pinkwashing, as a way of improving its image in the international arena. Azahálea Solís of the Autonomous Women's Movement (MAM) analyzed the Ortega administration's LGBTQ policies.

> I think there is an opportunistic vision regarding the issue [of LGBTQ rights] because it is profitable in economic terms, in political terms, in terms of international image. I think that if we look at the moment [when the FSLN reached out to the LGBTQ community] . . . it is the moment in which there

is the most repression and intimidation directed against the women's move-ment. . . . How can anyone who eliminated therapeutic abortion, who re-presses women, be a revolutionary? There had to be a way out; the way out was not to go back to permitting abortion. I don't see any chance of going back on [the ban on therapeutic abortion]. Nor were there real possibilities of the FSLN co-opting the most visible and recognized feminist leaders. The FSLN could not show the international community a democratic, modern, and revolutionary face with respect to women. But it could put forth that image with respect to the LGBTQ movement, which turns out to be a grow-ing movement. (Interview, June 9, 2011)

The FSLN's LGBTQ policies helped it to present a modern and progressive face to the world, to paint over the stains of the total ban on abortion, credi-ble allegations of electoral fraud, and the consolidation of the institutions of governance and the mass media in the hands of the ruling family. That mat-tered since, for a small country like Nicaragua, maintaining relative domestic peace and prosperity was always dependent on maintaining good relations with international donors, lending institutions, and powerful countries, es-pecially the United States.

At a domestic level, those policies were a way to gain influence over some of the LGBTQ groups and to rein in their demands by co-opting them. One activist, whose organization was affiliated with Zoilamérica Ortega Murillo's CEI, explained that many LGBTQ leaders did not immediately realize that the FSLN was encroaching upon their work. While their organizations were never formally part of the FSLN (as was, for instance, the Sandinista Youth), some individuals "were associated with the FSLN's community work in one way or another, and with the naming of the Ombudsperson for Sexual Diver-sity, one could feel a bit more of the presence of the FSLN in LGBTQ spaces." That expanding partisan presence had an impact on their work.

It is not a coincidence that since we started to associate ourselves with [groups associated with the FSLN] we have lost some of our political presence. We have not organized a single demonstration [plantón] in more than a year, for different reasons. Now we have more money, thanks to the [Norwegian] Embassy project, but we can't organize the demonstrations that we did when we were penniless. . . . What we do in the public sphere, is linked to the decisions of the Center for International Studies, along with the FSLN. . . .

Personally, I feel deceived, because I expected an alliance to fight for human rights with accountability. Now what I see is that they call upon sexual diversity groups to give little talks . . . with doctors, in some district in Managua, and to travel to represent Nicaragua regarding international LGBTQ issues. (Interview, 2011)

This of course was how clientelism was supposed to work, from the perspective of the patron. In exchange for material benefits, the clients cede political control to the patron. So, the groups that were affiliated with Zoilamérica found themselves with more material benefits but also with greater political constraints.

Another reason for reaching out to members of the LGBTQ community was that it was one more way to build legitimacy for the Ortega-Murillo government. This was certainly true for some members of the LGBTQ community who repeatedly and publicly expressed gratitude to the presidential couple. Consider this excerpt from a gushing letter to the first lady, thanking her for her support for the upcoming 2013 Miss Gay pageant.

Dear First Lady,

Before anything else we want to thank you again for all of the support and trust that you placed in us, and for making our big dreams a reality.

You have taught us that, in life, it is not bad to dream, and whatever your goal may be, God needs to be there. . . . People like you and our Commander, forgive us if we are too bold to say that you are our angels.

But for LGBTQ people you are an angel, it is difficult for us to describe the love and trust you have offered us, if we had to describe it, it would be like the love of a mother for her child, that is the most sublime love. . . . [F]or us it is extremely important that you attend or delegate someone to represent you the day of the event, for we wish to feel rocked in your arms during our pageant. (Miss Gay Nicaragua 2013b)

According to the Miss Gay Nicaragua website (2013a), the Ortega-Murillo administration, along with several state agencies and several LGBTQ organizations, was an official sponsor of the event, though neither the first lady nor the president attended the pageant. Nonetheless, in the years that followed, members of the Miss Gay Nicaragua organization continued its praise. "Julio Sánchez, Public Relations spokesperson for Miss Gay Nicaragua, asserted that Nicaragua is now practically free of discrimination thanks to the inclusive policies of the administration" (Álvarez 2016; Radio Primerísima 2010; La Voz del Sandinismo 2012).

Ortega and Murillo's clientelistic efforts in the LGBTQ community were particularly aimed toward working-class trans women and their organizations (though the FSLN reached out to some gay and lesbian groups as well). That may be because trans women, as an especially vulnerable sector of the population, were simply easier to co-opt than many other people. But it is also likely that the government's interest in reaching out to the trans population built upon Nicaragua's long-standing, although usually unacknowledged, trans tradition (see González-Rivera forthcoming).

Legitimacy and the LGBTQ Community

Offering material help to some LGBTQ groups helped bolster the legitimacy of the government in the eyes of many members of the LGBTQ community and perhaps those of other socially liberal Nicaraguans. The dilemma, from a legitimacy perspective, was that while pro-LGBTQ rights policies could increase legitimacy among certain sectors of the population, the same policies could alienate other potential supporters of the Ortega-Murillo administration, especially leaders of the Catholic and evangelical churches with whom the administration was often allied.

Amy Lind and Christine Keating argued that the Ecuadoran government of Rafael Correa addressed this dilemma through a combination of homophobic and homoprotectionist strategies. For instance, the 2008 Constitution forbid "discrimination based on gender identity [and revised] the legal definition of 'the family' from one based on blood kinship to one based on a notion of diverse families," which included LGBTQ families as well as those separated by long-distances due to migration (2013, 522). But "the Constitution also [stated] that marriage exists only between a man and a woman and adoption can only take place among 'couples of the opposite sex' (Art. 68) . . . putting in place restrictions not present in the 1998 Constitution" (2013, 524–25). Apparent contradictions in the Ortega-Murillo government's LGBTQ policies could be seen as examples of an ambivalent inclusion of LGBTQ people, or a dual homoprotectionist and homophobic strategy. "Although seemingly opposed, these homophobic and homoprotectionist approaches are closely linked and political authorities often rely on a complex interplay of both approaches in order to mobilize consent" (Lind and Keating 2013, 520; also see Wilkinson 2018).

In chapters 4 and 5, I identified numerous examples of the state tacking back and forth between homoprotectionism and homophobia. One of the Ortega-Murillo government's earliest acts (promised to the LGBTQ community during the 2006 campaign) was to revise the Penal Code, and in so doing, to eliminate the antisodomy law Article 204, and to add a series of articles (36, 427, 428, and 315) that banned discrimination based on sexual orientation, to the Penal Code. Yet when it came time to ratify a new Family Code, diverse families were explicitly omitted, despite significant lobbying from LGBTQ and feminist organizations. Similarly, despite a multiyear campaign in favor of a gender-identity law (which would have allowed people to request new identification cards using the names with which they identified) no such a law was ever even considered by the National Assembly.

The state's relationship with the organizations linked to Zoilamérica Ortega Murillo, the role of LGBTQ people within the Sandinista Youth, and the relationship between the government and the Miss Gay pageants, all shifted over time. On the one hand, extending privileges to LGBTQ people made the FSLN seem more progressive. On the other hand, when push came to shove, the government's alliance with the Catholic Church and evangelical churches was more important than the alliance with the less powerful LGBTQ community. A gay FSLN party member told me he had spoken about this problem at party meetings: "Of course one must recognize that . . . the government has a stronger system of alliances with the churches than with the sexual diversity movements. That is a reality that we cannot deny. There are situations when they are going to prefer them" (interview, July 2017). The FSLN's efforts to maintain a balance between its different alliances meant there was a repeated pattern of steps forward, followed with steps back.

Despite all the many changes that had occurred to the LGBTQ community since Daniel Ortega was reelected in 2006, an electoral forum held at Managua's Holiday Inn in October 2016 was much like the electoral forum that was held in October 2006, which I discussed in chapter 3. Both events were sponsored by LGBTQ activists to lobby for the inclusion of LGBTQ issues in electoral politics. Both were events in which activists lamented the fact that none of the candidates had introduced such issues into the political debate. Comparing the two electoral events, things were slightly worse in

2016: in 2006 two small parties sent representatives to the electoral event, compared to none in 2016. Similarly, there was one openly gay candidate for National Assembly, Norman Gutiérrez from the *Partido Alternativa por el Cambio* (PAC) in 2006, and no openly LGBTQ candidates in 2016 (EFE 2016b; El Nuevo Diario 2006).

Despite the disappointment expressed by many at the electoral forum, in 2016, many LGBTQ individuals and groups campaigned for the FSLN, including an FSLN electoral event specifically for LGBTQ people, in which trans women performed on the stage, while a gay man played the role of master of ceremonies. The winner of the 2016 Miss Gay Nicaragua contest, Lisette Sandino, "expressed the support of the gay community for the Sandinista government, whose work has made it possible for [LGBTQ people] to live with more respect. 'Thanks to President Daniel and *Compañera* Rosario Murillo for supporting us. Step by step we have made gains, and the community's acceptance of us has advanced,' [Sandino] observed" (La Voz del Sandinismo 2016).

Luis Carlos Estrada told a reporter, "We are here to support the presidential ticket of Commander Daniel Ortega and *Compañera* Rosario Murillo. We have a big change thanks to them, and we hope this will continue." Another participant in the event, Norman Gaitán, thanked the presidential couple for its support, noting: "They gave us time off from work so we could be here, to speak out with peace and joy, for that reason: Long live the Commander and *Compañera* Rosario! We are going to cast our vote for box 2, the box of the people!" (La Voz del Sandinismo 2016).

By late 2016, many may have felt little choice but to support the FSLN's campaign, as there was no longer a viable electoral opposition. In late 2017, it might have seemed like support for the FSLN was starting to pay off when many LGBTQ Nicaraguans celebrated the swearing in of *fiscales* (legal advisors) by the Vice-Presidential Magistrate of the Supreme Court, Rafael Solís Cerda, in a ceremony at the Supreme Court. The trans rights organization ANIT announced the induction of "30 volunteer advocates who carry out the work of legal advisers as they themselves are LGBTQ people and people who are openly living with HIV" (Facebook post, December 13, 2017).

While the legal advisers were not to be paid anything for their work, they were provided with t-shirts, baseball-style caps, and black cloth bags printed with the logo of the Supreme Court, along with those of the Organization of American States, and the Kingdom of the Netherlands. The shirts, caps, and bags all identified them as "legal advisers" (*facilitadores judiciales*). The swearing in of legal advisors had been the culmination of the work of many organizations, as noted in a post that same day on the Facebook page of the LGBTI Roundtable (*Mesa Nacional LGBTI Nicaragua- Oficial*).

On July 9, 2015, during a meeting in the Hotel HEX between members of the LGBTI National Roundtable, and the Special Ombudsperson for Sexual Diversity, there was a discussion of the need to recognize the work for access to justice that LGBTI people had already been doing for many years; Harvey Maradiaga from Adis Nic proposed at that time that Legal Advisers be named. Today we succeeded with the swearing in at the Supreme Court of Legal Advisers who are committed to change the way in which cases are registered to identify the peculiarities of cases that affect LGBTI people. The LGBTI Roundtable has proposed a list of 30 people from all over the country. We congratulate Adis Nic, Amodisec Racn, ADISEX Siuna, Feminist Ideas Collective, Mojuds Ciudad Sandino; members of the LGBTI National Roundtable for their involvement in this process.

It was a happy day. According to ANIT's Facebook page, "lesbians, gays, feminine and masculine trans people, bisexuals, and people with HIV" were integrated into the judicial system in a respectful way (also Solórzano 2017).

But the happiness only lasted a few hours. The next day this short announcement appeared on the website of the Judicial Branch:

NOTE FOR THE PRESS
Thursday, December 14, 2017
Written by the Editorial Board
The Supreme Court announces to the public that the swearing in of 24 members of the LGBTQ community as Legal Advisers, which occurred on Wednesday the 13th of the current month, has been revoked, and the accreditation is voided, with no legal effect. Managua, Nicaragua, December 14, 2017 (Poder Judicial 2017).

That was it: no explanation, or apology, was ever offered. A reporter contacted Roberto Larios, the spokesperson for the judicial branch, but he refused to give any information, simply saying "that is the decision that has been made" (Gutiérrez 2017). Ludwika Vega of ANIT explained that there were close to forty people who were sworn in as legal advisers for the LGBTQ community or for HIV positive people. "'But they only mentioned 23 legal advisers, which is to say that they are only voiding the induction of the sexual diversity group.' Vega explained that on the day of the swearing in they took photos of her colleagues for their identification cards, gave them documentation, and explained to them that they would receive training four times a year to keep up to date with the current laws. Vega declared that none of her colleagues was personally informed about the decision, and they do not know why their induction was voided" (Gutiérrez 2017). So once again, a step forward was followed by a step back; homoprotectionism was undercut with homophobia.

Marching with Pride 2017

The decade (2007–17) in which the Ortega-Murillo government consolidated its power was also the decade of the LGBTQ boom. In June of 2017, the end of that decade was marked with a series of pride events across the country, including the panel on LGBTQ contributions to Nicaraguan culture that I discussed in chapter 5. The centerpiece of pride month was Managua's parade, which was notably larger than in previous years. Some accounts estimated the size of the crowd in the hundreds (Mojica and Villavicencio 2017; Velásquez 2017b), but photos and videos were consistent with other press reports that thousands marched (Canal 10 2017; EFE 2017a). Activist estimates ranged from five thousand (ANH 2017) to ten thousand (*Cuerpos Sin-Vergüenzas* 2017c).

That parade attracted more press attention than some previous parades, especially from those media outlets that were most closely linked to the FSLN, and that attention was overwhelmingly respectful. "Colorful" was the word that found its way into almost all journalistic accounts, referring to the rainbow flags (some were tiny, some were conventional flag size, some so huge that they were carried horizontally by a dozen people). "Colorful" also referred to the personal styles of the march participants.

Many wore black or white t-shirts with images of rainbow volcanoes shooting rainbow lava into the air. Some looked like Miss Gay contestants as they marched or rode on top of vehicles—waving beauty queen style—splendid in their evening gowns. Others, like Elyla (who wore a filmy black dress and high heels, their face made up with purple and green eyeshadow

FIGURE 9 Antonia Reyes and Jaika Gradiz at the pride celebration in Managua, June 2017. Courtesy of Jaika Gradiz and Antonia Reyes.

and red lipstick, their beard colored bright purple), played with gender binaries.

Many wore the clothes they might wear on an ordinary day, but this was no ordinary day, and so they also adorned themselves with streamers, yellow and orange mouse-style ears, brightly colored wigs, or helium balloons. Some danced in matching turquoise and purple costumes, others beat drums in unison, some marched in a brass band. Many carried the banners that identified their organizations. Nobody carried a party flag, though a group from the MRS's LGBTQ network wore matching t-shirts with bright orange trim evoking the MRS's signature color. Some women carried babies or pushed them in strollers; some people purchased drinks and snacks from the vendors pushing carts. Many more reminded reporters and other parade watchers that this was a day not only to celebrate but also to demand the rights they deserved as Nicaraguans (EFE 2017b; VOS TV 2017).

One of the innovations of the 2017 pride parade was the visible presence of family members. Tania Irias from the lesbian collective Artemisa explained that she was there with her family, and that there were many reasons they marched that day. "We march because our sons and daughters have the right to feel proud of our families; we march so that our mothers and fathers no longer feel ashamed because their children are lesbian, gay, bisexual, trans; we march because we want decent work, because we deserve to be treated well, because we deserve employment, health, education, and family policies [that include us] also" (Niú 2017; for another interview with Irias see Arévalo Contreras 2013, 25–48).

One group of children carried a banner reading "Kids Pride: We have the right to feel proud of our family." Another group of adults carried a banner reading: "March for dignity and love for our LGBTIQ daughters and sons: Families for sexual diversity." Additionally, many individuals carried small signs proclaiming their support and love: "I love my gay brother," "Proud of my gay son," "Gay or heterosexual, I love my son," "Who am I too judge? (Pope Francis)," "Try not to offend, my daughter is a lesbian, and I am going to defend" (Niú 2017; Vásquez López 2017b). These family marchers were part of a bigger trend. By 2017, several campaigns had featured parents and other relatives of LGBTQ people speaking out (e.g., *Cuerpos Sin-Vergüenzas* 2016; Vásquez López 2017c).

Starting at the St. Teresa School (*Colegio Teresiano*), thousands marched, bicycled, skateboarded, and danced down Managua's Highway to Masaya

(*Carretera a Masaya*), until they finally stopped at the Metrocentro traffic circle, the site of so many demonstrations during the previous decade. There they listened to music and speeches, including an essay written and read by David Rocha, entitled "Our memories, our revolutions: Nicaragua, another zero hour."

On June 28, 1969, in the New York bar, the Stonewall Inn, the piercing voice of a trans women of Latina descent would call out: Gay Power! With this cry Sylvia Rivera would initiate a series of violent occurrences that would lead to the liberty of the LGBTI movement in the United States. The echo of that trans woman would give birth to diverse groups that take to the streets today, every June 28th, to celebrate their pride in being different. In Nicaragua the first occurrence in our recent history that marks the struggle for our difference, is the 1956 assassination of Anastasio Somoza García at the hands of Rigoberto López Pérez, since, even though the official historiography does not identify him as homosexual, it is an open secret that the poet from León was in a loving relationship with Rafael Corrales. This event marked the zero hour of the struggle for a different desire.

During the 1960s and 1970s the Somoza dictatorship constructed a discourse that criminalized homosexuality. Many *locas* and lesbians were jailed and exhibited in the newspaper *Novedades* as dishonorable criminals. Nonetheless, gay power always rose from below. In the streets we had a thousand and one names that took the shape of a baroque *cochón* alphabet: Anita of the Sea, la Chanel or Chanela, la Guillermina, Murillo the Frog, the Queen of the Twist, the Peruvian, the Morning Star, Black Selina and Little Selina, Cinnamon Skin, the Hen, the Queen of the Tartars, la Bamba, the Deer, Rocío, Flor, the Gay Sondy, Pretty Chinese Girl or the Gay Chinese Girl, la Giorgina, la Carmen Belanllevis, Chacha, Evil Struggle and the most important and well-known: la Sebastiana who along with la Caimana would come to form two inextricably linked historical references in that city. Also, in this parade of names one sees the face of the Somoza dictatorship: Bernabé Somoza Urcuyo, son of Luis Anastasio Somoza Debayle and Isabel Urcuyo, Bernabé or la Barnabi. The elite also took on a face and shape in the names of Carlos Manfut, Jimmy Tefel, Conny Mercado and Elvir Espinoza better known as la Elvira. And in this era a learned *cochona* city appeared in drag within the national culture: José Debb Mcnell, Alberto Ycaza, Omar DLeón, Rolando Steiner and Leoncio Saenz are some of the essential artists who managed to survive the discourse that criminalized our affection.

We plunged ourselves into the clandestine struggle against the Somoza dictatorship while [elsewhere] in Latin America, groups for sexual liberation were forming. We plunged ourselves into the revolutionary effervescence and after July 19, 1979, we applauded the speeches about the New Man from our corners, nourishing the ideal of a different option, our option, with our false eyelashes. Nonetheless, our difference began to be seen as a Somoza-era wrong, a wrong that threatened the future of the New Man. Still, some of us managed to include ourselves in artistic spaces, and we even made it onto the governmental stage. Many homosexual artists swelled the ranks of the FSLN during those years, and Commander Dora María Téllez ended up being the highest lesbian symbol of our revolutionary history. And we also served in the military to defend the interests of the red-and-black fatherland. Then in 1987 the stain of AIDS arrived. Some began to die because of the pink pandemic and others organized with the Commander Minister of Health [Dora María Téllez] and we began to create clandestine collectives as a way of counteracting what now is remembered as the hardest years of the pink cancer. In that decade, precisely in 1989, gays and lesbians were out publicly in what, at least symbolically, was our first pride parade. On the 10th anniversary of the Sandinista People's Revolution, 50 gays and lesbians wearing black t-shirts with pink triangles, were seen in the parade. That was the zero hour for making ourselves visible, and displaying alternatives to the New Man.

And then peace came, democracy, and neoliberalism with its discourse of wiping the slate clean. And while the president raised her arms to the heavens as a sign of victory, we were criminalized with Article 204 of the Penal Code, the article against sodomy. The state's view of our differences, combined with the virus, made us unite our forces even more. At that time fundamental organizations that would make room for what came later appeared: Xochiquetzal founded by the lesbian feminists Hazel Fonseca and Mary Bolt González and Nimehuatzin directed by Rita Aráuz. Others that made their appearance were SHOMOS, Nosotras, The Group for Lesbian Visibility, Puntos de Encuentro and Ixchen. For his part, the gay activist Sergio Navas created ASONVIHSIDA, continuing to express the demands of HIV positive people. Thanks to those collective efforts diverse spaces would open their stages to our voices. Among those was the *Coro de Angeles* Cultural Center where the first LGBTI cultural festival was held. At the same time the Minister of Education, Humberto Belli, labeled sexual education plans as morally repugnant and compared our affection with sex among animals. At the same time, in its homilies, the Catholic Church attacked "sodomites" and presented HIV as the price of sin. It was zero hour for our collective struggle.

Today we celebrate the 12th LGBTI Pride March. Nonetheless, our memories reveal a long period of constant struggle. It is zero hour to realize that without feminism there is no pride, that without sisterhood there is no pride, that if we do not stop with the lesbo-, homo-, trans-phobia within our movement, there is no pride, that if we do not make bisexual and intersexual pride visible, there is no pride, that without critical stances, there is no pride. It is the zero hour to think from the perspective of our differences, and to know that we are not a marketable mallet to be used to attract international funding, that we are more than initials, that we are not homogenous, and that we have diverse demands, that we are subjects who are capable of being free. It is the zero hour to stop resisting and to get on the political stage so as to subvert the present and to advance toward the future. (Rocha Córtez 2017b)

As David Rocha noted, the date of pride day—June 28—marked the anniversary of the Stonewall uprising, far away in New York City. That day Nicaraguans, like people all over the world, celebrated the most important holiday on the global queer calendar. Yet, as Rocha also recognized, what they remembered on that day was not global history but rather Nicaraguan history. At the march they celebrated their country's history, and they demanded a more just future. Nicaragua's history and future were very much their own.

Epilogue

Pride Day of 2017 was a massive outdoor event in which activists made many demands for political and social change. It was also a joyous occasion. After 2017, Pride Day was never the same. There was a small public demonstration in 2018, despite a cloud of fear: participants were warned to travel in groups and to wear flat shoes to be able to run from the police and paramilitaries. From 2019 onward, organizers did not think even that was possible, so the holiday was commemorated behind closed doors.

By 2017, Daniel Ortega and Rosario Murillo had consolidated their power. For a decade, they governed as a team, effectively taking over the state with the help of trusted allies, especially their own children, who they put in charge of major businesses and much of the media. Rosario Murillo wielded power in a far more populist way than Daniel Ortega, her husband. He was the legitimate elected president and tended to quietly work behind the scenes. She lacked legitimate power from 2007 to 2017, but she easily stepped outside the bounds of formal institutions to project her presence practically everywhere, through daily radio and television shows, starting in 2013; through her photo, alongside that of her husband, on ubiquitous billboards proclaiming Nicaragua to be "Christian, Socialist, and in Solidarity"; and through her signature Trees of Life, some 140 illuminated multicolored metal trees that towered over most real trees, making Managua look like an impoverished Disneyland.

When she was sworn in as vice president in January 2017, she was able to combine her informal power with formal power since, as vice president, she would become president were anything to happen to Ortega. Then, in April of 2018, her plans were threatened. Early in the month, environmentalists protested what they saw as governmental indifference or incompetence regarding a huge fire in the *Indio Maíz* reserve, one of the biggest reserves of tropical forest in Central America. Then just as the fire was contained, on the morning of April 18, retired people and students protested reforms to the social security system that would have had increased the amount that workers owed and decreased the pension paid to retired people.

Protests like this had occurred before. While they were sometimes repressed through roadblocks, threats, and even killing individual activists, they were often permitted. After all, hybrid regimes maintain a balance between authoritarianism and democracy by tolerating protest, at least to a point. But in April there was little balancing.

Men in t-shirts proclaiming "United in Victory! Daniel, Rosario," printed in Murillo's signature colors (hot pink, blue, and yellow), attacked protesters and onlookers, bloodying journalists and destroying their cameras and beating protesters with metal bars. Much of the violence was broadcast live on Facebook, as well as on live television. The next day, protests extended to cities beyond Managua, protesters were shot, and three people died (E.P./C.S. 2018).

What happened? Why did the government respond differently than in the past, in a way that had the unintended consequences of creating a massive nationwide protest movement? One theory was that Ortega was absent from the country, attending the presidential inauguration in Cuba, and so Murillo acted on her own, ordering that the demonstrations be stopped with violence. Supposedly, Ortega did not know what was going on. Once he returned, he withdrew the social security reforms, but it was too late (Belli 2018; Miranda Aburto 2018).

It may be that Murillo ordered the initial violence conducted by the t-shirt wearing men whom many called the Sandinista Youth, paramilitaries, parapolice, or simply "the t-shirts." Some sources document Murillo's coordination of the violent attacks on the opposition in the following months (del Cid 2019; Miranda Aburto 2018). But it is a bit too easy to "blame the woman"—to treat Ortega and Murillo as a team when things went well, and to blame Murillo when things went very badly. In particular, the claim that Ortega was unaware of what was going on starting on April 18th is hard to believe. People like me, with no inside information, watched the police and paramilitaries attack protesters (and sometimes bystanders) live on Facebook, and it seems unlikely that Ortega had less access to information than

I did. It is implausible to claim that he could not have made a phone call to rein in the violence within the first few hours of the April protests.

LGBTQ people were integral to the new politics of state violence and grassroots resistance, just as they had been for hundreds of years. On the very first day of the April demonstrations against the government, long-time activist Ana Quirós was beaten with metal pipes on the head and hand by armed bands wearing t-shirts that identified them as supporters of the first lady. The attacks left her with head injuries and two fractured and displaced fingers, which required several surgeries. As Quirós explained the next day on the television program *Esta Noche*, it seemed that her attackers targeted her because they recognized her, since none of the others demonstrating near her were attacked (*Esta Noche* 2018; Nicaragua Actual 2019).

Was she targeted because she was a widely known democracy activist who had appeared multiple times on shows like *Esta Noche*? Was she targeted because she was foreign-born, holding both Costa Rican and Nicaraguan citizenship? Was she targeted because she was a feminist? Or because she was lesbian? Or perhaps for all those reasons?

In the weeks that followed, more protesters (and to a much lesser extent, government supporters) were attacked. Massive marches, sometimes reaching the hundreds of thousands, protested government violence and, more broadly, the lack of democracy in the country (E.P./C.S. 2018). Over the course of 2018, thousands were wounded, hundreds were killed, hundreds more were imprisoned. Most were charged with nothing at all. Many of the people who were attacked, imprisoned, tortured, and forced into exile were members of the LGBTQ community.

One way in which the political crisis affected LGBTQ people was a homophobic social media campaign. One meme showed photos of eight members of the opposition to the FSLN, on an orange background, the color of the MRS party. The meme read "MRS, Apparently, the coup plotters are all homosexuals." Those words were spoken by the image of a man in outline, wearing a suit and tie, and holding a cigarette. The bottom of the meme explained "It is a conspiracy of FAGGOTS [MARICONES] and LESBIANS." In another meme, two young men stood near each other, the background decorated with hearts and smiles. The captions named the two men, claimed one was the "active [partner]" and the other the "passive [partner]" and then noted "The little couple from 19th of April Movement. Those gays don't represent me" (Anonymous 2018, 1–2).

Many LGBTQ activists were attacked personally. In the first two months of the uprising, seventeen members of the LGBTQ community were watched in their houses, fifteen were threatened by members of their families, twenty-six were persecuted, and twenty-four were threatened with death (Anonymous 2018, 4). Additionally, as the authors of that study noted, one LGBTQ person was raped and three were murdered as part of the wave of persecution following the April uprising against the government (Anonymous 2018, 4).

According to another study of over seventy LGBTQ political prisoners who spent more than six months in prison, "the physical and psychological torture was more severe if the torturers became aware of their sexual orientation. In fact, 30% of the former prisoners had to be treated by doctors for the damage and physical lesions suffered during torture in the prisons and others had to be treated for mental health problems. . . . Some of the testimonies were so harsh that many people could not stand to listen to them and had to leave the room" (Anonymous 2020, 4). Among LGBTQ people, transgender women were especially targeted by government agents. Some were kidnapped by law enforcement, brutally beaten, and left in the streets (Institute on Race, Equality, and Human Rights 2018). Other transgender women were held in men's prisons for periods of up to a year, where they were subjected to physical abuse (leading one of them to lose her teeth), obligatory nudity, repeated rape threats, and rape with objects (Espinoza 2019; Gómez 2019; Romero 2019).

As of this writing, demonstrations of any sort (except those supporting the government) are banned. Many nongovernmental organizations were stripped of their legal standing and their property seized, including CISAS, the feminist health rights organization directed by Ana Quirós (who had been beaten on the first day of the protests in April), and Quirós herself was illegally expelled from the country in late 2018 (del Cid 2018). Opposition media offices were ransacked, and their shows were taken off the air. In some cases, television broadcasters were imprisoned and charged with terrorism. Dozens of journalists fled the country rather than waiting to see if the death threats they received would be carried out.

Most of the political prisoners who were arrested in 2018 were released, though new ones were captured regularly, and several former prisoners who had been granted amnesty were arbitrarily detained and imprisoned months after being released. Observers counted "more than 300 murders, thousands of wounded, more than 700 political prisoners, of whom 90 are still

FIGURE 10 Yolanda Valverde holding a sign in front of *La Modelo*, the Managua men's prison where her daughter, Victoria Obando, was held for over nine months in 2018 and 2019. The sign reads: "We want her free! Victoria Obando." Obando was one of several trans women who were imprisoned because of their participation in protests against the Ortega-Murillo regime. In demanding her daughter's liberty, Yolanda Valverde joined a long tradition of Latin American mothers who led protests against political imprisonment and disappearance. Courtesy of Victoria Obando and Yolanda Valverde.

in prison, and 100,000 living in exile" (Munguía 2020a; Munguía 2020b). Nicaragua, which had been considered a hybrid regime from 2007 to early 2018, had become a brutal dictatorship. By some accounts, it had become the worst dictatorship in Latin America (Flores 2020; Magazine 2018; Navas 2019; Núñez 2018).

The events that began in April 2018 had terrible consequences for all Nicaraguans. They were especially consequential for the LGBTQ community as many of Nicaragua's most courageous and skilled sexual diversity activists were victims of political violence, sometimes forced into hiding within the country, sometimes forced to live in exile. In other cases, LGBTQ rights groups broke up as their members were divided over how to respond to the crisis, with some choosing to cast their lots with the Ortega/Murillo government, and others joining the opposition. As hard as promoting rights always was, it became ever more difficult after April 2018, and the decade of the LGBTQ boom sometimes seemed like a distant memory. Yet those memories have not been erased, and a new, even stronger, version of the movement will return one of these days, as it always does.

REFERENCES

ACAN-EFE. 2013. "Zoilamérica en protesta." *La Prensa*, May 3, 2013. Available at https://www.laprensa.com.ni/2013/05/03/nacionales/145071-zoilamerica-en-protesta.

Acevedo, Azucena. 2014. "Grupos LGBTI reciben sus equipos de oficina," February 4, 2014. https://comunicacionrds.wordpress.com/2014/02/04/grupos-lgbti-reciben-sus-equipos-de-oficina/.

Adam, Barry. 1993. "In Nicaragua: Homosexuality without a Gay World." *Journal of Homosexuality* 24, no. 3/4: 171–83.

Agence France Presse (AFP). 2012. "Nicaragua elige a su Miss Gay." *El Nuevo Diario*. April 29. https://www.elnuevodiario.com.ni/nacionales/249696-nicaragua-elige-su-miss-gay/.

Agence France Presse (AFP). 2013. "Nuevo Miss Gay Nicaragua impulsará reformas legales en defensa del gremio." *El Nuevo Herald*. April 29. https://www.elnuevodiario.com.ni/variedades/284510-miss-gay-nicaragua-impulsara-refomas-legales-defen/.

Agüero, Arnulfo. 2004. "El 'mago' de la revolución." *El Nuevo Diario*. July 25. http://archivo.elnuevodiario.com.ni/especiales/148972-mago-revolucion/.

Aizenman, N. C. 2006. "Nicaragua's Total Ban on Abortion Spurs Critics." *Washington Post*. November 28. https://www.washingtonpost.com/archive/politics/2006/11/28/nicaraguas-total-ban-on-abortion-spurs-critics/f4e17dd1-448a-497b-be42-53f96c7d0360/.

Altman, Dennis. 1997. "Global Gaze/Global Gays." *GLQ*. Vol. 3. pp. 417–436.

Alvarado, Samuel. 2013. "Ultimas Noticias de Nicaragua." *Diver-Radio Honduras*. May. http://grupodiverradiohn.blogspot.com/2013/05/.

Alvarenga López, Cristhian. 2013. "Coordinadora Civil-Red Managua se une al Grito de los Excluidos/as Continental." January 11. http://red-managua-coordinadora-civil.blogspot.com/2013/01/coordinadora-civil-red-managua-se-une.html.

Álvarez, Carlos Fernando. 2016. "Miss Gay Nicaragua 2016, un evento por la igualdad." *El 19 Digital*. June 21. https://www.el19digital.com/articulos/ver/titulo: 43322-miss-gay-nicaragua-2016-un-evento-por-la-igualdad.

Álvarez, Leonor. 2017. "Una década de acoso a las ONG." *La Prensa*. February 27. https://www.laprensa.com.ni/2017/02/27/politica/2189531-una-decada-acoso-las-ong.

Álvarez, Leonor. 2018. "MRS exige personería desde hace nueve años." *La Prensa*. January 17. https://www.laprensa.com.ni/2018/01/17/politica/2361937-mrs-exige-personeria-desde-hace-nueve-anos.

Andersson, Susanne. 1993. "Embracing a Sexual Right: The Fight against Penal Code Article 204"; "We Don't Play Roles in Sex Either: Lesbian Feminists." *Barricada Internacional* 13, no. 365 (September): 22–23, 23–24.

ANDISEX. (Alternativa Nicaragüense de Diversidad Sexual) n.d. "Nicaragua y el 28 de Junio" *ANDISEX-Nicaragua Alternativa Nicaragüense de Diversidad Sexual*. Available at http://andisexnicaragua.blogspot.com/.

Antillón, Camilo. 2015. "Memorias del porvenir y sitios de memoria en la Nicaragua post-revolución." *Carátula*. December 2. http://ihnca.edu.ni/files/doc/camilo/2015%20-%20Antillon%20-%20Memoria%20post-revoluci%C3%B3n%20-%20Car%C3%A1tula.pdf.

Anonymous. 2018. "Incidencia y afectaciones a personas LGBTIQ en el periodo de la crisis socio política en Nicaragua." April–June. Unpublished manuscript, 1–4.

Anonymous. 2020. La Comunidad LGBTIQ de Nicaragua de las redes a las calles. Unpublished manuscript, 1–8.

AP (Associated Press). 2014. "Miss Gay Nicaragua luchará contra la homofobia en su país: Tiene el objetivo de concienciación social sobre la diversidad sexual y la identidad de género." June 26. https://www.larepublica.ec/blog/2014/06/26/miss-gay-nicaragua-luchara-contra-homofobia/.

Aráuz, Rita. 1994. "Coming Out as a Lesbian Is What Brought Me to Social Consciousness." In *Sandino's Daughters Revisited: Feminism in Nicaragua*, edited by Margaret Randall. New Brunswick: Rutgers University Press. 265–85.

Aráuz, Rita. 1999. "Salir a la luz como lesbiana es lo que me llevó a la conciencia social." In *Las Hijas de Sandino: Una Historia Abierta*. edited by Margaret Randall, 350–73. Managua: Anamá Ediciones Centroamericanas.

Araya Molina, Keller. 2019. "'Quiero ser mujer': La construcción de la identidad en un grupo de mujeres trans en Costa Rica." *Identidades* 9, no. 15 (July/December): 254–77. http://www.cultura.gob.sv/revista-identidades-15/.

Areas Esquivel, Norely. 2016. "Diversidad Sexual expresa su apoyo al Presidente Daniel Ortega y la Compañera Rosario Murillo." *El 19*. October 21. https://www.el19digital.com/articulos/ver/titulo:48046-diversidad-sexual-expresa-su-apoyo-al-presidente-daniel-ortega-y-la-companera-rosario-murillo.

Arévalo, Amaral, and Andre Solorzano. 2019. "Alianzas y agencias políticas de la disidencia sexual y de género: ¿Una forma para sobrevivir en El Salvador?" *Periódicos* 11, vol. 1 (May–October):8–111. https://portalseer.ufba.br/index.php/revista periodicus/article/view/29244.

Arévalo Contreras, Cristina. 2011. *Ser mujer más allá del cuerpo: Cuatro Mujeres, Cuatro Historias*. https://www.yumpu.com/es/document/view/29857931/iqxox9.

Arévalo Contreras, Cristina, ed. 2013. *Cuando las Lesbianas Hablamos Managua: La Corriente*. http://lacorrientenicaragua.org/wp-content/uploads/2014/02/Historias -de-Vida-Lesbianas.pdf.

Arias, Leopoldo. 2000. "En el 2020 saldrán autores de asesinato" *La Prensa*. July 6. https://www.laprensa.com.ni/2000/07/06/nacionales/735952-en-el-2020-saldrn -autores-de-asesinato.

Armstrong, Elizabeth A., and Suzanna M. Crage. 2006. "Movements and Memory: The Making of the Stonewall Myth." *American Sociological Review 71* (October): 724–51.

ARTEMISA (*Grupo Lésbico Artemisa*). 2013. "Video ARTEMISA final." October 10. https://www.youtube.com/watch?v=jE6gtUcgQzI.

Asamblea Nacional de la República de Nicaragua. 1992. "Ley de Reformas al Código Penal." *La Gaceta*. September 9. Year 96, no. 174. http://sajurin.enriquebolanos .org/docs/G-1992-09-09.pdf.

Asamblea Nacional. 2007–09. "Asociación por los derechos de la diversidad sexual Nicaragüense," ADESENI. https://www.facebook.com/pages/category/Nonprofit -Organization/Asociacion-por-los-derechos-de-la-diversidad-sexual-Nicaraguense -Adeseni-352837382052364/.

Asociación por los derechos de la diversidad sexual nicaragüense (ADESENI). 2010. "Estudio Línea de Base con Población TRANS y Mujeres Lesbianas de 4 Municipios Intervenidos," 1–75. http://www.prevensida.org.ni/index.php/documentos/send/4 -investigaciones/217-lb-con-poblacion-trans-y-mujeres-lesbianas-adeseni.

Asociación Nuevos Horizontes (ANH). 2017. "Nicaragua se lució con más de 5000 personas en la marcha del orgullo LGBTI 2017. Y por supuesto que #ANHNic-aragua estuvo presente." June 29. Facebook post.

Avellán, Héctor. 2002. *Las ciruelas que guarde en la hielera 1994–1996*. León, Nic-aragua: Editorial Universitaria, UNAN-León.

Babb, Florence. 2003. Out in Nicaragua: Local and Transnational Desires after the Revolution. *Cultural Anthropology* 18, no. 3: 304–28.

Babb, Florence. 2004. "Out in Public: Gay and Lesbian Activism in Nicaragua." *NACLA Report on the Americas* 37, no. 6 (May/June): 27–30.

Babb, Florence. 2020. "Nicaraguan Legacies: Advances and Setbacks in Feminist and LGBTQ Activism." In *A Nicaraguan Exceptionalism? Debating the Legacy of the Sandinista Revolution*, edited by Hilary Francis, 165–78. London: University of London Press.

Baca, Gaby. n.d. "Mujeres Brujas." Lyrics and music by Gaby Baca. https://soundcloud .com/gabriela-baca-vaughan/02-mujeres-brujas-gaby-baca.

Baldwin, Anne. 1990. "An Unknown Quantity: AIDS in Nicaragua." *Barricada Inter-nacional*. (August 25):18–20.

Banco Mundial. 2006. "Reduciendo la vulnerabilidad al VIH/SIDA en Centroamérica Nicaragua: Situación del VIH/SIDA y respuesta a la epidemia." América Latina y el

Caribe Programa Global de VIH/SIDA. http://documents.worldbank.org/curated /en/258681468137093903/Reduciendo-la-vulnerabilidad-al-VIH-SIDA-en-Centro america-Nicaragua-situacion-del-VIH-SIDA-y-respuesta-a-la-epidemia.

Bazán, Osvaldo. 2016. *Historia de la Homosexualidad en la Argentina*, 4th ed. Buenos Aires: Editorial Marea.

BBC Mundo. 2017. "Rosario Murillo, la poderosa y extravagante mujer de Daniel Ortega que se convirtió en vicepresidenta de Nicaragua." BBC Mundo. January 11. https:// acento.com.do/bbc-news-mundo/rosario-murillo-la-poderosa-y-extravagante-mujer -de-daniel-ortega-que-se-convirtio-en-vicepresidenta-de-nicaragua-8418611.html.

Belli, Gioconda. 1998. "En el escándalo NO está el pecado." *El Nuevo Diario*. September 30. http://firmandogoldber.blogspot.com/2010/07/en-el-escandolo-no-esta -el-pecado.html.

Belli, Gioconda. 2018. "How Daniel Ortega Became a Tyrant: From Revolutionary to Strongman." *Foreign Affairs*. (August 24). https://www.foreignaffairs.com/articles /nicaragua/2018-08-24/how-daniel-ortega-became-tyrant?cid=soc-fb-rdr.

Benavides, Gabriela. 2011. "Grandes Pasos contra la homofobia y la discriminación," *El Nuevo Diario*. March 21. https://www.elnuevodiario.com.ni/especiales/97654 -grandes-pasos-homofobia-discriminacion/.

Berger, Susan A. 2006. *Guatemaltecas: The Women's Movement, 1986–2003* Austin: University of Texas Press.

Bienal Centroamericana. 2016. "Operación Queer/Cochona." http://www.bienalcentro americana.com/2016/08/08/operacion-queercochona/.

Bimbi, Bruno. 2010. *Matrimonio Igualitario: Intrigas, tensiones y secretos en el camino hacia la ley*. Buenos Aires: Editorial Planeta.

Blandón, Erick. 2003. *Barroco descalzo: Colonialidad, sexualidad, género y raza en la construcción de la hegemonía cultural en Nicaragua*. Nicaragua: Uraccan.

Blandón, María Teresa, and Cecilia Medal Salaverry. 2015. *Cuerpos y desafíos que confluyen: diez años de trabajo del Programa Feminista La Corriente*. Managua: Programa Feminista La Corriente. http://lacorrientenicaragua.org/wp-content /uploads/2015/03/SISTEMATI_LACORRIENTE_FINAL.pdf.

Bolt González, Mary. 1996. *Sencillamente Diferentes: La autoestima de las mujeres lesbianas en los sectores urbanos de Nicaragua*. Managua: Centro Editorial de la Mujer (CEM).

Borge, Tomás. 1989. *La paciente impaciencia*. Havana, Cuba: Ediciones Casa de las Américas.

Borge, Tomás. 1992. *The Patient Impatience: From Boyhood to Guerrilla: A Personal Narrative of Nicaragua's Struggle for Liberation*. Willimantic: Curbstone Press.

Borland, Katherine. 2006. *Unmasking Class, Gender, and Sexuality in Nicaraguan Festival*. Tucson: University of Arizona Press.

Bosworth, James. 2012. "How Teustepe was won—Election fraud in Nicaragua." *Bloggings by boz Foreign Policy, Latin America, etc.* November 8. http://www.bloggings byboz.com/2012/11/how-teustepe-was-won-election-fraud-in.html#!/2012/11 /how-teustepe-was-won-election-fraud-in.html.

Brenes, María Haydée. 2014. "La lesbiana más pública de Nicaragua" *Metro*. November 17.

Broadbent, Lucinda. 1991. "Sex and the Sandinistas." (Film) 25 minutes.

Caballero López, Venus. 2016. "Somos iguales a vos." *El Nuevo Diario*. January 10. https://www.elnuevodiario.com.ni/opinion/381764-somos-iguales-vos/.

Cabezas, Omar. 1986. *Fire from the Mountain: The Making of a Sandinista*. New York: Crown Publishers.

Calero Sequeira, Antonia. 2015. "Mujeres trans de Jalapa se organizan." *La Boletina*. September 27, no. 98: 49. https://documen.site/download/mortalidad-materna -una-realidad-silenciada_pdf.

Campaña Somos Iguales a Vos. 2016. "Historias de éxito: Doctora René Villalobos." November 16. https://www.facebook.com/SOMOSIGUALESAVOS/videos/1316 743465002860/.

Canal2Nicaragua. 2012. "Miss Gay Nicaragua." Xiomara Blandino interview of Ladieska Diedrick. https://www.youtube.com/watch?v=dGraoFRsnVg.

Canal2Nicaragua. 2013. "Entrevista a Miss Nicaragua Gay 2013." Xiomara Blandino interview of Elizabeth Ríos. https://www.youtube.com/watch?v=yVTNI mmmxOk.

Canal 10. 2017. "Comunidad LGBTI celebra el Día del Orgullo Gay." http://www.canal 10.com.ni/accion-10/comunidad-lgbti-celebra-dia-orgullo-gay-managua-29334.

Cannon, Barry, and Mo Hume. 2012. "Central America, civil society and the 'pink tide': democratization or de-democratization?" *Democratization* 19, no. 6 (December) 1039–64.

Cañada, Ernesto. n.d. (1999?) "Los grupos de hombres contra la violencia de Nicaragua: Aprendiendo a construir una nueva masculinidad." https://www.europrofem .org/contri/2_05_es/es-masc/13es_mas.htm. Accessed April 30, 2015.

Cardenal, Ernesto. 1974. *In Cuba*. Translated by Donald Walsh. New York: New Directions Books.

Carranza, Miguel. 2015. "M&R: Población satisfecha con democracia." *El Nuevo Diario*. January 17. http://www.elnuevodiario.com.ni/politica/339498-mr-poblacion -satisfecha-democracia.

Carranza Mena, Miguel. 2015. "Mujeres lideran simpatías políticas." *El Nuevo Diario*. January 17. https://www.elnuevodiario.com.ni/politica/339500-mujeres-lideran -simpatias-politicas/.

Carrillo, Héctor. 2001. *The Night is Young: Sexuality in Mexico in the Time of AIDS*. Chicago: University of Chicago Press.

CEJIL (Coordinación del Centro por la Justicia y el Derecho Internacional). 2013. *Diagnóstico sobre los crímenes de odio motivados por la orientación sexual e identidad de género en Costa Rica, Honduras y Nicaragua*. San José, Costa Rica: CEJIL.

Centro Cultural de España en Nicaragua (CCEN). 2014. "Colectivos de Cine con MOVFEMD X la diversidad." http://www.ccenicaragua.org/2014/06/30/colectivos -de-cine-con-movfemd-x-la-diversidad/.

Centro de Derechos Constitucionales "Carlos Núñez Téllez." 1992. "Recurso por inconstitucionalidad: Penalización de la sodomía." November 9: 1–21.

Centro de Estudios Internacionales (CEI). 2008. "Informe Anual 2008." http://biblio teca.clacso.edu.ar/Nicaragua/cei/20120809044532/informe2009.pdf.

Centro de Estudios Internacionales (CEI). 2009. "2009 annual report." http://biblio teca.clacso.edu.ar/Nicaragua/cei/20120809044532/informe2009.pdf.

Cerda, Arlen. 2017. "Murillo 'manda', pero tiene 'peor' opinión que Ortega." *Confidencial.* (May 24). https://confidencial.com.ni/murillo-manda-pero-tiene-peor -opinion-que-ortega/.

Cerón Méndez, Tania. 2014. "Diversidad Sexual celebra la restitución de sus derechos." *El Pueblo Presidente.* June 29. noticias/ver/titulo:6993-diversidad-sexual -celebra-la-restitucion-de-sus-derechos.

Chaguaceda, Armando. 2012. "Régimen político y estado de la democracia en Nicaragua: Procesos en desarrollo y conflictos recientes." *Nueva Sociedad.* July/August. Issue 240, p.163–174. https://nuso.org/articulo/regimen-politico-y-estado -de-la-democracia-en-nicaragua-procesos-en-desarrollo-y-conflictos-recientes/.

Chamorro, Carlos Fernando. 2018. "¿Modelo Cosep, o el régimen de Ortega?" *Confidencial.* (January 2). https://confidencial.com.ni/modelo-cosep-regimen -ortega/.

Chamorro, Emiliano. 2010. "Iglesia dice no a matrimonios homosexuales." *La Prensa.* August 29.

Chamorro, Emiliano and Elízabeth Romero. 2016. "Obispos llaman a Ortega 'a la cordura': 'Se les está pasando la mano', asegura obispo Solórzano." *La Prensa.* (December 1). https://www.laprensa.com.ni/2016/12/01/politica/2143862-obispos -llaman-ortega-la-cordura.

Chamorro, Pedro Joaquín. 1980 [1957]. *Estirpe Sangrienta: Los Somoza.* Second Edition. México: Editorial Diogenes, S.A.

Chan, Sewell. 2017. "Russia's 'Gay Propaganda' Laws Are Illegal, European Court Rules." *The New York Times.* June 20. https://www.nytimes.com/2017/06/20/world /europe/russia-gay-propaganda.html.

Chauncey, George. 1994. *Gay New York: Gender, Urban Culture, and the Making of the Gay Male World, 1890–1940.* Basic Books: New York.

Chavarría, Nicole. 2008. "Se cancela personalidad jurídica del MRS y del PC: Consejo Supremo Electoral confirmó." *El Nuevo Diario.* June 11. https://www.elnuevo diario.com.ni/nacionales/18305-se-cancela-personalidad-juridica-mrs-pc/.

Chávez, Kenneth. 2016. "Comunidad LGTBI y juventud nicaragüense impulsan campaña 'En mi país no hay discriminación.'" *El 19.* ver/titulo:43590-comunidad -lgtbi-y-juventud-nicaraguense-impulsan-campana-en-mi-pais-no-hay-discrim inacion.

CHRICA (National Central America Health Rights Network [U.S.]; Committee for Health Rights in Central America). 1987?. V North America Nicaragua Colloquium on Health: November 5–15, 1987, Managua, Nicaragua: a project. San Francisco: CHRICA.

CINCO (Centro de Investigación de la Comunicación). 2016. "La otra oposición y las protestas sociales." *Confidencial.* April 8. https://confidencial.com.ni/la-otra -oposicion-las-protestas-sociales.

Ciudadanía Regional de la Juventud Centroamericana. 2015. "Chester Córtez, líder de la sociedad civil en Nicaragua." June 3. http://ciudadaniaca.blogspot.com/2015 /06/chester-cortez-lider-de-la-sociedad.html.

Close, David, and Kalowatie Deonandan. Eds. 2004. *Undoing Democracy: The Politics of Electoral Caudillismo,* Lexington Books.

Close, David. 2016. *Nicaragua: Navigating the Politics of Democracy.* Boulder: Lynne Rienner Press.

Comisión Interamericana de Derechos Humanos (CIDH). 2015. "Violencia contra Personas Lesbianas, Gay, Bisexuales, Trans e Intersex en América." November 12. http://www.oas.org/es/cidh/informes/pdfs/violenciapersonaslgbti.pdf.

Comunidad Homosexual de Nicaragua. 2010–14. Blog. http://comuhomonicaragua .blogspot.com/2014/.

Comunidad Homosexual de Nicaragua. 2010a. "Procuraduría de la Diversidad Sexual o pretendidas cochinadas???" February 23. https://comuhomonicaragua.blogspot .com/2010/02/procuraduria-de-la-diversidad-sexual-o_23.html.

Comunidad Homosexual de Nicaragua. 2010b. "Aprender en el camino y aprender de nuestros propios errores (. . . al andar se hace camino y . . . se hace camino al andar . . .)." February 24. http://comuhomonicaragua.blogspot.com/2010/02 /aprender-en-el-camino-y-aprender-de.html.

Comunidad Homosexual de Nicaragua. 2010c. "Movimiento de la Diversidad Sexual de la Juventud Sandinista: hacia qué apuestan las nuevas tretas del dictador Daniel Ortega?" September 1. https://comuhomonicaragua.blogspot.com/2010/09/movi miento-de-la-diversidad-sexual-de.html.

Comunidad Homosexual de Nicaragua. 2013a. "Miembros de la Alianza Diversidad Sexual Nicaragua se reúnen con personeros de instituciones del Estado." February 13. https://comuhomonicaragua.blogspot.com/2013/02/miembros-de-la-alianza -diversidad.html.

Comunidad Homosexual de Nicaragua. 2013b. "En estos tiempos tan difíciles para las expresiones de LGBTI, no estaría de más una revisión de nuestro trabajo a profundidad—afirma el activista Ebén Díaz." April 8. https://comuhomonicaragua .blogspot.com/2013/04/en-estos-tiempos-tan-dificiles-para-las.html.

Comunidad Homosexual de Nicaragua. 2013c. "Grupos y activistas de LGBTI no lograron ponerse de acuerdo sobre comunicado de denuncia contra el gobierno de Nicaragua." April 15. http://comuhomonicaragua.blogspot.com/2013/04/grupos -y-activistas-de-lgbti-no.html.

Comunidad Homosexual de Nicaragua. 2013d. "Alianza Diversidad Sex =ual Nicara- gua en 'veremos.'" April 22. https://comuhomonicaragua.blogspot.com/2013/04 /alianza-diversidad-sexual-nicaragua-en.html.

Comunidad Homosexual de Nicaragua. 2013e. "Activistas Transgéneras y lesbianas de dos grupos LGBTIQ intentan linchar a personal del CEI." May 10. https://

comuhomonicaragua.blogspot.com/2013/05/activistas-transgeneras-y-lesbianas
-de.html.

Comunidad Homosexual de Nicaragua. 2013f. "CEI anuncia cierre de operaciones."
July 30. http://comuhomonicaragua.blogspot.com/2013/07/cei-anuncia-cierre-de
-operaciones.html.

Comunidad Homosexual de Nicaragua. 2014. "Reconocido activista LGBTIQ pro-
movido a responsabilidades mayores." (February 20). http://comuhomonicaragua
.blogspot.com/2014/02/reconocido-activista-lgbtiq-promovido.html.

Conducta Impropia. 1992. "Nicaragua: Gays Denuncian Recorte de Derechos." *Conducta Impropia* 2 (Lima, Perú): 26.

Coordinadora Civil. 2013? "Estamos en toda Nicaragua: Construyendo Ciudadanía
para incidir en las políticas públicas," 1–6. http://www.gritodelosexcluidos.org
/media/uploads/brochure_presentacion_cc.pdf.

Coordinación del Centro por la Justicia y el Derecho Internacional (CEJIL). 2013.
Diagnóstico sobre los crímenes de odio motivados por la orientación. San José,
Costa Rica: CEJIL.

Córdoba, Matilde. 2006. "Diversidad Sexual Demanda Respeto." *El Nuevo Diario.* October 13. http://archivo.elnuevodiario.com.ni/politica/192613-diversidad-sexual
-demanda-respeto/.

Córdoba, Matilde. 2014. "El suplicio de ser yo: Discriminación. Puede ser verbal,
física y sexual, La violencia contra gays, lesbianas, transexuales, bisexuales e intersex es reiterada y vista de un lado por la sociedad." *El Nuevo Diario.* June 22.
https://www.elnuevodiario.com.ni/nacionales/322986-suplicio-ser-yo/.

Córdoba, Matilde. 2015. "Mayoría de nicas contra el matrimonio homosexual." *El
Nuevo Diario.* June 25. https://www.elnuevodiario.com.ni/nacionales/363149
-mayoria-nicas-matrimonio-igualitario/.

Corrales, Javier, and Mario Pecheny, eds. 2010. *The Politics of Sexuality in Latin
America: A Reader on Lesbian, Gay, Bisexual, and Transgender Rights.* Pittsburgh:
University of Pittsburgh Press.

Córtez Ruiz, Israel. 2019. "La otredad insurgente: consideraciones sobre la homosexualidad en el conflicto armado salvadoreño (1978–1992)." *Identidades* 9, no.
15. (July/December): 278–91. http://www.cultura.gob.sv/revista-identidades-15/.

Cowan, Benjamin. 2016. *Securing Sex: Morality and Repression in the Making of Cold
War Brazil.* Chapel Hill: University of North Carolina Press.

Crane, Rachel. 2015. "La búsqueda de una agenda en común: Una mirada feminista
a las organizaciones LGBTI en Nicaragua." Fall. https://digitalcollections.sit.edu
/cgi/viewcontent.cgi?article=3297&context=isp_collectin.

Cronio. 2018. "Rosario Murillo, primera dama de Nicaragua y su historia de 'ár-
bol de la vida.'" *Cronio.* May 3. http://cronio.sv/internacionales/rosario-murillo
-primera-dama-de-nicaragua-y-su-historia-de-arbol-de-la-vida/.

Cruz, Eduardo. 2016. "¿Quién es Pedro Reyes?" *La Prensa.* June 9. https://www.laprensa
.com.ni/2016/06/09/politica/2049207-quien-es-pedro-reyes.

Cuadra, Elvira, Angel Saldomando, and Sofía Montenegro. 2013. "Las lógicas ocultas de los nuevos conflictos sociales: Nuevos conflictos, viejas causas." *Perspectivas* 71 (April): 1–4. Managua: Centro de Investigaciones de la Comunicación (CINCO).

Cuerpos Sin-Vergüenzas. 2014a. "Diversidad Sexual en Nicaragua ¿Un movimiento unido?" June 27. Podcast. http://lacorrientenicaragua.org/diversidad-sexual-en-nicaragua-un-movimiento-unido/.

Cuerpos Sin-Vergüenzas. 2014b. "Homosexuales y lesbianas en la Revolución" July 24. Podcast. http://www.ivoox.com/homosexuales-lesbianas-revolucion-audios-mp3_rf_3351092_1.html.

Cuerpos Sin-Vergüenzas. 2015. "Cuando las lesbianas hablamos." June 19. Podcast. http://lacorrientenicaragua.org/cuando-las-lesbianas-hablamos-2/.

Cuerpos Sin-Vergüenzas. 2016. "Soy lesbiana, soy homosexual: ¿Qué piensa mi familia?" Podcast. http://www.ivoox.com/soy-lesbiana-soy-homosexual-que-piensa-mi-familia-audios_mp3_rf_12016985_1.html?utm_source=audio_title&utm_medium=email&utm_campaign=mail_subscription.

Cuerpos Sin-Vergüenzas. 2017a. "Todo comenzó con la rebelión de nuestros cuerpos." June 30. Podcast. https://www.ivoox.com/todo-comenzo-rebelion-nuestros-cuerpos-audios-mp3_rf_19562396_1.html.

Cuerpos Sin-Vergüenzas. 2017b. "Celebramos nuestro orgullo." July 1. Podcast. http://www.ivoox.com/celebramos-nuestro-orgullo-audios-mp3_rf_12092423_1.html.

Cuerpos Sin-Vergüenzas. 2017c. "Lesbianas rebeldes y visibles." October 13. Podcast. https://www.ivoox.com/lesbianas-rebeldes-visibles-audios-mp3_rf_21434980_1.html.

Cupples, Julie, and Kevin Glynn. 2018. *Shifting Nicaraguan Mediascapes: Authoritarianism and the Struggle for Social Justice.* New York: Springer.

Curry, Colleen. 2018. "I Thought Gay Rights Were Safe. Now I Know I Was Wrong." *Washington Post.* February 5. https://www.washingtonpost.com/news/postevery thing/wp/2018/02/05/i-thought-gay-rights-were-safe-now-i-know-i-was-wrong/.

de la Dehesa, Rafael. 2010. *Queering the Public Sphere in Mexico and Brazil.* Durham: Duke University Press.

Decena, Carlos Ulises. 2016. "Sujetos Tácitos," 217–39. In Diego Falconí Trávez, Diego, Santiago Castellanos, and María Amelia Viteri. Eds. Resentir lo queer en América Latina: diálogos desde/con el Sur. Barcelona and Madrid, Spain: Editorial Egales.

Del Cid, Amalia. 2018. "Ana Quirós: 'Los Ortega Murillo no van a sobrevivir cinco años'" *La Prensa*. December 2. https://www.laprensa.com.ni/2018/12/02/suplemento/la-prensa-domingo/2501658-ana-quiros-los-ortega-murillo-no-van-a-sobrevivir-cinco-anos.

Del Cid, Amalia. 2019. "Padre Augusto Gutiérrez: 'Rosario Murillo dirigía la represión'" *La Prensa*. May 19. https://www.laprensa.com.ni/2019/05/19/suplemento/la-prensa-domingo/2550672-padre-augusto-gutierrez-rosario-murillo-dirigia-la-represion.

del Val, Jaime. 2011. "COMISARIOS QUEER: Sobre los límites en la asimilación institucional del activismo." December. http://www.reverso.org/comisarios-queer.htm.

D'Emilio, John. 2007. "Capitalism and Gay Identity." In *Culture, Society and Sexuality: A Reader*, 250–58. Edited by Richard Parker and Peter Aggleton. New York: Routledge.

D'Emilio, John, and Estelle B. Freedman. 2012. *Intimate Matters: A History of Sexuality in America*, 3rd ed. Chicago: The University of Chicago Press.

Diez, Jordi. 2015. *The Politics of Gay Marriage in Latin America: Argentina, Chile, and Mexico*. New York: Cambridge University Press.

Drucker, Peter. 1996. "In the Tropics There Is No Sin: Sexuality and Gay-Lesbian Movements in the Third World." *New Left Review* 218: 75–101.

E.P./C.S. 2018. "Nicaragua: tres meses de protestas y más de 300 muertos: Las manifestaciones iniciadas en contra de una reforma de la Seguridad Social canalizaron el descontento de la población en contra del presidente sandinista Daniel Ortega." *El País* (July 19). https://elpais.com/internacional/2018/07/18/america /1531921411_489786.html.

EFE. 2008. "El Gobierno de Nicaragua multa a 17 ONG críticas con Daniel Ortega por 'ilegalidad.'" *elmundo.es*. September 25. https://www.elmundo.es/elmundo /2008/09/25/solidaridad/1222339987.

EFE. 2013. "Lesbianas de Nicaragua reclaman la capacidad de adoptar niños." *crhoy. com*. April 25. *El EconomistaAmérica.com*. https://www.eleconomistaamerica .com/sociedad-eAm/noticias/4779203/04/13/Lesbianas-de-Nicaragua-reclaman -la-capacidad-de-adoptar-ninos.html.

EFE. 2016a. "Transgéneros de Nicaragua y El Salvador piden ley de identidad." *La Patria*. April 17. http://lapatriaenlinea.com/?t=transga-neros-de-nicaragua-y-el -salvador-piden-ley-de-identidad&nota=253615.

EFE. 2016b. "Nicaragua | Comunidad LGBTI no se siente representada en elecciones." *W Radio*. October 11. https://www.wradio.com.co/noticias/internacional /la-comunidad-lgbti-no-se-siente-representada-en-elecciones-de-nicaragua/2016 1011/nota/3271345.aspx.

EFE. 2017a. "Miles de nicaragüenses participan en Marcha del Orgullo Gay en Managua." *La Vanguardia*. June 29. https://www.lavanguardia.com/vida/20170629 /423754447482/miles-de-nicaraguenses-participan-en-marcha-del-orgullo-gay -en-managua.html.

EFE. 2017b. "Miles de nicaragüenses participan en Marcha del Orgullo Gay en Managua." June 29. *Alianza Metropolitan News*. http://noticias.alianzanews.com/187 _america/4641995_miles-de-nicaraguenses-participan-en-la-marcha-del-orgullo -gay-en-managua.html.

EFE 2018. "Nicaragua espera 1,424 millones de dólares por remesas en 2018: Un 20% de la población nicaragüense reside fuera de su país." *Confidencial*. January 2. https://confidencial.com.ni/nicaragua-espera-1424-millones-dolares-remesas -2018/.

El Nuevo Diario. 2006. "Diversidad Sexual demanda respeto." *El Nuevo Diario*. October 12. http://archivo.elnuevodiario.com.ni/politica/192613-diversidad-sexual-demanda-respeto/.

El Nuevo Diario. 2008. "Culmina primer seminario sobre diversidad sexual: Managua albergó a 75 delegados de Centroamérica." *El Nuevo Diario*. December 15. https://www.elnuevodiario.com.ni/contactoend/35191-culmina-primer-seminario-diversidad-sexual/.

El Nuevo Diario. 2010. "¿Cuánto se acepta diversidad sexual en Nicaragua?" *El Nuevo Diario* March 21. https://www.elnuevodiario.com.ni/especiales/70778-cuanto-se-acepta-diversidad-sexual-nicaragua/.

El Nuevo Diario. 2011a. "Marcha por la diversidad sexual en Bluefields: Estamos hartos que nos insulten y agredan, expresaron los manifestantes reclamando respeto y derechos." June 4. https://www.elnuevodiario.com.ni/departamentales/106785-marcha-diversidad-sexual-bluefields/.

El Nuevo Diario. 2011b. "La metamorfosis de Daniel Ortega." December 27. https://www.elnuevodiario.com.ni/politica/236955-metamorfosis-daniel-ortega/.

El País. 1992. "¿Cómo viven los Gays en Nicaragua? El País analiza a fondo el controversial tema de la homosexualidad." (Managua). Year 1, no. 4: 5–10.

Elyla. n.d. "Elyla." https://www.elyla.studio/bio/. Accessed February 15, 2021.

Encarnación, Omar. 2016. *Out in the Periphery: Latin America's Gay Rights Revolution*. New York: Oxford University Press.

Envío. 2006. "Daniel Ortega Presidente: Del poder 'desde abajo' al gobierno." *Envió* 25, no. 296–97: 3–5. https://www.envio.org.ni/articulo/3418.

Envío. 2009a. "Persecución Contra ONG." in *Envío* 322 (January). http://www.envio.org.ni/articulo/3929.

Envío. 2009b. "Persecution of NGOs Changes Tack." *Envío* 330. January. https://www.envio.org.ni/articulo/3418.

Epstein, Steven. 1999. "Gay and Lesbian Movements in the United States: Dilemmas of Identity, Diversity and Political Strategy." In *The Global Emergence of Gay and Lesbian Politics*, edited by Barry Adam, Jan Willem Duyvendak, and André Krouwel. Philadelphia: Temple University Press. pp. 3090.

Equipo Envío. 1998. "El caso Zoilamérica en la voz de los protagonistas." *Envío* 192 (March). https://www.envio.org.ni/articulo/346.

Equipo Nitlápan-Envío. 1998. "Un test ético para una sociedad en crisis." *Envío* 192. http://www.envio.org.ni/articulo/345.

Espinoza, Carlos Mikel. 2019. "Homofobia en Nicaragua: Cuando te criminalizan y discriminan por ser opositor y de la comunidad LGBTI." https://redcolectiva.com/2019/08/07/homofobia-en-nicaragua-cuando-te-criminalizan-y-discriminan-por-ser-opositor-y-de-la-comunidad-lgbti/.

Espinoza, María José. 2017. "La violencia electoral en Nicaragua empezó en 2008." *La Prensa*. November 19. https://www.laprensa.com.ni/2017/11/19/politica/2333211-la-violencia-electoral-nicaragua-empezo-2008.

Esta Noche. 2015. "La exposición de Operación Queer en Managua." https://www.you tube.com/watch?v=4btT0ivzDHQ.

Esta Noche. 2016a. "Rosario Murillo es nombrada candidata a vicepresidente: Dora María Téllez y Luis Callejas analizan." August 3. https://www.youtube.com/watch ?v=fDEcUDtr0H0.

Esta Noche. 2016b. "Vilma Núñez: 'Nicaragua sufre la peor situación de derechos humanos en los 25 años del CENIDH.'" May 4. https://confidencial.com.ni/vilma -nunez-nicaragua-sufre-la-peor-situacion-derechos-humanos-los-25-anos-del -cenidh/.

Esta Noche. 2018. "Miguel Mora, Patricia Orozco, Ana Quiros." April 19. https:// confidencial.com.ni/esta-noche-19-de-abril-2018/.

Esta Semana. 2015. "¿Hay respeto por la diversidad sexual en Nicaragua?" May 4. https://www.youtube.com/watch?v=fnhMwXS3cac.

EuroPROFEM. n.d. "Nicaragua: Los Grupos de Hombres Contra la Violencia." https://www.europrofem.org/contri/2_05_es/es-viol/08es_vio.htm.

Fondo Centroamericano de Mujeres (FCAM). 2018. "Nicaragua." https://fcmujeres .org/copartes/nicaragua/.

Ferguson, Ann. 1991. "Lesbianism, Feminism, and Empowerment in Nicaragua." *Socialist Review* 21 (3/4): 75–97.

Flores, Casey. 2020. "Amnistía Internacional: 'Nicaragua vive una de las peores crisis de DDHH del continente.'" *La Mesa Redonda.* December 10. https://www.lamesa redonda.net/amnistia-internacional-nicaragua-vive-una-de-las-peores-crisis-de -ddhh-del-continente/?fbclid=IwAR2uMbec6tp47HEcC55Uh73xsjueA5kEcwBb nzMfayUCvSewJu28ji5y78o.

Flores, Judith. 2017. "Freedom House: Nicaragua vive 'autoritarismo moderno:' Organismo de DD.HH. analiza situación de democracia en el mundo." *La Prensa.* June 8. http://www.laprensa.com.ni/2017/06/08/politica/2242830-freedom-house -nicaragua-vive-autoritarismo-moderno.

Francis, Hilary. 2012. "Que se rinda tu madre! Leonel Rugama and Nicaragua's Changing Politics of Memory." *Journal of Latin American Cultural Studies* 21, no. 2: 235–52.

Friedman, Elisabeth Jay. 2009. Gender, Sexuality, and the Latin American Left: Testing the Transformation. *Third World Quarterly* 30, no. 2: 415–33.

Friedman, Elisabeth Jay. 2012. "Constructing 'The Same Rights with the Same Names': The Impact of Spanish Norm Diffusion on Marriage Equality in Argentina." *Latin American Politics & Society* 54, no. 4 (Winter): 29–59.

Friedman, Elisabeth Jay. 2014. "Room for Debate: Why Is Latin America So Progressive on Gay Rights?: In Latin America, Human Rights Causes Resonate." *New York Times.* January 29. <-progressive-on->gay-rights/in-latin-america-human-rights -causes-resonate.

Friedman, Elisabeth Jay, ed. 2018. *Seeking Rights from the Left: Gender, Sexuality, and the Latin American Pink Tide.* Durham: Duke University Press.

Fundación Xochiquetzal. 1993. "Créditos," in *Fuera del Closet* 0 (June): 3.

Fundación Xochiquetzal. 1997. "VI Jornada: Por una sexualidad libre de prejuicios." 1–4. http://puntosmovrec.org/sidoc_new/images/books/03706/03706_00.pdf.

Fundación Xochiquetzal. 2015. "La revista fuera del closet." http://www.xochiquetzal .org.ni/index.php/joomla-topmenu-95.

Garay, Josué. 2014. "Ser mujer más allá del cuerpo." *El Hidalgo*. https://www.cisas.org .ni/story/ser_mujer_m%C3%A1s_all%C3%A1_del_cuerpo.

Garay, Josué. 2018. "¿Sabías que Managua tiene más de 40 sitios 'gay friendly'?" *Vosdale*. January 11. https://www.facebook.com/VosDaleni/posts/2402697131 70410.

García, Melissa. 2011. "Las mujeres transgéneras: Creando espacios y una identidad colectiva para combatir la discriminación y la violencia." ISP Collection. Paper 1041. https://www.yumpu.com/es/document/read/34706550/creando-espacios -y-una-identidad-colectiva-para-combatir-la-sidoc.

Gardella, Annalise. 2019. "El derecho al luto: estrategias del activismo para combatir la violencia contra la población LGBTI en El Salvador." 95–119. http://www .cultura.gob.sv/revista-identidades-15/.

Gevisser, Mark. 2013. "Life under Russia's 'Gay Propaganda' Ban." *New York Times*. December 27. https://www.nytimes.com/2013/12/28/opinion/life-under-russias -gay-propaganda-ban.html.

Global Rights, Grupo Safo, International Gay and Lesbian Human Rights Commission (IGLHRC), International Human Rights Clinic, Human Rights Program, Harvard Law School, Red de LatinoAmerica y el Caribe de Personas Trans (Red LacTrans). 2008. "The Violations of the Rights of Lesbian, Gay, Bisexual and Transgender Persons in Nicaragua, A Shadow Report." October. https://www.outright international.org/sites/default/files/233-1.pdf.

Goett, Jennifer. 2017. *Black Autonomy: Race, Gender, and Afro-Nicaraguan Activism*. Stanford: Stanford University Press.

Gómez, Ángela. 2019. "Mujeres transgénero en Nicaragua denuncian abusos en las cárceles." *France 24* (January 4). https://www.france24.com/es/20193103-ellas -hoy-trans-nicaragua-carceles.

González-Rivera, Victoria. 2020. "Why My Nicaraguan Father Did Not 'See' His Blackness and How Latinx Anti-Black Racism Feeds on Racial Silence." *Confidencial*. June 15. https://confidencial.com.ni/why-my-nicaraguan-father-did-not-see -his-blackness-and-how-latinx-anti-black-racism-feeds-on-racial-silence/.

González-Rivera, Victoria. Forthcoming. *500 Years of LGBTQ+ History in Nicaragua*. Tucson: University of Arizona Press.

González-Rivera, Victoria, and Karen Kampwirth. Eds. 2001. *Radical Women in Latin America: Left and Right*. University Park: Penn State University Press.

González-Rivera, Victoria, and Karen Kampwirth. 2021. *Diversidad Sexual en el Pacífico y Centro de Nicaragua: 500 Años de Historia*. San Diego.

González Siles, Silvia. 2006. "Daniel Ortega ahora se compara con Cristo." *La Prensa*. October 31. https://www.laprensa.com.ni/2006/10/31/politica/1285423-daniel -ortega-ahora-se-compara-con-cristo.

Gorgeous, Holly. 2014. "Miss Gay 2014—Trajes de Fantasia." November 20. https://www.youtube.com/watch?v=YLrASS_mGpU.

Gould, Jeffrey. 1998. *To Die in This Way: Nicaraguan Indians and the Myth of Mestizaje, 1880–1965*. Durham: Duke University Press.

Grass, Jesse. 2011. "Pink Crude: Tar Sands Supporters Criticized for Using Gay Rights to Mask Environmental Disaster," *The Dominion: News from the Grassroots*. October 21. http://www.dominionpaper.ca/articles/4205.

Green, James. 1999. *Beyond Carnival: Male Homosexuality in Twentieth-Century Brazil*. Chicago: University of Chicago Press.

Green, James N. 2012. "'Who Is the Macho Who Wants to Kill Me?' Male Homosexuality, Revolutionary Masculinity, and the Brazilian Armed Struggle of the 1960s and 1970s." *Hispanic American Historical Review* 92, no. 3: 437–69.

Grupo de Hombres Contra la Violencia de Managua. 2013. "Cómplices del patriarcado, masculinidad obligada y heterosexualidad como norma." June 1. http://metiendoruido.com/2013/06/complices-del-patriarcado-masculinidad-obligada-y-heterosexualidad-como-norma/.

Grupo Safo. 2015. "Quienes Somos." http://gruposafo.doblementemujer.org/inicio/acerca-de/.

Grupo Venancia. 2015. "Hambre Cero: cómo les va a las mujeres." *Envío* 396. March. https://www.envio.org.ni/articulo/4972.

Guerra, Lillian. 2010. "Gender Policing, Homosexuality, and the New Patriarchy of the Cuban Revolution, 1965–70." *Social History* 35, no. 3: 268–89.

Guevara, Alberto. 2014. *Performance, Theater, and Society in Contemporary Nicaragua: Spectacles of Gender, Sexuality, and Marginality*. Amherst NY: Cambria Press.

Gutiérrez, Noelia Celina. 2017. "Miembros de la diversidad sexual no podrán ser facilitadores judiciales." *El Nuevo Diario*. December 16. https://www.elnuevodiario.com.ni/nacionales/449787-miembros-diversidad-sexual-no-podran-ser-facilitad/.

Hedrick, Tace. 2013. "Neoliberalism and Orientalism in Puerto Rico: Walter Mercado's Queer Spiritual Capital." *Centro Journal* 25, no. 1 (Spring): 180–209.

Heumann, Silke. 2014. "The Challenge of Inclusive Identities and Solidarities: Discourses on Gender and Sexuality in the Nicaraguan Women's Movement and the Legacy of Sandinismo." *Bulletin of Latin American Research* 33, no. 3 (July): 334–49.

Heumann, Silke, et al. 2017. "Dialogue: Transgendered Bodies as Subjects of Feminism: A Conversation and Analysis about the Inclusion of Trans Personas and Politics in the Nicaraguan Feminist Movement." In Wendy Harcourt, ed. *Bodies in Resistance: Gender and Sexual Politics in the Age of Neoliberalism*, 163–87. London: Palgrave Macmillan.

Hispantv. 2018. "Sondeo: Daniel Ortega, presidente mejor evaluado de Latinoamérica." *Hispantv*. February 13. https://www.hispantv.com/noticias/nicaragua/368452/daniel-ortega-popularidad-presidente-latinoamericano.

Hobson, Emily. 2012. "Si Nicaragua Venció: Gay and Lesbian Solidarity with the Revolution." *Journal of Transnational American Studies* 4, no. 2: 1–26. https://cloudfront.escholarship.org/dist/prd/content/qt9hx356m4/qt9hx356m4.pdf?t=mftbx8.

Hobson, Emily. 2016. *Lavender and Red: Liberation and Solidarity in the Gay and Lesbian Left*. Berkeley: University of California Press.

Holiday Travel. 2021. "Rubén Darío National Theatre (Teatro Nacional Rubén Darío)." http://www.holidaytravel.cc/Article/travelguides/northamerica/nicaragua/201602/73095.html.

Hooker, Juliet. 2005. "'Beloved Enemies:' Race and Official Mestizo Nationalism in Nicaragua." *Latin American Research Review* 40, no. 3: 14–39.

Horn, Maja. 2010. "Queer Dominican Moves: In the Interstices of Colonial Legacies and Global Impulses." In Amy Lind, ed *Development, Sexual Rights and Global Governance*. New York: Routledge.

Horst, Ian Scott. 2010. "Echoes of a past life: Gay Libre / Patria Libre." http://thecahokian.blogspot.com/2010/01/echoes-of-past-life-gay-libre-patria.html.

Horton, Lynn. 1998. *Peasants in Arms: War and Peace in the Mountains of Nicaragua, 1979–1994*. Athens: Ohio University Press.

Howard, Joanna, and Luis Serra Vasquez. 2010. "The Changing Spaces of Local Governance in Nicaragua." *Bulletin of Latin American Research* 30, no. 1 (January): 64–79.

Howe, Cymene. 2002. "Undressing the Universal Queer Subject: Nicaraguan Activism and Transnational Identity." *City and Society*: 237–79.

Howe, Cymene. 2009. "The Legible Lesbian: Crimes of Passion in Nicaragua." *Ethnos: Journal of Anthropology* 74, no. 3 (September): 361–78.

Howe, Cymene. 2013. *Intimate Activism: The Struggle for Sexual Rights in Postrevolutionary Nicaragua*. Durham: Duke University Press.

Hoyt, Katherine. 2004. "Parties and Pacts in Contemporary Nicaragua." In David Close and Kalowatie Deonandan. eds., 1742. *Undoing Democracy: The Politics of Electoral Caudillismo*, Lexington Books.

Human Rights Campaign (HRC). 2017. "Global Partners with LGBTQ Advocates in Nicaragua." March 2. https://www.hrc.org/news/hrc-global-partners-with-lgbtq-advocates-in-nicaragua.

Human Rights Watch. 2007. "Nicaragua: Blanket Ban on Abortion Harms Women: Women Afraid to Seek Life-Saving Treatment." August 29. https://www.hrw.org/news/2007/08/29/nicaragua-blanket-ban-abortion-harms-women.

Hutton, Jeffrey. 2017. "Indonesia's Crackdown on Gay Men Moves from Bars into the Home." *New York Times*. December 20.

IDSDH. (Iniciativa desde la Diversidad Sexual para los Derechos Humanos). 2009. "Presentación idsdh." October 27. https://www.youtube.com/watch?v=5ejCubvW4ew.

Iglesias de la Comunidad Metropolitana (MCC/ICM) en Iberoamérica. N.d. (2012?). "ICM paz y alegría de Nicaragua: Cronología de 'Una comunidad de fe donde Dios No

Discrimina a Nadie.'" 9–11. Accessed March 5,2015. http://ftpmirror.your.org/pub/wikimedia/images/wikipedia/commons/8/85/IGLESIAS_DE_LA_COMUNIDAD_METROPOLITANA_MCC-ICM_EN_IBEROAM%C3%89RICA.

Institute on Race, Equality, and Human Rights. 2018. "LGBTIQ Community is More Vulnerable After the Start of the Crisis in Nicaragua According to Activists." *Race and Equality*. November 30. https://raceandequality.org/blog/lgbti-en/lgbtiq-community-vulnerable-crisis-nicaragua/o.

INSSBI (Nicaragüense de Seguro Social y Bienestar). 1987. *Prostitución en Nicaragua: Una experiencia de reeducación*. Managua: INSSBI.

Jackson, Peter A. 2009. "Capitalism and Global Queering: National Markets, Parallels Among Sexual Cultures, and Multiple Queer Modernities." *GLQ: A Journal of Lesbian and Gay Studies* 15, no. 3: 357–95.

Jarquín, Carlos Daniel. 2017. "Diversidad sexual demanda más inclusión laboral." Canal 2. June 15. http://canal2tv.com/diversidad-sexual-demanda-mas-inclusion-laboral/.

Jarquín C, Edmundo. 2016. "Construcción Democrática Revertida y Pervertida." In *El Régimen de Ortega: ¿Una nueva dictadura familiar en el continente?*, 17–64. Edited by Edmundo Jarquín C. Managua: PAVSA.

Jiménez Bolaños, José Daniel. 2016. "La criminalización de la diversidad sexual y el inicio del activismo gay en Costa Rica, 1985–1989." *Revista Rupturas* 6, no. 1. January–June: 61–90. https://ucr.academia.edu/JoseJimenez.

Jiménez Bolaños, José Daniel. 2017a. "Matrimonio igualitario en Costa Rica: Los orígenes del debate, 1994–2006." *Revista de Ciencias Sociales* 155: 157–72. https://ucr.academia.edu/JoseJimenez.

Jiménez Bolaños, José Daniel. 2017b. "De lo privado a lo público: La celebración del orgullo LGBTI en Costa Rica, 2003–2016." *Diálogos Revista Electrónica de Historia* 18, no. 1: 65–90. https://ucr.academia.edu/JoseJimenez.

Kampwirth, Karen. 1996. "Confronting Adversity with Experience: The Emergence of Feminism in Nicaragua." *Social Politics: International Studies in Gender, State, and Society* 3, no. 1. (Summer/Fall): 136–58.

Kampwirth, Karen. 1998. "Legislating Personal Politics in Sandinista Nicaragua, 1979–1992." *Women's Studies International Forum*. 21, no. 1: January / February: 53–64.

Kampwirth, Karen. 2002. *Women and Guerrilla Movements: Nicaragua, El Salvador, Chiapas, Cuba*. University Park: Penn State University Press.

Kampwirth, Karen. 2003. "Arnoldo Alemán Takes on the NGOs: Antifeminism and the New Populism in Nicaragua." *Latin American Politics and Society* 45, no. 2 (Summer): 133–58.

Kampwirth, Karen. 2004. *Feminism and the Legacy of Revolution: Nicaragua, El Salvador, Chiapas*. Athens: Ohio University Press.

Kampwirth, Karen. 2010, *Gender and Latin America's New Left: Lessons from Nicaragua*. New York: Springer.

Kampwirth, Karen. 2012. "Feminismo, Derechos LGBT y la segunda Revolución Sandinista en Nicaragua." In *Nicaragua. Problemas, estudios y debates de la historia reciente,1979–2011*, 125–80. Edited by Paula Fernández Hellmund. Rosario, Argentina: Ediciones del Colectivo de Estudios e Investigaciones Sociales (CEISO) / Centro de Estudios de América Latina Contemporánea.

Kampwirth, Karen. 2014. "Organizing the *Hombre Nuevo Gay*: LGBT politics and the second Sandinista Revolution." *Bulletin of Latin American Research* 33, no. 3 (July): 319–33.

Kaufman, Chuck. 2014. "Nicaragua Vive! 35 Years Since the Triumph of the Sandinista Revolution." July 18. *NicaNet*. https://afgj.org/nicaragua-vive-35-years-since -the-triumph-of-the-sandinista-revolution.

Kennon, Isabel. 2020. "Costa Rica Legalized Same-Sex Marriage. Where Does the Rest of Latin America Stand on Marriage Equality?" *Atlantic Council*. June 2. https:// www.atlanticcouncil.org/blogs/new-atlanticist/costa-rica-legalized-same-sex -marriage-where-does-the-rest-of-latin-america-stand-on-marriage-equality/.

Kramer, Andrew. 2017. "Russians Protesting Abuse of Gay Men in Chechnya Are Detained." *New York Times*. May 1. https://www.nytimes.com/2017/05/01/world /europe/russia-gay-rights-chechnya.html.

La Boletina. 1991a. "Abriendo Brecha," "Enfoque del Mes," "El día internacional del orgullo lesbiana y gay." No. 1 (July): 5, 16, 17–19.

La Boletina. 1991b. "Se forma Red de Lesbianas Feministas Latinoamericanas." "¿Qué decís?: Cartas a La Boletina." No. 2 (September–October): 21, 29–30.

La Boletina. 1992a. "Aunque Ud. No lo crea . . ." No. 6 (May–June): 25–26.

La Boletina. 1992b. "204, 208 . . . En el Tapete." "Felicitaciones a la Fundación Xochiquetzal" "Reflexión de una lesbiana feminista." "La Iglesia de la Comunidad Metropolitana." Nos. 7–8 (July, August, September): 22–23, 26, 34–35.

La Boletina. 1993. "Editorial: el derecho humano a decidir," "Jornada por una sexualidad libre de prejuicios." "Fuera del Closet." No. 13 (July, August, September): 2–3, 25, 39. http://sidoc.puntos.org.ni/publicacionesptos/boletina/boletina-13.

La Boletina. 1994. "Se forma comisión de derechos humanos para lesbianas y homosexuales." No. 17 (June, July, August): 22.

La Boletina. 1996. "Lo que cocinamos: Inauguran centro de mujeres 'Acahual'" No. 25 (March). http://webmil.puntos.org.ni/index.php/es/lo-que-cocinamos-boletina25.

La Boletina. 2005. "Un festival diverso y diferente" No. 60 (May): 59.

La Boletina. 2006. "Una jornada llena de arte y libre de prejuicios." No. 65: 81.

La Boletina. 2007. "Marcha por una sexualidad libre de prejuicios." No. 69 (September): 66.

La Boletina. 2011. "Contracorriente: televisión para hacer pensar en familia." No. 84: 45.

La Costeñísima. 2018. "Diversidad sexual de Bluefields demanda más respeto." June 29. https://lacostenisima.com/2018/06/29/diversidad-sexual-demanda-mas-respeto/.

La Nación. 2014. "Iglesia y Gobierno de Nicaragua iniciarán diálogo en procura de limar diferencias" *La Nación*. May 21. https://www.nacion.com/el-mundo/politica /iglesia-catolica-de-nicaragua-descarta-encuentro-con-daniel-ortega-antes-de -las-elecciones/3LH7VPV64NGVPP7KRT3FPBX4ME/story.

La Nueva Radio Ya. 2017. "Sepultan a devoto de Santo Domingo tras ser golpeado por un desconocido en Managua." *La Nueva Radio Ya*. November 19. https://nuevaya .com.ni/sepultan-a-sordo-mudo-devoto-de-santo-domingo-tras-ser-golpeado -por-un-desconocido-en-managua/.

La Prensa. 2011. "La iglesia de Daniel Ortega." *La Prensa*. October 10. https://www .laprensa.com.ni/2011/10/10/nacionales/76310-la-iglesia-de-daniel-ortega.

La Prensa. 2017. "Un decenio de orteguismo en Nicaragua: La prensa presenta un resumen de los diez peores actos y las diez mejores obras del gobierno de Daniel Ortega (2007–2017)." *La Prensa*. (January 10). Available at https://www .laprensa.com.ni/2017/01/10/politica/2162961-un-decenio-de-orteguismo-en -nicaragua.

La Voz del Sandinismo. 2012. "Trabaja Movimiento Juvenil por la Diversidad Sexual en restitución de derechos." La Voz del Sandinismo. July 24. http://www.lavoz delsandinismo.com/nicaragua/2012-07-24/trabaja-movimiento-juvenil-por-la -diversidad-sexual-en-restitucion-de-derechos/.

La Voz del Sandinismo. 2014. "Amerika Berdrinadxy es coronada Miss Gay Nicaragua 2014: Elegida nueva soberana de la Diversidad Sexual." June 22, 2017. https:// www.lavozdelsandinismo.com/espectaculo/2014-06-22/amerika-berdrinadxy-es -coronada-miss-gay-nicaragua-2014/.

La Voz del Sandinismo. 2016. "Comunidad de la Diversidad Sexual nicaragüense patentiza su respaldo al Presidente Daniel y la Compañera Rosario: Agradecieron los beneficios de las políticas promovidas por el Gobierno Sandinista." La Voz del Sandinismo. (October 22). http://www.lavozdelsandinismo.com/nicaragua/2016 -10-22/comunidad-de-la-diversidad-sexual-nicaraguense-patentiza-su-respaldo -al-presidente-daniel-y-la-companera-rosario/.

La Voz del Sandinismo. 2018. "Gestión del Presidente Daniel es aprobada por mayoría de los nicaragüenses: El estudio de opinión realizado por la firma encuestadora CID Gallup refleja, además, que el 54 por ciento de los encuestados asegura que Nicaragua avanza por el camino correcto." *La Voz del Sandinismo*. (February 14). http://www.lavozdelsandinismo.com/nicaragua/2018-02-14/gestion-del -presidente-daniel-aprobada-mayoria-los-nicaraguenses/.

La Voz del Sandinismo. 2020. "La tierra es un satélite de la Luna: la poesía siempre viva de Leonel Rugama." *La Voz del Sandinismo*. Available at: https://www.lavoz delsandinismo.com/nicaragua/2020-01-15/la-tierra-es-un-satelite-de-la-luna -la-poesia-siempre-viva-de-leonel-rugama-libro/#:~:text=15%2F01%2F2020- ,Cuando%20se%20cumple%20el%2050%20aniversario%20del%20tr%C3%A1 nsito%20a%20la,compromiso%20con%20las%20causas%20justas.

Lacombe, Delphine. 2010. "El escándalo Ortega-Narváez o la caducidad del 'hombre nuevo': volver a la controversia." Istor, año X, núm. 40. (Spring). pp. 81–107. http://www.istor.cide.edu/archivos/num_40/dossier5.pdf.

LaFeber, Walter. 1986. "Afterward, Nicaragua: The Historical Framework to 1979," 223–33 Omar Cabezas. *Fire From the Mountain: The Making of a Sandinista*. New York: Crown Publishers.

Lancaster, Roger. 1988. *Thanks to God and the Revolution: Popular Religion and Class Consciousness in the New Nicaragua*. New York: Columbia University Press.

Lancaster, Roger. 1992. *Life is Hard: Machismo, Danger, and the Intimacy of Power in Nicaragua*. Berkeley: University of California Press.

Lara, Rafael. 2009a. "En II Encuentro Centroamericano por la Diversidad Sexual: Gays buscan su reconocimiento." (September 4). http://gruposafo.doblemente mujer.org/ii-encuentro-centroamericano-por-la-diversidad-sexual/.

Lara, Rafael. 2009b. "Procuradora especial de diversidad sexual," *El Nuevo Diario*, (November 30). https://www.elnuevodiario.com.ni/nacionales/62977-procura dora-especial-diversidad-sexual/.

Larracoechea Bohigas, Edurne. 2018. "Nicaragua and Ortega's 'Second' Revolution: 'Restituting the Rights' of Women and Sexual Diversity?" 235–68. In Elisabeth Jay Friedman. Ed. *Seeking Rights from the Left: Gender, Sexuality, and the Latin American Pink Tide*. Durham: Duke University Press.

Levins Morales, Aurora. 1983. "Gays in Nicaragua: An Interview with Roberto Guardian." *Coming up!* (July), 1, 7.

Lind, Amy, and Christine (Cricket) Keating. 2013. "Navigating the Left Turn: Sexual Justice and the Citizen Revolution in Ecuador." *International Feminist Journal of Politics* 15, no. 4 (December): 515–33.

Liptak, Adam. 2018. "In Narrow Decision, Supreme Court Sides with Baker Who Turned Away Gay Couple." *New York Times*. June 4. https://www.nytimes.com /2018/06/04/us/politics/supreme-court-sides-with-baker-who-turned-away-gay -couple.html.

Lobanov, Vladislav. 2017. "Singer Still Missing after Chechnya's Anti-Gay Purge Russia Should Investigate Zelim Bakaev's Disappearance." *Human Rights Watch*. (November 7). https://www.hrw.org/news/2017/11/07/singer-still-missing-after -chechnyas-anti-gay-purge#.

Lodola, Germán, and Margarita Corral. 2010. "Apoyo al matrimonio entre personas del mismo sexo en América Latina: Perspectivas desde el Barómetro de las Améri-cas (No. 44)." https://www.vanderbilt.edu/lapop/insights/I0844.esrevised.pdf.

López, Julio. 2017. "Los medios de la familia presidencial nicaragüense." *Onda Local*. October 10. https://ondalocal.com.ni/especiales/305-los-medios-de-la-familia -presidencial-nicaraguense/.

López Chavarría, Julio. 2015. "Operación Queer 2015 celebra la diferencia." *Onda Local*. August 6. https://ondalocal.com.ni/producciones/199-operacion-queer -2015-celebra-la-diferencia/.

Luna Garay, Carlos. 2013. *Debajo de la Cama*. Managua: Fondo Editorial ANE.

Macías-González, Victor. 2001. "A Note on Homosexuality in Porfirian and Postrev-olutionary Northern Mexico." *Journal of the Southwest* 43, no. 4: Border Cities and Culture (Winter): 543–48.

Macías-González, Victor. 2014. "The Transnational Homophile Movement and the Development of Domesticity in Mexico City's Homosexual Community, 1930–70." *Gender & History* 26, no. 3 (November): 519–44.

Managua Furiosa. 2019. ¿Qué significa ser Queer? (April 27). https://www.managua furiosa.com/que-significa-ser-queer/.

Magazine. 2018. "Edición Especial: Los Muertos de la Crisis." *La Prensa*. (December 12). https://www.laprensa.com.ni/multimedia/los-muertos-de-la-crisis/.

Manalansan, Martin. 2003. *Global Divas: Filipino Gay Men in the Diaspora*. Durham: Duke University Press.

Marenco, Cristhian. 2008. "'Gorra' de agua a multitud de Purísima oficial: Bomberos usaron sus mangueras ante muchedumbre descontrolada." *El Nuevo Diario*. December 12. https://www.elnuevodiario.com.ni/nacionales/34570-gorra-agua -multitud-purisima-oficial/.

Marsiaj, Juan P. 2006. "Social Movements and Political Parties: Gays, Lesbians, and Travestis and the Struggle for Inclusion in Brazil." *Canadian Journal of Latin American and Caribbean Studies* 31, no. 62: 167–96.

Martí i Puig, Salvador. 2016. "Nicaragua: Desdemocratización y Caudillismo." *Revista de Ciencia Política* 36, no. 1: 239–58.

Martínez, Erick Vidal. 2012. Apertura del Miss Gay Nicaragua. April 30. http://www .youtube.com/watch?v=3jmZMlDi8P0.

Marx, Karl. 1848. *Manifesto of the Communist Party*. https://www.marxists.org /archive/marx/works/download/pdf/Manifesto.pdf.

Masaya para todxs 2015. "Primer video donde se habla sobre la ordenanza municipal a favor de la NO discriminación hacia los gay, lesbiana y transgeneras de #masaya." https://www.facebook.com/1542077979392402/videos/15670613 53560731/.

Matthews, Tede. 1989. "Without the Participation of Lesbians and Gays . . . There Is No Revolution." *NICCA Bulletin*. September, October: 8.

McCaskell, Tim. 1981. "Sex and Sandinismo: Gay Life in the New Nicaragua." *Body Politic*. 73. May: 19–21.

McCaughan, Edward J., and Ani Rivera. 2018. "Queerly Tèhuäntin | Cuir Us." *Social Justice: A Journal of Crime, Conflict & World Order*. January 11. http://www.social justicejournal.org/queerly-tehuantin-cuir-us/.

McGee, Marcus J., and Karen Kampwirth. 2015. "The Co-optation of LGBT Movements in Mexico and Nicaragua: Modernizing Clientelism?" *Latin American Politics and Society*. 57, no. 4 (Winter): 51–73.

Medina, Fabián. 2013a. "Mi verdad está intacta." *La Prensa*. May 12. https://www.la prensa.com.ni/2013/05/12/reportajes-especiales/146278-mi-esta-intacta.

Medina, Fabián. 2013b. "Las Andanzas de Pastora." *Magazine*. October 13. https:// www.magazine.com.ni/reportaje/las-andanzas-de-eden-pastora/.

Medina, Fabián. 2015. "Voy a regresar a mi país: Entrevista con Zoilamérica Ortega Murillo, Exiliada." *La Prensa*. June 21. https://www.laprensa.com.ni/2015/06/21 /poderes/1853747-15890.

Medina, Fabián, and Alejandra González. 2016. "Ortega y Murillo: Una pareja de poder." *La Prensa*. August 7. http://www.laprensa.com.ni/2016/08/07/suplemento /la-prensa-domingo/2079241-ortega-murillo-una-pareja-poder.

Mendoza, Elizabeth. 2017. "Realizan primer conversatorio en Nicaragua sobre aportes de la comunidad LGBTI a la cultura nacional." June 27. http://www.tn8 .tv/nacionales/424077-realizan-primer-conversatorio-nicaragua-sobre-aportes -comunidad-lgbti-cultura-nacional/.

Mendoza M., Tammy. 2014. "Regreso de los 'rotonderos': Empleados del Estado y juventud sandinista se toman de nuevo calles y rotondas." *La Prensa*. December 28. http://www.laprensa.com.ni/2014/12/28/nacionales/1670864>-regreso-de -los-rotonderos.

Miller, Francesca. 1991. *Latin American Women and the Search for Social Justice*. Hanover: University Press of New England.

Miller, Liz. 2004. "Novela, Novela." Documentary film. Frameline studio. 29 minutes.

Miranda Aburto, Wilfredo. 2014. "Zoilamérica lanza videoblog en Costa Rica: Tras once meses de exilio, la hijastra del Comandante Ortega da la cara públicamente arropada por un medio de comunicación tico." *Confidencial*. June 6. http://confidencial.com .ni/archivos/articulo/17728/zoilamerica-lanza-videoblog-en-costa-rica.

Miranda Aburto, Wilfredo. 2016. "M&R: Cae confianza en la transparencia de elecciones: Daniel Ortega con una simpatía de casi 80%; la primera dama Rosario Murillo suma un 73% de agrado." *Confidencial*. https://confidencial.com.ni/mr -cae-confianza-en-la-transparencia-de-elecciones/.

Miranda Aburto, Wilfredo. 2017. "Latinobarómetro: Solo 30% de nicas confía en CSE." *Confidencial*. October 30. https://confidencial.com.ni/latinobarometro -solo-30-nicas-confia-cse/.

Miranda Aburto, Wilfredo. 2018. Una década de asedio a la libertad de prensa en Nicaragua. *Confidencial*. January 17. https://confidencial.com.ni/una-decada-de -asedio-a-la-libertad-de-prensa-en-nicaragua.

Miranda Aburto, Wilfredo, and Octavio Enríquez. 2013. "Capturan y deportan a pareja de Zoilamérica." *Confidencial*. June 25. http://www.confidencial.com.ni /archivos/articulo/12446/capturan-y-deportan-a-pareja-de-zoilamerica.

Miss Gay Nicaragua 2013a. Official website. http://missgaynic.wixsite.com/missgay nicaragua.

Miss Gay Nicaragua. 2013b. "Estimada Primera Dama." http://missgaynic.wixsite .com/missgaynicaragua/agradecimientos.

Miss Nicaragua Gay. 2013. Facebook page.

Missgaynic nicaragua. 2013. "Miss Gay Nicaragua 2012 (Trajes de Fantasia)." February 8. http://www.youtube.com/watch?v=YsmhrV6dZjo.

Mock, Carlos T. 2005. "The Power of the Internet in Latin America." June 1. http:// www.windycitymediagroup.com/m/APParticle.php?AID=8095&i=19&s=News.

Mogrovejo, Norma. 2000. *Un amor que se atrevió a decir su nombre: la lucha de las lesbianas y su relación con los movimientos homosexual y feminista en América Latina*. México: Plaza y Valdés.

Mojica, Yamlek, and Franklin Villavicencio. 2017. "Esto pasó en la Marcha de la Diversidad Sexual 2017 en Nicaragua." *Niú*. June 29. Available at http://niu.com.ni /diversidadsexual2017/.

Molyneux, Maxine. 1985. "Women." In *Nicaragua: The First Five Years*, 145–62. Edited by Thomas W. Walker. New York: Praeger.

Montenegro, Sofía. 2000. "La Cultura Sexual en Nicaragua." Managua: CINCO (Centro de Investigaciones de la Comunicación). http://cinco.org.ni/archive/6.pdf.

Montenegro, Sofía. 2006. "Nicaragua: El aborto en la batalla electroal del 2006." August: 1–3. http://cinco.org.ni/archive/39.pdf.

Montoya, Osvaldo. 1992a. "Hombre y Género" *La Boletina* 8.

Montoya, Osvaldo. 1992b. "Los Hombres Rompiendo el Silencio" *La Boletina* 9 (October–November): 15–18.

Moraga Peña, Bismarck, et al. 2010. *Una Mirada a la Diversidad Sexual*. Managua: Grupo Estratégico por los Derechos de la Diversidad Sexual (GEDDS). http://www.oie-miseal.ifch.unicamp.br/pf-oiemiseal/public-files/una_mirada_a_la_diversidad_sexual_en_nicaragua.gedds_2010.pdf.

Morales, Amalia. 2015. "La huella verde de Félix Pedro." *La Prensa*. (June 11). https://www.laprensa.com.ni/2015/06/11/boletin/1848275-la-huella-verde-de-felix-pedro.

Morales Carazo, Jaime. 1989. *La Contra*. Mexico City: Editorial La Planeta.

Morgan, Martha. 1995. "The Bitter and the Sweet: Feminist Efforts to Reform Nicaraguan Rape and Sodomy Laws." *University of Miami Inter-American Law Review* 26, no. 439 (July 1). http://repository.law.miami.edu/umialr/vol26/iss3/3.

Morris, Courtney Desiree. 2016. "Toward a Geography of Solidarity: Afro-Nicaraguan Women's Land Activism and Autonomy in the South Caribbean Coast Autonomous Region." *Bulletin of Latin American Research*, 35, no. 3 (July): 355–69.

Morris, Courtney Desiree. Forthcoming. *To Defend this Sunrise: Black Women's Activism and the Geography of Race in Nicaragua*. New Brunswick, NJ: Rutgers University Press.

Morris, Kenneth. 2010. *Unfinished Revolution: Daniel Ortega and Nicaragua's Struggle for Liberation*. Chicago: Lawrence Hill Books.

Movimiento Feminista de Nicaragua. 2010a. "Su amor NO daña, tu rechazo SÍ." http://www.movimientofeministanicaragua.org/index.php?option=com_content&task=view&id=54&Itemid=1.

Movimiento Feminista de Nicaragua. 2010b. "Colectivo Feminista Panteras Rosas." October 29. http://movimientofeministanicaragua.org/index.php?option=com_content&task=view&id=59.

Movimiento Feminista de Nicaragua. 2011. "Grupo Lésbico Artemisa." August 30. http://movimientofeministanicaragua.org/index.php?option=com_content&task=view&id=79.

Movimiento Nacional Mnacxdssrr and Fondo Centroamericano de Mujeres (FCAM). 2012. "Por este medio tenemos el agrado de invitarte a la conferencia de prensa." https://www.facebook.com/fcmujeres/posts/10150451536771879.

MSM & HIV Global Forum (MSM GF). N.d. "Organizations Directory." http://msmgf.org/info-hub/organizations-directory/nahomy-club-tttt.

Mugen Gainetik. N.d. (2017?). "Directorio de Organizaciones Centroamericanas que trabajan por los derechos del colectivo LGTBI+." http://www.gehitu.org/images

/gehitu/convenios/MugenGainetik/diagnostico/Directorio-organizaciones-centro americanas-es.pdf.

Munguía, Ivette. 2020a. "Ortega amenaza con cadena perpetua a la mayoría Azul y Blanco." *Confidencial*. September 16. https://confidencial.com.ni/ortega-amenaza -con-cadena-perpetua-a-la-mayoria-azul-y-blanco/.

Munguía, Ivette. 2020b. Régimen orteguista recaptura a más expresos políticos. *Confidencial*. September 19. https://confidencial.com.ni/regimen-orteguista-recaptura -a-mas-expresos-politicos/.

Murguialday, Clara. 2017. Diagnóstico de Situación de la Comunidad LGBTI en 4 Países Centroamericanos (El Salvador, Guatemala, Honduras y Nicaragua). (January to June). http://mugengainetik.org/es/noticias/247-diagnosticolgtbicas.

Murillo Zambrana, Rosario. 2008. "La conexión 'feminista' y las guerras de baja intensidad . . ." *La Voz del Sandinismo*. August 25. http://www.lavozdelsandinismo .com/nicaragua/2008-08-28/la-conexion-feminista-y-las-guerras-de-baja-inten sidad/.

Murillo, Rosario. 2006. "Extracto de la entrevista ofrecida por Rosario Murillo, jefa de campaña del Frente Sandinista de Liberación Nacional, a la emisora Nueva Radio Ya." August 21. http://www.izquierda.info/modules.php?name=News&file =print&sid=1498.

Murillo, Rosario. 2017. "Declaraciones de la Compañera Rosario Murillo, Vicepresidente de Nicaragua (22/12/2017) (Texto íntegro)." *La Voz del Sandinismo*. December 22. http://www.lavozdelsandinismo.com/nicaragua/2017-12-22/declara ciones-la-companera-rosario-murillo-vicepresidenta-nicaragua-22-12-2017-texto -integro/.

Nacho. 2008. "Colegios nicaragüenses denunciados por discriminación." *Ambiente G*. March 4. http://www.ambienteg.com/integracion/homosexuales-nicaraguenses -denuncian-a-tres-colegios.

Narváez, Zoilamérica. 1998. "Testimonio de Zoilamérica Narváez contra su padrastro Daniel Ortega." May 31. *El Nuevo Herald*. http://www.latinamericanstudies .org/nicaragua/zoilamerica-testimonio.htm.

Navas, Lucía. 2017. "MRS elige nueva directiva en Managua." *La Prensa*. June 19. https://www.laprensa.com.ni/2017/06/19/politica/2249059-mrs-elige-nueva -directiva-en-managua.

Navas, Lucía. 2019. "Nicaragua está entre los países menos democráticos del mundo, según Funides." *La Prensa*. June 28. https://www.laprensa.com.ni/2019/06/28 /politica/2564900-nicaragua-esta-entre-los-paises-menos-democraticos-del -mundo-segun-funides.

New York Times. 2013. "Mr. Putin's War on Gays." July 27. http://www.nytimes.com /2013/07/28/opinion/sunday/mr-putins-war-on-gays.html.

Newman, Lucía. 2011. "Activists urge abortion rights in Nicaragua: issue of legalisation gains prominence in run-up to presidential polls in staunchly Catholic country." *Al Jazeera*. November 2. www.aljazeera.com/video/americas/2011/11 /201111214451363244.html.

Newsweek Global. 2014. "Putin to Russia: We Will Bury Ourselves." *Newsweek Global* 162, no. 24 (June 20): 1–8.

Nicaragua Actual. 2019. "Ana Quiros, la primera persona agredida el 18 de abril." https://www.facebook.com/watch/?v=309196046426509.

Niú. 2017. "Marcha orgullo 2017." https://www.facebook.com/RevistaNiu/videos/4713 84749876302/?hc_ref=NEWSFEED.

Núñez, Leticia. 2018. "Rosario Murillo es la persona más rechazada de Nicaragua." *Alnavio.* (December 18). https://alnavio.com/noticia/15129/actualidad/rosario -murillo-es-la-persona-mas-rechazada-de-nicaragua.html.

Ocampos Ortega, Alfredo. 2013. "Vidas Diversas." https://www.youtube.com/watch ?v=6HTLF-iHUo0.

Oettler, Anika. 2009. "Nicaragua: orteguismo y feminismo." *Iberoamericana* 9, no. 33: 178–81. https://journals.iai.spk-berlin.de/index.php/iberoamericana/article /viewFile/784/467.

Ortega, Zoilamérica. 1996. *Desmovilizados de guerra en la construcción de la paz en Nicaragua.* Managua: Centro de Estudios Internacionales (CEI).

Ortega Ramírez, Pedro. 2018. "Gobierno de Daniel y Rosario Murillo es un ejemplo continental." *El 19 Digital.* February 15. https://www.el19digital.com/articulos/ver /titulo:66588-gobierno-de-daniel-y-rosario-murillo-es-un-ejemplo-continental.

Other Sheep. 2000. "Other Sheep: Multicultural Ministries with Sexual Minorities." Spring. http://www.othersheep.org/Newsletter_2000_Spring.html.

Palevi, Amaral. 2017. "Hilando Memorias: Organización de Mujeres Lesbianas en El Salvador." *Estudos de Sociologia* 2, no. 23: 125–94.

Palevi Gómez Arévalo, Amaral. 2016. "Del orgullo gay a la Diversidad Sexual: organización de identidades sexuales disidentes en El Salvador." *Diálogos Latinoamericanos* 25. (December): 99–116.

Palma, Milagros. 2004. "Memoria nicaragüense. El carnaval del toro venado en Nicaragua; simbolismo del mestizaje y representación de la relation de géneros." *Cahiers du CRICCAL.* http://www.persee.fr/doc/ameri_0982-9237_2004_num _31_1_1644.

Peraza C., José Antonio. 2016. "Colapso del Sistema Electoral." In *El Régimen de Ortega: ¿Una nueva dictadura familiar en el continente?* 116–40. Edited by Edmundo Jarquín C. Managua: PAVSA.

Peri Rossi, Cristina. 2001. *Julio Cortázar.* Barcelona: Ediciones Omega, S.A.

Peña, Susana. 2013. *Oye Loca! From the Mariel Boatlift to Gay Cuban Miami.* Minneapolis: University of Minnesota Press.

Perla, Héctor. 2016. *Sandinista Nicaragua's Resistance to US Coercion: Revolutionary Deterrence in Asymmetric Conflict.* Cambridge: Cambridge University Press.

Petrus, John. N.d. "The Transformative Power of Performance Art in Contemporary Managua." http://istmo.denison.edu/n33/articulos/09_petrus_john_form.pdf.

Pineda, Uriel. 2016. "Protesta y Represión: El Monopolio Privado de la Violencia." In *El Régimen de Ortega: ¿Una nueva dictadura familiar en el continente?* Edited by Edmundo Jarquín C., 160–85. Managua: PAVSA.

Poder Judicial. 2017. "Nota de prensa." *Poder Judicial.* December 14. https://www
.poderjudicial.gob.ni/prensa/notas_prensa_detalle.asp?id_noticia=8460.

Portalsida. N.d. "Gay Gas: Grupo Gay de Actores Sociales para la Incidencia Municipal y la Integración Centroamericana." http://www.portalsida.org/Organisation
_Details.aspx?orgid=2434.

Portillo Villeda, Suyapa. 2014. "Honduras: Refounding the Nation, Building a New
Kind of Social Movement." In *Rethinking Latin American Social Movements: Rad-
ical Action from Below,* edited by Richard Stahler-Sholk, Harry E. Vanden and
Marc Becker, 121–146. Lanham, MD: Rowman and Littlefield.

Pousadela, Inés. 2013. "From embarrassing objects to subjects of rights: The Argentine LGBT movement and the Equal Marriage and Gender Identity laws." *Development in Practice.* 23, nos. 5 and 6: 701–20.

Poveda, Javier. 2016. "Fiesta de Operación Queer a pocos días." *El Nuevo Diario.*
http://www.elnuevodiario.com.ni/suplementos/weekend/407787-fiesta-operacion
-queer-pocos-dias/.

Puntos de Encuentro. 2015. "Comunicación Masiva." http://puntosdeencuentro.org
/index.php/es/que-hacemos/comunicacion-masiva.

Radio Primerísima. 2010. "Juventud Sandinista debate sobre diversidad sexual." *Radio
Primerísima.* May 8. http://www.radiolaprimerisima.com/noticias/76164/juventud
-sandinista-debate-sobre-diversidad-sexual/.

Rainsford, Sarah. 2018. "Chechnya gay rights activists 'make up nonsense for money'–
Kadyrov." *BBC News.* January 29. http://www.bbc.com/news/world-europe-428
54814.

Ramírez, Sergio. 2012. *Adiós Muchachos: A Memoir of the Sandinista Revolution.*
Translated by Stacey Alba D. Skar. Durham: Duke University Press.

Randall, Margaret. 1978. *Doris Tijerino: Inside the Nicaraguan Revolution, As told to
Margaret Randall.* Vancouver: New Star Books.

Randall, Margaret. 1993. "To Change Our Own Reality and the World: A Conversation with Lesbians in Nicaragua." *Signs: Journal of Women in Culture & Society* 18
no. 4 (Summer): 90–24.

Red de Desarrollo Sostenible (RDS). 2012a "Cortometraje sobre prostitución en la
diversidad sexual de Nicaragua." https://www.youtube.com/watch?v=06-EXU
mXnmU.

Red de Desarrollo Sostenible (RDS). 2012b. "Encuentro de 3 Generaciones de la Diversidad Sexual Nicaragüense." https://www.youtube.com/watch?v=ox4YaMYs_sE.

Red de Desarrollo Sostenible (RDS). 2012c. "Presentación de la mesa nacional con la
diversidad sexual." March 16. https://www.youtube.com/watch?v=0e7NIeHGgj4
&feature=share.

Red de Desarrollo Sostenible (RDS). N.d. (2013?). Claves para una comunicación en
un mundo diverso: guía de comunicación para el abordaje de temas LGBTI con
enfoque de derechos. http://www.hirschfeld-eddy-stiftung.de/fileadmin/images
/laenderberichte/Nicaragua/GUIA_COMUNICACION_ULTIMA_VERSION
_22022013.pdf.

Red de Desarrollo Sostenible (RDS). 2014. "Miss Gay Nicaragua 2014 habla sobre la plataforma social durante su reinado." September 2. https://www.youtube.com /watch?v=PSn1A26YZdI.

Red de Desarrollo Sostenible (RDS). 2015a. "Qué es RDS." https://comunicacionrds .wordpress.com/que-es-rds/.

Red de Desarrollo Sostenible (RDS). 2015b. "Intro RDS." https://www.youtube.com /user/rdsnicaragua/featured.

Reno, R. R. 2014. "Global Culture Wars: When It Comes to Culture, America and West- ern NGOs Are Global Aggressors." First Things: A Monthly Journal of Religion and Public Life. https://www.firstthings.com/article/2014/04/global-culture-wars.

Restoy, Enrique. 2016. "Human Rights Appropriation in the Development of Trans* Organizations' Membership: The Case of Honduras." LGBTQ Policy Journal vol. 6. 33–44. http://theprojectx.org/wp-content/uploads/2015/02/2016-LGBTQ-full -journal.pdf#page=35.

Reuterswärd, Camilla, Pär Zetterberg, Suruchi Thapar-Björkert and Maxine Moly- neux. 2011. "Abortion Law Reforms in Colombia and Nicaragua: Issue Networks and Opportunity Contexts," Development and Change 42(3): 805–31.

Reyes, Ruben. 1994. "Cómo llegué a ser un hombre violento sin querer . . ." La Bolet- ina no. 18 (September–December): 36–40.

Ring, Trudy. 2016. "Belize High Court Strikes Down Sodomy Law." The Advocate. August 10. https://www.advocate.com/world/2016/8/10/belize-high-court-strikes -down-sodomy-law.

Ríos, Julia. 2007. Rosario Murillo, el poder tras el 'orteguismo'. El Nuevo Diario. Jan- uary 10. http://archivo.elnuevodiario.com.ni/nacional/199749-rosario-murillo -poder-orteguismo/.

Ríos Vega, Juan. 2020. "Una Mariposa Transnacional: Memorias desde el Sexilio." Cuadernos Nacionales 26 (January–June): 28–53.

Roberts, Tifani. 2016. Interview with Zoilamérica Ortega Murillo on the program Aquí y Ahora. November 5. https://www.youtube.com/watch?v=12vYdlZaMmg.

Rocha Córtez, David. 2012a. "Segunda carta de amor." Crónicas de la ciudad: Un hombre y la ciudad, un hombre y lo cotidiano, un hombre y su entorno, un hom- bre y otros hombres. September 3. https://cronicashmsx.blogspot.com/2012/09 /segunda-carta-de-amor.html.

Rocha Córtez, David. 2012b. "Cristiano y homosexual: humano." Crónicas de la ciu- dad: Un hombre y la ciudad, un hombre y lo cotidiano, un hombre y su entorno, un hombre y otros hombres. May 22. https://cronicashmsx.blogspot.com/2012/05/.

Rocha Córtez, David. 2013. "He arreglado mis libros." Crónicas de la ciudad. No- vember 8. http://cronicashmsx.blogspot.com.es/2013/11/he-arreglado-mis-libros .html.

Rocha Córtez, David. 2015. "Ciudad, memoria, sexualidad: Cartografía de homo- socialización, espacios en fuga Managua, 1968–1975." Revista de Historia 33–34: 49–60.

Rocha Córtez, David. 2017a. "Lirismo Cochón." Crónicas de la ciudad: Un hom- bre y la ciudad, un hombre y lo cotidiano, un hombre y su entorno, un hombre y *otros hombres.* February 2. https://cronicashmsx.blogspot.com/2017/02/lirismo-cochon.html.

Rocha Córtez, David. 2017b. "Nuestras memorias, nuestras revoluciones: Nicaragua otra hora cero." *Crónicas de la ciudad.* June 29. http://cronicashmsx.blogspot.com/2017/06/nuestras-memorias-nuestras-revoluciones.html.

Rocha Córtez, David. 2019. "La cochona ciudad letrada: arte y discursos homoeróticos en Nicaragua." *Identidades* 9, no. 15. July / December: 68–94. http://www.cultura.gob.sv/revista-identidades-15/.

Rocha, José Luis. 2016. "El proyecto Ortega-Murillo: cuatro claves de un éxito volátil." *Envío.* 416. November. http://www.envio.org.ni/articulo/5274.

Rogers, Tim. 2008. President Ortega vs. the Feminists. *Time.* October 16. http://content.time.com/time/world/article/0,8599,1850451,00.html.

Rogers, Tim. 2013. "NGO Protests Give New Twist to an Old Family Feud: President Ortega's Stepdaughter Claims the Sandinista Government Is Interfering in Her Organization's Efforts to Secure Foreign Funding" *Nicaragua Dispatch.* April 10. http://www.nicaraguadispatch.com/news/2013/04/ngo-protest-gives-new-twist-to-old-family-feud/7307.

Romero, Elizabeth. 2010. "Avales CPC los otorgan en los barrios." *La Prensa.* May 12. https://www.laprensa.com.ni/2010/05/12/nacionales/24313-avales-cpc-los-otorgan-en-los-barrios.

Romero, Elizabeth. 2013. "Ortega reprime y 'ahoga' a las ONG." *La Prensa.* April 24. https://www.laprensa.com.ni/2013/04/24/ambito/143817-ortega-reprime-ahoga-a.

Romero, Elizabeth. 2015. "Policía no tramita denuncias de delitos por discriminación." *La Prensa.* January 14. https://www.laprensa.com.ni/2015/01/14/nacionales/1765063-policia-no-aplica-delito-por-discriminacion.

Romero, Elizabeth, and Vladimir Vásquez. 2013. "'A mí no me pueden callar' Zoilamérica denuncia represalia y acoso de su propia madre." *La Prensa.* June 27. https://www.laprensa.com.ni/2013/06/27/nacionales/152445-a-mi-no-me-pueden-callar.

Romero, Keyling T. 2019. "El infierno de las mujeres trans en prisión: Nicaragua." *Viento Sur.* June 22. https://vientosur.info/el-infierno-de-las-mujeres-trans-en-prision/.

Rosenberg, Tina. 2009. "The Many Stories of Carlos Fernando Chamorro." *New York Times.* March 20. https://www.nytimes.com/2009/03/22/magazine/22Nicaragua-t.html?searchResultPosition=1.

Sáenz, Enrique. 2016. "La Gestión Económica: ¿Despilfarro de oportunidades?" *El Régimen de Ortega*: ¿*Una nueva dictadura familiar en el continente?* Managua: PAVSA. 209–65.

Saldaña-Portillo, María Josefina. 2003. *The Revolutionary Imagination in the Americas and the Age of Development.* Durham: Duke University Press.

Salinas Maldonado, Carlos. 2009. "Guerra abierta entre Daniel Ortega y la Iglesia católica: La filtración de unas declaraciones atribuidas a un sacerdote levanta ampollas en el episcopado nicaragüense." *El País.* May 7. https://elpais.com/internacional/2009/05/07/actualidad/1241647201_850215.html.

Salinas Maldonado, Carlos. 2016a. "El 'familismo amoral' de Daniel Ortega: Salvador Martí Puig analiza la transformación del Frente Sandinista." *Confidencial*. June 21. https://confidencial.com.ni/familismo-amoral-daniel-ortega/.

Salinas Maldonado, Carlos. 2016b. "La 'eternamente leal' Rosario Murillo: La heredera." *Confidencial*. http://confidencial.com.ni/rosario-murillo-la-heredera/.

Salinas Maldonado, Carlos. 2016c. "Cenidh: 'se profundizó la impunidad en Nicaragua'" *Confidencial*. June 10. https://confidencial.com.ni/cenidh-se-profundizo-la-impunidad-nicaragua/.

Salinas, Carlos. 2017. "La madre que desafía a Daniel Ortega: Elea Valle, una campesina nicaragüense, reclama justicia tras una matanza del ejército que costó la vida a dos de sus hijos." *El País*. December 11. https://elpais.com/internacional/2017/12/10/america/1512944034_910320.html.

Salvatierra, Elvis G. 2015a. "A propósito del 8 de marzo y la lucha por los derechos LGBTI." *Managua Furiosa*. March 8. http://www.managuafuriosa.com/a-proposito-8-marzo-lucha-lgbti/.

Salvatierra, Elvis G. 2015b. "A propósito de la diversidad y las crianzas . . ." *Managua Furiosa*. March 16. http://www.managuafuriosa.com/proposito-diversidad-crianzas/.

San Francisco Sentinel. 1988. "State Dept. Denies Visas to Nicaraguan AIDS Educators." *San Francisco Sentinel*16, no. 32 (August 5): 8.

Schulenberg, Shawn. 2012. "The Construction and Enactment of Same-Sex Marriage in Argentina." *Journal of Human Rights* 11, 106–25.

Schulman, Sarah. 2011. "Israel and 'Pinkwashing.'" *New York Times*. (November 22). https://www.nytimes.com/2011/11/23/opinion/pinkwashing-and-israels-use-of-gays-as-a-messaging-tool.html.

Schulman, Sarah. 2012. *Israel / Palestine and the Queer International*. Durham: Duke University Press.

Seaman, Barrett. 1988. "Good Heavens! An astrologer dictating the President's schedule? So says former White House Chief of Staff Donald Regan in an explosive book" *Time Magazine*. http://content.time.com/time/magazine/article/0,9171,967389,00.html#ixzz2dUtwTFCG.

Sequeira, Carlos. 2017. "1er Encuentro Latinoamericano y el Caribe, LGBTI: Inclusión Laboral." January 27. http://idwfed.org/en/updates/nicaragua-lgbti-labor-inclusion-convening/1er-encuentro-laboral-lgtbi-version-final-27-enero.pdf.

Sequeira Malespín, Guadalupe, and Javier Antino Berríos Cruz. 1993. "Investigación sobre la situación lésbica homosexual en el norte, centro y costa del Pacífico de Nicaragua." April. Unpublished manuscript.

Setright, Aynn. 2013. "Creating Space or Co-opting a Movement? Zoilamérica Ortega and the LGBT Community in Nicaragua." Prepared for presentation at the 2013 Congress of the Latin American Studies Association (LASA), Washington D.C. May 28–June 2.

Sindicato de Trabajadoras Domesticas y Oficios Varios Transgénero (SITRADOVTRANS). 2016. "Sindicato de Trabajadores Domesticas y Oficios Varios Transgénero

SITRADOVTRANS Plan Estratégico 2016–2020." May. Managua, Nicaragua. Unpublished document, 1–31.

Sirias, Silvio. 2009. *Meet Me Under the Ceiba*. Houston: Arte Público Press.

Sokirianskaia, Ekaterina. 2017. "Chechnya's Anti-Gay Pogrom." *New York Times*. May 3. https://www.nytimes.com/2017/05/03/opinion/chechnyas-anti-gay-pogrom.html.

Solórzano, Edgar. 2017. "Notas de Prensa: Comunidad LGBTI se integrará al Servicio de Facilitadores Judiciales." *Poder Judicial*. November 29. https://www.poderjudicial.gob.ni/prensa/notas_prensa_detalle.asp?id_noticia=8431.

Spalding, Rose J. 2017. "Los Empresarios y el estado posrevolucionario: El reordenamiento de las èlites y la nueva estrategia de colaboración en Nicaragua." *Anuario de Estudios Centroamericanos* 43, 149–88. http://www.redalyc.org/pdf/152/15253710006.pdf.

Sperling, Valerie. 2015. *Sex, Politics, and Putin: Political Legitimacy in Russia*. New York: Oxford University Press.

TeleSUR tv. 2014. "Diversidad sexual es cada vez más aceptada en Nicaragua." https://www.youtube.com/watch?v=8ZX5yDzwXnI&feature=share.

Tempo.co. 2016. "Minister: LGBT Movement More Dangerous than Nuclear Warfare." *Tempo.co*. February 23. https://en.tempo.co/read/news/2016/02/23/055747534/Minister-LGBT-Movement-More-Dangerous-than-Nuclear-Warfare.

Thayer, Millie. 1997. "Identity, Revolution, and Democracy: Lesbian Movements in Central America." *Social Problems* 44, no. 3: 386–407.

Torres-Rivas, Edelberto. 2007. "Nicaragua: el retorno del sandinismo transfigurado." *Nueva Sociedad* 207 (January–February): 4–10.

Unidad de VIH. 2017. "Clínicas Vicits Nicaragua." http://www.vihces.com/index.php/en/ubicacionesnc.

Univisión. 2011. "Familia de Daniel Ortega en puestos clave." September 13. http://www.youtube.com/watch?v=zh2doIc5Ihg; https://www.youtube.com/watch?v=SffE2S3Hu9w.

USAID. 2015. *USAID ASSIST Project: Nicaragua Country Report FY15*. http://pdf.usaid.gov/pdf_docs/PA00M58H.pdf.

Vásquez López, Mario Santiago. 2017a. "Mesa Nacional LGBTI denuncia nuevos crímenes de Odio en Nicaragua." https://elblogdemariosvl.wordpress.com/2017/01/25/mesa-nacional-lgbti-denuncia-nuevos-crimenes-de-odio-en-nicaragua/.

Vásquez López, Mario Santiago. 2017b. "Agenda LGBTI del Orgullo en Nicaragua." June 19. https://elblogdemariosvl.wordpress.com/2017/06/19/agenda-lgbti-del-orgullo-en-nicaragua/.

Vásquez López, Mario Santiago. 2017c. "Madres y Padres con hijos de la diversidad sexual." June 26. https://elblogdemariosvl.wordpress.com/2017/06/26/madres-y-padres-con-hijos-de-la-diversidad-sexual/.

Vásquez López, Mario Santiago. 2017d. "#ObituarioLGBTINica: En homenaje a Manoly López." https://elblogdemariosvl.wordpress.com/2017/06/20/obituariolgbtinica-en-homenaje-a-manoly-lopez/.

Vásquez López, Mario Santiago. 2007–11. Various posts. *Espacio Comunicación Alternativa.* https://espacionicaragua.blogspot.com/.

Vásquez López, Mario Santiago. 2011–17. Various posts. *El blog de Mariovsl.* https:// elblogdemariosvl.wordpress.com/.

Vásquez, Trinidad. 2010. "Tercer Encuentro Centroamericano de Diversidad Sexual demanda respeto y no discriminación." October 11. http://ciudadaniasx.org/10 -nicaragua-tercer-encuentro-centroamericano-de-diversidad-sexual-demanda -respeto-y-no-discriminacion/.

Vásquez, Vladimir. 2013a. "Excluyen a Zoilamérica: Gobierno presiona a noruegos para sacar ONG de cooperación." *La Prensa.* April 8.

Vásquez, Vladimir. 2013b. "Rechazan presiones para recortar fondos al CEI." *La Prensa.* April 18. https://www.laprensa.com.ni/2013/04/18/nacionales/142930 -rechazan-presion-para-cortar-fondos-al-cei.

Vásquez, Vladimir. 2013c. "Vuelve represión a las ONG." *La Prensa.* April 9. https:// www.laprensa.com.ni/2013/04/09/nacionales/141642-vuelve-represion-a-las-ong.

Vásquez, Vladimir. 2013d. "Exigen al Gobierno No Condicionar Apoyo." *La Prensa.* April 10. https://www.laprensa.com.ni/2013/04/10/nacionales/141798-exigen-al -gobierno-no-condicionar-apoyo.

Velásquez, Uriel. 2017a. "Proponen declarar Managua como zona libre de discriminación" *El Nuevo Diario.* June 28. https://www.elnuevodiario.com.ni/nacionales /managua/432223-proponen-declarar-managua-zona-libre-discriminacio/.

Velásquez, Uriel. 2017b. "Marchan por la igualdad." *El Nuevo Diario.* https://www.el nuevodiario.com.ni/nacionales/managua/432347-marchan-igualdad/.

Velásquez, Uriel. 2017c. "Nicas son más tolerantes a la diversidad sexual" *El Nuevo Diario.* July 27. https://www.elnuevodiario.com.ni/nacionales/435082-nicas-son -mas-tolerantes-diversidad-sexual/.

Velásquez Villatoro, Antonio. 2015. "Miradas sobre la representación de la homosexualidad en la literatura centroamericana y el caso de Trágame Tierra de Lisandro Chávez Alfaro." *The Latin Americanist* 59, 2. June: 51–66.

Vilas, Carlos 1986. *The Sandinista Revolution: National Liberation and Social Transformation in Central America.* New York: Monthly Review Press.

Vilas, Carlos. 1995. *Between Earthquakes and Volcanoes: Market, State, and the Revolutions in Central America.* New York: Monthly Review Press.

Vilchez, Dánae. 2017. "Athiany Larios, la primera mujer trans en un cargo partidario." *Niú.* June 28. http://niu.com.ni/athiany-larios-la-primera-mujer-trans-cargo-parti dario/.

Villavicencio, Franklin. 2017. "Critican 'represión' del gobierno en marcha contra la violencia: Organizaciones de mujeres hacen balance del 25 de noviembre." *Confidencial.* November 28. https://confidencial.com.ni/critican-represion-del -gobierno-marcha-la-violencia/.

Viteri, María Amelia, Diego Falconí Trávez, and Santiago Castellanos, eds. 2016. *Resentir lo queer en América Latina: diálogos desde/con el Sur.* Barcelona and Madrid: Editorial Egales.

Viterna, Jocelyn. 2012. "The Left and 'Life' in El Salvador." *Politics and Gender* 8, no. 2: 248–54.

VOS TV. 2017. "#LoÚltimo [Noticias] Managua se llena de colores con la marcha de la diversidad sexual." https://www.facebook.com/vostv/videos/137281023943 4864/.

Walker, Thomas, and Christine Wade. 2011. *Nicaragua: Living in the Shadow of the Eagle*. Boulder: Westview Press.

Webber, Jude. 2016. "El Salvador's Anti-abortion Laws: 'An Aggressive, Punitive Attack on Women's Rights Groups Have Denounced the Draconian Laws Under which Women Can Be Put Behind Bars for Aggravated Murder." *Financial Times*. November 16. https://www.ft.com/content/68064cac-a484-11e6-8898-79a99e2a4de6.

Weiss, Meredith L., and Michael J. Bosia, eds. 2013. *Global Homophobia: States, Movements, and the Politics of Oppression*. Urbana: University of Illinois Press.

Welsh, Patrick. 2010. "Desarrollo comunitario: ¿un activismo de género? La cuestión de las masculinidades." *Community Development Journal*. http://cdj.oxfordjournals .org/content/suppl/2010/06/28/bsq023.DC1/bsq023_supp.pdf.

Welsh, Patrick. 2014. "Homophobia and Patriarchy in Nicaragua: A Few Ideas to Start a Debate." *IDS Bulletin* 45, no. 1. January: 39–45.

Wessel, Lois. 1991. "Reproductive rights in Nicaragua: from the Sandinistas to the government of Violeta Chamorro." *Feminist Studies* 17, 537–49.

White, Melanie. 2014–15. "As Long as You're a Black Wo/Man You're an African: Creole Diasporic Politics in the Age of Mestizo Nationalism." University of Pennsylvania. Undergraduate Humanities Forum, 1–58. https://repository.upenn.edu /uhf_2015/11/.

Wikipedia. 2017. "Colectiva Casa de los Colores." Last edited October 19, 2017. https:// es.wikipedia.org/wiki/Colectiva_Casa_de_los_Colores.

Wilkinson, Annie. 2018. "Ecuador's Citizen Revolution 2007–17: A Lost Decade for Women's Rights and Gender Equality." In Elisabeth Jay Friedman, ed. *Seeking Rights from the Left: Gender, Sexuality, and the Latin American Pink Tide*. Durham: Duke University Press.

Wilkinson, Tracy. 1992. "20 Years After Quake, Poor Still Live in Managua's Ruins." *Los Angeles Times*. December 27. http://articles.latimes.com/1992-12-27/news /mn-5120_1_quake-ruins.

Wundram Pimentel, Maria Alejandra. 2015. "Negotiating trans activism in Guatemala City: The case of Redmmutrans." Purdue University M.A. thesis. https://docs .lib.purdue.edu/cgi/viewcontent.cgi?article=1651&context=open_access_theses.

Yellow-Place. N.d. "Movimiento de la Diversidad Sexual Alexis Montiel Alfaro." https://yellow.place/en/movimiento-de-la-diversidad-sexual-alexis-montiel-alfaro -bluefields-nicaragua.

Zeledón, Jaquelin. 2013. "Estudiantes del Instituto Rigoberto López Pérez realizan Conversatorio sobre Diversidad sexual." *El 19*. August 2. http://juventudpresidente .el19digital.com/index.php/noticias/ver/176/estudiantes-del-instituto-rigoberto -lopez-perez-realizan-conversatorio-sobre-diversidad-sexual.

INDEX

94, 118, 164, 283; and elite allies pocketed external aid for 1972 earthquake, 44; appropriated twenty-five per cent of Nicaragua, 45; built opulent performance center, 49; dictator, 3, 32, 40, 46, 49, 56, 61, 86, 87, 93, 95, 111, 150, 245, 283, 284; extravagant birthday party for Sampson, Dinorah, 40; fled from Nicaragua (1979), 45; FSLN overthrew (1979), 3, 34; gay nephew, 47; homosexuality as legacy of Somoza era and capitalism, 62; imprisoned and tortured Chamorro, Pedro Joaquín, 44; involved in torture of political prisoners, 45; liberal elements within dictatorship, 47; murder of U.S. citizen, 45; National Guard of, 38; ruled through clientelism and violence, 45; social, religious, and institutional repression under, 46; teachers strike against, 41; United States patrons, 49. *See also* Carter, Jimmy (President); Chamorro, Pedro Joaquín; Contra War; FSLN; homosexuality as legacy of capitalism; Ortega, Daniel (President); United States

Téllez, Dora María (FSLN Commander), 53, 96, 102, 103, 104, 105, 106; access to subsidized food politicized, 265–66; addressed the delegates at the AMNLAE conference, 115; considered a hero of the guerrilla struggle, 104; highest level lesbian in Revolution, 284; Minister of Health, 33; on FSLN not having a policy on homosexuals, 50; prominent political figure in Nicaragua, 103–104; provided some protection from the state for CEP-SIDA activists, 105; Sandinista Assembly accepted lesbians and gays in the Party, but not in leadership positions, 50. *See also* AMNLAE; CEP-SIDA

Thayer, Millie, 20, 28, 29, 56, 114, 121; 1991 public event aimed at reaching the broader Nicaraguan society, 116
Torrez, Aldrín, 132; co-founded *Trans-Deseo* (Trans Desire Feminist Collective), 180; politicized within feminist movement, 132. *See also* Vargas, Dámaso
trans (trans women, trans men), xv, xvi, xvii, xviii; abbreviated as T in LGBTQ, 3; defined, 184n1. See also cisgender; *cuir* (queer)
transmission belt concept: defined, 98; FSLN actions as, 102; *Grupo Inicio* not conforming to, 98. *See also Grupo Inicio* (Initial Group)

UCA (Universidad Centroamericana (Central American University), xviii, 53, 180–81, 187n2, 221, 246
UNE (Una Nueva Esperanza; A New Hope), xviii, 139, 139n7, 140, 143, 144, 145, 176, 199n5, 209–10n7, 220; directed by Ríos, Ricardo. *See also Asociación de Mujeres Acahual* (Acahual Women's Association)
United States of America (US/USA): 9, 10, 16, 17, 24n7, 26, 27, 35, 43, 45, 46, 55, 56, 75n2, 77, 80, 83, 84, 85, 88, 91, 92, 93, 94, 95, 98, 137, 146, 156, 211, 212, 250, 254, 255, 274, 283; denied visas for Nicaraguan activists planning to attend conference in Boston, 105n9; encouraged Sandinista defection to the U.S., 81; funding of Contra War, 5; history of sexuality in, 12; important ally to Somoza Debayle, Anastasio (President), 85; large-scale migration to, 13; migration and gay and lesbian politics in US and Latin America, 14, 17; parallel impact of Contra War regarding emergence of gay and lesbian actions, 13; withdrew support for Contras, 29;

ABOUT THE AUTHOR

Karen Kampwirth is the Robert W. Murphy Professor of Political Science at Knox College. She holds a bachelor of arts in political science and Spanish from Knox College and a doctorate in political science from the University of California, Berkeley. Kampwirth is the author or editor of five books on Latin American politics.